To Be Suddenly White

Steven J. Belluscio

To Be Suddenly White

Literary Realism and Racial Passing

University of Missouri Press
Columbia and London

Library of Congress Cataloging-in-Publication Data

Belluscio, Steven J.
   To be suddenly white : literary realism and racial passing / Steven J. Belluscio.
      p.   cm.
Summary: "Explores the challenges of subjective passing narratives written during the
height of literary realism. Discusses racial and ethnic differences, assimilation, passing,
and identity by comparing African-American narratives of James Johnson, Nella Larson,
and George Schuyler and "white" ethnic (Jewish-American and Italian-American) narra-
tives by Mary Antin, Anzia Yezierska, and Guido d'Agostino"—Provided by publisher.
   Includes bibliographical references and index.
   ISBN-13: 978-0-8262-1619-9 (alk. paper)
   ISBN-10: 0-8262-1619-6 (alk. paper)
   1. American prose literature—African American authors—History and criticism.
2. American prose literature—Minority authors—History and criticism.   3. Minorities—
United States—Biography—History and criticism.   4. African Americans—Biography—
History and criticism.   5. Assimilation (Sociology) in literature.   6. Identity (Psychology)
in literature.   7. African Americans in literature.   8. Passing (Identity) in literature.
9. Human skin color in literature.   10. Race awareness in literature.   11. Group identity
in literature.   12. Ethnicity in literature.   13. Realism in literature.   14. Race in
literature.   15. Autobiography. I. Title.
   PS338.N4B45 2005
   810.9'3552—dc22   2005028036

Designer: Douglas Freeman of Foley Design
Typesetter: Phoenix Type, Inc.
Printer and binder: The Maple-Vail Book Manufacturer
Typefaces: Palatino and Rotis

To Vanessa

Contents

Acknowledgments

Since the ideas presented in this study were first explored in my dissertation at Purdue University, I would like first to thank my wonderful committee: Susan Curtis, Wendy Stallard Flory, Fred L. Gardaphè, Robert Paul Lamb, and Anthony J. Tamburri, each of whom has provided invaluable advice, guidance, and encouragement over the years. I also would like to acknowledge the Purdue Research Fund, the American Italian Historical Association Memorial Scholarship Fund, and the Purdue Departments of English and American Studies for their financial support, as well as Borough of Manhattan Community College, which allowed me release time to complete this project. I certainly should mention Benjamin Lawton, for his conversation, his sense of humor, and his insights into the world of academia. Warm thanks go to Clair Willcox, Jane Lago, John Brenner, and the rest of the University of Missouri Press—along with their tough, honest anonymous reviewers—for their indispensable assistance. Finally, I would like to thank my wife, Vanessa, my parents, John and Marilyn, and my brother, Chris, for their continual love and encouragement.

I am grateful for permission to quote from the following works:

Bread Givers by Anzia Yezierska. Copyright © 1952 by Anzia Yezierska, transferred to Louise Levitas Henriksen in 1970. Reprinted by permission of Persea Books, Inc. (New York).
Whiteness of a Different Color: European Immigrants and the Alchemy of Race by Matthew Frye Jacobson, pp. 3–4, 6, 56, 174. Cambridge, Mass.:

Harvard University Press, Copyright © 1998 by the President and Fellows of Harvard College.

Haunch, Paunch and Jowl by Samuel Badisch Ornitz. Reprinted with the permission of Markus Wiener Publishers, Princeton, New Jersey.

Along This Way by James Weldon Johnson, copyright 1933 by James Weldon Johnson, renewed © 1961 by Grace Nail Johnson. Used by permission of Viking Penguin, a division of Penguin Group (USA) Inc.

Black No More by George Schuyler, selections from pp. 13–222. © 1989 Northeastern University Press/University Press of New England. Hanover, Mass., and London.

A Man Called White by Walter White. Reprinted by Permission of Rights Holder, Jane White Viazzi.

Elaine Ginsberg, "Introduction: The Politics of Passing." Reprinted by permission of Duke University Press.

Deborah E. McDowell, Introduction, and Nella Larsen, *Passing*. Reprinted by permission of Rutgers University Press.

Everett Stonequist, *The Marginal Man: A Study in Personality and Culture Conflict*. Reprinted by permission of Martha Stonequist.

Fred L. Gardaphè, *Italian Signs, American Streets: The Evolution of Italian American Narrative*. Reprinted by permission of Duke University Press.

Richard Gambino, *Blood of My Blood: The Dilemma of the Italian-Americans*. Guernica Editions. Reprinted by permission of Guernica Editions.

Giuseppe Cautela, *Moon Harvest*. Reprinted by permission of Random House, Inc.

Marie Hall Ets, *Rosa: The Life of an Italian Immigrant*. Reprinted by permission of the University of Wisconsin Press.

Jessie Redmon Fauset, *Plum Bun*. Reprinted by permission of Beacon Press.

Frantz Fanon, *Black Skin, White Masks*. Reprinted by permission of Mary Flower.

Helen Barolini, *Umbertina* and *the Dream Book*. Reprinted by permission of Helen Barolini.

To Be Suddenly White

Introduction

In many ways, American literary history traces a continual narrative of the relationship between dominant and marginal groups in colonial America and the United States. American subgenres as diverse as colonial histories, slave narratives, immigrant autobiographies, and African American literature deal willy-nilly with infinite variations on this perennially relevant theme, the seemingly impermeable divide it suggests, and the means by which this divide can be advantageously manipulated, even violated. The passing narrative is no exception, as it involves an extreme example of crossing the boundary that separates dominant and marginal cultural, racial, and/or ethnic groups—usually with the purpose of "shed[ding] the identity of an oppressed group to gain access to social and economic opportunities."[1]

Passing has traditionally been treated as an exclusively African American phenomenon; however, such a conception relies upon a generally reductive but long-enduring definition such as the one found in Gunnar Myrdal's *An American Dilemma: The Negro Problem and Modern Democracy* (1944), in which "[f]or all practical purposes 'passing' means that a Negro becomes a white man, that is, moves from the lower to the higher caste." Since passing is typically viewed by scholars as centered around a black/white racial binary, critics have tended to locate literary passing

---

1. Elaine K. Ginsberg, "Introduction: The Politics of Passing," 3. In this study, "ethnic American" is generally used as an umbrella term for all culturally marginal persons.

1

exclusively in the works of African American writers, such as Jessie Fauset, Nella Larsen, George Schuyler, Pauline Hopkins, James Weldon Johnson, Frances E. W. Harper, and Walter White. This focus upon the African American canon is unsurprising given the great number of passing narratives written by both nineteenth-century and early-twentieth-century writers of this tradition. However, this study will argue that the critical apparatus of passing should also be applied to the literature of white ethnic immigrant groups who came to the shores of the United States, most numerously from the 1880s until the racist immigration restriction of the 1920s stemmed the tide of southern and eastern European immigration. During this time period, as scholars such as David Roediger, Noel Ignatiev, Matthew Frye Jacobson, and Desmond King have demonstrated, non–Anglo-Saxon European immigrants found themselves in racially in-between subject positions from which they could escape only by adopting the social, religious, economic, and intellectual mores of the better-established white dominant culture. One might say, then, that many first- and second-generation ethnics, in an attempt to achieve occupational security and social acceptance, passed for white. Although the idea of white ethnic passing is not a new one, there is a dearth of research on the subject, particularly in the field of ethnic American literary history. As Earl Lewis correctly notes, "The story of European immigrants 'passing' for white is one of the little-explored chapters in late nineteenth and early twentieth-century U.S. history."[2]

In order to counteract the silence on the subject, I hope to initiate a critical dialogue on selected Jewish American and Italian American novels and autobiographies as passing narratives in their own right. I do not, however, intend to conflate the passing figure as it develops in white ethnic works with that found in the African American tradition, for there are clear distinctions I find regarding the intrinsic and extrinsic changes required of each culturally specific passing figure discussed. I am focusing upon the aforementioned white ethnic groups in particular for a number of reasons. First, more Italians and Jews entered the United States in the late nineteenth and early twentieth centuries than immigrants of any other origin group, and they soon entered the literary imagination of American authors, both "ethnic" and "mainstream," often with the rhetorical purpose of posing a number of questions about identity and citizen-

---

2. Gunnar Myrdal, *An American Dilemma: The Negro Problem and Modern Democracy,* 683; Earl Lewis, "To Turn as on a Pivot: Writing African Americans into a History of Overlapping Diasporas," 785.

ship. Second, Italian Americans and Jewish Americans consequently were situated at the center of debates on racial aptitude during this era. Initially, both groups officially and popularly were granted a racially in-between status they could not shed until the mid–twentieth century, and narratives of both the Italian American and Jewish American literary traditions detail and dramatize the circumstances of this unique subaltern status. Third, and most importantly, American writers of Italian and Jewish descent published fictional works that examined, even interrogated, ideas of identity, ethnicity, assimilation, and (occasionally) passing—ideas central to this study. The reason for the inclusion of African American texts is nearly self-evident, as African Americans were thought to set the absolute standard of racial inferiority in the United States. Consequently, for African American writers, the passing narrative served as a framework for not only a realistic depiction of the black experience but also an examination of the limits of the idea of race itself. Comparatively speaking, the differences in assigned racial status arguably generated distinctions in the racial rhetoric used in white ethnic narratives on one hand, and that used in African American narratives on the other, with the former making use of tropes more in accordance with prevailing American myths of race and nationhood—oftentimes adopting a now ideologically suspect racial romanticism—and the latter (though not immune to the racial foibles of the former) more likely to attempt a wholesale deconstruction of race and race ideologies. In either case, this study reads the selected works textually, contextually, and comparatively for their respective engagements with discourses of racial and/or ethnic difference, assimilation, passing, and identity—all of which have profound implications for our understanding of American literary history.

Before proceeding further, I would like to make clear that while I invoke notions of both "ethnic experience"—as a context for the works considered here—and "ethnic literature"—as the primary focus of the present study—I do not wish to be understood to mean that the latter proceeds necessarily, naturally, and directly from the former as if the former were the only influence to bear upon the ethnic writer and the latter could be understood simply through the application of a sociological model or two. Rather, I view matters of ethnicity, race, assimilation, migration, American nationalism, and the like—that is, anything and everything pertaining to "ethnic experience"—as one part of the ethnic writer's literary arsenal. But given that these matters were often of personal importance to the ethnic writer, and given that American publishers of the early twentieth century often all but required the ethnic author to write only of ethnic themes, "ethnic experience" became not only a *possible* literary discourse for the ethnic writer but also a very *likely*, if not central, discourse. I will address matters of ethnic textuality in more detail later in the introduction.

To date, the vast majority of major studies on literary racial passing focus upon performativity and epistemology: for example, what passing says about modern subjectivity or what it says about race ideologies. Insofar as this study considers those very issues, it is undoubtedly indebted to the work of scholars such as Samira Kawash, Gayle Wald, Cheryl Wall, Deborah McDowell, and Pamela Caughie. However, my focus is somewhat different in that I am interested in how representations of racial and ethnic identities—which are consistently foregrounded in passing narratives—effect generic change in African American, Italian American, and Jewish American literature. I focus upon realism largely because white ethnic and African American authors writing between the 1890s and the 1940s generally chose literary social realism as an artistic means by which to represent accurately and truthfully the living experiences of their co-ethnics.[3] While some scholars, such as Thomas Ferraro, George Hutchinson, and Delia Caparoso Konzett, have made a convincing case for the *modernism* of early-twentieth-century white ethnic and African American authors—a modernism derived not so much from the formalistic qualities of the writing as from its introduction of discourses of difference into the American literary tradition—an equally convincing case could be made for the *realism* of these works, a realism that dates back to the thickly described social milieus represented by Henry James and William Dean Howells. So while I am examining the representative works for their creative engagements with a number of American social discourses, I am also concerned with how these very engagements influence the uses of genre.

For a number of reasons, realism is a useful lens through which to view the works of white ethnic and African American authors in the late nineteenth and early twentieth centuries. First is realism's devotion to mimetic verisimilitude, which gave white ethnic and African American

3. Of course, there are notable exceptions, such as Jean Toomer's *Cane* (1923), Henry Roth's *Call It Sleep* (1934), and Pietro di Donato's *Christ in Concrete* (1939). For discussions on the predominantly realistic style of African American and white ethnic American literature in the early twentieth century, see George Hutchinson, *The Harlem Renaissance in Black and White*, 118–19; Delia Caparoso Konzett, *Ethnic Modernisms: Anzia Yezierska, Zora Neale Hurston, Jean Rhys, and the Aesthetics of Dislocation*, 1–18; and Thomas J. Ferraro, "Avant-Garde Ethnics."

authors the opportunity to describe closely and accurately typical living and working conditions of co-ethnics. Second is realism's foregrounding of the Enlightenment concept of the free-willing individual, which allowed white ethnic and African American authors to depict their co-ethnics as fully competent and capable of shouldering the burdens of American citizenship during a time when prevailing racial discourses questioned their ability to do so. As I will argue—and as many others have argued—classic texts of American realism from the late nineteenth century generally feature this free-willing individual adapting to his or her social milieu and exercising moral agency when confronted with any number of dilemmas.

However, it would be inaccurate to suggest that ethnic literature proceeded directly and exclusively from American literary realism, because during the early twentieth century, when white ethnic and African American literary production was in full swing, literature was also feeling the effects of 1890s American literary naturalism, which questioned, even rejected, Enlightenment notions of free will in its representation of characters deterministically controlled by primal instinct, environment, racial predispositions, and the quotidian demands of an increasingly modern United States.[4] Characteristic works such as Stephen Crane's *Maggie* (1893), Frank Norris's *McTeague* (1899), and Theodore Dreiser's *Sister Carrie* (1900), while retaining some of the formal and thematic characteristics of realism, such as a commitment to verisimilitude and social relevance, break radically with the realist notion of the free-willing self in favor of a more hardline, often pessimistic, determinism that sees little hope for meaningful human choice so long as contemporary problems of racial violence, monopolization, labor unrest, and urban corruption went unaddressed.[5]

Consequently, white ethnic and African American writers from the 1890s to the 1940s had two significant literary precedents from which to choose when they turned to fiction writing. The result, I argue, is a highly problematic realism in which the desired free will of the ethnic subject,

4. On free will and American naturalism, see Donald Pizer, *Twentieth-Century American Literary Naturalism;* John J. Conder, *Naturalism in American Fiction: The Classic Phase;* and June Howard, *Form and History in American Literary Naturalism.*

5. On the distinction between realism and naturalism vis-à-vis determinism, see Lee Clark Mitchell, *Determined Fictions: American Literary Naturalism,* preface and chapter 1. Mitchell's special contribution to our understanding of naturalism lies in his description of not only epistemological but also *formal* distinctions between the two modes.

while foregrounded to some degree, comes into direct and ultimately irresolvable conflict with the determinisms of, among other things, harsh
living and laboring conditions, socially and legally sanctioned discrimination, and the burdens of racial and/or ethnic inheritance (which are
often conceived in *biological* terms by white ethnic and African American
authors themselves). To be sure, "mainstream" realists, such as Henry
James, William Dean Howells, and Mark Twain, themselves never fully
resolved the paradox of the realist subject: that is, the subject, who as free-
willing as he or she would wish to be, nevertheless confronts seemingly
insurmountable barriers of economic necessity, environmental influence,
and social convention. However, I argue that for white ethnic and African
American writers in the late nineteenth and early twentieth centuries—
some of whom, such as Abraham Cahan and Charles Chesnutt, were professionally and aesthetically assisted by William Dean Howells—the
problem of the realist subject is especially acute. In a time of racist
pseudoscience, racial violence, and fervent anti-immigrant sentiment,
American writers of Italian, Jewish, and African descent wrote in part to
counter popular and official narratives of racial aptitude and to demonstrate the ability of their co-ethnics to participate fully in the fundamen-
tals of American citizenship.[6] Thus, the capable, competent, and ultimately moral free-willing agent of realism becomes a useful rhetorical
tool for demonstrating this. However, for the white ethnic author who
devotes him or herself to representing accurately all the exigencies of
ethnic subjectivity, the realist subject is immediately problematized, as it
runs into direct conflict with a dizzying array of social, economic, political, racial, and gendered realities that call into question any notion of the
free-willing ethnic self. Thus, as we shall see in the works of writers such
as Giuseppe Cautela, Abraham Cahan, and Anzia Yezierska, the result
for the white ethnic author is very frequently an interesting, if incoherent, mixture of realist agency and naturalistic determinism. I argue that
these subjective contradictions, for some authors, lead directly to generic
innovations, most notably a sustained irony that critiques notions of ethnic or racial affiliations, as in Samuel Ornitz's *Haunch, Paunch, and Jowl*
(1923) and George Schuyler's *Black No More* (1931), or a nascent (even
full-blown) modernism that abandons a consistent linear narrative of
ethnicity in favor of a more fragmented, disjointed narrative seen to be

6. For a discussion of Harlem Renaissance artistic production as a nationalistic,
culturally pluralistic endeavor, see Hutchinson, *The Harlem Renaissance in Black and
White*, chapters 2 and 3.

more capable of representing ethnic subjectivity's many conflicting and contradictory strands, as in Nella Larsen's *Passing* (1929) and part three of Helen Barolini's *Umbertina* (1979).

Still, while ideologies of racial difference troubled both Italian Americans and Jewish Americans, they were also more forgiving than they would ever be for more visibly marked racial groups, such as African Americans. Indeed, the well-documented racial in-betweenness of Jewish Americans and Italian Americans was as much a barrier as a motivator to assimilation, and both ethnic groups would fully join the ranks of white America in the increased social, educational, and economic opportunity of the post–World War II era. Thus, while the early-twentieth-century literature of Italian Americans and Jewish Americans unavoidably narrates the circumstances of racial in-betweenness, it also has a tendency to represent racial ideology less problematically in passing narratives that describe a character's attempted transition from a position of ethnic difference to one of full American citizenship and, more frequently, in acculturation narratives that idealize a relatively simplistic, if theoretically incoherent and essentialistic, combination of "ethnic" and "American" influences. In the case of both Italian American and Jewish American narratives, the relative "safeness" of race vis-à-vis both groups is evidenced in the relative ease with which such writers adopt, first, a casual racial romanticism in order to explain ethnic difference and, second, an affinity for mainstream American mythologies of success and citizenship.

Arguably more than white ethnic authors, African American authors also delved into cuttingly ironic (George Schuyler) and decidedly modernistic (Nella Larsen) territory in order to convey the many conflicting strands of ethnic subjectivity. However, one of the most fundamental differences between African American literature and white ethnic literature of the time period under consideration is the former's tendency to openly critique ideas of race. In the labor market, the social arena, the legal realm, and elsewhere, the experiences of African Americans compared with those of white ethnics tell the story of a group more adversely affected by ideologies of race, as witnessed by, among other things, the era's racial violence, legalized segregation, and miscegenation laws: none of which affected white ethnics as much as it did blacks.[7] Thus, African American authors, insofar as they are aware of the ideological problems

7. For a discussion of Italian immigrants' racial status and their subsequent treatment, see Thomas A. Guglielmo, "'No Color Barrier': Italians, Race, and Power in the United States" and *White on Arrival: Italians, Race, Color, and Power in Chicago,*

of race and render them into narrative, have a decidedly greater tendency than their white ethnic counterparts to critique race and racial subjectivity as ideas. For as novelistic discourses of free will (acculturation, passing, and the American success myth) come into direct conflict with novelistic discourses of determinism (discrimination, subaltern status, biological essentialism, racial affiliation, racial ideologies), African American authors, far more than white ethnic authors, find that the realistic aesthetic begins to expend its usability and gives way either to a strident irony that undercuts ideologies of race or to a modernism that replaces unitary, "centripetal" narratives of subjectivity with a more inclusive, if contradictory, "centrifugal" narrative capable of representing all the conflicting strands of modern (racial) subjectivity.[8]

While it might be argued that I could have traced these generic trends in other varieties of realist texts, I believe the passing narrative offers a number of unique opportunities. First, passing is in many ways an archetypically realist act: that is, a freely willed exchange of one set of circumstances for another not unlike that often found in classic realist texts of social mobility and adaptation. Second, the passing narrative, more than any other kind of narrative, brings into high relief questions of ethnic and racial identity—both their practical consequences and their theoretical problematics—and allows us to see how their literary representation often leads directly to changes in realistic mimesis. Third, given that passing narratives represent the attempted erasure of both internal and external discourses of ethnicity and/or race, they require the reader to think about these discourses in their entirety: that is, every represented notion of appearance, tradition, religion, folkways, and affiliation that contributes to a perceived sense of ethnic and/or racial "difference" in literature. In the end, my overall purpose in this study is to use the passing narrative to provide one more insight into the ways the representation of ethnic and/or racial subjectivity can contribute to generic change in American literary history.[9]

1890–1945. Guglielmo argues that while Italians were undeniably racialized both popularly and officially, they were also to some degree always white, as they could claim to be of "white" color on naturalization forms.

8. The terminology of centripetal and centrifugal narratives is Bakhtin's. See M. M. Bakhtin, *The Dialogic Imagination,* 272.

9. For an example of a study that links questions of racial identity with questions of genre, see Walter Benn Michaels, *Our America: Nativism, Modernism, and Pluralism.* According to Michaels, it is impossible to fully appreciate literary modernism without understanding concomitant American notions of race, identity, and culture.

What Is Passing?

It has lately become customary to distinguish between two understandings of passing. There is a "commonsense understanding" advanced by sociologists such as Gunnar Myrdal (*An American Dilemma*, 1944) and St. Clair Drake and Horace R. Cayton (*Black Metropolis*, 1945), in which passing means to conceal a unitary, essential, and ineffaceable racial identity and substitute it with a purportedly artificial one, as in the oft-discussed case of a light-skinned black person passing for white "for social, economic, or political reasons." This conception is what Pamela Caughie refers to as passing "[i]n its literal or first cultural sense," which "carries certain pejorative connotations of deception, dishonesty, fraudulence, or betrayal" and "designates an effort to disguise or suppress one's racial heritage, racially marked body, or sexual orientation." This has given way to an understanding of passing that is linked to performativity and that refers not to an assumption of a fraudulent identity but more broadly to "the condition of subjectivity in postmodernity," in which our Lyotardian distrust of totalizing metanarratives, when applied to identity, has caused us to focus not so much upon identity as a unitary, essentialized entity, but rather as a process-oriented performance drawing upon a seemingly infinite number of cultural texts, "ethnic" or otherwise. The signified of "identity" has thus given way to the signifier of "performativity." To be sure, William Boelhower's comments on postmodern ethnicity certainly could be applied to postmodern subjectivity: "In the postmodern context it is useless to speak of authentic as opposed to false ethnic culture, implying that only one deserves cultivation... Authenticity now pertains to the pragmatics of simulation rather than to a process of literal representation." Thus, if the "first cultural" notion of passing relies upon a "binary logic of identity, the logic that says if A is white, A cannot be not white," then the latter cultural notion shatters this binarism and offers in its stead multiplicity and performative possibility.[10]

While Caughie correctly reminds contemporary critics not to promote the former notion—or at least not to privilege the former to the neglect of the latter—I would also caution against the opposite. That is, while the latter notion of passing carries more critical currency in the postmodern era, we as critics cannot forget that many passing narratives written in the

10. Samira Kawash, *Dislocating the Color Line: Identity, Hybridity, and Singularity in African-American Narrative*, 125–26; Pamela Caughie, *Passing and Pedagogy: The Dynamics of Responsibility*, 6, 20, 21, 24; William Boelhower, *Through a Glass Darkly: Ethnic Semiosis in American Literature*, 132.

late nineteenth and early twentieth centuries are governed by the logic of the first cultural notion, and our readings must be ever aware of this. For in reality, the first cultural notion never really "goes away" because its patent essentialism informs the writings of late-nineteenth and early-twentieth-century African American and white ethnic writers even as it informs contemporary popular thought. Only with this kind of intellectual nimbleness can we understand the meaning of literary passing as it once existed while at the same time retaining a critical awareness of its theoretical problematics. So while the passing narrative requires of contemporary readers one kind of intellectual feat—that is, a paradigmatic move from the latter cultural notion to the first cultural notion—it also requires the opposite—that we imagine the subject of the latter cultural notion emerging from the strictures of the first cultural notion, something that occurs generally over time and sometimes individually within texts.

The intellectual history suggested by terms such as "first cultural notion" should not misguide us into thinking that African American and white ethnic writers of the time period were wholly unaware of the latter cultural notion. Indeed, a sense of subjective play, a trying on of multiple identities, figures into many passing narratives of the time period. Moreover, it could be argued that *any* passing narrative—given the idea that a subject can so effortlessly exchange one racial identity for another—necessarily calls into question any notion of racial fixity and, willy-nilly, suggests the latter cultural notion. However, as I shall demonstrate, most white ethnic and African American passing narratives of the time period never completely shed the racialisms of the first cultural notion—a fact that would continually problematize these narratives' realism, a literary genre that privileges both the free-willing agency and the essential, self-consistent core being of the individual. But by way of comparison, I will argue that given the differing experiences with race ideologies between blacks and white ethnics, African American authors of passing narratives have a greater tendency to critique the very idea of race, thereby de-essentializing it and pointing toward the latter cultural notion of passing. And while white ethnic authors are not wholly unaware of this latter cultural notion—as we shall see in, for example, Helen Barolini's *Umbertina*—they historically show a greater tendency to cling to racially romantic, essentialistic notions of authentic ethnicity, often using the first cultural notion to reject passing as an unethical fraud and to promote an Aristotelian mean of "ethnicity" and "Americanism" that essentializes both and resolves none of the pressing debates either term provokes. Given that progressives and, eventually, conservatives would warmly extend this assimilative option to white ethnics in the twentieth century, it is unsurprising that so many white ethnic writers would arrive at this thesis. Although they were no doubt aware of immigrants' subaltern status, Jewish American and Italian American authors would use the space opened by the culturally pluralistic theories advanced during immigration debates of the early twentieth century to realistically describe, humanize, and often valorize their ethnic protagonists. If the theoretical problematics of "ethnicity" or "race" went unresolved, it did not matter, because the racial ideologies contained therein were becoming increasingly less threatening to white ethnics than they were to other, more racially marked Americans. African Americans enjoyed no such luxury, and while black authors of passing narratives did make use of the very same kinds of racial romanticisms to explain black cultural difference, they also knew that to identify as biologically black meant to write oneself into a history of slavery and a contemporary reality of Jim Crow, miscegenation law, one-dropism, and racial violence. Thus, while African American writers of passing narratives in many cases shape their stories according to the logic of the first cultural notion, they are more likely than their white ethnic counterparts to engage with the idea of race itself, to transcend the first cultural notion of passing, and in doing so, to transcend the orderly aesthetics of realism. In the final analysis, we as critics must retain an awareness of both cultural notions, for in the history of the passing narrative, they are always in implicit (if not explicit) and productive (if irresolvable) dialogue.

What Is Literary Racial Passing?

The most immediate (and admittedly simplistic) answer to this question is to state that literary racial passing is a creative rendering of the act of racial passing into narrative. However, I will need to further detail this study's understanding of narrative before attempting a more precise definition. I share M. M. Bakhtin's notion of the novel as an arena of "internal dialogization," where, ideally, the author gives creative and strategic voice to the "significant" "social and ideological voices of [the] era" and "welcomes the heteroglossia and language diversity of the literary and extraliterary language into his own work not only not weakening them but even intensifying them." I also share Roland Barthes's analogous notion of the text as a "polysemic space where the paths of several possible meanings intersect." The single most obvious identifying characteristic of textuality is in fact *intertextuality*. In the case of any text, "other texts are present in it, at varying levels, in more or less recognisable forms: the texts of the previous and surrounding culture. Any text is a new tissue of past citations. Bits of codes, formulae, rhythmic models, fragments of social languages, etc. pass into the text and are redistributed in it."[11] Taken from this perspective of the text, the *ethnic* text can be viewed as a creative tapestry of multiple and often competing literary and social discourses: generic conventions, such as realism and naturalism; plot conventions, such as the bildungsroman and the acculturation narrative; and social discourses, such as gender, class, sexuality, and nationalism—indeed, all are featured prominently in the literature of the time period considered. And while I am hesitant to draw impassable barriers between "ethnic" and "mainstream" literature, I would also suggest that what seems to distinguish "ethnic" literature from "mainstream" literature is its foregrounding of discourses of ethnic difference, indeed, its tendency to distribute "ethnic signs with a greater...degree of frequency and intensity."[12] However, discourses of ethnic difference (and by extension the very term "ethnic American") implicitly and explicitly raise questions of American civic nationalism: to what degree is the "ethnic" able to "be American"? Are "ethnic" and "American" discourses mutually exclusive? Are they one and the same? I argue that these questions are central in attempting a definition of literary racial passing applicable to all the literature I discuss in this study.

In *American Crucible: Race and Nation in the Twentieth Century*, Gary Gerstle argues that two mutually dependent discourses of inclusive nationalism and exclusive racialism formed during the turn-of-the-century wave of "new" immigration and have existed to varying degrees of con-

---

11. Bakhtin, *The Dialogic Imagination* 284, 411, 298; Roland Barthes, "Theory of the Text," 36, 39.

12. Boelhower, *Through a Glass Darkly,* 36. Another useful work on revisionist theories of ethnic literature is Werner Sollors, *Beyond Ethnicity: Consent and Descent in American Culture.* Boelhower and Sollors view ethnicity as central to both the American experience and American literature and, likewise, caution against ghettoizing either and thereby failing to appreciate the ways "ethnic" and "American" literatures dialogue and, in many cases, are one and the same. See both texts for clear and nuanced theories on ethnic literary production. In both cases, the authors are careful to draw more attention to the discursive, rather than the essential, nature of both "ethnic" and "American." While Boelhower views ethnic literature as an author's creative rearticulation of cultural discourses drawn from an ever-changing ethnic "encyclopedia," Sollors views ethnic literature as a dramatization of the conflict between discourses of descent (or what our cultural inheritances dictate we must do) and consent (or what we personally wish to do).

flict, consonance, and intensity until the present. Thus, while the early-twentieth-century notion of American civic participation was, in theory, applicable to everyone, in practice it was to some degree racialized and not completely available to white ethnics and even less so to African Americans. Unsurprisingly, white ethnic and African American litera-ture of the time period engages, even foregrounds, these very questions of American nationalism and ethnic difference, and I argue that certain typological differences in ethnic literature emerge from this very debate. For example, the *acculturation narrative* involves bringing discourses of ethnicity and Americanness into equilibrium, or at least managing, even suppressing, the conflict between the two. While white ethnic writers such as Abraham Cahan and Giuseppe Cautela made use of this literary mode, I would submit that it is nearly absent from African American lit-erature due to the fact that blacks' ascribed racial status precluded such a comfortable coexistence of "ethnic" and "American." Italians and Jews, at the very least, could be classified as "Caucasian"—even if their *whiteness* was contestable—and eventually be able to participate in a cul-turally pluralistic American scene. However, the more visibly and in-delibly racialized African Americans would not be extended the same opportunities: as we shall see, even pluralistic early-twentieth-century commentators, such as Randolph Bourne and Horace Kallen, would ex-clude African cultural inheritances in their Eurocentric theories of multi-cultural America. Early-twentieth-century African American authors were fully aware of this and were thus more likely to use the *passing narrative* in order to imagine the African American's attempt at full assimilation.

In the *racial passing narrative,* a character attempts (successfully or not) to shed all overt evidence of racial difference and imperceptibly enter mainstream society. From the perspective of the author, this involves depicting one or more characters in such a manner that all discourses of racial difference (especially ones that would easily be read by other characters) are overwritten by discourses of American civic national-ism.[13] As I will argue, Italian American and Jewish American authors made use of this literary device, but given that they also had the credible

13. Of course, literary passing involves a certain amount of dramatic irony that precludes the *total* erasure of racial discourses. In other words, even though other characters might not be able to detect another character's racial passing, the reader is almost always made aware of it, and very typically, the character's ostensible racial difference reemerges periodically throughout the text. Thus, literary passing is never absolute: I can think of no example in American literary history in which it is. This study limits itself to considerations of *racial* passing. However, a broader definition

option of the acculturation narrative, they were less likely than their African American counterparts to do so. Indeed, African American authors, given their awareness of blacks' designated racial status, more frequently resorted to the passing narrative—in which a light-skinned character of African descent attempts to suppress all overt evidence of racial and cultural inheritances—in order to imagine black civic participation and simultaneously draw attention to the limitations therein. But in any case, the tension between the presence and presumed absence of ethnic and/or racial difference implicitly, and, usually in the case of African American writers of the time period, explicitly, raises questions about the very nature of "ethnicity" and "race" and what it means, if anything, to attempt to erase their palpable effects. What is ethnicity? What is race? Are the two distinct, or is ethnicity, cultural emphasis notwithstanding, merely a more fashionable restatement of race, given its dependency upon birth? The inevitable contradictions inherent between ethnicity and race as essentialistic traits and ethnicity and race as negotiable constructs (or, as Pamela L. Caughie might have it, between first and latter cultural notions of passing) chafes at the straightforward, mimetic veneer of realism, and when notions of race are explicitly engaged, as they are most frequently in African American passing narratives, the result is generically perceptible.

Literary Passing in the Eyes of the Critics

Given that black authors most frequently used the trope of passing in their narratives, it is unsurprising that most scholarship on literary passing deals with African American literature. But even as theory on literary passing progressively has built upon the arguably reductive definitions established by Myrdal and Drake and Cayton to view passing as a crossing of not only racial but also class, gender, ethnic, and sexual barriers, and even as scholarship on whiteness by the likes of Noel Ignatiev, David Roediger, Matthew Frye Jacobson, and Desmond King has questioned the veracity of racial binarism, the tendency to examine passing

---

of literary passing narrative might read like this: "any narrative in which a character attempts to obliterate overt evidence of *any* undesirable trait perceived as natural and permanent. From the perspective of the author, this involves depicting a character in such a way that these undesirable traits are overwritten by other, presumably more desirable, ones."

almost exclusively in the African American literary tradition has had the unintended effect of reifying this very binary to the detriment of potential explorations of, among other things, white ethnic racial rebirth in literature. This is not to say the black/white racial boundary has no significance whatsoever: indeed, white ethnic characters who lay claim to a more purely white identity are exploiting its very power. However, the racialism suggested by the black/white boundary could distract us from an understanding—particularly from the perspective of early-twentieth-century America—of many *racialisms* that affected all ethnic groups, white or otherwise.

While it was only of sporadic interest to critics throughout the 1970s and early 1980s, the late 1980s and 1990s witnessed a flurry of interest in the passing narrative. With the following brief review of representative literary critics' definitions of passing, I hope to demonstrate that the manner in which it is currently conceived *theoretically* has opened up the possibility for it to be considered in broader terms than ever before and, by extension, the possibility for the present study—even if *practically* it is only applied to African American literature and the familiar black/white racial binary. Since the late seventies, literary passing seems to have moved through three definitional stages: the first, which focuses centrally upon racial transgressions, though not at the total expense of other categories of social repositioning, especially class (e.g., Berzon and Carby); the second, a transitional stage in which racial passing is stripped of its conceptual primacy and linked firmly with sexual and narratological transgressiveness (e.g., McDowell); and the third, which, building upon the revolutionary influence of Deborah McDowell, associates passing with any of a wide array of boundary crossings and makes use of ever-broader definitions, even to the point of vagueness, so as to encompass the act's infinite narrative possibility (e.g., McLendon, C. Wall, Ginsberg, and Sollors).

The first stage tends to define literary passing almost exclusively vis-à-vis race, and admittedly, this is often because the studies in which such definitions are advanced, such as this one, limit their scope to race. *Neither White nor Black: The Mulatto Character in American Fiction* (1978), by Judith Berzon, is a representative example, in which the author defines passing sociologically and literarily as the most extreme potential consequence of the mulatto's resolution of the tension between his or her black and white cultural influences. According to Berzon, if one is given a clear-cut choice between the "two extremes" of "black nationalism" or "assimilationism," "passing," then, "is the most extreme form of the impulse toward assimilation." For Berzon, however, the implications of passing do not end with racial identification. Class is an extremely important consideration as well, as passing cannot be separated from "the American dream of upward mobility" and the ultimate goal of full "identification with white middle-class America."[14] Thus, as early as 1978, Berzon yokes racial passing with its concomitant class component, thereby complicating our understanding of what we might initially think to be an exclusively *racial* act.

Hazel Carby's definition of passing reflects this class-influenced understanding. In *Reconstructing Womanhood: The Emergence of the Afro-American Woman Novelist* (1987), Carby defines passing as "the conscious decision to use a white appearance to hide a black heritage *for social advancement.*"[15] Thus, while the act of passing involves a primarily "racial" action—namely, the vacating of one racial subject position for another—this very act contains an inseparable economic component. Accordingly, while most of the passing narratives I shall examine essentially have the structure of "mainstream" literary realism—which often contains the classic story of moral and socioeconomic ascent—white ethnic and African American characters have the additional burden of aligning themselves with the dominant racial group before they can hope to improve their lot in any such way. Thus, while the protagonist's means are largely racial, his or her ends are at least in part socioeconomic. In any case, these first-stage definitions of literary passing consider race to be the first and foremost concern: that is, a racial transformation must take place before any other transformation becomes remotely possible.

During the last two decades, much attention has been drawn to the sexual implications of literary passing: a trend that can be traced to Deborah E. McDowell's introductory essay to Rutgers' 1986 reprint of Nella Larsen's *Quicksand* (1928) and *Passing* (1929), in which the author argues that *Passing* not only tells the story of protagonist Clare Kendry's full absorption into the white middle-class culture of Chicago and New York, but, through indirection, also tells of a latent sexual desire between Kendry and her friend Irene Redfield. In effect, then, *Passing* is a story of masked lesbian attraction that passes as a passing narrative. According to McDowell, in Larsen's narrative technique:

14. Judith Berzon, *Neither White nor Black: The Mulatto Character in American Fiction*, 3–4, 141, 162.

15. Hazel Carby, *Reconstructing Womanhood: The Emergence of the Afro-American Woman Novelist*, 158.

"safe" themes, plots, and conventions are used as the protective cover underneath which lie more dangerous subplots. Larsen envelops the subplot of Irene's developing if unnamed and unacknowledged desire for Clare in the safe and familiar plot of racial passing. Put another way, the novel's clever strategy derives from its surface theme and central metaphor—passing. It takes the form of the act it describes. Implying false, forged, and mistaken identities, the title functions on multiple levels: thematically, in terms of the racial and sexual plots; and strategically, in terms of the narrative's disguise.[16]

Thus, in McDowell's second-stage assessment, passing embodies not only racial actions but sexual and narratological ones as well. McDowell's hugely influential observations have paved the way for a wide array of critical approaches to passing, and the last ten years of scholarship have yielded increasingly generous definitions of the act's possibility.

For example, in *The Politics of Color in the Fiction of Jessie Fauset and Nella Larsen* (1995), Jacquelyn Y. McLendon uses readings of *Plum Bun: A Novel Without a Moral* (1928), *Comedy: American Style* (1933), *Quicksand*, and *Passing* to demonstrate how both Fauset and Larsen use passing as one possible literary device to interrogate societal assumptions regarding boundaries of class and gender, in addition to race. In this study, McLendon broadly defines passing "as any form of pretense or disguise that results in a loss or surrender of, or a failure to satisfy a desire for, identity, whether racial, cultural, social, or sexual." Ultimately, "passing is as much a state of mind as a physical act," an assertion that, once again, opens up passing to nontraditional examinations of the subject.[17]

In *Women of the Harlem Renaissance* (1995), by Cheryl A. Wall, the theoretical basis upon which the author discusses the lives and works of Jessie Fauset and Nella Larsen further exhibits a broader conception of passing. Like McLendon, Wall argues that the implications of passing extend beyond race to gender and cultural concerns, as the female protagonists of *Quicksand* and *Passing* undergo "quest[s] for selfhood" in which "racism and sexism" are "inextricably tied." Like McDowell, Wall argues that Larsen's use of passing reaches to the level of narrative: "Perhaps Larsen's most effective act of passing," she writes, "was masking the subversive themes that frequently simmered beneath the surface of the fiction." In a

16. Deborah E. McDowell, Introduction to Quicksand *and* Passing, xxvi, xxx.
17. Jacquelyn Y. McLendon, *The Politics of Color in the Fiction of Jessie Fauset and Nella Larsen*, 7, 96.

statement describing Larsen's protagonists' "assum[ption of] false identities"—a statement that is clearly a critical sign of the time—Wall writes that "[p]assing for white . . . is only one way this game is played"—one implication being, of course, that there is simply more than one kind of passing.[18]

Over the last seven years, literary studies devoted exclusively to passing and interracial literature have made conscious efforts to define passing as broadly as possible—even at the risk of vagueness—and thereby have expanded ever further our understanding of the act's implications. In Elaine K. Ginsberg's introduction to *Passing and the Fictions of Identity* (1996), the author asserts that passing is quite generally "about identities: their creation or imposition, their adoption or rejection, their accompanying rewards or penalties. Passing is also about the boundaries established between identity categories and about the individual and cultural anxieties induced by boundary crossing. Finally, passing is about specularity: the visible and the invisible, the seen and the unseen." While Ginsberg acknowledges that passing has typically been associated with the exchange of a socially constructed black identity for a presumably false white identity, she also points out that "[b]y extension, 'passing' has been applied discursively to disguises of other elements of an individual's presumed 'natural' or 'essential' identity, including class, ethnicity, and sexuality." Most significantly, according to Ginsberg's conception, passing is "[n]ot always associated with a simple binary," a fact that theoretically paves the way for this present study and others with nontraditional approaches to the subject.[19]

With *Neither Black Nor White Yet Both: Thematic Explorations of Interracial Literature* (1997), Werner Sollors sought to provide readers with a simultaneously more precise and more generous definition of passing than ever before. In a thorough chapter devoted to passing in American literature, Sollors defines passing as simply "the crossing of any line that divides social groups," which can clearly be applied to situations beyond those operating along the familiar black/white racial binary. Like Ginsberg, Sollors acknowledges that the term "passing" is usually taken to mean a move from the black to the white side of the color line. Also like Ginsberg, Sollors argues that passing is not restricted to this kind of action only but occurs whenever and wherever "descent characteristics"

18. Cheryl A. Wall, *Women of the Harlem Renaissance*, 89.
19. Ginsberg, "Introduction," 2–3.

are viewed essentialistically and are judged to be detrimental to a person's potential for success. According to Sollors, passing was especially prevalent in the United States in the late nineteenth and early twentieth centuries, when both the anonymity of the city and the possibility of social mobility provided the impetus for many to pass.[20] Therefore, as I argue, the logic of passing, while obviously applicable to the experience of African Americans, is also relevant to the experience of Italian and Jewish immigrants of the very same time period Sollors explores.

Still, despite the current understanding of passing in theory, there is also an urgent need in practice to explore its many varieties other than the familiar black-to-white journey. For even though recent studies of passing are unequivocal in their attempts to reveal the artificiality of the color line, their many examinations of black-to-white passing serve to reiterate the familiar terms "black" and "white" and thereby unwittingly reify the very color line thought to be destabilized. As Gayle Wald writes, "The durability of the black/white paradigm may in certain cases be abetted rather than undermined by its instability, insofar as this quality lends it a discursive mobility and flexibility. In short, whereas passing is conditioned on the radical instability of the racial sign, the fluidity of race that it appropriates is a function of its (socially produced) stability in marking out the binary possibilities of the national narrative." Wald's *Crossing the Line: Racial Passing in Twentieth-Century U.S. Literature and Culture* (2000) is doubly innovative in that it examines not only black-to-white but also white-to-black racial passing and in that it reads these phenomena in not only literature but also in musical culture, film, and confessional narratives. Furthermore, the study initiates a dialogue on a potential role of the white ethnic in the national drama of racial passing: in this case, Jewish American jazz saxophonist "Mezz" Mezzrow, who so identified with African American culture and musical form that he came to identify as a "'Negro' musician" himself.[21] Laura Browder's *Slippery Characters: Ethnic Impersonators and American Identities* (2000) is perhaps the first study to live up to the full potential of recent theory on literary passing, as it discusses a broad range of narrative passing acts pertaining to many racial and ethnic groups and social classes. The present study proposes to go even further in its examination of white ethnic

20. Sollors, *Neither Black nor White yet Both: Thematic Explorations of Interracial Literature*, 247–48.
21. Gayle Wald, *Crossing the Line: Racial Passing in Twentieth-Century U.S. Literature*, 187, 53.

literary racial passing: a very real part of late-nineteenth and early-twentieth-century American prose that deserves closer examination, that has profound implications for American literary history, and that further challenges our binaristic understanding of American racial discourse.

Of course, I am suggesting neither that the color line does not exist nor that it has had no palpable effects in American history. But while this binaristic conception of race was certainly a product of the concurrent forces of advanced white ethnic assimilation and the black civil rights movement of the mid–twentieth century, and in some ways still informs our thinking on race today, it is an inadequate lens through which to read the history of African Americans and immigrants in the late nineteenth and early twentieth centuries. Most problematically, it ignores the possibility of Italian Americans and Jewish Americans (and other white ethnics) occupying an in-between racial status—legally white, yet popularly nonwhite and still on their way to reaching a state of fully Americanized whiteness. This is where Pamela Caughie's antibinaristic notion of passing is especially helpful. For while late-nineteenth and early-twentieth-century American literature often fictionalizes identity according to currently suspect dualisms—white/black, authentic/fraudulent, etc.—that necessitate our continual awareness of the first cultural notion of passing, such binaries should not exclusively dictate the direction of scholarship on the subject. Indeed, the vast majority of the criticism devoted to literary passing ignores, or deals only tangentially with, white ethnic characters,[22] a critical absence which, perhaps counterintuitively, does a great disservice to African American studies: Earl Lewis is correct to say that "[t]he telling of this story [the assimilation of European/American immigrants] has profound implications for the study and writing of African-American history." To be sure, any examination of how some ethnic groups, such as Irish Americans, Italian Americans, and Jewish Americans, can become white speaks volumes about why other more indelibly racialized groups, such as African Americans and Asian Americans, cannot. Eric Lott has argued that nineteenth-century working-class Irish, by participating in and consuming blackface minstrelsy, used dominant racial discourses in order to lay claim to whiteness—a fact that "displaces . . . the binary emphasis on 'the' black-white relationship in America" and draws attention to the racial indeterminacy of the white

22. Some notable exceptions to this include the work of Laura Browder, Meredith Goldsmith, and Susan Koppelman.

ethnic. I believe that what holds for American cultural history also holds for American literary history: that the fictional stories of racially in-between ethnics (whether or not this racial in-betweenness is explicitly stated) laying claim to whiteness unavoidably complicate our binaristic understandings of race in American literature.[23]

Toward this end, the present study will trace authorial negotiations of race, ethnicity, passing, and genre in four separate traditions: white ethnic male-centered narratives, African American male-centered narratives, white ethnic female-centered narratives, and African American female-centered narratives. Of course, I am not unaware that such groupings may, at first glance, seem suspiciously arbitrary; however, they rely more upon textual commonalities therein than any preconceived or artificially imposed sense of "tradition." Thus, white ethnics are grouped together not because there are no differences between Italian American and Jewish American literatures (as we shall see, quite the opposite is often the case), but rather because both share certain understandings of race, assimilation, and national identity that can be fruitfully and tellingly compared to those encountered in African American literature. Moreover, both Jewish American and Italian American literatures can be viewed as part of a broader phenomenon of mostly realistic European immigrant literature of the late nineteenth and early twentieth centuries. And while white ethnic and African American passing narratives possess, as their primary conceptual nucleus, the notion of seamlessly acculturating to white, middle-class standards, in white ethnic narratives there is more of a tendency to gloss over the theoretical problematics of identity suggested by these narratives' inevitable engagements with ethnicity, race, "Americanness," and the equally inevitable essentialisms of each. Aesthetically speaking, the result for white ethnic acculturation and passing narratives tends to be a comparatively pat, earnest immigrant realism in which some dominant discourses are challenged—as they often are in "mainstream" realism—while others, often pertaining to American myths of success and citizenship, are unquestioned, even privileged. On the other hand, African American passing narratives, while not free of the facile racialisms and nationalisms of white ethnic acculturation and passing narratives, have a greater tendency explicitly to critique myths of racial affiliation, race, and American social mobility. The aesthetic result

23. Earl Lewis, "To Turn as on a Pivot," 785; Eric Lott, *Love and Theft: Blackface Minstrelsy and the American Working Class*, 94.

in black passing narratives is an eventual break with the more straight-forward mimesis of earlier novels in favor of anti-realistic satire in the case of the African American male-centered narrative (George Schuyler) and existential modernism in the case of the African American female-centered narrative (Nella Larsen).

And this race-based distinction indicates my rationale for grouping the literatures I consider according to their "gender-centeredness": namely, that discourses, and by extension, determinisms of female gender add a layer of generic complexity to both white ethnic and African American narratives. To be sure, the "double marginalization" (as Mary Dearborn would phrase it) of female gender increases the ethnic burdens of characters in both Italian American and Jewish American acculturation and passing narratives—a reality that adds a discourse of determinism that does not exist in white ethnic male-centered narratives and further complicates the realism of these female-centered narratives. And while characters in white ethnic female-centered passing narratives—especially in the Jewish American women's tradition—often react against the gender-based strictures of their cultural milieus by attempting to pass, the determinisms of ethnic affiliation usually provoke some kind of return. In any case, the aesthetic result is still a relatively straightforward ethnic realism that, while undoubtedly more complex and conflicted than that of white ethnic male authors, does not achieve the level of myth interrogation encountered in African American passing narratives. As we shall see, African American female-centered passing narratives, while every bit as generically complex as their white ethnic female-centered counterparts, exhibit a greater tendency to critique received, presumably stable, notions of race and even subjectivity itself. The aesthetic result is not so much the cutting irony we find in the African American male tradition as an existential modernism that carries the stable aesthetic and epistemological categories of realism to their logical extremes.

Admittedly, the literary history that emerges is by no means a linear narrative. However, it does provide potential insight into the means by which conflicting discourses of race, ethnicity, gender, and nationalism effect palpable change in the genres (and subgenres) of American prose. Toward that end, chapter 1 further develops the connections between literary passing and literary realism, arguing that the attempt by the "ethnic" to resituate him or herself as a white, middle-class American re-hearses some classically realist themes: namely, the exercise of free will and the adaptation to the mores of a particular social milieu. Chapter 1

also discusses the often unspoken theme of whiteness in American literature and briefly summarizes the pressures brought to bear upon Americans of Jewish, Italian, and African descent to achieve white status in a
late-nineteenth- and early-twentieth-century context that viewed whiteness as a prerequisite to American citizenship.

Chapter 2 contains a discussion of *An Imperative Duty* (1892), by William
Dean Howells, and *Iola Leroy, or Shadows Uplifted* (1892), by Frances E. W.
Harper. Since Howells was the most vocal proponent and theorist of literary realism, it seems appropriate to introduce this study with a reading of his fictional treatment of racial passing. Harper, as a literary contemporary of Howells and an African American female activist who
herself confronted the perennial dilemma of whether or not to pass, balances the perspective in a number of ways. Both texts are among the
earliest examples of realist passing narratives and, despite their authors'
differences in viewpoint, both exhibit the inherent difficulty of realistically depicting the passing act: an act that not only connotes at least as
much determinism as free will, but that also defies social decorum. Indeed, the limits of both decency and verisimilitude continually hindered
the ability of literary realists to bring closure to tales of passing and
mixed-race marriage.[24]

These two texts complement each other well not simply because of
their contemporaneity and thematic similarities, but also because, considered together, they encompass, with regard to aesthetics and tone, a
broad range of literary options and pose a number of pressing questions
for the author of passing narratives. While *An Imperative Duty* is simple,
detached, and thinly described, *Iola Leroy* is ornate, polemical, and thickly
described. Also, while *An Imperative Duty* is classically realistic and somewhat pessimistic in its conclusion, *Iola Leroy* is arguably melodramatic
and overly optimistic. My intent is not to suggest that one approach is
always better than another, even though I do contend that *Iola Leroy*'s
optimistic tale of uplift was, at the time, more rhetorically useful than
An Imperative Duty's sparsely ironic tale of escape. Rather, by reading
these two works that could certainly be seen as polar opposites in many
ways, I wish to demonstrate the seemingly irresolvable aesthetic dilemma
of authorship vis-à-vis passing narratives. Is it best to use a cool, detached
tone as Howells does? Is it best to be polemical and passionate like

24. Cathy Boeckmann, *A Question of Character: Scientific Racism and the Genres of
American Fiction, 1892–1912,* 141, 176.

Harper? Is it best to conclude pessimistically, so as to be realistic about the hardships nineteenth-century African Americans encountered? Or, is it best to be optimistic, so as to imagine creatively and dramatically Hamlin Garland's notion of the democratic future heralded by literary realism? While I do not purport to have the final answers to these questions, I do hope the reader will notice their continued relevance throughout the many passing narratives I discuss in this study.

Chapter 3 is an examination of male white ethnic passing narratives, in which characters attempt to overcome the burden of ethnic status and become materially successful participants in the American socioeconomic mainstream. I begin the chapter with readings of Madison Grant's *The Passing of the Great Race* (1916) and Gino Speranza's *Race or Nation: A Conflict of Divided Loyalties* (1925) in order to describe the antagonistic intellectual climate ethnic writers encountered and the obvious need for realistic accuracy as a counternarrative to popular and official stereotyping. I then provide readings of representative Italian American and Jewish American male-centered novels of acculturation, so as to distinguish them from full-blown passing narratives, which can in some ways be characterized as acculturation narratives of a quite distinct and extreme kind. The passing narratives—the central texts of the chapter—are *Up Stream* (1922), by Ludwig Lewisohn, and *Olives on the Apple Tree* (1940), by Guido d'Agostino, both of which feature a male character who attempts to shed completely his "other" status as a first- or second-generation Jewish American or Italian American in favor of a new "American" self. While I do not intend to conflate the Italian American and Jewish American literary traditions—for clearly there are cultural and aesthetic differences between the two—the early-twentieth-century narratives in both these traditions share a number of notable characteristics. Structurally and stylistically, the texts resemble "mainstream" realism; yet as I will argue, the nativist and racially prejudiced social arena in which these characters freely will their own admission into the American mainstream adds a layer of determinism that does not plague more "conventional" examples of social realism. Both the acculturation and passing narratives of this chapter show a tendency toward racialism, even racial romanticism, that underscores a key difference between white ethnic and African American narratives of the early twentieth century vis-à-vis race: namely, that the rhetoric of race has safer implications for the white ethnic than it does for the African American. Finally, the chapter concludes with a discussion of Samuel Ornitz's *Haunch, Paunch and Jowl* (1923), which addresses issues of assimilation and passing yet does so with a sense of irony uncommon to most contemporary European immigrant narratives but central to black male passing narratives.

In chapter 4, the deterministic ante is upped as African American male characters attempt a transition similar to that of the male white ethnic characters of the third chapter. The representative texts are Charles W. Chesnutt's "The Wife of His Youth" (1899) and *The House behind the Cedars* (I look at John Walden's story, leaving Rena Walden's for later) (1900), James Weldon Johnson's *The Autobiography of an Ex-Coloured Man* (1912), and George Schuyler's *Black No More* (1931). In both the third and fourth chapters, however, the idea of cultural betrayal figures heavily as characters find they must decide between loyalty to their ancestral heritage and the ways of their new American selves. Additionally, I shall demonstrate that as one proceeds from text to text in chapter 4, one notices a move away from simplistic notions of cultural betrayal, toward irony, and toward a pointed critique of race that only begins to be hinted at in the Jewish American tradition—with Ornitz's *Haunch, Paunch, and Jowl*—and that is utterly absent from this early stage of the Italian American tradition.

In chapter 5, gender adds another complicating factor to what are still, in many fundamental ways, works of social realism. While no doubt sharing many characteristics with their counterparts in chapter 3—and I do not intend to suggest they always be considered separately—the main characters of these works face a different set of circumstances and ponder different domestic, and when possible, professional alternatives than the characters of works read in the earlier chapters. Thus, the rationale for separating the texts into gender-specific chapters lies in the fact that female-centered texts are frequently structured around different sets of desires, motivations, and actions than male-centered texts. Furthermore, white ethnic female-centered texts are infused with deterministic discourses of gender that tend not to complicate male-centered texts. In Mary Antin's *The Promised Land* (1912), Anzia Yezierska's *Bread Givers* (1925), Marie Hall Ets's *Rosa* (1970), and Helen Barolini's *Umbertina* (1979), the authors find they must narratologically confront issues of both ethnicity and gender as they construct tales of assimilation, professional success, and/or marriage that still manage to fall within the realm of American social realism. As we find when comparing the early Italian American and Jewish American male literary traditions, this analysis reveals the Italian American women's tradition to be thematically and aesthetically "behind" the Jewish American women's tradition in some regards. For example, while Antin's and Yezierska's works are both passing narratives, Ets's *Rosa*, a latent ur-text of sorts, is a narrative of acculturation in which complete assimilation is not even entertained as a possibility. In fact, we do not even encounter a passing character in the Italian American women's oeuvre until 1979 with Clara of *Umbertina*. As I argue, this discrepancy underscores social, economic, and educational differences between Italian American and Jewish American women in the twentieth century. In any case, when we consider both ethnic female traditions on the whole, it seems that passing is an assimilative option that, given the double burdens of both ethnicity and gender, is considered but ultimately rejected, as the ineludible warmth and lure of ethnic community prove too powerful to ignore. Thus, while white ethnic American women's texts often depict a "trying on" of different identities, this almost inevitably results in some kind of ethnic return.

In chapter 6, I offer readings of Chesnutt's *The House behind the Cedars* (this time focusing upon Rena Walden's story), Walter White's *Flight* (1926), Jessie Redmon Fauset's *Plum Bun* (1928), and Nella Larsen's *Passing* (1929), demonstrating that the tale of an early-twentieth-century African American woman attempting to take control of her own destiny through passing comes dangerously close to expending the usefulness of the realist genre in order to tell the story. As decorum, believability, and agency are problematized more greatly than in any of the other works discussed, the author of the African American women's passing narrative finds that she must render her character indeterminate in such a manner that she might escape socioeconomic confinements and be allowed a degree of self-determination that black women might not have enjoyed in the "real world." At its most successful, the result is a text that stretches the boundaries of literary realism, takes a decisive step toward modernism, and is also in some ways decades ahead of its time in American literary history. Beyond a simple "trying on" of new identities, then, African American women's passing narratives engage not only in a thoroughgoing critique of race—as do their male-centered counterparts—but also eventually in a critique of subjectivity as it is traditionally (and realistically) conceived. Finally, the epilogue reflects upon recent projects of ethnic literary recovery and their significance for ethnic subjectivity in contemporary times.

The title of this study comes from Frantz Fanon's *Black Skin, White Masks* (1952), a groundbreaking series of essays on psychology, sexuality, and the social construction of race. Chapter 4 begins, "Out of the blackest part of my soul, across the zebra striping of my mind, surges this desire to be suddenly *white*"—a desire that becomes for Fanon utterly irrational given his rejection of "whiteness" and "blackness" as incoherent and ultimately "unacceptable."[25] The desire "to be suddenly white" is nonetheless real and will serve as a continual point of reference for this study, in which writers, even when overtly aware of the problematic nature of race (especially the African American writers), are also aware of the conditions it creates, the transformations it provokes, and the consequences of both.

25. Frantz Fanon, *Black Skin, White Masks*, 63, 197.

1

Assimilation, Whiteness, and Realism

"The Pull Factor": The Continuing Significance of Whiteness

The flourishing of whiteness studies in the 1990s, due particularly to its focus upon European immigration, provides much of the justification for the present study because it helps us understand what is at stake in late-nineteenth- and early-twentieth-century literary discourses of assimilation. On the one hand, the notion of light-skinned African Americans crossing the racial line and substituting a black identity for a white one is obvious to us, and the volume of sociological, literary, and critical work on the subject is ample evidence of this. We view the change as not only ethnic—that is, a product of *cultural* differences associated with group status—but racial—that is, a perceived change of status from the *biological* category of black to white. On the other hand, when the theme of passing is deployed by white ethnic writers in a late-nineteenth/early-twentieth-century context (and, admittedly, white ethnic writers were far less likely to incorporate passing into their works), the connotations are not merely ethnic as they are often assumed exclusively to be, but racial, for the ethnic subject, as recent studies in whiteness would tell us, is attempting to exchange a racially in-between status for an unimpeachably white one. Thus, it is almost impossible to consider the theme of acculturation and subjectivity in white ethnic literature without considering the racial negotiations this necessarily involves, and this is certainly a notable shortcoming in much of the scholarship on white ethnic writers. As we shall see, many of the theories advanced by whiteness scholars have a direct bearing on our reading of ethnic literature, in which whiteness is one of the greatest "pull factors" in characters' subjective migration from racial difference to racial parity.

Roediger's *The Wages of Whiteness: Race and the Making of the American Working Class* (1991) was a significant landmark in working-class studies, African American studies, and whiteness studies, for it provoked a re-examination of the traditional racial binary at the same time that it set out to demonstrate how race was used by white workers to explain both their experiences and those of blacks. Roediger locates American racial formation within the arena of labor, in which working-class whites, in an attempt to garner what W. E. B. DuBois called the psychological "wages of whiteness," viewed themselves as free and productive whites in opposition to allegedly unproductive, servile, and morally depraved African Americans. Roediger also views this as part of a historical pattern in the United States, in which "[b]lackness and whiteness were . . . created together," from colonial times when European settlers needed a convenient excuse for their mistreatment of indigenous peoples, to the mid–nineteenth century when working-class whites increasingly "identified their freedom and their dignity in work" in not being slaves, to the increasingly industrialized period when assimilated white workers began to prize their disciplined "industrial morality" as opposed to the undisciplined "preindustrial morality" ostensibly exhibited by blacks, Native Americans, Asian Americans, and the more recent European immigrants. Thus, at different points in European immigrant history, it was quite possible that "immigrants could be Irish, Italian, Hungarian, and Jewish . . . without being white." This provided the impetus, indeed the "pull factor" of which I speak, for "not-yet-white" ethnic groups to take the necessary social, cultural, political, and economic measures to ensure their instatement as whites—in other words, to "[fight, work and vote] their ways into the white race."[1] Very significantly, this very process of fighting, working, and voting one's way into the white race is exactly the story told by so many ethnic fictional and autobiographical narratives.

More recent work in the field of whiteness theory has drawn further attention to the once in-between racial status of some European immigrant groups and the process by which they became "white" in the eyes of America. *Whiteness of a Different Color: European Immigrants and the*

1. David Roediger, *The Wages of Whiteness: Race and the Making of the American Working Class*, 5, 95, 49, 95–96, 97; Roediger, *Towards the Abolition of Whiteness. Essays on Race, Politics, and Working Class History*, 184. For a discussion of racial formation and European encounters with Native Americans, see *The Wages of Whiteness*, 21.

Alchemy of Race (1998), by Matthew Frye Jacobson, is perhaps the most detailed and comprehensive account of how European immigrant groups assimilated and transcended racial statuses such as "Celtic," "Mediterranean," and "Hebraic" in order to claim new statuses as white Americans or "Caucasians" in a mid-twentieth-century United States where continuing inequalities and civil rights agitation recast the country's racial map in a decidedly more dualistic light. In the book's introduction, Jacobson expands upon a discussion of "racial 'Jewishness'" by arguing that "[t]he vicissitude of Jewish whiteness is intimately related to the racial odysseys of myriad other groups—the Irish, Armenians, Italians, Poles, Syrians, Greeks, Ruthenians, Sicilians, Finns, and a host of others—who came ashore in the United States as 'free white persons' under the terms of the reigning naturalization law, yet whose racial credentials were not equivalent to those of the Anglo-Saxon 'old stock' who laid proprietary claim to the nation's founding documents and hence to its stewardship. All of these groups became Caucasians only over time." Jacobson is rightfully critical of studies on immigration that inaccurately apply contemporary understandings of "ethnicity" to what was once thought to be "race" and would not cease to be thought so until the ardent anti-racialism in the wake of World War II. This understanding of difference lends credence to the idea that, in many cases, immigrants and second-generation "ethnics," in order to abide by socially prescribed standards of whiteness, engaged in *racial* passing.[2]

Jacobson further opens a space for my readings of white ethnic texts as passing narratives in his division of the history of American whiteness into three epochs. In the first epoch, which lasts from 1790 to 1840, there existed an uncomplicated consensus on whiteness largely the result of the Naturalization Act of 1790, under which anyone deemed to be "free" and "white" was eligible for naturalization. The second epoch lasted from 1840 until 1924, during which the tremendous wave of immigrants from first Ireland and then southern and eastern Europe complicated the national perception of whiteness as the white race was splintered into many unequal "white races." The third epoch, which lasts from 1924 until the present, witnesses many white races becoming a "unitary Caucasian race" as white ethnic assimilation, black northern migration, and civil rights agitation reformed race in dualistic terms.[3] The present study

2. Matthew Frye Jacobson, *Whiteness of a Different Color: European Immigrants and the Alchemy of Race*, 3–4, 6.
3. Ibid., 7, 8.

is obviously most concerned with the second epoch, during which white ethnics, such as Italian Americans and Jewish Americans, were ascribed separate *racial* statuses to explain what we now understand to be *ethnic* differences: differences that either become acceptable to the dominant culture or were eliminated through acculturation. But what Jacobson says about Italians and Jews as groups over decades of time could certainly be said about individuals who very rapidly make the attempt "to be suddenly white" by passing. They were, to be sure, traversing *ethnic* ground, but that era's understanding of southern Italian and Russian Jewish difference requires that we see such individuals—and in literature, such characters—as *racially* passing.

In scope, Desmond King's *Making Americans: Immigration, Race, and the Origins of the Diverse Democracy* (2000) is more akin to Jacobson, who is socially and ethnically comprehensive, than to Roediger, who focuses primarily on the Irish working class. However, King is like neither in that he locates white racial formation primarily in immigration policy and legislation, which fostered a primarily Anglo-Saxon conception of American identity that worked temporarily to the disadvantage of "not-yet-white" European Americans (as evidenced by the racist immigration restriction of the 1920s) and perennially to the disadvantage of African Americans, Asian Americans, Native Americans, and others more visibly marked by "race." According to this top-down approach, the most significant landmarks of scientific racialism vis-à-vis European immigrants were congressional: the research and findings of the 1911 U.S. Immigration Commission (also known as the Dillingham Commission, as it was headed by Senator William P. Dillingham) and the resultant Emergency Quota Act of 1921 and Johnson-Reed Act of 1924—all of which worked to minimize southern- and eastern-European immigration. King believes the Dillingham Commission's forty-two-volume report did three things: establish a distinction between old, "superior" northern and eastern European immigration and new, "inferior" southern and eastern European immigration; neglect African Americans, thereby "emphasi[zing] a vision of the United States's identity as a white one"; and express "anxieties" about the assimilability of new immigration, thereby solidifying "the United States's dominant ethnic identity as an Anglo-Saxon one, traceable to the English settlers and subsequent northern European immigrants." King notes that much of the political discourse regarding the racial capabilities of southern and eastern Europeans and their consequential desirability as immigrants was mysteriously silent about African Americans. According to King, this is clear evidence of blacks' presumably permanent racial inferiority as opposed to the contested, probationary racial inferiority of southern and eastern Europeans, for whom "whiteness" would become "a sociological and historical process that enabled formerly reviled immigrants . . . to become part of the U.S. nation."[4]

Whether one favors Roediger's working-class, Jacobson's comprehensive, or King's legislative approach to whiteness, it is clear that race is central to not only African American history but European American history as well. However, I would like to extend these useful insights to European American *literary* history, in which authors have historically attempted to demonstrate the readiness of their co-ethnics for American citizenship, sometimes through the tropes of assimilation and full-blown passing, or, more covertly, through a character's unstated claim of the wages of whiteness.

"The Push Factor": Historical Pressures to Assimilate

Having covered the "pull factor" to assimilation experienced by Italian, Jewish, and African Americans, I now turn briefly to the "push factors." To be sure, the context (or contexts) into which each of the groups was placed—not to mention how group members have been understood to respond to these contexts—is necessary in order to understand the motives of passing characters in the Italian, Jewish, and African American literary traditions. Sociological and historical studies of these groups reveal that passing became one rare option exercised by the members of these groups most willing to sacrifice the cultural attributes of their ancestral heritage in order to achieve full entry into the white bourgeois world.

The Italian Americans

Between 1891 and 1920, four million Italians emigrated to the United States. Mostly southern Italian, this massive migratory wave consisted almost entirely of peasant-class Italians escaping the famines, diseases,

---

4. Desmond King, *Making Americans: Immigration, Race, and the Origins of the Diverse Democracy,* 3, 42, 79, 80, 81, 295–96. The 1921 Emergency Quota Act "limited immigration to 3 percent per annum of each European nationality already resident in the United States, taking the 1910 census as a baseline." Given the ethnic breakdown of the United States in 1910, this obviously discriminated against southern and eastern Europeans. The Johnson-Reed Act, scheduled for implementation in 1927, reduced European immigration to 2 percent annually of each European nationality present in the United States according to the 1890 census. This further reduced the numbers of "undesirable" southern and eastern Europeans allowed into the country.

natural disasters, agricultural depressions, overtaxation, and racial prejudice that had grown steadily worse since Risorgimento had fully unified the Italian state in 1870. Throughout the late nineteenth century, it became increasingly apparent that the economic freedom for which many southern Italians had fought against Bourbon rule was not to be. Southern Italians, who were for the most part peasant sharecroppers (*contadini*) working on bourgeois landowners' property, were taxed heavily by the industrialized north in order to fund further development. By 1910, southern Italians owned a mere 27 percent of the nation's wealth, yet paid 32 percent of its taxes. This imbalance of wealth, combined with already oppressive natural disasters and diseases, created a situation southern Italians referred to as *la miseria*. In the Italy of the late nineteenth and early twentieth centuries, southern Italy occupied a socially, politically, and economically subservient position to the more industrialized north, which refused to aid the south partially due to the widely held belief in innate southern Italian racial inferiority.[5]

As unskilled laborers and peddlers relegated to ghettoes in northeastern and midwestern urban areas of the United States, Italians felt the pangs of both poverty and nativist prejudice. For example, during the first decade of the twentieth century, the Italian American family averaged an income of six hundred dollars, 45 percent of the average income of mainstream American families. As before in Italy, Italian American poverty was attributed partially to racial inferiority, which was used as evidence of southern Italians' innate unfitness for standardized work hours and self-government. Acts of violent anti-Italian hatred became commonplace, as a series of lynchings took place between 1891 and 1911 in places as widespread as West Virginia, Colorado, Louisiana, Mississippi, Florida, and Illinois. The most famous case is the 1891 lynching of eleven New Orleans Italian immigrants accused of murdering the city's police chief, which Matthew Frye Jacobson offers as evidence of Italians' perceived racial "otherness" due to their appearance, their free association with blacks, and their ostensible "innate criminality."[6]

Stereotypical beliefs in southern Italian inferiority, many of which

5. Joseph Lopreato, *Italian Americans*, 14; Richard Gambino, *Blood of My Blood: The Dilemma of the Italian-Americans*, 47–58, 70. For a detailed survey of the Italian American experience, see also Herbert J. Gans, *The Urban Villagers: Group and Class in the Life of Italian-Americans*; Luciano Iorizzo and Salvatore Mondello, *The Italian Americans*; Andrew Rolle, *The American Italians: Their History and Culture*; Patrick Gallo, *Ethnic Alienation: The Italian-Americans*; and Jerre Mangione and Ben Morreale, *La Storia: Five Centuries of the Italian American Experience*.

6. Gambino, *Blood of My Blood*, 87; Jacobson, *Whiteness of a Different Color*, 56–58.

originated in Italy, were given official sanction by the aforementioned Dillingham Commission, which provided in its forty-two-volume report a *Dictionary of Races or Peoples,* listing geographical, cultural, and biological characteristics of all the known peoples of the world. The purpose of the dictionary was to "promot[e] a better understanding of the many different racial elements that [were] being added to the population of the United States through immigration." Italian immigrants were, by far, the most numerous at the time, and given the popular assumption of Italian criminality, also the most troublesome. While the dictionary describes Italians of the more industrialized and cosmopolitan north as "cool, deliberate, patient, practical, and . . . capable of great progress in the political and social organization of modern civilization," the southern Italian, coming from a region of crippling poverty and widespread illiteracy, is described as "excitable, impulsive, highly imaginative, impracticable, [and] as an individualist having little adaptability to highly organized society." The dictionary notes that "all crimes, and especially violent crimes, are several times more numerous among the South than the North Italians"—gambling, Mafia activity, and the vendetta are all provided as evidence of southern Italian criminality. "The immense capacity of the Italian race to populate other parts of the earth," coupled with the "belief that certain kinds of criminality are inherent in the Italian race," made Italian immigration a most troubling issue to ordinary citizens and politicians alike.[7]

In *Italian American: The Racializing of an Ethnic Identity,* the first major work to deal extensively with Italian racial difference in the United States, David A. J. Richards argues from the perspective of legal and constitutional theory that the relegation of southern Italians to positions of inferiority in both Italy and the United States was nothing short of a failure of liberal constitutionalism in both cases. More of a theoretical treatise than a narrative history of Italian American racial formation, *Italian American* nonetheless aptly details the racist culture into which Italians immigrated in the late nineteenth and early twentieth centuries, when pseudo-scientific race theories, influential politicians, and public opinion conspired to devalue Italian American subjectivity. In this context Italian Ameri-

7. Joseph P. Cosco, *Imagining Italians: The Clash of Romance and Race in American Perceptions, 1880–1910,* 176. The Dillingham Commission's 1911 study was hugely influenced by Italian ideas of southern Italian racial inferiority and drew heavily upon social anthropologist Alfredo Niceforo's *L'Italia Barbara Contemporanea (Contemporary Barbarian Italy)* (1898). U.S. Congress, *Dictionary of Races of Peoples,* 2, 82, 83, 84. King, *Making Americans,* 73. Desmond King is here citing U.S. Congress, *Emigration Conditions in Europe,* 209.

cans essentially became "nonvisibly black"—a descriptor that glosses over experiential differences between African Americans and white ethnics but that nonetheless depicts the chasm of racial difference separating white ethnics from the more authentically white dominant culture.[8]

While Richards's version of Italian American racial formation is more or less aligned with Roediger's, King's, and Jacobson's, Thomas A. Guglielmo—who characterizes the former scholars' work as the "wop to white" paradigm—tells a somewhat different story in *White on Arrival: Italians, Race, Color, and Power in Chicago, 1890–1945*. According to Guglielmo, Italians never became white at all: rather, they always were in many fundamental ways. For while naturalization papers would require that immigrants identify their "race," which for most Italian immigration to the United States would mean "South Italian" (and all the connotations of inferiority that went with this), they would also require immigrants to identify their "color," which for "South Italians" was "white." This mere fact would provide Italian Americans, their dubious racial credentials notwithstanding, with social, political, and economic benefits unknown to more visibly racialized Americans. However, rather than self-consciously claim "the wages of whiteness," Italians themselves would first learn to identify (socially, politically, and personally) as *Italians* before they would learn to identify themselves as *white* in the post–World War II period when theories of intra-European racial difference were discredited.[9]

For whiteness scholars, there is unlikely to be a simple resolution to this debate. Were Italians (and, by extension, Jews) initially nonwhite only later to become white? Or were they always white and only in need of assimilation and, eventually, white consciousness? For our purposes, it may be best to imagine a confused consensus—if one could indeed call it that—between the two models, in which the Italian (or Jew) *is* white (and thereby more likely to be able to pass) and yet *not* white, at least not by American standards of Nordic perfection (and thereby in need of a number of acculturative gestures so as to abide by these very standards). It may be that the tension between the two is irresolvable. Our very use of the loaded term "white ethnic" is evidence of this, for while "white" modifies "ethnic" and thereby expresses the limits of the Jew's or Italian's perceived difference, the reverse also unavoidably occurs: that is, "ethnic" indicates our reticence to call the Italian or Jew

8. David A. J. Richards, *Italian American: The Racializing of an Ethnic Identity*, 12.
9. Thomas Guglielmo, *White on Arrival: Italians, Race, Color, and Power in Chicago, 1890–1945*, 6–8. For a concurring view, see Jennifer Guglielmo, "Introduction: White Lies, Dark Truths."

unimpeachably "white." But also for our purposes—that is, the examination of racial passing in white ethnic literature—the distinction between the two models may be, as they say, academic. For whether we view white ethnic authors as fictionalizing the move from "wop to white" or the move from "South Italian/white" to "white," we know they arguably are still covering the same amount of narrative ground, still detailing the same kinds of assimilative processes, and still struggling to find the proper artistic means to do all of this, and this is our primary focus anyway. Furthermore, any whiteness scholar, despite their stance, would agree that the plot structure of an immigrant passing narrative traces the movement of a character from a status of racial inferiority—the specifics of which would generate some disagreement: "South Italian/white," "not yet white," "invisibly black," etc.—to a status of white racial parity—the specifics of which would generate very little disagreement. To put it another way, the white ethnic passing character begins in some kind of racial limbo and attempts to transform him or herself so as to be perceived as purely white by American standards.

It has become a historical commonplace to argue that Italian Americans felt strong social, political, and economic pressures to assimilate to contemporary standards of whiteness. Most sociological and historical accounts of Italian American immigration hold that while full assimilation for first-generation Italians was rare, it became a soul-wrenching concern for their second-generation progeny. Irvin Child identified three potential second-generation reactions to assimilative pressures: the in-group response, the apathetic response, and the rebel response. With the in-group response, the Italian American "resolves the conflict arising from contact with two mutually incompatible cultures [Italian and American] by striving primarily for acceptance by the Italian group." A minority of second-generation Italian Americans, "in-groupers," "turn inward" not so much "to reject American society and culture" as to remain geographically, socially, and spiritually one with his fellow Italian Americans. According to Child, the most common response is the "apathetic," in which the second-generation ethnic devotes little intellectual or emotional energy toward resolving the conflict of Italian and American impulses, instead biding his or her time as a full array of social forces slowly work their assimilative effect.[10]

10. Lopreato, *Italian Americans*, 69, 71, 72–73. For an in-depth discussion of this concept of Italian American assimilation, see also Irvin L. Child, *Italian or American? The Second Generation in Conflict* and Lydio F. Tomasi, *The Italian American Family*.

It is the "rebel" response with which I am most interested in this study. Representative of a minority of second-generation Italian Americans, it involves a rejection of Italian associations in favor of "complete acceptance by the American group." The rebel attempts to rid him or herself of telltale Italian ethnic attributes, associates rarely with fellow Italian Americans in social organizations, and holds a notable degree of animosity toward his or her first-generation parents for their unassimilability, hoping to assimilate fully "in the shortest period possible." One way this happens is by passing for a mainstream white American, and Lopreato actually uses the term "passing" to describe a kind of minority-group "avoidance" behavior.[11] The Italian American literary tradition contains a number of "rebels," some who go so far as to pass for white by using a variety of assimilative strategies.

The Jewish Americans

Jewish Americans were part of the great wave of "new immigrants" that brought millions of Italians to the United States. It is a well-documented fact that Jews had existed in the Americas as early as colonial times, most of them Spanish and Portuguese Sephardim. From 1840 to 1880, the Jewish population in the United States increased from 50,000 to 250,000 as German Ashkenazim escaped the social, political, and economic upheavals that characterized nineteenth-century Europe. Mostly lower-middle-class immigrants, German Jews possessed the resources to settle as far inland as the Midwest and West and were able to use their proficiency as small entrepreneurs to assimilate. Some, such as Levi Straus, even became major retailers.[12] By all accounts, however, the bulk of Jewish American immigration was of Russian origin.

Relegated to the Polish Pale of Settlement since Catherine the Great's eighteenth-century reign, Russian Jews lived a peasant existence detached from the mainstream of Russian culture. Throughout the nineteenth and early twentieth centuries, a series of hostile czars initiated anti-Jewish pogroms that led to a mass migration of more than three million Jews from the shtetls of Russian Poland to the United States from the 1880s through 1920s. This wave of Russian Jewish immigration is characterized most by the fact that, unlike other southeastern European immigration

---

11. Ibid., 69, 70, 168.
12. Max Dimont, *The Jews in America: The Roots and Destiny of American Jews*, 125–26.

of the time, it was family oriented, young, relatively skilled, and inclined toward permanent residency. Once in the United States, many now-urban Russian Jews, particularly of New York, created formidable intellectual communities interested in literature, philosophy, and social theory. Given their veneration of literacy, the Torah, and Talmudic tradition, Russian Jews possessed the intellectual raw materials to become excellent writers in the New World, and this they did in astonishingly disproportionate numbers. However, upon arrival Jewish Americans mostly joined the ranks of factory laborers in the urban Northeast, becoming especially prominent as skilled and semi-skilled laborers in the clothing industry. They were also known, however, to become pushcart peddlers and small shop owners. Contrary to popular stereotypes that viewed Jews as lazy and opportunistic, Jewish Americans were like other contemporary immigrants in that they were hardworking, and arguably unique in that they derived their industriousness and "self-denial" from the values of their Old Testament–based faith.[13]

Nevertheless, this wave of Jewish immigration found itself arriving in an America where nativism, theories of Anglo-Saxon racial superiority, and anti-immigrant sentiment constituted the social and intellectual norm. Predictably, popular notions of Jewish racial distinctiveness were given official sanction. For example, the Dillingham Commission writes of the "Hebrew" that he is most assuredly "not Aryan" and that "[t]he 'Jewish nose' ... [is] found well-nigh throughout the race." There are, of course, countless other examples of official "scientific" accounts of Jewish "biological" and cultural characteristics coinciding with popular stereotypes of Jewish opportunism, guile, selfishness, and laziness. The result was

13. Ibid., 58–59, 160, 164–65. Alexander II, who reigned from 1855 to 1881, promoted Russian nationalism and was not opposed to using force to achieve it. After his assassination, Alexander III, who ruled from 1881 to 1894, turned violently upon Russia's Jewish population through expulsions and pogroms. The repressive reign of Nicholas II, which lasted from 1894 to 1917, was met with the Russian Revolution.

Irving Howe, *World of Our Fathers: The Journey of the East European Jews to America and the Life They Found and Made* and Dimont, *The Jews in America* are both solid histories of the Jewish experience in America. Dimont's study efficiently covers the full spectrum of Jewish immigration, both Sephardic (Spanish and Portuguese) and Ashkenazi (German and Russian), from colonial times through the 1970s, but examines Jewish American culture primarily from the perspective of religious assimilation. Howe's study focuses mainly upon the Russian Jews of New York City, but does so in a more comprehensive manner, covering not only Jewish American religious expression but also Jewish American culture, politics, labor, literature, and scholarship. See also Jeffrey Gurock, *When Harlem Was Jewish, 1890–1925* and Deborah Dash Moore, *At Home in America: Second Generation New York Jews.*

something Irving Howe termed "social anti-Semitism," or an "informal system of exclusion" that was at its worst in the last two decades of the nineteenth century, when Russian Jewish immigration began in earnest. This was promptly followed by the period after World War I when "100% Americanism" was the rallying cry of the day and a general distrust of all things foreign and radical produced a Red Scare. No less significant was the 1920s resurgence of the Ku Klux Klan, which had shifted its focus from African Americans to include Jews and Catholics. In many ways, Jews sharply bore the brunt of American nativism and racialism, often with violent consequences, such as the aftermath of the Leo Frank murder trial of 1915, in which the Jewish defendant, accused of the murder of a female employee at his Atlanta factory, was convicted on spurious evidence and then lynched. Whiteness scholars have viewed this as evidence of Jews' perceived racial difference from other whites—and a very extreme, though real, consequence of it. But when American anti-Semitism did not result in overt, violent discrimination, the "structure of prejudice" more subtly affected the social and economic opportunities afforded Jews and allowed them "to become Americans" only "at arm's length."[14]

In any case, like the Italian Americans, Jewish Americans constituted a racialized minority in the late-nineteenth and early-twentieth-century United States and hence experienced enormous pressure to assimilate. As was the case with their Italian American ethnic counterparts, Jewish Americans' assimilation could become as extreme as passing, and as early as 1937, "passing" was indeed used to describe the experiences of Jews who wished to merge seamlessly and imperceptibly with the dominant American culture. In *The Marginal Man: A Study in Personality and Culture Conflict*, a seminal study on race, national origins, and assimilation, Everett Stonequist devotes an entire chapter to "Assimilation and Passing." To Stonequist, passing is one option of the ethnic or racial "marginal man" who finds himself uneasily straddling the border between cultures (for example, Jewish and American, Italian and American, black

14. U.S. Congress, *Dictionary*, 74; Jacobson, *Whiteness of a Different Color*, 62; Howe, *The World of our Fathers*, 409. For a discussion of the confluence of race and popular Jewish stereotypes, see King, *Making Americans*, 62. Also, see Karen Brodkin, *How Jews Became White Folks* for a study of the process by which Jewish Americans were initially afforded a status of racial inferiority only later to join the ranks of the white American mainstream. It is like David Richards, *Italian American* not only in its specificity to the racial experience of one ethnic group, but also in some of the conclusions it draws—particularly with regard to the Jewish American historical adoption of mainstream racial views in order to enter that very mainstream.

and American). Stonequist explains this concept in a manner that speaks directly to the experience of Jewish Americans: "Partial or complete incorporation into the dominant culture . . . may take the form of assimilation, as with the immigrant and his children; it may take the form of 'passing' as a member of the dominant group where such assimilation is possible. In order to pass the individual must possess the general physical and social traits of the dominant group. The Jew who is not accepted on terms of equality can pass provided his language, name, and other social characteristics do not betray him; but the person of mixed blood must be able to conform physically as well as culturally." Thus having underscored both the physiognomic and cultural components of passing, Stonequist provides a number of case studies of Jewish Americans who passed in order to secure employment. According to one Jewish American subject from Chicago, "I had been working all my life—and now nationality stood between me and starvation. I resolved to change my nationality and go to work—I went into another employment bureau, changed my name, nationality, etc., and got a job—right away, mind you! It was easy for me to get along as a Gentile as I had mostly Gentile habits—not having lived amongst members of my own race for any great length of time, and fortunately I looked like a German and that helped— You can bet." As this subject is at least unconsciously aware, given his reference to the Jewish "race" to which he belongs, this change of "nationality" amounted to a perceived change of race, from the reviled Jewish "race" to the favored German "race." Hence, an ethnic subject, whom we would now consider to be self-evidently "white," actually engaged in a kind of *racial* passing in order to achieve acceptance in American society. But what was readily palpable to Everett Stonequist and his contemporaries has become obscured by contemporary conceptions of ethnicity in which any Irish American, Italian American, or Jewish American claim to difference is based purely on matters of culture and national origin, not race; therefore, "passing" tends not to be applied to the experience of such white ethnic groups. However, for Stonequist passing had much broader implications than it has today. He reveals, "in Jewish districts in Chicago there are individuals of Italian origin who have passed as Jews. Among Germans, a Polish girl may prefer to be German. A Swedish young man on an Irish baseball team passes as Irish. A white child among coloured children wishes she were dark so that she would not be excluded. During the World War many Germans found it more comfortable to be Scandinavians or Dutch. The principle seems to be that of the minority wishing to share the advantages of membership in the majority, or to escape its discriminations and antagonisms."[15] Nevertheless, presentist notions of race have unfortunately narrowed critical attention regarding passing almost exclusively upon the group to which we now turn our attention, African Americans: a fact that almost certainly has hindered our understanding of the African American experience, especially from a comparative perspective.

The African Americans

The 1860s era saw the passing of the Thirteenth, Fourteenth, and Fifteenth Amendments, which freed the slaves, gave blacks equal protection under the law, and afforded them equal male voting rights. However, after the end of Reconstruction, African American dreams turned into nightmares as rabid racism, lynching, Jim Crow laws, and Ku Klux Klan terrorism left blacks little better off than they were under slavery. Historians have identified a number of pivotal historical events in African American race formation, most importantly the 1896 Supreme Court decision in *Plessy v. Ferguson*, which gave legal sanction to segregation and bolstered a system of Jim Crow that "became a powerful instrument of oppression, denying Southern blacks the American dream of upward mobility through education and effort." By the 1910s, this trend was fully entrenched and pressured many African Americans into passing.[16]

Many African Americans in the South chose escape and new beginnings. Between 1916 and 1930, some one million African Americans left the South for the urban North and Midwest, a movement that, in a very limited sense, provided migrants with employment in the burgeoning industries north of the Mason-Dixon line. This massive wave of African American migration (later termed the "Great Migration") left the failing agricultural economy, Jim Crow legislation, and underdeveloped industrial economy of the South for the employment opportunities and presumed socioeconomic egalitarianism of the urban North. These black migrants were akin to the southern and eastern European migrants who preceded them in that they tended to be young, male, and in search of

15. Everett V. Stonequist, *The Marginal Man: A Study in Personality and Culture Conflict*, 184, 194, 199. Sollors, *Neither Black nor White*, 247, mentions a number of these circumstances of unconventional passing as they appear in *The Marginal Man*.

16. F. James Davis, *Who Is Black?: One Nation's Definition*, 56.

better economic opportunities. Northbound African Americans filled the labor void created by the temporary halt in European immigration that occurred during World War I, which was followed by a more permanent stemming of the tide courtesy of the 1920s immigration restriction. But by and large, African American laborers were held in lower regard than their ethnic counterparts, despite their level of skill and the fact that southern blacks were generally more literate than the European immigrants of the time.[17]

As Desmond King has argued, African American inferiority to European immigrants was so self-evident to the mainstream that there is little mention of blacks in the intellectual and political discourses regarding assimilation in the early twentieth century. Furthermore, theories of race science consistently placed African Americans at the bottom of the racial totem pole in the United States. For example, a major psychological study for the U.S. military determined in 1921 that while "[t]he darker people of southern Europe and the Slavs of eastern Europe are less intelligent than the fair peoples of western and northern Europe," African Americans were considered to have a lower "mental age" than every other ethnic group in the United States. The earlier Dillingham Commission had concurred, assigning the "Negro" "to the lowest division of mankind from an evolutionary standpoint."[18] Popular opinion also tended to place blacks beneath even the lowly southern and eastern Europeans. This has been well documented in a number of studies that compare the experiences of blacks and white ethnics in late-nineteenth and early-twentieth-century urban American schools, workplaces, and social settings. The story is almost always the same: African Americans experi-

17. Carole Marks, *Farewell—We're Good and Gone: The Great Black Migration*, 1–2, 94, 169–70; Blyden Jackson, "Introduction: A Street of Dreams," xiv-xv. On the causes and consequences of the Great Migration, see also Alfredteen Harrison, ed., *Black Exodus: The Great Migration from the American South*, a collection of essays that offers a more traditional treatment of the subject matter, and Joe William Trotter, Jr., ed., *The Great Migration in Historical Perspective: New Dimensions of Race, Class, and Gender*, which attempts to bring the scholarship on African American migration more theoretically up to date.

18. Stephen Jay Gould, *The Mismeasure of Man*, 225, 227; U. S. Congress, *Dictionary*, 100. *The Mismeasure of Man* is a survey of the a priori biases of European and American race science and eugenics. It reveals that while southern and eastern Europeans were not exactly treated kindly by race theories of the late nineteenth and early twentieth centuries, African Americans generally bore the brunt of "scientifically" determined inferiority.

ence the harshest racial prejudice and are consistently denied more opportunities than even their white ethnic counterparts.[19]

Although it would seem that African Americans experienced even more pressure to assimilate than European immigrants, this would prove more difficult for those lacking any potential future claim to whiteness. Changing "class, ethnic origin, and sexual orientation" is one thing, but changing social statuses that have more obvious biological connotations—"race and gender," for example—is quite another, and thus passing is generally unachievable for those ethnics whose "racial marks" too easily distinguish them from the white mainstream. Given the incontrovertible stigma of visible "racial" difference, and given that one-drop racial logic—which grew in national power from the Civil War to World War I—did not allow for a comfortable coexistence of both "ethnic" and "American" attributes, passing became a legitimate option only for those light-skinned blacks who could most easily take shelter in the namelessness of the modern city and become "full-time" whites.[20] Unsurprisingly, it is the modern city where most of the literary saga of African American passing takes place.

Although statistics on the subject are scarce and tend to vary wildly, one credible estimate has ten thousand to twenty-five thousand African Americans passing for white each year from 1880 to 1925, when the practice was at its zenith.[21] St. Clair Drake and Horace R. Cayton, in their 1945 study of race relations in Chicago entitled *Black Metropolis,* indicate that at the time of their writing, between twenty-five thousand and three hundred thousand had passed fully into "white society." However, Drake's and Cayton's study is perhaps useful not so much for statistical certainty on passing, but rather for its detailed exploration of the five varieties of passing, each accompanied by real-life examples culled from

19. See, for example, John Bodnar, Roger Simon, and Michael Weber, *Lives of Their Own: Blacks, Italians, and Poles in Pittsburgh, 1900–1960,* 264; Joel Perlmann, *Ethnic Differences: Schooling and Social Structure among the Irish, Italians, Jews, and Blacks in an American City, 1880–1935,* 168; and Christopher M. Sterba, *Good Americans: Italian and Jewish Immigrants during the First World War,* 189.

20. Ginsberg, "Introduction," 41; Stonequist, *The Marginal Man,* 185. Very interestingly, particularly from our contemporary perspective of white ethnic racial in-betweenness, Stonequist assigns Jews a mixed-race status that renders racial identification difficult, if not impossible. St. Clair Drake and Horace R. Cayton, *Black Metropolis: A Study of Negro Life in a Northern City,* 159. For a brief history of the "one-drop rule" in the United States, see Davis, *Who Is Black?* 12–13, 58.

21. Davis, *Who Is Black?* 22.

case studies: "unintentional" passing, in which an African American is unwittingly mistaken for a white (by way of example, Drake and Cayton tell of one woman who was mistaken for a Jew; as we shall see, the literature of African American passing is replete with instances of blacks being taken for darker-skinned ethnics); "passing for convenience," for example to escape periodic encounters with discrimination and Jim Crow; "passing for fun," significant because it can supposedly be done without remorse; passing "out of economic necessity or advantage" (the most common reason); and, finally, "crossing over completely to the other side of the color-line"—complete absorption into white, middle-class culture in both its public and private realms.[22] Each of these "types" of passing, which Drake and Cayton present as stages of increased social transgression, is fictionalized in the literature of African American passing.

When it comes to the likelihood of success in passing, visible racial difference—as perceived in one's hair, skin, or bodily characteristics— best determines whether one may be "taken for white." Thus, clearly not every African American could pass, and it is the problem of visible difference that made passing for African Americans more difficult and restrictive than it ever could be for Jewish Americans and Italian Americans. Drake and Cayton recognize that the more easily the African American passer might be confused with a white, the more likely his or her passing will meet with success. Furthermore, any racial difference ascribed to "such marginal persons is sociological rather than biological; and what really determines their 'race' is how much the public knows about their ancestry."[23] This assessment, however, applies to Italian Americans and Jewish Americans as well; for "racial differences" attributed to members of both groups were most often conceived retroactively—only *after* it was known that the particular subject was Italian American or Jewish American. The fundamental difference between black and white ethnic passing, however, lies in the fact that however light the African American or however dark the ethnic, African ancestry created a heavier legal and social burden than southern or eastern European ancestry, even though none were held in favorable regard during the relevant time period. African American passing simply held different implications, carried greater risks, violated more strictly policed boundaries, and was

22. Drake and Cayton, *Black Metropolis*, 160–63. On economic necessity as the most common reason for passing, see Davis, *Who Is Black?* 56.
23. Drake and Cayton, *Black Metropolis*, 164, 165.

thus arguably a very different sort of action than white ethnic passing. This distinction becomes quite significant when considering the dynamics of determinism—and its narrative foil, free will—in ethnic literature.

Genre and the Imperative Duties of Passing

In this study, I will examine the passing figure through the lens of American literary realism, a historical genre that often features protagonists who freely will a transformation of themselves into morally and materially successful Americans—exactly the motive of so many characters in passing narratives. My sense of realism is informed not so much by the influence of any one literary figure or theorist as it is by the realist zeitgeist of American literary culture in the 1880s and 1890s. I am aware of both the diversity of understandings of realism among practitioners and theorists such as Henry James, William Dean Howells, Mark Twain, and Hamlin Garland, and of the chronological shift from the arguably "optimistic" realism of the 1880s to the more pessimistic determinism of Frank Norris, Theodore Dreiser, and Stephen Crane. Still, my sense of realism in American literary production is generous, includes works published outside the main era of American realism, and is not intended to be exclusive. That is, it allows that generic intermixing can be more the rule than the exception, with realist elements operating alongside romantic, naturalistic, and modernistic ones. However, for clarity's sake, and admittedly for simplicity's sake, my understanding of realism relies upon well-documented common trends in the genre, such as a commitment to social verisimilitude, an engagement with the idea of the individual as possessing an authentic inner self, and a concomitant engagement with, even belief in, the moral agency of the individual. Such concerns pervaded "mainstream" realism of the late nineteenth century and would continue to preoccupy white ethnic and African American writers throughout the time of modernism, even when such writers as James Weldon Johnson, Jean Toomer, Nella Larsen, and Samuel Ornitz also could be thought to be writing in a more modernist vein.

I believe that this generic approach is appropriate because even during the early-twentieth-century heyday of modernism, white ethnic texts were preoccupied with the decidedly *realist* endeavor of closely describing ethnic cultures and challenging American cultural narratives (particularly racist ones)—even as they reaffirmed others, most significantly the

American success myth. Mainstream American realists' treatment of the success myth was by no means uncomplicated and uncritical, but its centrality to the genre suggests a kind of optimistic faith in American democracy that many white ethnic and (earlier) African American writers would adopt to demonstrate the morality, ability, and fundamental "Americanness" of their respective peoples. Indeed, this abiding optimism is arguably the primary distinction between realism and naturalism. For an American realist such as Hamlin Garland, "it was the responsibility of the novelist to depict not only society's wrongs but also man's finer nature struggling toward an inevitably brighter day." Indeed, Garland believed that through the ennobling effects of American democracy, such a day was possible, as he proclaims in his 1894 realist manifesto *Crumbling Idols:*

> If the past was bond, the future will be free. If the past was feudalistic, the future will be democratic. If the past ignored and trampled upon women, the future will place them side by side with men. If the child of the past was ignored, the future will cherish him. And fiction will embody these facts. If the past was dark and battleful and bloody and barbarous, the future will be peaceful and sunny. If the past celebrated lust and greed and love of power, the future will celebrate continence and humility and altruism. If the past was the history of a few titled personalities riding high on obscure waves of nameless, suffering humanity, the future will be the day of high average personality, the abolition of all privilege, the peaceful walking together of brethren, equals before nature and before the law. And fiction will celebrate this life.

In no uncertain terms, Garland believed that "[t]he realist . . . is really an optimist, a dreamer. He sees life in terms of what it might be as well as in terms of what it is." This brand of critical optimism was a central feature of the realist zeitgeist of late-nineteenth-century American literary culture, which is to say that while the realism of Mark Twain, William Dean Howells, Henry James, and the like could no doubt be "satirical" at times, it also exhibited a "basic devotion to American republicanism, science, and the doctrine of progress": a democratic credo that was held in opposition to the aristocratic foibles of sentimentalism.[24]

---

24. Jane Johnson, Introduction, xvii, xx; Hamlin Garland, *Crumbling Idols: Twelve Essays on Art Dealing Chiefly with Literature, Painting and the Drama,* 39, 43; Everett Carter, *Howells and the Age of Realism,* 68.

All the narratives I will discuss are either predominantly realist in theme and style or, at the very least, contain notably realist elements, but the generic connection is more specific than this. Classic realist texts are often structured around scenes of agency in which a character, presented with a dilemma, can exercise free will and make a moral, if difficult choice.[25] This presents a potential contradiction in that while the realist must truthfully represent societal wrongs, he or she also clings to a belief in human agency that might in reality be undercut by the very wrongs he or she describes. Thus, in the drive to depict "a more favorable adaptation to a sordid environment," realist writers run the risk of being profoundly *unrealistic,* even though investing characters with moral agency undoubtedly serves important rhetorical purposes for the ethnic writer. Nevertheless, the more specific questions raised by the passing narrative concerning agency and morality make it particularly attractive for a reading from the perspective of literary realism. One of the moral dilemmas white ethnic and African American characters encounter is whether or not to abandon completely the trappings of their ancestral heritage in favor of a new "American" identity; hence, to pass or not to pass becomes the moral dilemma of the passing narrative's scene of agency. Yet, the realism of so many white ethnic and African American authors is tempered with a heavy infusion of naturalism, in which the hard logic of determinism coerces characters into the decisions they make and the actions they perform. For white ethnic and African American characters alike, this coercion can come in the form of prejudice, discrimination, barriers of gender, and the seemingly ineludible presence of ancestral heritage. These characters, then, are trapped between opposing sets of duties: to ethnicity on the one hand and to success in the American mainstream on the other. The problem of agency as revealed in these works is the result of the passing character's free-willing agency coming into conflict with the more deterministic and coercive elements of his or her story. Indeed, making sense of the "ethnic self" according to realist logic may, in fact, be impossible. What Lee Clark Mitchell says about the naturalist self in literature could certainly be said about the ethnic self with its irresolvably dizzying array of both self-determined and externally determined components: "the closer one attends to the self, the less it tends to cohere— as if the very process of depiction somehow dismantled subjectivity, breaking the self apart piece-by-piece and absorbing it into an indifferent

25. Lee Clark Mitchell, "Naturalism and Languages of Determinism," 530; Mitchell, *Determined Fictions: American Literary Naturalism,* xii.

world."[26] I contend that the more acute the conflict between free will and determinism, the more conflicted the realism, and the more sophisticated the narrative must be—even to the point of avoiding straightforward realist mimesis—in order for the author to create a sense of rhetorical freedom for the protagonist and critique the ideologies of race that oppress him or her. This is most evident in the African American literary tradition, where among male-centered passing narratives, we encounter an increasingly potent ironic critique of race, and perhaps more so in black female-centered passing narratives, especially Nella Larsen's *Passing*, in which the double-marginalization of race and gender is at its most deterministic, yet the narrative's modernist evolution beyond the representational and ideological strictures of realism creates freedom for its enigmatic protagonist Clare Kendry. I will provide readings of novels and autobiographies by white ethnic male and women writers, as well as African American male and female writers, demonstrating that the different challenges of ethnicity, race, and gender described therein require different kinds of passing acts, which in turn produce realist narratives with varying degrees of complexity and generic conflictedness.

Agency, already a complex subject in classic realist texts such as *The Rise of Silas Lapham* (1885), by William Dean Howells; *Adventures of Huckleberry Finn* (1885), by Mark Twain; and *The Portrait of a Lady* (1881), by Henry James, is rendered even more complicated by race, ethnicity, and gender.[27] To be sure, agency is a problematic idea not easily resolved within the confines of any text, but this fact underscores an important aspect of the realist enterprise—bringing literary closure to situations that most resist it. Recent studies of realism that focus on the "social constructedness" of the genre have posited that realist texts use their presupposed mimetic legitimacy to reconcile the more troubling aspects of American society with the realist's own idealized vision or sense of representational propriety. This might explain why many ethnic texts written in the style of realism create a sense, if only illusory, of agency for the characters contained therein. From a social constructionist standpoint, it could be argued that authors of these works struggle rhetorically to create a sense

26. Jane Johnson, Introduction, xvii; Mitchell, *Determined Fictions*, 17.
27. For a discussion of James's *A Portrait of a Lady* and Isabel Archer's *actual* degree of free will versus her *ideal* conception of it, see Miles Orvell, *The Real Thing: Imitation and Authenticity in American Culture, 1880–1940*, 66. Also, for a discussion of the limits of Silas's agency in *The Rise of Silas Lapham*, see Edwin H. Cady, *The Road to Realism: The Early Years of William Dean Howells, 1837–1885*, 231.

of free will for characters despite a social context that might dictate otherwise. Priscilla Wald's exploration of "the limits of storytelling" in *Constituting Americans* might be helpful here: that is, the notion that the ostensible seamlessness of narrative form—in this case, realism—can be used, if imperfectly, to mask substantial contradictions in meaning, which for our purposes are created when the ethnic character's agency comes into conflict with his or her deterministic circumstances.[28]

Illusory or not, this privileging of agency explains, in part, why realism's most vigorous theorist and advocate, William Dean Howells, was so fascinated by "character," not merely as a textual ingredient, but as the driving force behind the moral choices people and literary characters make. Edwin H. Cady has argued that "[r]ealists were concerned first and last with character, sacrificing every fictional consideration to present their vision of personhood." Indeed, the writings of mainstream realists confirm the notion that character, and not circumstance, propels the plot of a realist text. For example, Henry James, in his 1908 preface to the New York Edition of *The Portrait of a Lady*, writes that the entire novel was inspired by "the sense of a single character, the character and aspect of a particular engaging young woman," Isabel Archer. The logic of realism encourages such a creative approach, for according to Howells, "The true plot comes out of the character; that is, the man does not result from the things he does, but the things he does result from the man, and so plot comes out of character." Praising Mark Twain's characterization and comparing realism favorably to romanticism, Howells writes that "one of the differences between the romantic and the realistic was that the realistic finds a man's true character under all accidents and under all circumstances." Character, for the realists, is best exemplified through the moral exercise of free will; thus, according to Howells, "When men are bent upon sin," they are "saved" not "by melodramatic accident," but by "their own free wills." Similarly, James's germinal idea of Isabel Archer—before she is brought into the deterministic embroilments that would weigh in against her—is of a freely willing individual "not confined by the conditions, not engaged in the tangle, to which we look for much of the impress that constitutes an identity." Then, after serious contemplation that dramatizes the moral epitome of realist personhood, the classically realist character, given a moral crisis, is able to exhibit solid character and to "do the right thing," so to speak: Twain's Huckleberry

28. Priscilla Wald, *Constituting Americans: Cultural Anxiety and Narrative Form*, 1.

Finn tears up the letter that would have sent Jim back to Miss Watson, Howells's Silas decides not to cheat the English investors, and James's Isabel Archer decides not to divorce her husband.[29]

The precise degree of agency exercised by these characters is debatable, but nowhere does the indeterminacy of agency become more problematic than when race, ethnicity, and gender become factors, not simply because these are deterministic forces in the lives of literary characters, but because each can be simultaneously the impetus for and the target of significant lifestyle changes. In many white ethnic and African American narratives, and especially passing narratives, the primary question of agency concerns the character's ability to pass from a racially "other" white ethnic or African American subject position to that of a mainstream, white American. Everett Stonequist's concept of the *parvenu*, or the individual who leaves one social class for a more prestigious one, is very helpful here not only because it essentially describes the motive of the passer but also because the manner in which it is described underscores the free-willing agency of the *parvenu*. Stonequist believes that the milieu of the United States is particularly conducive to *parvenu* activity: "In a society of relatively open classes, where ancestors count less heavily in the balance sheet of the individual's present status, the *parvenu* is the rule instead of the exception. Instead of being regarded with suspicion, as in an old country like England, in America he becomes glorified in the doctrine of the 'self-made man' and immortalized in the epic 'from log-cabin to White House.'"[30] However, implicit in the very act of leaving one ethnic or racial subject position for another is the seemingly ineludible determinism of ancestry, as well as a prejudicial social context that

---

29. Edwin H. Cady, *The Light of Common Day: Realism in American Fiction*, 102; James, Preface, 1071, 1076; William Dean Howells, *Selected Literary Criticism*, 283, 290, 77. On the scene from *The Rise of Silas Lapham*, see Cady, *The Light of Common Day*, 142: "the truest force of a realist's morality in *The Rise of Silas Lapham* bears upon Silas's repentance. His turning again at the price of pride and fortune wins him only the grace of a rise from the pit up to the plane of free humanity. His vision cleared, he may begin the good, humble life, once more a man." On the scene from *The Portrait of a Lady*, see James, Preface, 1084. James himself considered Isabel Archer's "extraordinary meditative vigil" to be an aesthetically pleasing and thematically important "vigil of searching criticism" that is, in effect, "the best thing in the book." For a discussion of the scenes of deliberation and moral agency in *The Rise of Silas Lapham, The Portrait of a Lady*, and *Adventures of Huckleberry Finn*, see Mitchell, *Determined Fictions*, 4–10.

30. I am here indebted to Werner Sollors, for his application of the idea of the parvenu to literary passing in chapter 9 of *Neither Black nor White*. Stonequist, *Marginal Man*, 6.

provoked the change in the first place; indeed, the passing character's "choice" is almost always "condition[ed] . . . on factors outside of the subject's own individualized choosing."[31] Furthermore, the act of passing itself essentializes the ancestral subject position that is vacated, effectively "run[ning] against the notion that ancestry . . . should not matter in a true democracy." To be sure, there is much determinism implicit in passing, however freely willed and arduously attained the act may appear to be, and this immediately problematizes a central myth of American egalitarianism, as well as a central feature of American literary realism. Werner Sollors, using the language of Stonequist and Melville, argues that the idea of having to privilege one ancestry type (for example, "white") over another ("black," "Italian," or "Jewish") also "seems at particular odds with a social system that otherwise cherishes social mobility[;] espouses the right of individuals to make themselves anew by changing name, place, and fortune[;] and that has produced famous *parvenus* and confidence men." Thus, the ethnic *parvenu*—the one who, through great exercise of will, effects a personal change that is in many ways forced and negotiated under terms beyond the control of the *parvenu*—presents a unique problem for the realist, who, to use Judith Butler's terms, would rather believe in the "voluntarist subject who exists quite apart from the regulatory norms which she/he opposes" but who, especially through the creation of the ethnic character, and more specifically the passing character, may in fact be "locat[ing that character's] agency as a reiterative or rearticulatory practice, immanent to power."[32]

Another way of understanding the indeterminate agency of the passing act in literature is by examining how it relates to assimilation theory. In his seminal study, *Assimilation in American Life: The Role of Race, Religion, and National Origin*, Milton M. Gordon usefully separates assimilation into two components: cultural assimilation and structural assimilation. In the former, the subject undergoes internal (religion, system of ethics, music, folk recreation, literature, language, and sense of common past) and external changes (dress, mannerism, patterns of emotional expression, and pronunciation) in order to adapt to the ways of the core society. For the most part, cultural assimilation is freely willed by the individual and "is likely to be the first of the types of assimilation to occur when a minority group arrives on the scene." Indeed, it involves all the cultural

31. Wald, *Constituting Americans*, 28.
32. Sollors, *Neither Black nor White*, 249–50; Judith Butler, *Bodies That Matter: On the Discursive Limits of "Sex,"* 15.

changes over which the individual has immediate control. The passing character, in a supreme exercise of free will that defines the realist passing narrative's scene(s) of agency, culturally assimilates and thereby undergoes the necessary changes of thought, manner, and appearance that will bring him or her full acceptance into the American dominant culture.

Structural assimilation, usually a consequence of cultural assimilation, embodies the more deterministic elements of assimilation: those that are beyond the reach of the individual. This aspect of assimilation involves the "entrance of" the assimilating individual "into primary group relationships with the" dominant culture and is dependent upon the willingness of the primary group to give full acceptance to the assimilating individual. Full structural assimilation, of course, is the ultimate goal of the passing character. However, in a country in which Anglo-conformity traditionally has been the primary assimilative option, groups have had varying degrees of success with *structural* assimilation, the ability to *culturally* assimilate notwithstanding; unsurprisingly, white ethnics accomplish structural assimilation—some by what Gordon calls "sociological 'passing'"—much more handily than nonwhite ethnics.[33] This is the assimilative reality that characters of the works here considered must confront: a hierarchy in which white ethnic eventually can achieve at least guarded acceptance—full acceptance if they can pass successfully—while those more visibly marked by race can never fully assimilate into the white dominant culture unless their appearance permits it. In any case, however freely willed the character's cultural assimilation, they must confront the uncertain external reality of structural assimilation and the inevitable link between agency and the power that both restricts and helps articulate it.

As I have tried to demonstrate, the question of agency—to pass or not to pass?—is so wrought with contradictions that the realism of each of the texts examined is unavoidably conflicted. The more deterministic the context in which the character operates, the more conflicted the realism becomes and the more narratologically clever the author must be in order to create a sense of self-definition and self-determination for the character. Thus, a case could be made that the African American male passing narratives of Charles Chesnutt and James Weldon Johnson embody a more conflicted realism than that of white ethnic male passing narratives by the likes of Guido d'Agostino and Ludwig Lewisohn, because,

33. Milton M. Gordon, *Assimilation in American Life: The Role of Race, Religion, and National Origins*, 79, 77, 70, 129.

given the social context, the idea of a white ethnic exchanging an Italian or Jewish racial position for a white one is not only more permissible but quite simply more likely than an African American shedding his or her black racial position. Despite outward appearances, the curse of "black blood" was far more burdensome than that of "Mediterranean" or "Hebraic blood," and the consequences that awaited the revealed African American passer could be more severe. Given that there is racially more at stake for the African American than for the white ethnic, who could eventually use whiteness to his or her advantage, there is, I argue, a concomitant tendency for white ethnic writers to *romanticize* their supposed racial attributes, while in African American literary history there is (admitting a troubling early tendency also to romanticize race) a far greater attempt to critique what Frantz Fanon called the "arsenal of complexes," indeed, the "absurd drama," that is race.[34] In the final analysis, the author who creates a sense of self-autonomy for the African American passer and brings closure to the text is performing a greater rhetorical feat than the author who does the same for an Italian American or Jewish American character.

As one might expect, female gender further complicates matters, adding an additional layer of "othered" subjectivity and all the gender-specific barriers that come with it.[35] In realist narratives, female characters find that the road to white bourgeois status is not only more difficult but also involves different strategies. For while the male passer must prove adept at negotiating the free market, the female passer customarily achieves her goal through success in the marriage market, a fact that has earned authors of female passing narratives, such as Nella Larsen and Jessie Fauset, a significant amount of criticism. Still, while the attempt to give self-definition and autonomy to white ethnic female-centered passing characters is difficult enough, as evinced by the work of Anzia Yezierska and Helen Barolini, nowhere is the narratological challenge greater than it is for authors of African American women's passing narratives, where both character and author must overcome the impossibility of the strictest racial and gender barriers. It is in the African American women's passing narrative where the logic of literary realism is stretched to the breaking point, and in order for the author to create the obligatory sense of free will required by literary realism, but otherwise nearly

34. Fanon, *Black Skin, White Masks,* 30, 197.
35. Mary V. Dearborn, *Pocahontas's Daughters: Gender and Ethnicity in American Culture,* 5.

impossible in the "real world," she must render the character unknow-able according to the conventional logic of the "real world." If success-ful, the result is a character whose indeterminacy opens the text, renders it more writerly, and takes it to places never before gone by realism, thereby anticipating the subjective and narratological "decenteredness" of postmodernism.

2

To Pass or Not to Pass?

William Dean Howells's and Frances E. W. Harper's "Not Very Black" Women

In 1892, two novels were published that laid the foundation for future passing narratives to be written in a realist vein. William Dean Howells's *An Imperative Duty* and Frances E. W. Harper's *Iola Leroy, or Shadows Uplifted* offer different versions of the same story: a young, light-skinned African American woman who believes she is white learns she has "black blood" and, in the tumultuous aftermath of this discovery, must decide whether to live her life as an African American, or even to become a vocal proponent of "racial uplift." In this chapter, I will examine both novels as realist texts and demonstrate that the manner in which they reveal the paradoxes of agency would set an example that passing narratives would follow throughout the twentieth century. Both novels are significant in that they establish "to pass or not to pass?" as a central moral dilemma and, in their dramatization of the consequent decision, suggest that this dilemma is resolved through either an act of perceived cultural betrayal or an act of perceived racial allegiance—an arguably simplistic dualism suggestive of the first cultural notion of passing that would nevertheless replicate itself throughout twentieth-century passing narratives until complicated by the more radically antiracialist rhetoric of the African American tradition.

Both *An Imperative Duty* and *Iola Leroy* have differing, yet likewise conflicted, realist credentials. However, despite Howells's firm belief that realism could work for social betterment, *Iola Leroy*, with its thick description of African American slave culture, its unabashed honesty about problems confronting nineteenth-century African Americans, and its comparatively explicit antiracialism, is of a more rhetorically effective kind of realism than Howells's own *An Imperative Duty*, which addresses race on a theoretical level but avoids some of the finer details of lived racial experience. Therefore, while *Iola Leroy* seems in some ways to be the more romantic text, it is also for the aforementioned reasons paradoxically more realistic and arguably a direct critique of Howells's abhorrence of "duty" in all its forms, particularly with regard to race. Furthermore, while Howells's work closes with a "cop-out" that belies the author's position of racial and literary cultural privilege, Harper's work bravely manages to negotiate a number of potential narratological obstacles, including the problem of agency, the ethics of passing, audience standards of "decency," and difficult decisions of narrative form.

Howells, Realism, and Passing

For Howells (1837–1920), realism served a number of significant and interrelated functions. During his career as editor of *Atlantic Monthly* from 1871 to 1881 and "Editor's Study" columnist for *Harper's Monthly* from 1886 to 1892, Howells routinely attacked the aristocratic extravagances of literary romanticism while advancing realism as an agent of favorable aesthetic, moral, social, and political change. In his May 1886 "Editor's Study" column, Howells writes that by exhibiting a "fidelity to experience and probability of motive," "realism seeks to widen the bounds of sympathy to level every barrier against aesthetic freedom." But for Howells, realism was to serve a function beyond mere aesthetics; additionally, it would "reflect and play a major role in encouraging the social and political progress that characterized nineteenth-century life." Thus, according to Howells, if fiction "cease[s] to lie about life" and remains "true to the motives, the impulses, the principles that shape the life of actual men and women," then it necessarily participates in both "the highest morality and highest artistry."[1]

For Howells realism also could foster the middle-class ethic of productiveness, prosperity, and progress that came to the fore in the rapidly

---

1. Eric J. Sundquist, "Realism and Regionalism," 503; Howells, *Selected Literary Criticism*, 21, 45–46, 49; Donald Pizer, "Introduction: The Problem of Definition," 6.

industrializing America in which he wrote: indeed, Howells in some ways "validates realism" by "locat[ing] it within the producer's ethos of the middle class." In this regard, realist literary production for Howells could not only promote but also become productive work in and of itself. Not coincidentally, many of Howells's novels focus upon the workaday life and moral beliefs of the middle class—perhaps most famously in *The Rise of Silas Lapham.* Insofar as the focal point of Howells's mimesis can be considered to be the "common people" of the middle class, realism can be viewed as nothing less than a reaffirmation of "the ideals of democracy" as understood by ordinary Americans.[2]

Perhaps most relevant to the idea of passing is realism's privileging of individual character and moral agency—exactly the sort of moral agency one would require to decide whether to pass. In his July 1891 review of William James's *The Principles of Psychology,* Howells praises the pragmatist philosopher's treatment of the subject of free will, equating the moral exercise of it with manly fortitude: "In fact the will of the weak man is *not* free; but the will of the strong man, the man who has *got the habit* of preferring sense to nonsense and 'virtue' to 'vice,' is a *freed* will, which one might very well spend one's energies in achieving." For William James and Howells alike, "character" was made up of the sum of one's moral choices, an idea that had both literary and social implications; to be sure, "[c]haracter for Howells and his contemporaries implied more than a neutral descriptive term for a structural element in a novel; it carried the moral connotations of personal integrity." Thus, if one had good "character," one held the power to act when confronted with a variety of moral dilemmas.[3]

However, despite the moral and representational optimism of realism, many critics have identified social and aesthetic limitations to the genre's mimetic project. As Donald Pizer has argued, Howells and other realists—their claims to honesty notwithstanding—found themselves unable to include in their representational panorama "areas of human nature and social life that were 'barbaric' in nature." This avoidance of "human degradation" rendered realists vulnerable to all manner of critical attacks

2. Amy Kaplan, *The Social Construction of American Realism,* 16; Sundquist, "Realism and Regionalism," 504; Elsa Nettels, *Language, Race, and Social Class in Howells's America,* 191.

3. Howells, *Selected Literary Criticism,* 176. See also David E. Shi, *Facing Facts: Realism in American Thought and Culture, 1850–1920,* 76, and John W. Crowley, "*The Portrait of a Lady* and *The Rise of Silas Lapham:* The Company They Kept," 129. Kaplan, *Social Construction of American Realism,* 24; Crowley, "*Portrait of a Lady,*" 129–30.

in the 1890s by hard-nosed naturalists such as Stephen Crane and Frank Norris. David Shi accounts for this perceived limitation nicely: "Realists often debated among themselves about how candid they should be in exposing the facts as they saw them. For all their claims of objectivity, [realists] viewed 'things out there' through a lens of confining social conventions and moral inhibitions." According to some critics, part of American realism's failure is its inability to represent class divisions in an industrializing and urbanizing America in which resurgent immigration and labor disputes made the gap between the elite and the workers all too obvious.[4] If we accept this line of critique, then it would seem that realism does more than simply reflect reality; it often reshapes it by literarily resolving conflicts and thereby rendering reality more benign to the reader.

It is not surprising, then, that an issue as ethically troubling as passing would present American realists with a unique representational quandary. The idea of a protagonist, let alone a living person, crossing the racial line obviously would have strained the limitations of the realist's sense of credibility, if not moral propriety. But this is to say nothing of the violent context in which this feat was performed. After all, Howells wrote *An Imperative Duty* in arguably the most racist time period of American history since slavery: the 1890s, a decade in which 1,111 African Americans, legally stripped of the rights they had begun to exercise during the aborted Reconstruction of the South, were lynched.[5] Yet, in many ways, the act of passing for the sake of financial security rehearses a central theme of the realist novel—the moral and material strivings of middle-class America. Furthermore, the agency the character exercises in raising his or her socioeconomic status is as relevant to a passing narrative such as *The Autobiography of an Ex-Coloured Man* as it is to a "mainstream" realist narrative such as *The Rise of Silas Lapham*. These commonalities are simply too obvious to ignore.

However, the act of passing to achieve this status admittedly brings a realist narrative such as *An Imperative Duty* into dangerous territory for two reasons well examined by critics. First, and most fundamentally, is the fact that representing a passing character involves also representing the "free-floating consciousness" of a person capable of shifting among racial subject positions—exactly the sort of indeterminate subjectivity

---

4. Pizer, "Introduction," 7; Kenneth S. Lynn, *William Dean Howells: An American Life*, 185; Shi, *Facing Facts*, 5; Kaplan, *Social Construction of American Realism*, 23.
5. Davis, *Who Is Black?* 53.

that Howells, who believed in an essential core being, would eschew. Second is the fact that African American protagonist Rhoda Aldgate—who upon discovering she has "black blood" elects to marry Dr. Olney, a white man, and live in Italy as an Italian—violates all popular notions of (inter)racial propriety and simply cannot be imagined by Howells to do so as an American citizen. And while this very evasion could be viewed as a testament to the fact that Howells's realism takes seriously, even allows itself to be dictated by, what was considered to be socially likely, in the very interest of realism one would also not want to suggest that mixed-race marriages did not occur, even in the hostile context of the post-Reconstruction United States.[6] This specific dilemma is emblematic of a more general problem in making narrative decisions in a realist text: that diametrically opposite outcomes are often both easily defensible on the grounds of realism, thereby rendering any kind of final judgment inconclusive. If anything is certain about realism—especially in its late-nineteenth-century heyday—it is that a number of social and aesthetic factors contributed to its ponderous difficulty as an enterprise. The realist wishes to "tell the truth," but must do so according to socially constructed and often confused notions of verisimilitude and decency. This, in turn, undercuts the very ability of the realist to "tell to truth"—something that becomes most frustrating when this very "truth" involves issues of great sociopolitical import to the writer. And while these many problems would especially present difficulties to African American women writers at the turn of the century—who were speaking more to power than from a position of one—they would even trouble members of the realist literary elite.

It is out of precisely these troubled, muddied waters of realist representation that *An Imperative Duty* emerges as Howells's only passing narrative. On the one hand, in the racist climate of the 1890s, passing was no doubt a dangerous subject for Howells to address. On the other hand, given the number of social taboos associated with passing—for example, race, "blood," miscegenation, and segregation—it was, among others, a tempting topic for realism's greatest proponent to "let the romantic steam out of." But while Howells had addressed American myths of social class, progress, and the self-made man in *The Rise of Silas Lapham*—indeed, had "challenged the comfortable optimisms of the Gospel of

---

6. Henry B. Wonham, "Writing Realism, Policing Consciousness: Howells and the Black Body," 703; Jeffrey A. Clymer, "Race and the Protocol of American Citizenship in William Dean Howells' *An Imperative Duty*," 48; Boeckmann, *A Question of Character*, 141.

Wealth and of Social Darwinism"—race was quite a different and decidedly "stickier" subject for his audience, if not for himself as well.[7] Still, despite the novel's representational and ideological shortcomings, in *An Imperative Duty* Howells manages at least to anticipate Mark Twain's *Pudd'nhead Wilson* (1894) in his attack (if somewhat limited) on one-drop racial logic, which would become part and parcel of a more generally antiracialist critique that African American authors issued throughout the early twentieth century in their own passing narratives.

Set in the mid-1870s, *An Imperative Duty* begins with a Dr. Olney returning to Boston from Europe, whereupon he is summoned by Rhoda Aldgate to attend to her ailing aunt, Mrs. Caroline Meredith. Having first met her in Italy, Dr. Olney eventually falls in love with Miss Aldgate, who we come to find out is the daughter of a middle-class white Northern man and an octoroon. Although the mixed-race marriage had ruined Rhoda's father socially, she was able to grow up in middle-class comfort with Mrs. Meredith and her husband, blissfully unaware of her ancestry. However, given what appears to be a potential love interest between Rhoda and a white acquaintance, Mr. Bloomingdale, Mrs. Meredith believes she has a "duty" to inform the prospective couple of her niece's "black blood." But for Howells, this romantic sense of "duty" toward irrational racial categories is a tempting social taboo to attack. In *Criticism and Fiction* (1891), Howells writes sneeringly of the classic romantic heroine who misguidedly values love over all other things in life. In what Howells took to have been a recent trend, he writes, "she has begun to idolize and illustrate Duty, and she is hardly less mischievous in this new role, opposing duty, as she did love, to prudence, obedience, and reason." Much of *An Imperative Duty* is devoted to scrutinizing such a romantic sense of "Duty" with a capital "D," particularly when it applies to race. Many critics have noted that Howells's treatment of race in the novella can be read as part of his campaign for realism. Nevertheless, given the racial assumptions of Howells's audience and his need to "portray men and women as they are," Howells, in his characterization, could not avoid reinscribing many of the racial taboos he would have liked to destabilize.[8] For example, Dr. Olney, despite being the voice of

---

7. Cady, *The Realist at War: The Mature Years, 1885–1920*, 159; Cady, *Road to Realism*, 231.

8. Howells, *Criticism and Fiction*, 326; Michele Birnbaum, "Racial Hysteria: Female Pathology and Race Politics in Frances Harper's *Iola Leroy* and W. D. Howells's *An Imperative Duty*," 51; Howells, *Selected Literary Criticism*, 49.

reason (and by extension realism) in his cool, rational approach to race, is not as free of racial prejudice as he would like to think.

Upon his return to the streets of Gilded Age Boston, Dr. Olney looks at the common immigrant laboring folk as having "average face[s] and figure[s]" that are "hardly American." Olney, though uncharacteristically freethinking for his time, shares the then popular notion of intra-European racial difference, by which Irish immigrants (and later southern and eastern European immigrants) could be marked as racially different from their Nordic predecessors and "beyond the pale of national identity."[9] The "not-yet-white" status of Irish immigrants is underscored by Olney's softly condescending observation that Irish women, "if they survived to be mothers[,] might give us, with better conditions, a race as hale and handsome as the elder American race" (ID 138). Rhoda Aldgate, who has yet to discover her African ancestry, is similarly racist in her views on Irish Americans—an irony Howells could not resist. "They seem to have *no* imagination," she exclaims, to which Olney responds, "Or too much," to begin a speech that smacks of romantic racialism:

> There is something very puzzling to us Teutons in the Celtic temperament. We don't know where to have an Irishman.... We can't call them stupid.... I think that as a general thing the Irish are quicker-witted than we are. They're sympathetic and poetic far beyond us. But they can't understand the simplest thing from us. Perhaps they set the high constructive faculties of the imagination at work, when they ought to use a little attention and mere commonsense. At any rate they seem more foreign to our intelligence, our way of thinking, than the Jews—or the negroes even. (ID 152)

Rhoda, also a romantic racialist, finds African American waiters to be "charming" with their "soft voices and gentle manners" (ID 153). Likewise, Dr. Olney professes to hate "race prejudice," but admires African American cheer and determination and believes that a "civilization" of blacks would surely be one of "sweetness and goodwill" (ID 153, 155). However, while he vehemently opposes segregation, he is unable to countenance intermarriage (ID 153–54).

Nevertheless, Olney, despite his prejudices, does fancy himself a scientist whose racial views presume to have biological and physiognomic backing. The scientific veneer of his language is certainly consistent with

9. Howells, *An Imperative Duty*, 137. Hereafter cited in the text as *ID*. Clymer, "Race and the Protocol of American Citizenship," 33.

the intellectual trend of the day, positivism, which was held in high regard by realists who held that all of knowledge was attributable to cautious and deliberate observation of external phenomena and aspired to mimetic accuracy based upon these perceptions.[10] Olney's intellectual posturing becomes evident when, responding to Rhoda Aldgate's request for medical assistance, "he recall[s] the particulars of her beauty" with the meticulous detail of a natural scientist:

> Her slender height, her rich complexion of olive, with a sort of under-stain of red, and the inky blackness of her eyes and hair. Her face was of almost classic perfection, and the hair, crinkling away to either temple, grew low upon the forehead, as the hair does in the Clytie head. In profile the mouth was firmly accented, with a deep cut outlining the full lower lip, and a fine jut forward of the delicate chin; and the regularity of the mark was further relieved from insipidity by the sharp winglike curve in the sides of the sensitive nostrils. Olney recalled it as a mask, and he recalled his sense of her wearing this family face, with its somewhat tragic beauty, over a personality that was at once gentle and gay. The mask, he felt was inherited, but the character seemed to be of Miss Aldgate's own invention, and expressed itself in the sunny sparkle of her looks, that ran over with a willingness to please and to be pleased, and to consist in effect of a succession of flashing, childlike smiles, showing between her red lips teeth of the milkiest whiteness, small, even and perfect. (*ID* 147)

This type of close physiognomic description is common in passing narratives and underscores the importance of appearances in both assigned and self-determined identity. Oftentimes when such passages pertain to a mixed-race person whose black ancestry is not easily visible, a subtle current of racial difference bubbles underneath the specifics of the description. Cathy Boeckmann writes that late-nineteenth-century American writers had two options when they wished to describe nonwhite characters: depict race visually or "characterize" it when it is invisible. This is a very helpful distinction, but we must be careful not to forget how a late-nineteenth-century readership would have understood visible racial difference: in other words, while a contemporary observer may not have seen a woman of Rhoda's appearance as black, per se, the above passage offers strong evidence that such an observer also may have not viewed

---

10. Shi, *Facing Facts*, 66. For a discussion on scientific positivism and American realism, see chapter 4 of Shi's book.

her as perfectly white. To be sure, Rhoda initially appears to be white, but she also has facial features of "classic perfection," "olive" skin "with a sort of under-stain of red," and "inky...eyes and hair"—all of which, to this author, are Italianate features and "not yet white" racial markers that can all too easily be overlooked if one thinks in terms of a black/white racial binary (*ID* 147). Boeckmann notes the "tension between the racially exotic and the classically perfect" in Rhoda's description, concluding that all the potential "markers" of Rhoda's blackness (or at least "nonwhiteness") are tempered by positive modifiers (for example, her skin is of a "rich" color).[11] Therefore, Rhoda's race, not being readily visible, must be *characterized* by Howells in her childlike behavior rather than *visualized* in her physiognomy. I would argue, however, that Howells's qualification of Rhoda's visible racial difference does not mitigate this passage's establishment of Rhoda as a visible racial "other." Whether one considers olive skin tone as becomingly "rich" or derogatorily "swarthy," the fact remains that Rhoda's description places her outside the realm of Nordic perfection into an area of racial in-betweenness that would have been all too familiar to Howells and his contemporaries. Furthermore, the distinction between "racially exotic" and "classically perfect" might not be so clear; for while "classic perfection" could refer to a physical ideal exhibited in ancient Greek statues, it could also have Roman connotations that further underscore Rhoda's *Italian* appearance. Admittedly, both the reader and Olney do not learn of Rhoda's racial status until later, after which, as Boeckmann points out, Olney retroactively attributes many of Rhoda's shortcomings to her black ancestry. However, this early description of Rhoda as Italian-looking visually marks her, in a late-nineteenth-century context, as racially "other" even if this racial difference was not "characterized" at all. The significance here is twofold: not only does the above passage further establish a convention of black/white passing narratives that would continue throughout the twentieth century—that of a light-skinned African American being taken for a white ethnic—but it also by implication requires the reader to become aware of how literary racial in-betweenness is articulated and how it necessarily disrupts conventional notions of "black" and "white."

This passage is further significant in the manner by which it underscores the act of passing and the performativity it embodies. For example, in the descriptive passage above, Olney remembers Rhoda's face

11. Ibid., 147.

"as a mask," which signifies the theatricality of her passing. According to Olney, this mask of a face reveals a "somewhat tragic beauty," obviously foreshadowing the "tragedy" of Rhoda's discovery that she is, in fact, not white. Olney further believes that Rhoda's face—her "mask"—"was inherited, but the character seemed to be of Miss Aldgate's own invention" (*ID* 147). Boeckmann argues that this demonstrates the distinction between race as physical and race as characterized—biologically, Rhoda's "mask" had been given to her, but her "good-natured, light-hearted gaiety" is her own contribution to her public persona.[12] Additionally, this passage serves as a restatement of the classic tension between "reality" and "appearances" that lies at the center of every passing narrative, but with one strange innovation: "the mask"—or what we would typically associate with performance—is in Olney's eyes actually the *inherited* part of Rhoda's being. This peculiarity underscores the dramatic irony of both Olney's and Rhoda's ignorance of Rhoda's ancestry. One does not inherit a mask; one puts on a mask. But in Rhoda's case, this seeming mischaracterization is entirely appropriate, for her passing is so unwitting—so "unintentional," to use Drake's and Cayton's terminology—that she may as well have directly inherited the means by which she accomplishes it. Taken as a metaphor of how Rhoda is perceived, this tension between the mask as voluntary (or, what the reader would expect the mask to be) and the mask as inherited (or, what Howells contributes to our understanding) is significant, as it conjoins both action and biology in the articulation of public persona and demonstrates Howells's unwillingness, his realism notwithstanding, to attribute all of it to that which is freely willed. Most literally, though, one thing becomes clear to the reader in this important passage—that the narrator is establishing a distinction between what Rhoda "is" and what she presents herself to be. This will come to a crisis later in the text.

In the meantime, Dr. Olney, despite his obvious prejudices, is presented as a cool-headed realist with regard to race. In a discussion regarding racial atavism, Mrs. Meredith subscribes to the popularly held belief that miscegenation produces in offspring a "reversion to the inferior race type," a notion Howells wishes to expose as romantic nonsense (*ID* 160). Dr. Olney's response to Mrs. Meredith's unwavering belief in a common racial myth is supremely realistic: "The child of a white and an octoroon is a sixteenth blood; and the child of that child and a white is a thirty-

12. Ibid.

second blood. The chances of atavism . . . are so remote that they may be said hardly to exist at all" (ID 161). Thus, the romantic racial hysteria of Mrs. Meredith (and arguably a sizable portion of the American mainstream at that time) is met with the calmly assured, even mathematical, racial realism of Dr. Olney.[13]

Like many of Howells's characters, however, Olney is flawed, even self-contradictory at times, and in the name of realism, Howells would not have it any other way. Olney may find the offspring of an octoroon and a white to be "only" one-sixteenth black, but when he discovers from Mrs. Meredith that Rhoda Aldgate is a "sixteenth blood," he "recoil[s] from the words" (ID 164). Exhibiting every sign of the romantic racial hysteria he disdains, Olney finds himself "in a turmoil of emotion for which there is no term but disgust" (ID 164–65). Further, "[h]is disgust was profound and pervasive. . . . He found himself personally disliking the notion of her having negro blood in her veins; before he felt pity he felt repulsion; his own race instinct expressed itself in a merciless rejection of her beauty, her innocence, her helplessness because of her race" (ID 165). These feelings pass, and Olney regains his rational composure. However, Mrs. Meredith is left with a very difficult choice. Who first to tell Rhoda's secret—Rhoda herself or her white suitor Mr. Bloomingdale? Having once considered her merely to be a "morbid sentimentalist," Olney gains respect for Mrs. Meredith because of the "heavy duty" she must bear (ID 170). However, in Howells's world, no "duty" is as great as the rational explanation that solves the dilemma "duty" presents. Olney reasons that since the secret is, in the end, Rhoda's, she should learn of her ancestry first so she may decide what to do. Once Rhoda does find out, she will be the one to confront the moral dilemma central to the realist passing narrative: to pass or not to pass? Dr. Olney understands the moral implications of this question but concludes, in irreverently realist fashion, that it may be permissible in some circumstances for someone to pass for personal gain. In effect, Dr. Olney gives sanction to the idea of Rhoda changing from "unintentional passing" to one of the more freely willed forms of passing Drake and Cayton identify, such as passing "out of economic necessity or advantage" (ID 162).

13. Giulia Fabi, "Reconstructing Literary Genealogies: Frances E. W. Harper's and William Dean Howells's Race Novels," 51. Fabi argues that it is not a coincidence that Howells attributes the rational view to a male character and the "hysterical," romantic view to a female character, thereby casting realism as inherently masculine and romanticism as inherently feminine.

This is again heavily implied when Dr. Olney says, "there may be worse things. It seems as if there might be circumstances in which it was one's *right* to live a lie . . . for the sake—" (*ID* 171). Olney, however, is interrupted by Mrs. Meredith, who, still insistent upon a romantic sense of duty, replies, "Never! . . . It is better to die—to kill—than to lie." (*ID* 171).

Soon enough, the problem indeed becomes Rhoda's concern, as Mrs. Meredith reveals that her niece is the daughter of a Creole and a Northern-educated octoroon. Upon hearing the news, Rhoda "was silent and motionless. With her head defined against the open window, her face showed quite black toward her aunt, as if the fact of her mother's race had remanded her to its primordial hue in touching her consciousness" (*ID* 184). This certainly could be read as an overtly romantic reaction caused by Mrs. Meredith's racial phobia. However, in this passage Howells also dramatizes the retroactive projection of racial characteristics—something that could have happened to both light-skinned African Americans and immigrants once their ancestry was learned. Rhoda is already somewhat marked by her "olive" skin, but with this new and troubling reminder of the girl's parentage, the skin appears darker to Mrs. Meredith than it actually is.

Rhoda's response to the news is hardly more composed: "The girl gave a little, low, faltering laugh, an articulate note of such pathetic fear and pitiful entreaty that it went through the woman's heart. 'Aunt Caroline, are you crazy? . . . And you mean to say—to tell me—that—that—I am—*black*?'" (*ID* 184). Rhoda immediately understands that by the prevailing one-drop rule, she is not simply a "sixteenth blood" as Olney would suggest, but fully black. Mrs. Meredith, not possibly believing herself, tries to tell Rhoda that she is as white as anyone, but Rhoda replies that having any of "that blood in me . . . is the same thing" (*ID* 184). Still more of a shame to Rhoda is the lie under which she has lived her entire life: "You let me pass myself off on myself and every one else, for what I wasn't" (*ID* 185). Rhoda, like Mrs. Meredith, abhors the idea of living a lie, so accepting Mr. Bloomingdale's advances and passing are both out of the question.

As she walks through Boston to mail a letter rejecting Bloomingdale, she encounters first "suburbans," whom to Rhoda seem "intense-faced" and purposeful—no doubt under the command of the dominant "industrial morality" of which David Roediger speaks (*ID* 191). When she begins to encounter more working-class folk, "the proper life of the street," Rhoda sees an increasing number of African Americans. Not surprisingly, if the "suburbans" were as "intense-faced" as a woman of her social class might expect them to be, the African Americans of Boston begin to take on all the stereotypical "pre-industrial" characteristics that a woman with her destabilized racial self-identity might fear they have. To Rhoda,

> [t]here was something in the way they turned their black eyes in their disks of white upon her, like dogs, with a mute animal appeal in them, that seemed to claim her one of them, and to creep nearer and nearer and possess her in that late-found solidarity of race. She never knew before how hideous they were, with their flat wide-nostriled noses, their out-rolled thick lips, their mobile bulging eyes set near together, their retreating chins and foreheads, and their smooth, shining skin; they seemed burlesques of humanity, worse than apes, because they were more like. But the men were not half so bad as the women, from the shrill-piped young girls, with their grotesque attempts at fashion, to the old grandmothers, wrinkled or obese, who came down the sloping sidewalks in their bare heads, out of the courts and alleys where they lived, to get the evening air. (*ID* 191)

Obviously upset over her recent discovery, Rhoda reacts by projecting grossly stereotypical racial characteristics she fears she might share onto more visibly black African Americans.[14] In her frantic state, lighter-skinned blacks "tragical[ly] approach . . . white," echoing Olney's earlier memories of her "tragic" mask (*ID* 192). According to Howells, Rhoda's response is clearly irrational and the stuff of romance. For while the realist ostensibly would consider Rhoda to be practically white, with one-sixteenth African ancestry, Rhoda obsessively thinks, "my mother was darker, and my grandmother darker, and my great-grander like a mulatto, and then it was a horrible old negress, a savage stolen from Africa, where she had been a cannibal" (*ID* 192). Rhoda's racial nightmare is capped off by visions of savage natives in the deserts of Africa.

To Howells, Rhoda's solution is not a rational consideration of her circumstances, but rather an appeal to "Duty," which Mrs. Meredith presumably had shirked in not disabusing Rhoda sooner. Feeling compelled to be among African Americans, she attends a black church meeting so as "to surround herself with the blackness from which she had sprung, and to reconcile herself to it, by realizing and owning it with every sense," as if one could "own" "blackness" (*ID* 196). As she sits in the church listening to the prayer and song, near her "Rhoda distinguished faces, sad, repulsive visages of a frog-like ugliness add[ing] to the repulsive black

14. Clymer, "Race and the Protocol of American Citizenship," 45.

in all its shades" (*ID* 197). As she continues to project racial caricatures onto the African Americans about her, Rhoda is aware of the variations in skin color she encounters. However, "these mixed bloods were more odious to her than the others, because she felt herself more akin to them; but they were all abhorrent" (*ID* 197). To be sure, one-drop racial logic holds that they are indeed all equally "abhorrent." Then, moved by a black preacher's call for love, Rhoda begins to cope with her discovery. She concludes, "Yes, that is the clew.... That is the way out; the only way. I can endure them if I can love them, and I shall love them if I try to help them" (*ID* 198). Mrs. Meredith, however, never recovers from the trauma of having performed her "duty"; she dies presumably from a self-administered overdose of sleeping medicine. Almost miraculously, even inexplicably, Rhoda grows more comfortable with her new racial identity, and, as we come to learn, had never really cared much for Mr. Bloomingdale, in spite of his sincere entreaties. Dr. Olney, however, still cares for Rhoda, but, ever the moralist, waits until Rhoda rejects Bloomingdale before he makes his feelings known. Once Olney asks Rhoda for her hand in marriage, the choice is presented as all-or-nothing, with Rhoda having to decide between life with Olney as a white woman and life as an African American.

The choice is by no means simple; for while Rhoda is morally inclined to claim black ancestry, she is not unprepared culturally to enter the white world. Throughout the early part of the narrative, Rhoda already had been passing unintentionally, her light skin supplemented by the bourgeois cultural refinement learned from her aunt and her Northern education.[15] However, now that Rhoda knows she is biologically part black and that marriage to Dr. Olney is a possibility, she believes she must decide between passing and finding her mother's family to live among and assist African Americans, "the humblest" of people—a seemingly irrational all-or-nothing dilemma that nonetheless reflects the Manichean absolutism of one-drop racial logic (*ID* 226). Dr. Olney reaffirms Rhoda's all-or-nothing plight when he insists that Rhoda not live among blacks but rather live with him in Florence (*ID* 226). At first Rhoda refuses Olney, for she is "a negress" and has a duty "to go down there and help them; try to educate them, and elevate them; give [her] life to them" (*ID* 227, 229). She earnestly asks Olney, "Isn't it base and cowardly to desert them, and live happily apart from them?" (*ID* 229). Olney replies, using terminology later employed by Werner Sollors to describe American

15. Ibid.

ethnogenesis, that she would have such a "duty" if she "had ever *consented* to be of their kind" (*ID* 229). To Sollors, ethnicity is an ongoing dialogue between consent, or one's voluntary cultural affiliations, and descent, or those biologically charged characteristics beyond a person's control. However, since Rhoda's *descent* is not readily apparent, or at least marks her as a racially suspect European, she is allowed nearly as much ethnic latitude as a similarly situated white ethnic. Still, given the psychological power of the one-drop rule—which continually reasserts itself in African American passing narratives—Rhoda believes her blackness to be an indelible matter of descent and her subjective options to be no more numerous than black or white. "I can't help it," she protests. "It's burnt into me. It's branded me one of *them*. I *am* one. No, I can't escape. And the best way is to go and live among them and own it. Then perhaps I can learn to bear it, and not hate them so. But I *do* hate them" (*ID* 230). But then, quite suddenly, and every bit as inexplicably as with her embrace of blackness, Rhoda decides to pass: she marries Dr. Olney, and the two live happily in Rome where Rhoda passes for (of all things) Italian and is "thought to look so very Italian that you would really take her for" one (*ID* 234). And with this turn of phrase, Howells unwittingly links the legacy of passing to the life and literary history of Italian Americans—those "not-yet-white" Americans still on their way toward full participation in the social mainstream of the United States. Howells also participates in a literary convention that dates back at least as far as William Wells Brown's *Clotel; or, the President's Daughter* (1853), the first African American novel, as well as the first African American novel of passing, in which the protagonist, a white-looking, out-of-wedlock daughter of Thomas Jefferson, attempts to find her own enslaved daughter in antebellum Virginia by passing as a gentleman invalid. To "American ladies," she "had the appearance of a fine Italian."[16]

In the end, it is very difficult to render a final judgment on the race critique presented by Howells in his passing narrative—a critique that is clearly mitigated by a view of race that, though vastly progressive for his time, still relied upon "innate, inherited differences between white and black."[17] A cursory examination of his reviews of African American authors is ample evidence of this. For example, in his introduction to

16. William Wells Brown, *Clotel; or, the President's Daughter*, 182.
17. Boeckmann, *A Question of Character*, 139. For other discussions of Howells, and realists in general, as flawed critics of race, see Nettels, *Language, Race, and Social Class*, 87, and Kenneth W. Warren, *Black and White Strangers: Race and American Literary Realism*.

Paul Lawrence Dunbar's *Lyrics of Low Life* (1896), Howells praises Dunbar's objective, thoughtful, and sensitive treatment of black subject matter. Yet while the craft of Dunbar, with his "pure African blood," is "evidence of the essential unity of the human race," Howells muses "that there is a precious difference of temperament between the races which it would be a great pity ever to lose." Similarly, in a review of Charles Chesnutt's *The Wife of His Youth and Other Stories of the Color Line,* Howells lauds the author's depictions of mixed-race characters, but does so in a manner that reflects the limits of his anti-racialism: "We may choose to think them droll in their parody of pure white society, but perhaps it would be wiser to recognize that they are like us because they are of our blood by more than a half, or three quarters, or nine tenths. It is not, in such cases, their negro blood that characterizes them; but it is their negro blood that excludes them" — as if "blood" ought to be the measure of human fellowship in the first place.[18] Nevertheless, despite Howells's unwitting reinscription of the fixity of racial "duty," much of *An Imperative Duty* serves as a critique of the romantic hysteria associated with the idea of race. Very significantly, the narrator at one point uses a metaphor of color to critique Mrs. Meredith's moral absolutism: "right affected her as a body of positive color, sharply distinguished from wrong, and not shading into and out of it by gradations of tint, as we find it doing in reality" (*ID* 158). As we have seen, Mrs. Meredith's ethical foil, Dr. Olney, is presented as a realist and rationalist who eschews Mrs. Meredith's and Rhoda's racial hysteria for a more calm, thoughtful approach to race. However, as we have also seen, Olney is anything but an ideal critic of race. Oftentimes he reaffirms the myth of race every bit as much as he deconstructs it, as evidenced by his revulsion upon discovering Rhoda's ancestry and his joke about her being at least "not a very black...negro" (*ID* 227). However much ironic distance Howells would have liked to place between himself and Olney, the fact remains that Olney's conceptual shortcomings are in many ways Howells's too.

At best, the social critique of *An Imperative Duty* is limited and certainly void of any program to assuage America's perennial obsession with race. This is perhaps best exemplified by Rhoda's decision not "to educate" and "elevate" poor African Americans (as we shall see, Iola Leroy comes to a very different conclusion). Furthermore, Howells's race

18. Howells, *Selected Literary Criticism,* 280; Howells, "Mr. Charles W. Chesnutt's Stories," 701.

narrative conspicuously lacks the details of African American experience that, by Howells's own realist standards, such a narrative would require. Everett Carter attributes this to Howells's belief that the realist should write mostly from experience, coupled with his relative lack of experience (compared with contemporaries such as Mark Twain and George Washington Cable) in matters of race.[19] This explanation is certainly plausible, but it does not change the fact that *An Imperative Duty* falls short of Howells's own demands, as a critic and theorist, for realistic detail to serve as the impetus for social reform. As we shall see, *Iola Leroy* would decisively surpass *An Imperative Duty* in this regard.

Among the accomplishments of *An Imperative Duty*, however, is its apt (though not unproblematic) theoretical probing of the idea of race. The novel is also important in that it exemplifies the troubled agency, and therefore the conflicted realism, of the passing act. As we have already established, Rhoda's "mask," or her public persona, is linked with familial inheritance and therefore can never be fully under her control. Also, Rhoda freely wills her transformation into a racially in-between Italian woman, but must do so outside the borders of the United States. Further mitigating the agency of Rhoda's passing act is both the social and ideological determinism of race that causes her to pass in the first place. Kenneth S. Lynn considers the notable determinism of *An Imperative Duty* as evidence of Howells's increased pessimism throughout the 1880s and 1890s, which had manifested itself first in *A Hazard of New Fortunes* (1890)—Howells's most detailed fictional treatment of labor unrest. Indeed, in *An Imperative Duty*, "a sense of entrapment is the predominating mood" with the protagonist "feel[ing herself] caught in the mesh of old evils."[20] More significant, though, is the novella's establishment of a central question—to pass or not to pass?—as the fundamental moral dilemma of the realist passing narrative. In this case, Rhoda's answer is not only to pass, but to do so outside the United States—a textual evasion that, on one hand, posits the irresolvability of American racial problems, but, on the other, seems a troubling "cop-out" in light of Howells's relative power in American literary culture—standards of decency notwithstanding. *Iola Leroy* presents the passing dilemma on a number of occasions, but its outcome in every case is quite different. And ultimately, Harper—despite writing from a position inferior to that of Howells,

19. Carter, *Howells*, 83.
20. Lynn, *William Dean Howells*, 303.

who was undeniably one of the great American cultural brokers of his day—more unequivocally rejects popular discourses of racism and does so while more deftly negotiating a number of narrative demands.

Lifting the "Veil of Concealment": Harper's Answer to Howells

With *Iola Leroy, or Shadows Uplifted* (1892), Frances E. W. Harper, despite her position of relative discursive weakness, supplies a more rhetorically potent—though not a perfect or absolute—critique of race than *An Imperative Duty* and does so all the while negotiating a number of problems with both audience and narrative form—some of which would never be brought to bear on Howells or his white male contemporaries. Like *An Imperative Duty*, the story is about a light-skinned African American woman's belated discovery that she is black and the decision she must make once confronted with this discovery. Also like Howells's novella, *Iola Leroy* offers a limited critique of the American idea of race. Unlike *An Imperative Duty*, though, Harper accomplishes this by far more explicit and numerous examples: for example, by having the darkest of African Americans prove to be as capable as any other character, by having light-skinned blacks go misidentified as white, and by giving multiple characters the option to cross the purportedly insurmountable barrier of race and pass in the United States. Also unlike *An Imperative Duty*, characters who are able to pass refuse to do so, and this refusal becomes part of an overall program of "racial uplift" that emphasizes African American intelligence, hard work, and culture. Further, Harper represents more elaborately than Howells many varieties of black experience, including slavery, the Civil War, the Northern urban labor market, and postbellum leadership of "racial uplift"—almost all of which are strangely absent from *An Imperative Duty* despite its author's fierce commitment to social realism. Finally, Harper improves upon Howells's clumsy treatment of characters' decisions regarding racial identity and passing, replacing the sudden changes of heart in *An Imperative Duty* with more rationally deduced courses of action reflecting a level of deliberation that realists traditionally believed should precede such decisions.

Still, while *Iola Leroy* shares many essential characteristics with mainstream American realism—even surpassing *An Imperative Duty's* own realist credentials in some fundamental ways—it is also undoubtedly a more generically mixed text that has much in common with the American sentimental and domestic traditions, particularly due to Iola Leroy's didactically expressed sense of racial ethics and her marriage to fellow activist Dr. Latimer. Critics universally view this as, in part, Harper's acquiescence to the aesthetic demands of her readership: quite simply, in the late nineteenth century, Americans still enjoyed a sentimental tale with strong romantic overtones. However, there is disagreement on the rhetorical potential of this appeal to sentimentality and domesticity. A minority of critics views this approach as self-stultifying and holds that Harper's incorporation of domestic and sentimental elements undercuts the political urgency of her story. Such objections are usually raised upon three grounds. First, those who view African American women's writing as, among other things, a corrective for stereotypical depictions of blacks in literature are often disappointed by the efforts of fin-de-siècle writers such as Harper and Pauline Hopkins, who ostensibly create romantic stereotypes that have little more basis in reality than the racist stereotypes they are supposed to replace. Such characters are thought to be "static, disembodied, larger-than-life," if unceasingly moral, and do more to comply with the socially and aesthetically restrictive "cult of true womanhood" than "substitut[e] reality for stereotype." Second, and from a purely aesthetic perspective, *Iola Leroy*'s heavy reliance upon "exposition and lofty sentiment" often runs counter to contemporary critical expectations of proper African American literary rhetoric. Finally, Harper's enlistment of a white-skinned, blonde-haired, blue-eyed mulatto Iola Leroy to play the role of the earnest racial activist strikes some readers as an unforgivable racial concession.[21]

Most critics, however, do not hold Harper's generic choice against her, but—in what has become an alternate critical approach to *Iola Leroy*—view the novel's blend of lofty romanticism and hard-hitting realism as a clever and important negotiation of audience expectations and political expediency. Mary Helen Washington aptly describes the context in which Harper wrote: "Black women writers at the turn of the century wrote under great pressures: to a white audience whose tastes were honed by the sentimental novel and whose conceptions of blacks were shaped by *Uncle Tom's Cabin;* to a limited black audience who desperately needed positive black role models; and to an audience whose notions of female propriety and female inferiority made it nearly impossible to

21. Deborah E. McDowell, "'The Changing Same': Generational Connections and Black Women Novelists," 284; Houston Baker, Jr., *Workings of the Spirit: The Poetics of Afro-American Women's Writing,* 25, 31; Kimberly A. C. Wilson, "The Function of the 'Fair' Mulatto: Complexion, Audience, and Mediation in Frances Harper's *Iola Leroy*," 105; and Diane Price Herndl, "Miscegen(r)ation of Mestiza Discourse?: Feminist and Racial Politics in *Ramona* and *Iola Leroy*."

imagine a complex woman character." Thus, there were clearly limits to what Harper could do and, likewise, to what she could be expected to do. Harper's work cannot be divorced from its context, and most critics give the author credit for creating a politically vital work despite the artistic demands of the day. The use of a mulatto protagonist, then, is not so much a passive acquiescence to audience demands as it is a clever "narrative device of mediation" between black and white races—a device specifically designed to attract the attention, sympathy, and assistance of white readers. A third critical approach refuses to accept that Harper's use of a sentimental heroine in a partially domestic plot is a concession of any kind at all and instead suggests that it is part of "a tradition of politicized motherhood that views mothers and the cultural rhetoric of maternity as instruments of social reform."[22]

Recently, critics have begun to compare *Iola Leroy* with *An Imperative Duty*, very frequently viewing the former as a progressive revision of the latter given Iola's refusal to pass as the wife of a white doctor. Some have suggested that *Iola Leroy*, because of its sociohistorical specificity, is more accurately mimetic than *An Imperative Duty*, despite the latter text's author and veneer of calm rationality. Indeed, the detailed literary depiction of African American culture and history—under slavery and during the postbellum period when the book was published—helps instruct a white, middle-class readership that might be ignorant of such realities. Furthermore, the wide variety of African American characters, nearly all of whom are given voice by Harper, allows for a "realistic treatment of black language" and consequently "more positive and complex versions of black women than those offered by previous writers."[23] Insofar as realist texts accomplish such tasks, they serve an important rhetorical function, for through mimesis they fill in gaps left untouched by main-

---

22. Mary Helen Washington, "Uplifting the Women and the Race: The Forerunners—Harper and Hopkins," 75. See also Carby, *Reconstructing Womanhood*, chapter 4 and p. 89; Claudia Tate, *Domestic Allegories of Political Desire: The Black Heroine's Text at the Turn of the Century*, 14. For other defenses of Harper on aesthetic and political grounds, see Elizabeth Young, "Warring Fictions: *Iola Leroy* and the Color of Gender"; Melba Joyce Boyd, *Discarded Legacy: Politics and Poetics in the Life of Frances E. W. Harper, 1825–1911*; and P. Gabrielle Foreman, "'Reading Aright': White Slavery, Black Referents, and the Strategy of Histotextuality in *Iola Leroy*."

23. Sarah B. Daugherty, "*An Imperative Duty*: Howells and White Male Anxiety," 62; Fabi, "Reconstructing Literary Genealogies," 55–56; John Ernest, "From Mysteries to Histories: Cultural Pedagogy in Frances E. W. Harper's *Iola Leroy*," 500–502; Marilyn Elkins, "Reading beyond the Conventions: A Look at Frances E. W. Harper's *Iola Leroy, or Shadows Uplifted*," 46. For further discussion of the realistic, myth-shattering function of *Iola Leroy*, see Boyd, *Discarded Legacy*, 177.

stream writers. I would go one step further and argue that because of this, and other reasons, Harper's text surpasses Howells's by the very standards of the latter author. However, I would also be hesitant to judge *Iola Leroy* as a perfect corrective to *An Imperative Duty*, for its ideological engagement with race retains a number of racialisms that seem to be unavoidably connected with its era of publication.

In an essay that calls for a "reconceptualization of American realism that holds at its center the principle of multiculturalism," Elizabeth Ammons argues that it is useful to think of American literary realism as more than simply a white, middle-class, male struggle to represent and reconstruct reality. Among the texts Ammons wishes to see included in an updated, "multicultural construction of American realism" is, not insignificantly, *Iola Leroy*, which given its more thorough foregrounding of African American culture and history is clearly of a more rhetorically forceful realism than *An Imperative Duty*.[24] However, one danger of this anticonstructionist stance is that it might hinder us from acknowledging that ethnic writers—though no doubt dealing with different concerns and writing from different perspectives than mainstream writers—themselves made authorial decisions that, in part, amounted to attempts to reconstruct reality in accordance with their own desires.

For example, perhaps most significant of all of Frances E. W. Harper's generic choices was one she avoided—naturalism, which in 1892 was enjoying its heyday. Clearly, Harper could not avoid presenting the more deterministic aspects of nineteenth-century African American life: slavery, poverty, rape, violence, illiteracy, and the breakup of innumerable families.[25] However, in order to fashion a countermyth of black racial uplift to replace the prevailing myth of black inferiority, Harper did not have the luxury—as did mainstream naturalists such as Frank Norris, Stephen Crane, and Theodore Dreiser—of creating hapless characters beleaguered by heredity, environment, and fate. Rather, Harper had to empower her characters with enough agency to allow them to negotiate the familiar American myths of hard work and self-reliance. This is not to mention that the barely concealed rage permeating the tone of many naturalist novels by ethnic authors—notably Michael Gold's *Jews Without Money* (1930), Pietro di Donato's *Christ in Concrete* (1939), and Richard Wright's *Native Son* (1940)—clearly was not a likely option for a

24. Elizabeth Ammons, "Expanding the Canon of American Realism," 95, 97–98. In the above quote, Ammons is citing T. J. Jackson Lears and Amy Kaplan, respectively.
25. For a further elucidation of this very point, see Boyd, *Discarded Legacy*, 173.

nineteenth-century black writer, let alone a nineteenth-century black *woman*. Witness, for example, the marked decline in William Dean How-ells's critical enthusiasm for Charles Chesnutt after the publication of *The Marrow of Tradition* (1901), "a distinctly negative, outraged," and arguably naturalistic novel of white racial hatred based upon the 1898 Wilmington, North Carolina, race riot.[26]

Therefore, the productive mix of romanticism and realism that defines *Iola Leroy* was not only among the most acceptable generic options for Harper but also among the most rhetorically effective. The lofty diction, the earnest didacticism, the domestic themes, the moral melodrama, and the prominence of the love story could be used to appeal to the white audience's emotions while the realistic depiction of African American speech, culture, and history could serve its pedagogical and political pur-pose. Harper can be forgiven for her romantic diversion from strict mime-sis, argues Claudia Tate, for "[t]o make the authenticity of black literary culture dependent on external social reality fundamentally reinscribes the authority of white patriarchal hegemony, which is precisely what has occurred in the critically acclaimed works of so-called 'black social realism.'"[27] This is not to mention the fact that the ethnic text—particu-larly when it closely represents the many vicissitudes and conflicting circumstances of ethnic experience, as does *Iola Leroy*—almost unavoid-ably becomes generically mixed with any number of authorial options ranging from romantic sentiment to realistic mimesis to naturalistic determinism and, eventually, modernistic innovation.

For example, the strategy of combining romance and realism in the African American novel dates back to a text as early as the aforemen-tioned *Clotel*, by William Wells Brown. To be sure, the novel is "melo-dramatic" and every bit as morally didactic as *Iola Leroy*. Furthermore, the novel's characterization deals generally, and somewhat predictably, in "types." However, proto-realist aspirations become apparent when the narrator directly addresses the reader and insists that the novel is "no fiction," is "founded in truth," and is "an unvarnished narrative."[28] I would submit that *Iola Leroy* takes a more decisive step in the direction of realism in, among other things, its decreased reliance upon first-person

26. Joseph R. McElrath, Jr., "W. D. Howells and Race: Charles W. Chesnutt's Dis-appointment of the Dean," 248.
27. Tate, *Domestic Allegories*, 109.
28. Henry Louis Gates, Jr., Introduction to *The Autobiography of an Ex-Coloured Man*, x, xi; William Wells Brown, *Clotel*, 127, 155, 188, 222.

appeals to the reader and in its politically astute subversion of raced and gendered stereotypes.

Drawing the often tenuous connection between politics and genre in *Iola Leroy* becomes more inviting when one recalls that William Dean Howells liked to think of literary realism as productive work in an era defined by a middle-class ethos of productivity and prosperity. Michael Davitt Bell has argued that part of this "work" was the exposure of injustice through the act of mimesis, or "[t]he idea that realism . . . can be legitimized . . . as part of a popular political struggle." Although Howells's idea of realism's work—both political and aesthetic—was inherently masculinist and arguably rooted in his own insecurities about the femininity of his own chosen profession, it still can be applied to Frances E. W. Harper's project in *Iola Leroy*, which "was rooted in the authority of Harper's experience as abolitionist, lecturer, poet, teacher, feminist, and black woman" and "was written to promote social change, to aid in the uplifting of the race."[29]

That much of *Iola Leroy* is devoted to the protagonist's rise to middle-class status, to a position of moral and material well-being, is clearly an indication that the novel is significantly akin to the classic "mainstream" realism, which "arose along with the middle class of a commercial, industrializing society."[30] Thus, given Iola Leroy's rise to bourgeois status and the novel's valorization of "talented tenth" African American "race leaders," *Iola Leroy* does clearly write itself into the tradition of realistic productivity as Howells viewed it. However, while realism often records a male's successful negotiation of the free market, the one arena of success and self-definition typically afforded to female characters is the marriage market. *Iola Leroy* features prominently a marriage between Iola and Dr. Latimer (also a light-skinned African American activist), and Harper has been criticized for bowing to this structural demand. To be sure, insofar as realist texts represent middle-class values, they will exhibit associated gendered notions of propriety and duty, especially through "cult of true womanhood" ideology and the idealized views of marriage that surround it. A number of American women's realist novels—notably

---

29. For a helpful discussion of literary realism as productive work and Howells's notable unease with being an artist during an era of manly enterprise, see chapter 1 of Michael Davitt Bell's *The Problem of American Realism: Studies in the Cultural History of a Literary Idea*. Bell, *The Problem of American Realism*, 27, 32; Carby, *Reconstructing Womanhood*, 63.

30. Louis J. Budd, "The American Background," 32.

Kate Chopin's *The Awakening* (1896) and Edith Wharton's *The House of Mirth* (1905)—have documented the pathologies inherent in such gendered ideologies. However, when domestic subject matter appears in nineteenth-century African American women's literature, it often does so in part to promote the idea that blacks are as capable of middle-class prosperity and morality as the white readers of the novel.[31] Furthermore, Iola Leroy's marriage is clearly not the reason for her success; rather, it comes at the end of the narrative only after she had already independently established herself as an African American activist. In fact, her marriage to Dr. Latimer becomes part of her activist project in that the two plan to work together as a married couple for the betterment of African Americans. Iola Leroy's promotion of the American myth of self-reliance is unequivocal and is given, by Harper, a decidedly feminist twist: "I have a theory that every woman ought to know how to earn her own living. I believe that a great amount of sin and misery springs from the weakness and inefficiency of women."[32] Thus, to make this stance appear plausible, Harper has Iola Leroy's story of freely willed success overshadow (without obscuring) the tales of violence and degradation that defined the lives of black women living under slavery. Harper gives Iola Leroy the leverage to make the moral decisions necessary for her own advancement, and such a presentation is consistent not only with the program of "racial uplift" but also in many ways with the course of Harper's life.

Harper was born Frances Ellen Watkins in Maryland on September 24, 1825. She was free, but was also orphaned at an unusually young age, whereupon she was raised by her aunt Henrietta and her uncle William Watkins, who was a vehement antislavery activist and member of the African Methodist Episcopal church. Harper generally lived within a significant degree of middle-class comfort and received a rigorous liberal education at home, where her father's lifework set an example of hard work, persistence, and charitable service. After advanced formal education, Harper taught in Ohio and Pennsylvania, but was radicalized when her home state passed a law in 1853 allowing any black person entering the state from the North to be sold into slavery.[33] In that same year, Harper gave her first antislavery lecture, which began a long, fruitful career of speaking, writing, and activism that would earn Harper

31. Tate, *Domestic Allegories*, 5.
32. Frances E. W. Harper, *Iola Leroy, or Shadows Uplifted*, 205. Hereafter cited as *IL*.
33. Boyd, *Discarded Legacy*, 34, 36, 40.

"the devotion of a sizeable audience of men and women, black and white, in the United States, Canada, and England." Throughout her literary career, Harper would publish a number of essay and poetry collections, as well as (most famously) the antiracist novel *Iola Leroy*—her only major work of fictional prose. Although the novel is written in a romantic, often sentimental style, it also has the decidedly realist endeavor of "refut[ing] . . . insidious stereotypes" of African Americans and replacing these stereotypes with fully realized characters who are, at the very least, intended to correspond more closely to African American history.[34] In this manner, *Iola Leroy* effectively combines the rhetorical strength of sentimentalism with the mimetic credibility of realism.

Early in the novel we are introduced to a number of such characters, including Tom Anderson, a servant of a wealthy North Carolina planter of the same name, and the more literate Robert Johnson. The mere juxtaposition of these two characters in the narrative is emblematic of the novel's verisimilitude, as it reveals two varieties of slave experience and thus immediately resists generalization. Tom is kind, altruistic, and earnest, but not as well educated as Robert, who had grown up with comparatively preferential treatment as his mistress's "favorite slave" (*IL* 7). Soon enough, the reader encounters Iola Leroy, who is also a servant of "Marster Anderson." Predictably, we are given a description of Iola that overtly underscores her visible racial status. Tom describes her as "putty. Beautiful long hair comes way down her back; putty blue eyes, and jis' ez white ez anybody's in dis place" (*IL* 38). Unlike Rhoda's description in *An Imperative Duty*, which establishes the protagonist as, at best, racially in-between, Iola is here presented as ineffaceably white looking.

The narrative begins during the Civil War as the tide turns irreversibly in favor of the North. When North Carolina is liberated, Iola becomes a nurse for Union soldiers. Soon, the reader is provided with an almost obligatory flashback to explain how such an incontestably white woman could have been remanded to servitude in the first place. The reader is taken back to the 1840s, when Eugene Leroy, a young, wealthy Creole heir, is explaining to his incredulous cousin Alfred Lorraine that he wishes to marry a part-black woman named Marie whom he is having trained in a Northern seminary (*IL* 61). Like much of the dialogue of *An Imperative Duty*, the conversation between these characters reverberates with much of the racial discourse of the era. Eugene Leroy, like Dr. Olney, is something of a realist: a critic of the social taboo of race, if he himself is

34. Frances Smith Foster, Introduction, xxx.

guilty of some of its consequent prejudices. Appealing to the United States's tradition of liberal constitutionalism, he protests, "We Americans boast of freedom, and yet here is a woman whom I love as I never loved any other human being, but both law and public opinion debar me from following the inclination of my heart. She is beautiful, faithful, and pure, and yet all that society will tolerate is what I would scorn to do." Lorraine, echoing the racial pseudo-science of the day, answers, "But has not society the right to guard the purity of its blood by the rigid exclusion of an alien race?" echoing a social, biological, and, frankly, emotional argument frequently used to sidestep questions of legality (*IL* 66).[35] Parroting one-drop racial logic, Lorraine explains that "if she is as fair as a lily, beautiful as a houri, and chaste as ice . . . still she is a Negro." Leroy replies, "Oh, come now; she isn't much of a Negro," but this response unwittingly lends credence to the biological and physiognomic calculus of race and eerily echoes Dr. Olney's insistence that Rhoda Aldgate is "not very black." Lorraine is unmoved and insists that "[o]ne drop of negro blood in her veins curses all the rest"—the one-drop rule in a nutshell (*IL* 67).

Upon his planned marriage to Marie, Leroy must decide whether to keep secret her black blood, for he is aware that despite her successful adoption of white cultural mores, he knows that her ancestry cannot become common knowledge in the South (*IL* 74). The newlywed couple is thus confronted with the dilemma of Marie's public identity: should she pass or not? Although the couple decides for Marie not to pass for white, she does pass as Leroy's *mistress,* which ironically attracts not nearly the public reprobation that a fully legal marriage would have. Children Iola and Harry, however, are not told of their heritage and thus begin a life of unintentional passing, much like Rhoda Aldgate of *An Imperative Duty.* Both are sent to school in the North because, according to Leroy, "a good education is an investment on which the law can place no attachment"—if nothing else, it can certainly provide Iola and Harry with the cultural refinement necessary to continue their lives as middle-class whites (*IL* 83).

When Leroy tragically becomes ill and dies, Albert Lorraine, who was never comfortable with Marie, finds flaws in both the marriage and the former slave's manumission. After winning a suit for Leroy's estate, Lorraine sells Marie and her children into slavery. Meanwhile, Iola has

---

35. See Eric J. Sundquist, *To Wake the Nations: Race in the Making of American Literature,* chapter 3, for a discussion of this rhetorical phenomenon.

attended school where she, ironically, has defended slavery from the attacks of Northern peers much like Rhoda Aldgate, who, ignorant of her racial status, openly professes racist views of African Americans and immigrants. After Iola is brought back south, Marie must tell her the truth of her heritage, and like the corresponding scene from *An Imperative Duty*, Iola's response is the stuff of sentimentalism: "An expression of horror and anguish swept over Iola's face, and, turning deathly pale, she exclaimed, 'Oh, mother, it can't be so! you must be dreaming!' . . . Almost wild with agony, Iola paced the floor, as the fearful truth broke in crushing anguish upon her mind" (*IL* 105). Iola then "burst into a paroxysm of tears succeeded by peals of hysterical laughter" (*IL* 106). After the initial shock, however, Iola Leroy is radicalized, much like Harper when she discovered that the law could be manipulated virtually to write her out of existence. Very significantly, Iola's hysteria—unlike Rhoda Aldgate's extended episode—quickly transforms into a rational and steadfast abolitionism.

Meanwhile, another character early in the narrative has faced the dilemma of passing: Robert Johnson, who becomes a vehicle for Harper's critique of racialism. Melba Joyce Boyd writes that *Iola Leroy* "is especially concerned with the 'myth of blood and race,' and contributes much of the text to argue against the absurdity of this social fiction"—the use of mulatto characters such as Robert Johnson is one means by which this is accomplished.[36] Although a black dialect speaker, he certainly has the intelligence, worldliness, and appearance to pass as white once liberated. Instead, he rises through Union ranks as a lieutenant of a "colored company." Fellow officer Captain Sybil cannot understand why Robert would do such a thing. The ensuing conversation allows for a cutting critique of race at the same time that it promotes loyalty to cultural ancestry. Sybil asks Johnson, "what is the use of your saying you're a colored man, when you are as white as I am, and as brave a man as there is among us. Why not quit this company, and take your place in the army just the same as a white man?" While Sybil's query underscores the two problematic components of race—the physiognomic ("white as I am") and the behavioral ("brave a man as there is among us"), Johnson's response critiques the popular racism of the day, if it also reifies some of race's central tenets: "Well, Captain, when a man's been colored all his life it comes a little hard for him to get white all at once. Were I to try it, I would feel like a cat in a strange garret. Captain, I think my place

36. Boyd, *Discarded Legacy*, 178.

is where I am most needed" (*IL* 43). Thus, Johnson defends his decision on ethical grounds, but also confirms that his "race" has enough of an influence upon him not to allow a rapid change of identity. Still, Johnson continues to critique popular racial notions. When Sybil says, "But, Johnson, you do not look like them, you do not talk like them. It is a burning shame to have held such a man as you in slavery," Johnson responds, "I don't think it was any worse to have held me in slavery than the blackest man in the South." He points out the nobility and bravery of Tom Anderson, who "is just as black as black can be" (*IL* 44). Thus, Robert's refusal to pass is viewed as not only a refusal to betray ancestral heritage but also a critique of skin color as the acid test of personal worth. Such characters as Tom Anderson serve a very important narrative function for Harper, for they "answer frequent charges made by whites of the period that talented and intelligent Negroes owed their capabilities to their white blood." Harper has Iola Leroy directly contradict this notion: "Every person of unmixed blood who succeeds in any department of literature, art, or science is a living argument for the capacity which is in the race" (*IL* 199).[37] Indeed, *Iola Leroy* seems unequivocal in its rejection of racial hierarchies based on skin color and in its belief in the natural ability of people of all races. An equally potent critique of racial logic appears later in the novel in the character of Dr. Latrobe, a racist Southerner who claims he "can always tell" if someone has black blood—even "niggers who are as white as I am" (*IL* 229). Latrobe, however, is unable to tell that Dr. Latimer—a light-skinned African American who intends to devote his life to helping the freed people of the South—is himself part black.

Iola Leroy is given the choice to pass when Dr. Gresham, who admires her work at the Union hospital and (after a while) is willing to overlook her African ancestry, offers his hand in marriage in the hope that he might bring her north where she could pass for white (*IL* 59–60). Iola's spoken decision embodies the problem of agency inherent in the passing act. She declines, itself an expression of free will, but on the grounds that "[t]here are barriers between us that I cannot pass"—a reply that references both the passing act and the deterministic forces that complicate it

37. Ibid., 179; Elkins, "Reading beyond the Conventions," 45. Although Harper devotes much space to deconstructing racial logic and elucidating social, rather than biological, explanations for character traits, speaking of "the capability...in the race" seems to reify that which she seeks to destabilize. I would argue, however, that in the final analysis Harper does far more to critique race as a biological category of social hierarchy than she does to does to reinforce it.

(*IL* 109). As Iola explains her life goals and her decision not to marry Gresham, she underscores the conflicted agency she exercises: "I did not choose my lot in life, but I have no other alternative than to accept it. . . . I intend, when this conflict is over, to cast my lot with the freed people as a helper, teacher, and friend" (*IL* 114). Rarely is the contradiction stated more succinctly than here: she will "cast [her] lot with the freed people," but largely because she has "no other alternative than to accept" this very lot (*IL* 114). Thus, the constraints of race and racism not only leave certain doors closed to Iola, but also guide the active decisions she is able to make.

Iola's decision is not yet final. During the narrative, Iola moves North and seeks employment for herself because "every woman ought to know how to earn her own living" (*IL* 205). Iola works a series of jobs in retail, passing to secure employment and being relieved of her duties every time it is discovered that she has black ancestry. Significantly, Harper does not allow Iola success until she manages to find a tolerant employer, Mr. Cloten, with whom she can be honest about her racial background (*IL* 211). From that moment in the narrative, Iola vehemently opposes passing, and the novel takes on a decidedly more didactic tone as she is given space to elucidate her antiracist, feminist views. Iola's brother Harry, also seemingly white, likewise rejects passing and elects to work for freed blacks in the South—a decision that provokes Dr. Gresham's disapproval. Indeed, by openly proclaiming his blackness, Harry is making an idealistic "martyr" of himself—exactly the sort of masochistic self-sacrifice William Dean Howells openly attacks in his novels.[38] However, Iola defends Harry's decision, explaining that "[t]o be . . . the leader of a race to higher planes of thought and action, to teach men clearer views of life and duty, and to inspire their souls with loftier aims, is a far greater privilege than it is to open the gates of material prosperity and fill every home with sensuous enjoyment" (*IL* 219). Thus, Harper is able to rationalize what Howells would label as romantic folly: she employs

---

38. As we have seen, Howells openly rails against a self-sacrificing sense of "duty" in *An Imperative Duty*. In *The Rise of Silas Lapham* (1885), which many take to be the consummate statement of Howellsian realism, Reverend Sewell—Howells's spokesman for realist ethics—proposes to resolve a love triangle through application of the "economy of pain." When it is discovered that Tom Corey loves Penelope Lapham and not sister Irene (both sisters love Tom), Penelope, out of a romantic sense of duty and self-sacrifice, initially refuses Tom for the sake of her sister. Reverend Sewell explains that under this scenario three people—Tom, Irene, and Penelope—would be rendered unhappy, while if Penelope were to accept Tom's hand in marriage, only Irene would be unhappy. Howells, *The Rise of Silas Lapham*, 241.

realist rationality to defend an altruistic sense of self-sacrifice and in so doing fills in a narrative gap Howells is unable to close: for while Howells depicts life-changing decisions of race as whimsically, even irrationally, sudden, Harper presents them in all their moral, rational, and practical difficulty. Ultimately, Harper cannot ethically countenance passing under any circumstances—even if, unlike Howells, she uses repeated examples of characters refusing to pass in order to suggest that it is very possible, if very unethical, to do so within the limits of the United States.

When Iola attacks passing, she serves as Harper's moral mouthpiece; but her refusal to pass—however potent an act of free will—still continues to embody the contradictory nature of the agency exercised in such a refusal. Late in the narrative, Dr. Gresham again proposes to Iola, and in the ensuing conversation, her responses make use of language that is at least as deterministic as it is evidence of a free will to do good. For example, she replies, "I feel now as I felt then, that there is an insurmountable barrier between us. . . . It is the public opinion which assigns me a place with the colored people" (*IL* 230–31). Dr. Gresham makes an appeal to free will: "But what right has public opinion to interfere with our marriage relations? Why should we yield to its behests?" Iola responds, "Because it is stronger than we are, and we cannot run counter to it without suffering its penalties" (*IL* 231). Intermixed with such statements of deterministic impossibility are statements of freely willed refusals and actions; Iola is "not willing to live under a shadow of concealment" and insists "[m]y life-work is planned. I intend spending my future among the colored people of the South" (*IL* 233, 234). Later, as Iola discovers her attraction to Dr. Latimer, she pronounces the novel's anti-passing manifesto: "when others are trying to slip out from the race and pass into the white basis, I cannot help admiring one [Dr. Latimer] who acts as if he felt that the weaker the race is the closer he would cling to it" (*IL* 263). Shortly thereafter, Iola and Dr. Latimer marry, as between the two there is "no barrier in [the] way" (*IL* 271). Iola and her fellow African American characters—both educated and uneducated—are able to overcome hardship through hard work; at the same time, there are also limits to what realistic description can allow.

Insofar as this is true, the novel must provide a troubling, but ultimately truthful, backdrop of social determinism against which African American characters leverage their moral agency. This conflicted sense of agency is directly linked to concerns of both female gender and racial allegiance. With regards to the former, Iola Leroy's domestic-plot marriage is, on one hand, a concession to external demands, both social and, from the perspective of Harper, aesthetic. On the other hand, it is no textbook sentimental marriage, for it is not simply an end in and of itself but, rather, a means by which Iola and Latimer mutually work for social justice. Marriage, then, is not only a prescribed convention but also an exercise of profound moral agency. Also, the conventional moralism embodied by the Iola Leroys of fin-de-siècle African American women's fiction would indicate that they were held to a higher standard than the Silas Laphams of mainstream fame and therefore would almost automatically be restricted in their textual destinies. Iola Leroy thus unavoidably becomes another example of the supremely moral female protagonist readers had come to expect. However, writers like Harper do not allow such protagonists to be passively shaped by social convention but rather apply these characters' moralism toward a larger program of social change.[39] Deterministic forces of social convention, again, coexist with exercises of agency.

Racial allegiance can also be viewed as part of this problematical but still realist exercise of agency. For example, M. Giulia Fabi argues that, like Howells in *An Imperative Duty*, Harper transforms race from a biological reality to an active *choice* one makes. Unlike Howells, however, this choice involves not only a "reconstructi[on of] black cultural distinctiveness" but also a reconfiguration of blackness as "a force for cultural change." Thus conceived, the choice to be black signifies agency not only in and of itself, but also in the political project that it suggests. However, *Iola Leroy's* figuration of ethnic allegiance is not quite so uncomplicated and, in the end, is not as perfect a corrective to Howells's as it may seem. Werner Sollors has written on ethnicity, agency, and the "aesthetic strategy" both imply, distinguishing between "ethnicity as romance (an idealized acceptance of descent)" and "ethnicity as realism (a truthful account of plausible behavior in new environments)."[40] *Iola Leroy* clearly embodies both: Iola actively adapts to the "new environment" of her latently discovered blackness (ethnicity as realism), but she also speaks of "barriers" that confine her to black subjectivity against her will (ethnicity as romance). Also, the other light-skinned black characters—Robert Johnson, Harry Leroy, Dr. Latimer—are given the choice to pass, and one by one they declare themselves black, but "by blood and choice," which is as succinct a renaming of determinism and agency as we are likely to

39. Washington, "Uplifting the Women and the Race," 78; Tate, *Domestic Allegories,* 8.
40. Fabi, "Reconstructing Literary Genealogies," 57; Sollors, *Beyond Ethnicity,* 161–62, 164.

encounter in a nineteenth-century context (*IL* 238). At the end of the novel, having devoted themselves to helping fellow African Americans, "[t]he shadows have been lifted from all their lives," implying that not to pass is to be closer to the light of truth (*IL* 281). Still, this moralistic proclamation, while satisfying, even exhilarating for the reader, cannot completely resolve all the contradictions previously introduced in the novel.

One could make the case that, like Howells, Harper can manage only a limited critique of race, even as she is certainly more extensive and explicit than Howells in this regard. Although fully black characters are shown to be as able as the light-skinned "talented tenth" characters and de jure blacks are depicted as indistinguishable from whites, there are the seemingly perennial racial "barriers" blacks are unable to cross despite their ability or efforts—Johnson's deterministically charged comparison of a black passing for white to "a cat in a strange garret" comes to mind. But given concerns of audience and their unavoidably limited, late-nineteenth-century understanding of race, black activists and authors of the time period, even when attacking the very idea of race, betray racialist leanings that, to the contemporary reader, seem to defeat their own purpose.[41] However, if one considers political change to be an important part of American literary realism's goals—and Howells certainly did— then there is little doubt that Harper, in *Iola Leroy*, has succeeded where Howells, in *An Imperative Duty*, has failed. And this distinction stems not from the fact that Harper rejects passing while Howells allows for it (if only on another continent). More importantly, while Howells sparsely describes, Harper thickly describes, giving her contemporary readership closer access to black experience (vis-à-vis slavery, the Civil War, Northern urban labor, and race-based activism); while Howells's racial critique is often indirect and implicit, Harper's is direct and explicit (if still problematic and limited); while Howells incongruously omits careful deliberation in decisions regarding passing, Harper gives direct voice to it; and while Howells contradicts his own socioliterary motives by having the protagonists escape to Italy, Harper allows them to remain in the United States and, further, allows them to participate in a program of "racial uplift" that would have resonated with her readership. This is rendered more impressive by the fact that Harper, from a position of relative powerlessness in the world of American letters, lends her narrative rhetorical force by carefully attending to all the aforementioned concerns

41. Kevin K. Gaines, *Uplifting the Race: Black Leadership, Politics, and Culture in the Twentieth Century*, xv.

of agency, "decency," and genre. And while her insistence upon racial duty arguably limits her critique of race—much as Howells's own critique was limited by racialism and racial determinism—Harper's approach to passing is certainly appropriate given its context and amounts to a bold stand while Howells's relies more upon evasion.

But perhaps the most significant in this discussion of *An Imperative Duty* and *Iola Leroy* is structural: namely, that in both novels, one question presents itself—to pass or not to pass?—and the manner in which it is answered not only propels the plot of the passing narrative but also speaks volumes about race and ethnic authorship itself. It is also a question that echoes throughout the history of the passing narrative in the United States and is one that I will return to throughout the remainder of this study. As we shall see, the answer to this question—a presumably malevolent "yes" or a presumably benevolent "no"—is not so significant as the larger forces that conspired to pose the question in the first place. As we shall also see, the multifarious aesthetic, rhetorical, and ideological choices presented to the author by this question and embodied by these two novels—sparse description versus thick description; pessimism versus optimism; realism versus romance; evasiveness versus openness; antididacticism versus didacticism; droll irony versus earnest polemicism; racialism versus racial deconstructionism—will also reassert themselves in significant ways throughout the remaining chapters. Given the ultimate difficulty in resolving many of these authorial dilemmas, it might be best to consider *An Imperative Duty* and *Iola Leroy* to be as productively dialogical as they are antithetical.

3

Race or Nation?

White Ethnics Upstream in the Writing of
Cautela, Cahan, D'Agostino, Lewisohn, and Ornitz

"We're Americans right now," I said. "Miss Zimmerman says if you're born here you're an American." "Aw, she's nuts," Joe said. He had no use for most teachers. "We're Italians. If y' don't believe me ask Pop." But my father wasn't very helpful. "Your children will be *Americani*. But you, my son, are half-and-half."

—Jerre Mangione, *Mount Allegro*

Late-nineteenth and early-twentieth-century white ethnic writers attempted to make their voices heard in a hostile maelstrom of popular, official, and intellectual racism. Racial pseudoscience, theories of Nordic supremacy, and popular nativism—all of which intensified in the last decade of the nineteenth century and rose to fevered pitch in the post–World War I era—reduced the socioeconomic subjugation of Italian Americans and Jewish Americans to a plain, brute fact of nature the immigrant was thought to be powerless to change. Given that the mainstream realistic literature of Howells, James, and Twain had depicted immigrants in a manner that veered toward the romantic when it did not reveal outright cultural anxiety on the part of the writer; that the mainstream naturalistic literature by such authors as Stephen Crane and Frank Norris had depicted immigrants as hereditarily flawed animals predestined for lives of violence, poverty, and degradation; and that sensationalist newspapers had featured racist political cartoons and had run sensationalist stories of inner-city crime that helped contribute to the overall zeitgeist of anti-immigrant sentiment, ethnic writers were left with the task of rescuing their co-ethnics from the representational one-dimensionality to which the American readership had grown accustomed.[1] But even by as late as the 1930s, American literary culture was overtly conscious of the racial in-betweenness of white ethnics—a fact that has not garnered nearly the attention it deserves. For example, James Weldon Johnson, Pauline Hopkins, Nella Larsen, and Jessie Redmon Fauset would all describe Italian-looking African Americans in their works—a testament to these authors' awareness, at least on some level, of the unique racial circumstances of European immigrants. Fauset is especially explicit about white ethnic racial status. In *There Is Confusion,* she catalogues a group of children by ethnic group: "Italians, Jews, colored Americans, white Americans," notably excluding Italians and Jews from the "white" race. *Comedy: American Style* features a light-skinned African American character Olivia Blanchard who passes for Italian at school. In turn, like the literature of fin-de-siècle African American women writers such as Anna Julia Cooper and Frances E. W. Harper, the work of male white ethnic writers from 1896 to 1940 was inevitably part of a revisionist project of "dislodging and debunking . . . stereotypes," such as innate Italian criminality and Jewish avariciousness. This very project, argues Louis Harap, allowed the American Jew in literature (and more generally, the ethnic) to be transformed from a stereotype to "full status as a human being."[2] Generally written in the style of social realism—with occasional aesthetic and thematic excursions into romanticism, naturalism, and modernism— these texts represent the daily experiences of Italian Americans and Jewish Americans and thus directly or indirectly plead their case and assert their fundamental humanity. Unwilling to accept the biologically

1. John Paul Russo, "From Italophilia to Italophobia: Representations of Italian Americans in the Early Gilded Age," 49. For a representative sampling of media representations of Italian Americans from 1890 to 1930, see Salvatore J. LaGumina, *Wop!: A Documentary History of Anti-Italian Discrimination,* chapters 3 and 5.
2. Jessie Redmon Fauset, *There Is Confusion,* 47; Fauset, *Comedy: American Style,* 6; Tamburri, *A Semiotic of Ethnicity: In (Re)cognition of the Italian/American Writer,* 4; Louis Harap, *Creative Awakening: The Jewish Presence in Twentieth-Century American Literature, 1900–1940s,* 2.

determined status afforded them by the American political, literary, and intellectual mainstream, white ethnic writers create characters who negotiate the exigencies of ethnic and civic identity and participate fully in the American myths of self-fashioning and self-reliance. This counter-mythmaking becomes especially pronounced in ethnic autobiography, in which the author often figures himself or herself as the protagonist of a Franklinian or Algerian success story—with ethnic difference. At the same time, however, these novelists and autobiographers, in their attempt to account benignly for this difference, often employ racialist, if *romantic* racialist, language that reifies the very deterministic logic that oppressed their fellow ethnics.

This chapter begins with brief readings of *The Passing of the Great Race* (1916), by Madison Grant, and *Race or Nation: A Conflict of Divided Loyalties* (1925), by Gino Speranza, which exemplify two varieties of anti-immigrant racialism that late-nineteenth- and early-twentieth-century Italian American and Jewish American authors almost necessarily had to address. By and large, when ethnic authors wrote, they wrote in response to the ideas encountered in these anti-immigrant texts, but their rhetorical efficacy could only go so far, for their opponents were powerful. Madison Grant, for instance, was a leading member of the highly influential Immigration Restriction League, which, founded in 1887, was instrumental in promoting ideas of immigrant racial inferiority that led to the immigration restrictions of the 1920s. In the tract, which was "widely embraced by restrictionists," Grant "distinguished three races in Europe, the Alpines, the Mediterraneans, and the Nordics, differentiating them in predictable ways and singing the praises of the last," which the author finds the most fit for American productivity, civic responsibility, and democratic leadership.[3] To remedy what was perceived as a racial crisis writ large, Grant recommends an immigration restriction policy sensitive to the inherent shortcomings of southern and eastern Europeans. Meanwhile, Speranza, son of northern Italian immigrants with a middle-class upbringing, wrote *Race or Nation* between the Emergency Quota Act of 1921 and the Johnson-Reed Act of 1924, arguing, in a marginally less racist fashion, that the former was not strict enough. Speranza rejects the notion of intra-European racial inferiority, but accepts the theory of intra-European racial *difference* and recommends harsh immigration restriction on the grounds that people of fundamentally different races cannot coexist peacefully.

3. King, *Making Americans*, 52, 69, 218.

Next in the chapter, for reasons of clarity, I will distinguish between acculturation and passing narratives. The former generally feature first- and second-generation ethnics who strive for spiritual, social, and professional stability in a context that pits their ancestral culture—often romanticized, even racialized—against the strange, enticing American milieu. Typically earnest, but sometimes slightly ironic—especially when a character engages in extreme ethnic self-erasure or hypocritically performs a false show of ethnic solidarity—these texts valorize an intelligent combination of ethnic and American cultural influences. In other words, they attempt to manage the conflict between ethnic allegiance and assimilationist striving. My representative male-centered ethnic novels of acculturation will be Giuseppe Cautela's *Moon Harvest* (1925) and Abraham Cahan's *Yekl* (1896) and *The Rise of David Levinsky* (1917). These novels are so categorized because they feature characters who acculturate—sometimes avariciously, sometimes precociously—in their appearance, language, beliefs, and manner of dress. However, these are not passing narratives because in them there is never a moment when the relevant characters attempt full absorption into the white mainstream. They unselfconsciously allow something to be visually or manneristically "other" about them, and therefore no ethnic—or in this context, racial—passing is performed. However, though race is not always explicitly foregrounded in these texts, there is still a decidedly racialist element to them that essentializes both ancestral heritage and the "Americanness" so many ethnic characters covet. These authors may advocate what Josiah Royce and, later, Werner Sollors would call a wholesome provincialism that balances both ethnic and civic responsibilities in the creation of a more pluralistic society, but the troubling racialism of these texts undercuts the concurrent "messages" of realist self-determination and ethnic egalitarianism. I include all three texts because they retain these thematic commonalities despite their subtle differences in aesthetic approach. To be sure, each of them possesses the aforementioned mixture of realist agency and naturalist determinism. However, *Moon Harvest* exhibits shades of romanticism, while *Yekl* is more bitterly naturalistic and *The Rise of David Levinsky* more completely within the realm of full-blown, densely described social realism.

The white ethnic male passing narratives I examine in this chapter are *Olives on the Apple Tree* (1940), by Italian American Guido d'Agostino, and *Up Stream* (1922), by German-Jewish American Ludwig Lewisohn. An autobiographical memoir and novel respectively, the two narratives contain male characters who deploy many of the same professional and assimilative strategies as the characters featured in ethnic novels of acculturation—with one fundamental difference. Both narratives feature male characters who attempt to *pass* seamlessly into the professional world of the white middle class. In both cases, the passing character fails and in his failure is forced into a reconsideration of the value of his abandoned ancestral culture. The implied thesis, once again, of such narratives is that the ethnic male could best forge an identity from the most useful strains of his ethnic past and his American present. Furthermore, both texts are emblematic of European immigrant literature's tendency not only to draw upon, but also to participate actively in, culturally pluralistic discourse.

The realism of these works is underscored not only by the trajectory of the characters' lives—that is, their Franklinian rise to a position of moral, material, and professional prominence—but also by the verisimilar description of the realities of ethnic life. Even in an era of high modernism, the subject matter of immigrant literature seems to demand a realistic treatment. Consequently, ethnic mimesis invariably reveals the tensions pulling at the ethnic male subject—both the bigotry of the dominant American culture and the seemingly inevitable call to ethnic allegiance. Given that the ethnic male subject runs the risk of becoming defined by the conflicting deterministic influences of both ethnic and American contexts, the author is presented with a significant narratological challenge: how to write the ethnic subject into the tradition of American success and still remain honest about the forces resisting this very success. The answer perhaps best lies in examining the constructedness of "mainstream" American literary realism. For while Howells and James deployed the mimetic transparency of their favored genre to reconcile the irreconcilable divisions of race and class of Gilded Age America, ethnic writers arguably used the same genre to weave together the conflicting narrative threads of ethnic subjectivity and invest their characters with an optimistic degree of free will and self-determination. This is not to cast ethnic literature as hopelessly naive or "pollyanish"; rather, it is to say that ethnic mimesis in and of itself could act as a powerful rhetorical tool to represent the competency of the writer's fellow ethnics and to imagine a more egalitarian, pluralistic American future. I conclude with a discussion of Samuel Ornitz's *Haunch, Paunch, and Jowl*, which shares many thematic features of the texts previously discussed in the chapter, but exchanges earnest mimesis for a sharp irony more common to the African American passing narratives to be discussed in chapter 4.

"A Race of Soldiers, Sailors, Adventurers, and Explorers":
Grant, Speranza, Anglophilia, and Immigration Restriction

Madison Grant's *The Passing of the Great Race* and Gino Speranza's *Race or Nation* are representative of two varieties of anti-immigrant racialism popular during the early twentieth century: the former more purely racist and the latter less aggressively, but no less restrictively, racialist. That is, while Grant believed lesser "races," including southern and eastern Europeans, to be inferior to the dominant Nordic American stock, Speranza believed they were merely different and incompatible: in either case, the authors argue that Italians and Jews are fundamentally incapable of the demands of American democratic citizenship. Italian American and Jewish American authors, then, wrote in part to counter these hugely influential ideas but, in the final analysis, were unable to shed the racialisms of both Grant and Speranza.

Madison Grant's *The Passing of the Great Race* set the intellectual standard for immigration restriction and theories of intra-European racial difference in the early twentieth century. Authored by the chairman of the New York Zoological Society, the Trustee of the American Museum of Natural History, and the Councilor of the American Geographical Society, *Passing of the Great Race* was greatly influential in shaping public and congressional debates regarding immigration restriction policy of the 1920s. Perfectly suited for a time of intense nativism and anti-immigrant sentiment, the work stood as a formidable challenge to any ethnic author who dared attempt to write his or her fellow ethnics into the American scene. For Grant and other such intellectual powerbrokers, there was little room for the southern and eastern European immigrants of the time. In their estimation, the United States was colonized, founded, and maintained by Nordic ingenuity, persistence, and leadership—in other words, by "a race of soldiers, sailors, adventurers, and explorers"—and therefore should not have served as a continual migratory destination for lesser European groups ill fit for American democracy and biologically incapable of true assimilation.[4]

Henry Fairfield Olson, in his "Preface to the New Edition" (1917) of the popular study, resoundingly states the central theme:

> Whatever may be its intellectual, its literary, its artistic or its musical aptitudes, as compared with other races, the Anglo-Saxon branch of

4. Madison Grant, *The Passing of the Great Race or the Racial Basis of European History*, 228. Hereafter cited in the text as *PGR*.

the Nordic race is again showing itself to be that upon which the nation must chiefly depend for leadership, for courage, for loyalty, for
unity and harmony of action, for self-sacrifice and devotion to an
ideal. Not that members of other races are not doing their part, many
of them are, but in no other human stock which has come to this
country is there displayed the unanimity of heart, mind and action
which is now being displayed by the descendants of the blue-eyed,
fair-haired peoples of the north of Europe.[5]

This focus upon physiognomy is appropriate, for in the introduction to
the study, Grant states that the prime motivating factor of history is not
to be found in the external material world, but rather in biology, which
directly determines the capability of the world's peoples to contribute to
civilization (*PGR* xix). Since not all racial groups in the United States
were created equal, only the best were suited to reap the fruits of American democracy: Grant, for example, points out that the "self-evident"
truths of the Declaration of Independence were not intended to apply to
American Indians and blacks (*PGR* xx-xxi). In the chapter entitled "The
Physical Basis of Race," Grant explicates the theory of hypodescent—
also known as the "one-drop rule"—whereby the admixture of one race
type and an inferior one results in a reversion to the "lower type": "The
cross between a white man and an Indian is an Indian; the cross between
a white man and a Negro is a Negro; the cross between a white man and
a Hindu is a Hindu; and the cross between any of the three European
races [Nordic, Alpine, and Mediterranean] and a Jew is a Jew" (*PGR* 18).
This effectively precludes the possibility of "inferior" racial types inter-
marrying their way into the mainstream.

Among the "inferior" racial types Grant identifies are many ethnic
groups now considered to be white, and his chapter entitled "The European Races in Colonies" follows the anti–"new immigration," pro–"old
immigration" bias of the time. Grant explains that while the once reviled
"Irish and German elements were for the most part of the Nordic race,"

[t]hese new immigrants were no longer exclusively members of the
Nordic race.... The result was that the new immigration, while it
still included many strong elements from the north of Europe, contained a large and increasing number of the weak, the broken and
the mentally crippled of all races drawn from the lowest stratum of
the Mediterranean basin and the Balkans, together with hordes of

5. Henry Fairfield Olson, "Preface to the New Edition," x.

the wretched, submerged populations of the Polish Ghettos. Our jails, insane asylums and almshouses are filled with this human flotsam and the whole tone of American life, social, moral and political has been lowered and vulgarized by them. (*PGR* 89–90)

More specifically to the present study, Grant allows that the "Mediterranean race," "while inferior in bodily stamina to both the Nordic and the Alpine, is probably the superior of both . . . in intellectual attainments," especially art, literature, and scientific research (*PGR* 229). However, "the south Italians," which formed the bulk of Italian immigration at the time of Grant's writing, "are very largely the descendants of the nondescript slaves of all races . . . who were imported by the Romans under the Empire to work their vast estates" (*PGR* 71–72). As for Polish Jews, who have questionable European racial credibility to begin with, this recent immigrant group is cursed with "dwarf stature, peculiar mentality and ruthless concentration on self-interest" (*PGR* 16).

Attempts by inferior racial types at assimilation, and by extension passing, were futile, for among blacks, "speaking English, wearing good clothes and going to school and to church does not transform a Negro into a white man" (*PGR* 16). In fact, whenever "the impulse of an inferior race to imitate or mimic the dress manners or morals of the dominant race is destroyed by the acquisition of political or social independence, the servient race tends to revert to its original status" (*PGR* 77). Therefore, no assimilative change made by an inferior racial group can ever be permanent; if anything, the absorption into society by such a group often results in a reverse melting pot scenario in which the original racial stock is rendered impure and thereby degraded (*PGR* 17). The only solution, therefore, is severe immigration restriction in order to avoid the plunge into the "racial abyss" that would signal the "Passing of the Great Race": no progressivist attempt at assimilating immigrants, however well meaning, would meet with success, and no comfortable coexistence of ethnic difference and civic belonging could be attainable (*PGR* 263).

It is perhaps not overly simplistic to describe *Race or Nation*, by Gino Speranza, as an Italian American version of *The Passing of the Great Race*; as, essentially, an anti-immigrant polemic whose vitriol is somewhat diluted only by Speranza's progressively tenuous attachment to his fellow Italian Americans. Speranza was the son of two members of "the prominent cultivated bourgeoisie of Verona." His father was a Columbia professor, and Speranza was born into middle-class comfort in 1872 in

Bridgeport, Connecticut. Significantly separated from the bulk of Italian immigration by class, region of origin (North), and his parents' time of immigration (1868), his "family environment," Olga Peragallo explains, "was almost exclusively American. The great influx of Italian immigration had not yet begun; there were, as yet, few 'Italian Colonies,' so that the immigrants were distributed among the American population and quickly absorbed." Speranza became a scholar of Italian literature, an attorney, the director of the Prison Association of New York Society for Italian Immigrants, and a special correspondent for the *Evening Post*. He also did a great deal of research on Italian American subject matter, and Aldo E. Salerno writes that "[d]uring the Progressive Era, he emerged as an ardent advocate of Italians and other immigrants and a leading defender of the melting-pot ideal." Once a strong proponent of Italian American causes, Speranza's transition from melting-pot idealist to immigration restrictionist reflected a general American transition from prewar optimism to postwar xenophobia. *Race or Nation* reveals Speranza in the midst of this transition. Researched and written upon the author's return to the United States from Rome, where Speranza temporarily worked at the American Embassy, *Race or Nation* is a surprisingly conservative assessment of the state of Italian immigration in the United States. Arguing that Italian immigrants were racially incompatible with Anglo Americans, Speranza calls for harsher immigration restrictions and naturalization requirements. Unsurprisingly, the book was met with great hostility among liberals, immigrants, and Catholics alike.[6] Decidedly less racist than *The Passing of the Great Race*, Speranza's work is still very likely the most blatant example of a tendency among Italian American authors of the early twentieth century to adopt unproductively the rac(ial)ist discourse of the dominant intellectual culture.

Speranza, like Madison Grant, racially distinguishes between "old immigration" and "new immigration," asserting that American democracy was built upon the efforts and attributes of the former. In an introductory chapter entitled "American and Other Peoples," Speranza writes, "this nation, in all the essentials of its life and character, was grafted upon a historically definite and distinguishable north-European or Anglo-Saxon stock. . . . [U]pon that graft there was developed a definite

---

6. Olga Peragallo, *Italian-American Authors and Their Contribution to American Literature*, 202, 203, 204–5; Aldo E. Salerno, "America for Americans Only: Gino C. Speranza and the Immigrant Experience," 133.

and distinguishable racial type—the historic American people."[7] This racial type is defined by not only by its "character and genius" but also its "like-mindedness"; that is, because of "the ennobling conditions of life and struggle in the new continent, they became a homogeneous people—the American stock" (*RN* 15). This "American stock," at the time of Speranza's writing, was in danger of racial dilution at the hands of those "other Americans." The warning Speranza issues sounds nothing short of hysterical to contemporary ears: "Immigration from foreign lands gradually expanded into such vastness of numbers that nothing in recorded history short of a race invasion equaled it. This immigration became appallingly diversified in racial characteristics, in political antecedents, in cultural traditions and history" (*RN* 19–20). According to Speranza, this "race invasion" on the "Protestant homogeneity of the nation" has resulted in a palpable "national weakness" (*RN* 102). Among the "other Americans" causing so much damage to American racial purity are "non-American-minded" Roman Catholics and the unassimilable Jew who "holds tenaciously to his racial and special culture and . . . realizes that he neither can, nor wants to, merge it with other cultures" (*RN* 102, 103).

Like Grant, Speranza maintains that attempts at assimilation are futile, as the racial divide that separates the new immigration from the old is immutable and impassable. Unlike Grant, however, Speranza, in making this argument, is unwilling to accept the doctrine of Anglo-Saxon superiority: "You cannot 'confer' [the Anglo-Saxon] psychology or moral outlook. It takes ages to develop and be able to transmit a racial 'point of view,' a point of view which necessarily underlies all opinions and all decisions. It is not claimed that the Anglo-Saxon point of view is better and finer than that of the stocks of our newer immigration which have flooded America . . . ; it is only claimed that it is *different*" (*RN* 52). Given that the national character is Anglo-Saxon, Speranza argues, then it only follows that Anglo-Saxons ought to be the prime movers of U.S. culture, politics, and society (*RN* 243).

Speranza's recommendations include the abolition of immigration and a residency requirement of twenty years for naturalization (*RN* 254, 258). For those immigrants already living in the United States, Speranza recommends something that sounds remarkably like passing, even as,

7. Gino Speranza, *Race or Nation: A Conflict of Divided Loyalties*, 14. Hereafter cited in the text as *RN*.

according to Speranza's logic of biological determinism, such an option is not immediately possible. Nothing but "conformity to the American spirit, to American life and history, to American ideals and aspirations," along with an abiding commitment "to be...in every possible way American—wholly American" will suffice (*RN* 263). In Speranza's view, the new immigrant must dedicate him- or herself to "complete American conformity," even at the risk of "racial self-effacement"—which is often figured in the literature I shall read as one of many negative consequences of passing (*RN* 266). Speranza's assessment presents the reader with a troubling contradiction: the new immigrant is biologically incapable of fully assimilating yet must nevertheless make every attempt to do so. Speranza's ultimate lack of confidence in the possibility of full immigrant assimilation is perhaps best revealed by the fact that during the time of *Race or Nation*'s publication, "most of his correspondents...consisted of nativists, restrictions, and racists."[8] The result is that the ethnic is placed within a near permanent state of limbo—indefinitely trapped between the legacy of (Italian, Jewish, etc.) race and the destiny of (American) nation. Ethnic writers would devote many novels and autobiographies to resolving this unenviable dilemma.

"Presentable in America": The White Ethnic Male Acculturation Narratives of Giuseppe Cautela and Abraham Cahan

Aldo E. Salerno argues that Speranza's alienation from his fellow Italian Americans was an outgrowth of both his middle-class status and his lack of experience with ethnic marginalization. Whatever the reason, it is undeniable that the vast majority of male ethnic authors of the late nineteenth and early twentieth century had little use for Speranza's program of Anglo-conformity. Typically, the autobiographies, novels of acculturation, and passing narratives male European American immigrant authors produced warned against the very "self-effacement" Speranza recommends. For example, even as ardent an assimilationist as Constantine Panunzio prefers a melting-pot theory of American assimilation to pure conformity. An emigrant from Molfetta, Italy, to New England, Panunzio's experiences as a laborer, student, social worker, and pastor gave him a fierce pride in American ideals and thought. However, in his autobiography *The Soul of an Immigrant* he cautions that "[l]ike myself,

8. Salerno, "America for Americans Only," 142.

every immigrant brings something with him from his native land which is worthy of perpetuation, and which, if properly encouraged and developed, may become a contribution to our national life. We would do well to afford to every newcomer an opportunity to develop and to contribute the best which he has brought with him, rather than to destroy it by any means, direct or indirect." Texts such as *The Soul of an Immigrant* advocate what turn-of-the-century Harvard philosopher Josiah Royce would call "wholesome provincialism," or a fluid attachment to both ethnic/regional and American identities that promotes amiable and productive interaction with other sociocultural groups. Royce's oft-cited essay "Provincialism"—delivered in 1902 and later published in 1908—advocates "wholesome provincialism...as a saving power to which the world in the near future will need more and more to appeal." His culturally pluralistic view of American culture allows provincialism and nationalism not only to coexist but also to enhance each other. Furthermore, in Royce's view, ethnic differences mitigate modernity's "tendency to crush the individual" in conformity and homogeneity. This ethnic ideal is similar to what Richard Gambino terms "creative ethnicity," or a willingness to allow the cultural inheritances of ethnicity to remain in productive dialogue with the American mainstream and other ethnic groups: "The creative ethnicist...uses his ethnic background as a point of departure for growth rather than as proof of his worth. By inquiry and reflection, he shapes his identity by building upon inherited ethnic characteristics he judges to be valuable. (He neither rejects his ethnicity—the transparent American—nor sets it and himself in solid unchanging rock—the chauvinistic ethnocentrist.) In shaping a true identity, he gains insight into himself that gives a sense of meaningful, realistic self-control of one's own life."[9]

Although it is unlikely that Gambino had literary genre in mind when he wrote of "realistic self-control," this productive negotiation of "ethnic" and "American" inheritances (or, to use Sollors's terminology, of "descent" and "consent") is part and parcel of the self-fashioning undertaken by ethnic characters of the realist mode. In order to effect this, ethnic authors of acculturation and passing narratives typically equip their characters with the power to become morally and materially successful Americans.

9. Ibid., 143; Constantine Panunzio, *The Soul of an Immigrant*, 189. For a full reading of this immigrant autobiography, see Fred L. Gardaphè, *Italian Signs, American Streets: The Evolution of Italian American Narrative*, 47–54; Sollors, *Beyond Ethnicity*, 179; Josiah Royce, *Race Questions: Provincialism and Other American Problems*, 62, 66–67, 75; Gambino, *Blood of My Blood*, 362.

Beleaguered by bigotry from the American social mainstream and the demands of their ethnic kin, successful characters are revealed to be those who refuse to neglect ethical concerns as they attend to matters related to professional and social advancement. Therefore, these tales of ethnic self-determinism can, in many ways, be viewed in direct opposition to the biological determinism of Grant and Speranza, which would forever banish "new immigrants" to the margins of American life. However, although these ethnic counter-narratives attempt to refashion the male ethnic subject as a free-willing individual, this attempt is also typically, if unwittingly, undercut by a pervasive racialist rhetoric, or at the very least, essentialized ethnic identity that immediately calls into question the very possibility of free will.

Moon Harvest (1925), by Giuseppe Cautela, is a good example of an acculturation novel that rehearses the themes of assimilation, free will, and wholesome provincialism—all with a strong undercurrent of racialism that renders problematical each of these themes. The story begins in 1912 in Ortanova, Italy, with Romualdo and Maria planning to leave Italy with their daughter for America. Romualdo's reasons for leaving represent the bitter social, economic, and political injustices visited upon southern Italy at the hands of the more industrialized, cosmopolitan north: as a southerner, Romualdo "wanted to breathe freely, he wished to expand his ideas of human progress and emancipation; but he found always an iron circle of opponents, who, fearful of their ill-gained positions at the expense of the peasantry, were biting his heels like a pack of hungry hounds."[10] Admittedly, much of the story that ensues is the stuff of romance. Not a common laborer for long, Romualdo is rather a poet, and his continual attachment to southern Italy is frequently figured in the most idyllic of terms. For example, during the premigratory harvest moon celebration of the novel's title, the narrator describes a quaint, naturally beautiful, and decidedly preindustrial Ortanova where "[l]ove is more felt than seen," where "children roll and fight," where crops are still hand-harvested, where "[s]ongs are made up and adapted to popular airs," where all the girls are unimpeachably beautiful, and where a sublime "harvest moon" casts a "sweet but flooding light" over all the proceedings (*MH* 33–36). Furthermore, there is throughout the narrative the pervasive, romantic sense of *destino* that Fred L. Gardaphè associates with the "poetic mode" of Italian American narrative.[11] Lured and repelled

10. Giuseppe Cautela, *Moon Harvest*, 2. Hereafter cited in the text as *MH*.
11. Gardaphè, *Italian Signs*, 24–54.

by the simultaneous beauty and injustice of southern Italy, Romualdo finally concludes that "[i]t is written in Heaven... that I shall go" (*MH* 12). The male centeredness of the text is thus signaled by Romualdo's desire as the impetus for the whole family's emigration; in fact, his desire—social, assimilative, and sexual—becomes the focus of *Moon Harvest*.

Upon the family's arrival in New York City, Romualdo strives with all his power to acculturate himself to the new urban/American milieu. He initially works at a tin factory, but—through attending lectures and reading English and American authors—quickly learns enough English to begin teaching Italian to American students. As is typical of many immigrant tales, Romualdo makes "gigantic strides" toward assimilation, while his wife "remain[s] stationary," woefully steeped in Old World tradition (*MH* 57).[12] Thus, Romualdo enters a plot of male self-fashioning, while Maria is unable to adjust fully to the mores of her newly adopted social milieu and enters a naturalistic plot of decline. Of course, the reason is obvious: Maria is so "wrapped up in the care of her home and baby"— plus the birthing of a second child—that she is simply unable to gain access to the assimilative forces of the public sphere as Romualdo does. Soon, "a gulf separated the thoughts of husband and wife"—a gulf that would never be bridged (*MH* 58). Shortly after Romualdo's plot of professional ascent is set into motion, he meets Vicenza di Dedda, a young, assimilated, second-generation Italian American woman who wishes to take Italian lessons from him. So assimilated is she that she claims not to have liked Italians at all before having met Romualdo (*MH* 105). The two fall in love in accordance with a convention of ethnic authorship that figures male assimilative desire in terms of an extramarital New World love interest. Vicenza takes Italian lessons from Romualdo to further her career as a vocalist, but also implicitly to explore her previously neglected Italian heritage: the two together come to embody the Roycean ethnic ideal. Maria, however, fails to adjust, and while she only suspects her husband's infidelity, her fears are confirmed one night when she follows her husband away from their home only to see Vicenza and Romualdo kiss. Maria soon falls ill, presumably of the trauma of a broken heart, but metaphorically due to her inability to adapt to the ways of the New World. As it turns out, illness in early Italian American literature is frequently figured this way: as Mary Jo Bona argues, "America is

12. For an examination of this male/New World, female/Old World dynamic in ethnic literature, see Sollors, *Beyond Ethnicity*, 160–66.

often perceived by first-generation Italians to cause illness and to infect Italian Americans with disease, the only cure of which is found in the original culture."[13] Thus, Maria decides to travel to Ortanova with the children in order to visit her parents and recoup; however, the illness is too advanced, and she dies just before her departure.

Maria's naturalist plot of decline thus concluded, Romualdo's struggle is depicted not so much as against a racist American environment, but rather as against his own inability to let go of some of his *italianità* ("Italianness.") Ever the tortured artist, Romualdo is haunted by poetic memories of a romanticized past in Ortanova, and in Romualdo's struggle to establish an identity for himself, he often cannot decide between embracing and jettisoning his Italian heritage.[14] Sorely wounded by guilt and his wife's death, Romualdo decides to leave Vicenza—most likely temporarily—to visit Italy with his children. Convinced of the value of Italian culture, Romualdo believes that if Vicenza were to visit with him, she would "absorb the simple, deep spiritual force that Maria had." However, as an Italian American, "[h]e would not stay very long in Italy. He could not; his future called him back to this land where his past had been buried" (*MH* 253). Thus, Romualdo's freely willed immigration to America and his subsequent creation of an Italian American identity are driven by the almost cosmically deterministic lure of the New World.

This idea of the ethnic individual conquering adversity is part of what Rose Basile Green considers to be the fundamental optimism of Italian American literature. Green's description of this literary phenomenon is directly related to realism in its appeal both to mimesis and agency. She argues that "while the Italian-American writer is a depicter in realistic fiction of a segment of American life, he gives to that fiction a distinctive interpretation: the individual has the moral power to triumph in the struggle against a hostile environment." Furthermore, for Green, "the Italian-American writer endows the literary protagonist with the faith to overcome obstacles by his struggles."[15] Green here reveals an important

---

13. Mary Jo Bona, *Claiming a Tradition: Italian American Women Writers*, 90.

14. Anthony J. Tamburri writes, "[i]talianità is indeed a term expressive of many notions, ideas, feelings, and sentiments. To be sure, it is any and all of these things which lead young Italian Americans back to their real and mythical images of the land, the way of life, the values and the cultural trappings of their ancestors. It could be language, food, a way of determining life values, a familial structure, a sense of religion; it can be all of these, as it can certainly be much more." Tamburri, *To Hyphenate or Not to Hyphenate: The Italian/American Writer: An Other Writer*, 21–22; Rose Basile Green, *The Italian-American Novel: a Document of the Interaction of Two Cultures*, 70.

15. Green, *The Italian-American Novel*, 19–20.

convention of early Italian American narrative, but her gender-slanted language is revealing when one considers that it is typically *female* characters who, like Maria, succumb to the deterministic forces of the New World.

Even if one focuses exclusively on Romualdo's male "success story," the novel is still complicated generically by the powerfully deterministic language of race that recurs throughout. Although the racialism is certainly of a more benign nature than that of Grant or Speranza, it is also effective in rendering problematic the image of the ethnic subject as a free-willing agent. For example, when Maria expresses an early wish to meet Vicenza, she expects to do so as a fellow Italian, for "[o]ur psychology may change here, but not the living traits of our race." Maria's aunt, Stella, agrees with this notion: "No, it's true, Maria. Look at my children for instance. Anyone can tell they are of Italian blood" (*MH* 69). When Romualdo first meets Vicenza, he views their interaction similarly: "Vicenza di Dedda is a lovely creature, who extends her welcome innocently to one of her race, and I must regard her only as such" (*MH* 75). As Romualdo later contemplates the sound of Vicenza's "soft, warm, sweet" voice, he marvels "that in a climate so severe such a voice had survived." He concludes that "[c]ertain values in a race are indestructible" (*MH* 90). Other ostensibly Italian traits are described racially. When Maria thinks jealously of Romualdo's lover, "[h]er innate Italian pride would not admit defeat" (*MH* 190). Still, "she would never reproach [Romualdo]; he would never know. She was too proud for that. Pride is traditional in her race. Italians, in a question of honour, either avenge themselves, or die in silence" (*MH* 191). Thus, if one follows the racial logic to its conclusion, Maria's death is due to her possession of an innate, racially Italian sense of honor that she is unable to overcome. An awareness of this acquiescence to contemporary racial logic is essential to an understanding of the generic conflictedness of the next author's works, as well as all of ethnic literary production from this time period.

Abraham Cahan (1860–1951) in many ways set the standard for European American ethnic male authorship in the early twentieth century. His connections with American literary realism are many, and his narratives of acculturation effectively dramatize the many aesthetic strands constituting immigrant writing. Born in a village near Vilna, Lithuania, in 1860, Abraham Cahan escaped the czarist pogroms of Russia and emigrated to the Lower East Side of New York City in 1882. Once there, he became part of a young Jewish intellectual elite "who differed from the great body of the more conservative and orthodox newcomers." As a "teacher, labor organizer, orator, editor, novelist, [and] the most gifted and resourceful of Yiddish journalists," Cahan was greatly concerned for the welfare of his fellow Jewish immigrants, many of whom were overworked and underpaid in semi-skilled jobs, often in less-than-favorable working conditions. When he first tried his hand at fiction, realism was the dominant representational mode. As an artist, Cahan appreciated realism's verisimilitude and pragmatism and believed that literature was pleasurable to the extent that it embodied both qualities. As an activist, Cahan believed, as Howells did, that literature had a responsibility to participate in the advancement of just social causes. To Cahan, telling the truth was important not simply for its own sake, but also for the very Howellsian reason that "the accurate portrayal of social conditions inevitably would lead to social change and revolution."[16]

Not surprisingly, when Cahan's novel *Yekl* was published in 1896, it was hailed as a masterpiece of urban American realism. In a *New York World* review dated July 26, Howells praised the novel as "intensely realistic," and scholars of ethnic American and Jewish American literature have since universally noted the seminal nature of the text. *Yekl* tells a story of stepped migration that very likely provided the model for later ethnic texts such as Garibaldi La Polla's *The Grand Gennaro* (1935) and Henry Roth's *Call It Sleep* (1934). At the beginning of the novel, Yekl Podvonik is a Russian immigrant who has been living in America for three years and now works in a New York clothing sweatshop. The narrator makes Yekl's assimilation readily apparent: Yekl has changed his name to Jake, has stopped practicing Orthodox Judaism, has Americanized his dress, has begun to follow American sports, and has even adopted a number of American slang expressions. Furthermore, "Jake" has been enjoying a number of uniquely American freedoms and vices and is hesitant to raise the money to bring Gitl and Yosselé, his wife and son, from Russia to New York. Jake is not a passing character, and his incomplete assimilation is even given racial overtones by his ineffaceably "Semitic smile."[17] Although he loves to talk baseball, his Yiddish accent causes him to mangle the American terms he tries to show off: "You must know

16. Bernard G. Richards, *Introduction to* Yekl *and* The Imported Bridegroom *and Other Stories of Yiddish New York*, iii, iv; Sanford E. Marovitz, *Abraham Cahan*, 61; Sam Girgus, *The New Covenant: Jewish Writers and the American Idea*, 69.

17. Howells, *Selected Literary Criticism*, 277. On *Yekl*'s seminal status, see, for example, Thomas J. Ferraro, *Ethnic Passages: Literary Immigrants in Twentieth-Century America*, 95, and Jules Chametsky, *From the Ghetto: The Fiction of Abraham Cahan*, 57. Abraham Cahan, *Yekl*, 5. Hereafter cited in the text as *Y.*

how to *peetch*," he lectures a co-worker (*Y* 6). Furthermore, he works among fellow Jews in a traditionally Jewish American place of employment, a cloak manufacturer. Nevertheless, Jake's alienation from his ethnic background is significant. Not nearly approaching Romualdo's respect for his past, Jake views "his Russian past" as a "charming tale, which he was neither willing to banish from his memory nor able to reconcile with the actualities of his American present." Ridiculously, "[h]e wished he could both import his family and continue his present mode of life" (*Y* 26). After his father's death places his family's survival in jeopardy, Yekl finally sends for them. Upon their arrival, Jake's "heart had sunk at the sight of his wife's uncouth and un-American appearance. She was slovenly dressed in a brown jacket and skirt of grotesque cut, and her hair was concealed under a voluminous wig of a pitch-black hue. . . . She was naturally dark of complexion, and the nine or ten days spent at sea had covered her face with a deep bronze, which combined with her prominent cheek bones, inky little eyes, and above all, the smooth black wig, to lend her resemblance to a squaw" (*Y* 34). Gitl seems so hopelessly Old World to Jake in manner, raiment, and appearance that his view of her places her in a distinct *racial* category from him. He would rather continue with his freewheeling American lifestyle, poignantly symbolized by his newfound preference for Americanized women. As the narrative progresses, Jake falls for one such woman, Mamie Fein, a beautiful blonde Pole who lends Jake money to furnish his home. It becomes clear to the reader that Jake is increasingly dependent upon Mamie's money—he must borrow hundreds of dollars from her in order to secure the divorce he desires from Gitl, whom he eventually grows to hate.

Meanwhile, Gitl stands by helplessly, unsuccessfully enlisting the help and counsel of neighbor Mrs. Kavarsky, who is well versed in the troubles of many immigrant marriages. As Gitl realizes she cannot keep her family together with Jake, she falls for Mr. Bernstein, a boarder at the Podvonik household. Bernstein is one of Jake's fellow employees at the garment factory; he is scholarly, religious, and more traditionally Jewish, yet still well adapted to American life. Once Jake and Gitl divorce, she marries Bernstein, and the two begin to make a happy life for themselves. At the same time, Jake, who marries Mamie, ends the novel riding a train away from the divorce proceedings; he seems doubtful and is uncertain he has made the right decision.

This novel of wholesome provincialism occupies a middle ground between realism and naturalism in a state of generic hybridity that would become typical of ethnic narratives written after the heydays of both

genres. If we focus upon Jake's story, we are confronted with a naturalistic plot of coercion and decline. However, if we focus upon Gitl, we
see the makings of a realist success story, in which free will and morality
conquer adversity—a reversal of what would become a convention of
male success and female decline in European immigrant literature. Many
critics, in an attempt to describe *Yekl* as a novel of urban realism, actually
describe a very naturalistic tale. For example, Sanford E. Marovitz terms
the moment Jake confronts Gitl and Yosselé on Ellis Island as the moment
where "Jake loses control of his life and future." Indeed, Jake is at the
mercy of Mamie Fein, both in his attraction to her Americanized good
looks and in the money he owes her. According to Marovitz, "Mamie has
total control over Jake from that time forward, though his increasing subservience to her leads to his commensurately hostile treatment of his
terrified wife." Jake is clearly trapped in a downward spiral of desire,
financial necessity, hatred, and circumstance from which there is no return.
Indeed, as chapter titles of *Yekl* suggest, Jake is "In the Grip of His Past"
as "Circumstances Alter Cases" in his life. Ronald Sanders goes so far as
to say that, in *Yekl*, "the corrupting force seems to be nothing else than
America itself, or at any rate some vision of America that captures the
souls of immigrants like Jake and Mamie." Werner Sollors's analysis of
Yekl further casts the novel in a naturalistic light. He writes that in the
novel, "fresh contact with new environments inevitably and inescapably
changes characters, their moral powers, and their allegiances. . . . Jake is
so thoroughly alienated from his past that he is unable to love his wife."
Thus, as Jake rides the train into his "dark and impenetrable . . . future"
(*Y* 89) "there is no getting off the deterministic cable car of history."[18]

By contrast, Gitl's story of assimilation is one of realist agency. Although
Gitl is cruelly shunned by her husband in a "terrible America" she initially hates, she willingly adjusts to her surroundings in a healthy manner
(*Y* 42). At her divorce hearing, Gitl's appearance has noticeably changed.
No longer the unassuming immigrant bride she once had been, Gitl has
steadily adjusted to her surroundings and—"greenhorn" no more—now
shows her own hair, wears more American-looking clothing, and, most
significantly, exhibits a "peculiar air of self-confidence" (*Y* 83). As further evidence of her assimilation, Gitl begins referring to Yosselé by the
more American-sounding "Joeyelé." Her free will is exemplified by her
choice to marry Mr. Bernstein, the intelligent, more traditional boarder

18. Marovitz, *Abraham Cahan*, 75, 77; Richard Sanders, *The Downtown Jews: Portraits of an Immigrant Generation*, 200; Sollors, *Beyond Ethnicity*, 163.

who is clearly more deserving of Gitl's love, and the couple comes to embody the epitome of wholesome provincialism. "Far from desolate," Gitl is clearly given a meaningful future in the New World. Meanwhile, Jake, "A Defeated Victor" as the final chapter title proclaims, ends up an unhappy, unsatisfied man whose life has declined in strict accordance with the logic of naturalism.

Sanford E. Marovitz argues that *Yekl* "approaches the naturalism of Stephen Crane," but has "the redeeming qualities represented by Gitl, Bernstein, and Mrs. Kavarsky" that one tends not to find in full-blown naturalism.[19] Cahan's unwillingness to write naturalistically probably has much to do with his position as an ethnic American writer and helps us understand why so many ethnic tales occupy this generic middle ground. Although Cahan was familiar with the American realists and naturalists popular in the 1890s, this body of literature was generated mostly by native-born American writers of the dominant culture—writers who could afford to observe urban America as outsiders and almost nihilistically consider it hopeless. William Dean Howells, for example, was poor as a child, but also well educated, and he was able to work his way into the intellectual and literary elites of Boston and New York. Stephen Crane's family had lived in America since the mid–seventeenth century, and Frank Norris first explored deterministic social theory as Louis Gates's student at Harvard. Both Norris and Crane worked as journalists in the late nineteenth century, so they came into close contact with the squalor and misery of urban life—just the sort of thing their yellow-journalism readership craved. Despite good intentions, most naturalists were distanced from their subject matter by ethnicity and class, so they could afford the bleak pessimistic determinism of works such as Crane's *Maggie: A Girl of the Streets* (1893) and Norris's *McTeague* (1899).

Abraham Cahan wrote in the aesthetic style of his day, but also as an ethnic writer. Using Thomas Ferraro's term, one could say that Abraham Cahan, as a Jewish American writing about Jews in America, had to undergo an "ethnic passage" in order to become accepted by the American literary mainstream. Marovitz writes that Cahan's "perspective on American life and literature differed significantly from that of such contemporary native realists as Howells, Twain, James, and the local colorists. Inevitably, his immersion in the culture of the Lower East Side as a Yiddish-speaking ... writer gave him access to attitudes and materials that were generally inaccessible to Gentile American authors." Of course, Cahan's

---

19. Marovitz, *Abraham Cahan*, 104.

contemporaries were also aware of his differing ethnic perspective. William Dean Howells, in an 1898 review of *The Imported Bridegroom and Other Stories of the New York Ghetto,* heavily praises the book, but offers cultural insights that range from the ethnically sensitive to the essentialistic, for he suggests that Cahan's abilities and aesthetic tastes come at least in part from being a Russian Jew.[20] Put simply, it would have been impossible for Cahan to forget who he was, not only as an immigrant writer but, more fundamentally, as an immigrant.

Given that Cahan was a Jewish American activist who sincerely believed realistic literature could better the lives of his fellow immigrants, it simply would not have made sense for him to create a completely hopeless and desolate urban American world, and thus to some degree, he found himself in an authorial position analogous to that of Frances E. W. Harper. Naturalism was a bitter pill for ethnic writers to swallow, and although they occasionally made use of its bleak urban landscapes and philosophical determinism, they were usually unwilling to declare their fellow ethnics as lost—for this was simply too much to lose. Thus, characters are given the moral agency (whether they make productive use of it like Gitl or misuse it like Yekl) necessary to forge meaningful ethnic identities for themselves.

This theme would remain the focus of Cahan's work, especially *The Rise of David Levinsky* (1917), arguably his consummate statement, and given its meticulously thorough description of Russian-Jewish American culture, his most purely realist statement. This becomes obvious from the very beginning when David Levinsky tells of his pre-American childhood and upbringing, thereby giving the reader insights into Russian-Jewish culture and into Levinsky's character that are generally unavailable to the reader of the more concise *Yekl.* In full confessional mode, David Levinsky tells of having been born in 1865 in northwestern Russia. Growing up in abject poverty, Levinsky is given a traditional Orthodox Jewish upbringing. He is schooled at *cheder*—or Jewish boys' school—where he studies Hebrew and religion: his mother hopes that he will one day become a renowned Talmudic scholar. When David is orphaned at a young age, he considers emigrating to America to escape both personal hardship and the increasing anti-Semitism of czarist Russia. Before his departure, he befriends a well-off secular married woman named Matilda who encourages him to Americanize as quickly as possible upon

20. Ferraro, *Ethnic Passages,* 8; Marovitz, *Abraham Cahan,* 68–69; Richards, Introduction, vii.

his arrival. She tells him, "When you are in America you'll dress like a Gentile and even shave. Then you won't look so ridiculous. Good clothes would make another man of you."[21] Matilda here underscores the performative nature of American identity; indeed, if David wishes to be taken for American, he must rid himself of his Orthodox sidelocks and conform to American standards of fashion.

Thus, when David arrives in Lower East Side New York, after being initially stung by his treatment as a "greenhorn," he meets a Talmudic scholar named Mr. Even who takes David shopping for American clothes: "He spent a considerable sum on me. As we passed from block to block he kept saying, 'Now you won't look green,' or, 'That will make you look American.' At one point he added, 'Not that you are a bad-looking fellow as it is, but then one must be presentable in America.'" Thus, the self-fashioning begins, but any understanding of David's agency is complicated by the obvious fact that in the American context in which he finds himself, he is not good enough "as [he] is" and must rid himself of the outward appearances of ethnic difference. Mr. Even takes David to a barber for a haircut, bath, and shaving of the side-locks. David is dazzled by the effect: "It was as though the hair-cut and the American clothes had changed my identity" (*RDL* 101).

David then very self-consciously and methodically attempts to assimilate American ways. He rents a pushcart and makes a meager living, but still manages to attend night school, learn English, and familiarize himself with American politics. When his business suffers from his voracious reading of English literature, he takes a series of jobs only to settle on learning a trade, cloakmaking. David rises in the business from laborer to owner to millionaire status, using a broad range of dubious business practices. When he is accused of being a "fleecer of labor," he cherishes being thus placed in the same class as other robber barons, "the Vanderbilts, the Goulds, the Rothschilds" (*RDL* 273). Assuming the worst motives and methods of American capitalism, David steals the designs of his competitors and then undersells them. Levinsky then justifies his behavior using the tenets of social Darwinism—a belief system very frequently referenced by fast-assimilating male characters "on the make" in ethnic literature. He reads Herbert Spencer's *Sociology* and begins to view union leaders as "so many good-for-nothings, jealous of those who had succeeded in business by their superior brains, industry,

21. Abraham Cahan, *The Rise of David Levinsky*, 75. Hereafter cited in the text as *RDL*.

and efficiency." To David, "[a] working-man, and every one else who was poor, was an object of contempt to me—a misfit, a weakling, a failure" (*RDL* 282, 283).

Levinsky's assimilative program becomes inextricably tied to his business endeavors, for the more American in dress and mannerism he seems to become, the more he appeals to the business community (*RDL* 260). He even takes up smoking cigars and learns "the importance of offering a cigar to some of the people I met. I would watch American smokers and study their ways, as though there were a special American manner of smoking and such a thing as smoking with a foreign accent" (*RDL* 326). He views his tendency to gesticulate while speaking—learned while praying as a youth—with horror: "It was so distressingly un-American. I struggled hard against it. I had made efforts to speak with my hands in my pockets; I had devised other means for keeping them from participating in my speech. All of no avail. I still gesticulate a great deal, though much less than I used to" (*RDL* 327). Levinsky is not a passing character: throughout the narrative he never changes his name and always identifies as a Russian Jew; he even takes pride in Russian Jews' business accomplishments and their adaptability to American business culture. Once ostracized by the business community, Russian Jews, according to Levinsky, had demonstrated their "energy, ability, and responsibility," so "[t]he American merchants . . . had gradually realized that we were a good risk, while we, on our part, had assimilated the ways of the advanced American businessman" (*RDL* 445).

Nevertheless, the whole of life becomes a performance for Levinsky, and he understands that "[w]e are all actors, more or less. The question is only what our aim is, and whether we are capable of a 'convincing personification'" (*RDL* 194). The problem is that beyond the performance, there is very little to Levinsky. Having all but abandoned the ways of his ancestral culture so as to pursue "Success! Success! Success! . . . the almighty goddess of the hour," Levinsky has done violence to what is taken to be his essential Jewish self (*RDL* 445). This social mobility comes at the cost of both his Jewishness and, to a large degree, his humanity. Perennially lonely, Levinsky's shortcomings as a human being are evinced by his pitiful inability to maintain successful relationships with women. Levinsky is forced to reconsider the value of his Jewish ancestral heritage, and the beginning and ending of the novel are very telling in this regard. The opening sentences of chapter 1 seem to betray the cocksureness of the first-person narrator; after all, his is an archetypical story of male rags-to-riches success: "Sometimes, when I think of my past in a superficial, casual way, the metamorphosis I have gone through strikes me as nothing short of a miracle. I was born and reared in the lowest depths of poverty and I arrived in America—in 1885—with four cents in my pocket. I am now worth more than two million dollars and recognized as one of the two or three leading men in the cloak-and-suit trade in the United States." Yet this "metamorphosis" has marred what Levinsky takes to be his essential Jewish self. He continues: "And yet when I take a look at my inner identity it impresses me as being precisely the same as it was thirty or forty years ago. My present station, power, the amounts of worldly happiness at my command, and the rest of it, seem to be devoid of significance" (*RDL* 3). In other words, Levinsky's assimilative strategies and the riches they bring are the purest of artifice and are not as valuable in human terms as the Jewish identity he has attempted to abandon. Furthermore, Levinsky's change "has resulted from weakness rather than strength of character."[22] After his reconsideration, Levinsky attempts to "revive . . . old friendships" with fellow Russian Jewish countrymen only to find that his prosperity has rendered him alien to them (*RDL* 529). The closing passage brings the narrative full circle and reasserts Levinsky's tragic alienation from himself: "I cannot escape from my old self. My past and my present do not comport well. David, the poor lad swinging over a Talmud volume at the Preacher's Synagogue, seems to have more in common with my inner identity than David Levinsky, the well-known cloak-manufacturer." When one considers Levinsky's attempt at self-fashioning, it is thus impossible to ignore the hostile environment that provoked his "metamorphosis" and his ineludible ancestral heritage. When Levinsky longs for the familiarity and comfort of his Jewish past, he "pit[ies] himself for a victim of circumstances" (*RDL* 530). Although Levinsky's attempt to figure himself as a naturalistic protagonist is somewhat comical, it does reflect a genuinely mournful sense of detachment from his Jewish ethnicity.

Jewish ethnic difference, however, is not only essentialized in the novel but also racialized—as one finds as well in *Moon Harvest*. When Levinsky recalls hearing the Jewish Prayer for the Dead as a child, he muses, "There is a streak of sadness in the blood of my race. Very likely it is of Oriental origin. If it is, it has been amply nourished by many centuries of persecution" (*RDL* 4). Similarly, when Levinsky relates the difficulty he had experienced learning American slang expressions, he compares his foreign birth to "a physical defect that asserted itself in many disagreeable

22. Murray Baumgarten, *City Scriptures: Modern Jewish Writing*, 37.

ways—a physical defect which, alas! no surgeon in the world was capable of removing" (*RDL* 291). Even his "Talmud gesticulations...worr[y him] like a physical defect" (*RDL* 327). Thus, Levinsky's realist tale of rags-to-riches success is complicated by the deterministic forces of anti-immigrant sentiment and an essentialized, even racialized, Jewish past he lacks the power to escape completely. The trope of the racialized ethnic inheritance is significant, for it would continue to provide a primary reason for why white ethnic passing characters generally fail in their attempts to merge with white, middle-class culture. It would also continue to complicate the realism authors would generally deploy to tell the story.

Olive No More: Guido d'Agostino and the White Ethnic Male Passing Narrative

Olives on the Apple Tree is a novel about a New York–area Italian American laboring community and the "danger of attempts at too-rapid assimilation," but it is also more than that, for it contains a character who tries—and fails—to pass completely into white middle-class society. The narrative begins by describing the Gardellas, an upwardly mobile family who live "in the village" away from the "poor Italians on Wop-Roost," the working-class immigrant community.[23] Federico, the father, supervises a number of Wop-Roost laborers, while his wife, Giustina— who cherishes the family's geographical and class distance from the poorer Italians—attends to household affairs. They have two children: Elena, an intelligent and sensitive young woman, and Emilio, arguably the most notorious passer in Italian American literature. Emilio is a doctor who, like David Levinsky, assimilates as part of an overall strategy of professional achievement. He fantasizes about Americanizing his name, impressing his medical superior Dr. Stone, and dating the wealthy Hazel Lambertson in order to achieve social acceptance in Anglo American high society. In order to do so, Emilio carries Levinsky's ethic of assimilation for professional success to an extreme—to the point of anti-Italian hatred and the erasure of visible and invisible *italianità*.

Throughout the narrative, Emilio mimics the mores and beliefs of the white middle class. Unlike his parents, he speaks self-consciously grammatical English and exhibits table manners that "ma[k]e him appear born

23. Green, *The Italian-American Novel*, 164; Guido D'Agostino, *Olives on the Apple Tree*, 1. Hereafter cited in the text as *OAT*.

to the part of the gentleman" (*OAT* 4). Having already changed his conspicuously Italian given name to Emile, the young doctor hates when his medical colleagues call him by his surname because it makes him "feel like a wop greenhorn" (*OAT* 33). He considers changing it to "Gardell." Once, when Emilio calls Hazel Lambertson, he introduces himself to the maid as "Doctor Gardella," "trying his best to kill the final *a*"—a gesture that heavily foreshadows his figurative and literal violence against *italianità* (*OAT* 78).[24] Emilio's ultimate goal is full structural assimilation, which for him would involve becoming familiar with boss Dr. Stone and his upper-crust socialites (*OAT* 5). In order to do so, he adopts many of the anti-immigrant views Dr. Stone and his contemporaries might share. Emilio cringes at the idea of "remain[ing] a little wop doctor in a one-jerk village all [his] life" and evinces outright hatred for immigrant Italians (*OAT* 7). In statements dripping with anti-Italian bigotry, Emilio advocates immigration restriction with language harsher but with fervor equal to Gino Speranza or even Madison Grant. He describes one Italian laborer as "the personification of that stagnant quality which makes the wop looked down upon by everyone else. Refuses to become assimilated, a part of the American way of life. Refuses to mold and shape to the new form of society. These fellows are dangerous, should be eliminated and kicked the hell back where they come from. Jesus, I can't stand those people who talk about the old country and the way things were different and better over there. Why do they come here in the first place?" (*OAT* 73). Emilio adopts the seemingly obligatory social Darwinist ethic, claiming that "[t]his is a world of dog eat dog, a survival of the fittest. If we [Italians] can't cut a niche for ourselves it's just too bad. We don't belong" (*OAT* 279). For Emilio, nothing but a strict adherence to Anglo conformity will do. When he enters Dr. Stone's home for a meeting—in a passage that is highly reminiscent of the close interior description found in many works of Anglo American realism—Emilio admires the décor of the study for its aesthetic representativeness, "English in effect," of an imagined white, middle-class ideal (*OAT* 182). Emilio desires all the things that exhibit white, middle-class learning and taste and is ashamed of the more humble immigrant living spaces he has always known.

24. On the significance of name-changing in Jewish American literature, see Susan Koppelman, "The Naming of Katz: Who Am I? Who Am I Supposed to Be? Who Can I Be? Passing, Assimilation, and Embodiment in Short Fiction by Fannie Hurst and Thyra Samter Winslow with a Few Jokes Thrown in and Various References to Other Others."

According to the conventions of the European immigrant narrative, Emilio's attempt at passing is destined for some kind of failure. He becomes too boastful, and both Dr. Stone and Hazel discover that Emilio has been using them for personal gain. Furthermore, Emilio has been involved in an affair with Angelina, a young Italian American woman who cares for the immigrant laborers. At one point, in an act symbolic of growing anti-Italian hatred, Emilio physically attacks Angelina, who was hitherto unaware of Emilio's involvement with Hazel. When the Italian immigrants hear about Emilio's and Angelina's affair, they call for an honor marriage, and in the novel's ambiguous conclusion Emilio drives off with her, seemingly forced into a reconsideration of the Italian past he had attempted to leave behind. The novel's thesis is, at least in part, the now familiar wholesome provincialism—the Aristotelian golden mean of possible literary immigrant identities. As I shall demonstrate, however, the wholesome provincialism of *Olives on the Apple Tree* has decidedly racialist overtones.

Throughout the novel, a few characters contradict, or even attempt to counter, Emilio's assimilative program. At one point, Emilio unabashedly dallies in attending to an injured Italian laborer named Nick, who notes, "when people is get lilla money they forget where they come" (*OAT* 21). Similarly, Emilio's sister Elena continually serves as her brother's conscience, reminding him, "you can't neglect those who depend on you just because you want to work yourself into the social set in town. The poor people need doctors too" (*OAT* 5). One Italian laborer, Marco, serves as an uneducated and bluntly eloquent foil to Emilio and underscores Guido d'Agostino's attempt to dramatize explicitly a debate that was obviously still important in 1940: Anglo conformity (Emilio) versus cultural pluralism (Marco). The living embodiment of wholesome provincialism, Marco advises fellow Italian Americans not to do violence to their *italianità*. Marco believes that Italian culture has much to offer the greater American culture—particularly the southern Italian devotion to land and labor he continually articulates. In Marco's eyes, American freedoms provide the opportunities that foster the southern Italian's devotion to hard, honest work.[25] Furthermore, Marco's concept of southern Italian labor and love of land is intertwined with his essentialist figuring of Italian identity:

25. For a discussion of southern Italian views on labor, see Gambino, *Blood of My Blood*, chapter 3.

Always I have looked for people like me—Italians. I have looked for the love of things that I love because I am me and my father was my father. Is something inside goes 'way, 'way back. The love of the work and what you do. The love of the ground and the good crops. The love of the grapes and the good wine. The love of the food and the table and the conversation, the laughing and everything else that makes the life worth while. I was so sure to find all this here. Better than over there, because here the man is free and can do what he wants and say what he wants—and the country is so big and so rich, with plenty for everybody. (*OAT* 26–27)

Thus, Italian Americans have freedoms unknown to southern Italians, but they are limited in the exercise of this freedom by a kind of biologically circular logic: "I am me and my father was my father." According to Marco, the self-erasure of *italianità* alienates Italian Americans from their ethnically (racially?) derived sense of work; the danger is that in America,

[e]verything is all mixed up. The farmer is no more farmer, he has become the businessman. The man who was good to handle stone, now he is a slave in the laundry. Is no more the work, but the money makes the man different one from the other. I look for the Italian. What have I found? No more the Italian but a bastard Italian. Quick he forgets everything from the old country to make money and have a car and buy food in cans and become just like the American he is working for. But he does not become the American and he is no more the Italian. Something in the middle—no good for himself and no good for the country. A real bastardo! (*OAT* 28)

Therefore, someone who attempts to do what Emilio does is doing irreparable damage to his or her *italianità*. They are former Italians, failed Americans, and *bastardi* whose Italian and American inheritances have yet to be properly married. Marco's idea of labor is clearly spoken from a working-class perspective, but this does not necessarily mean that Italian Americans should not pursue white-collar careers, as Emilio does: white-collar Italian Americans have traditionally chosen service-oriented professions that do not disrupt cherished folkways and family duties.[26] Emilio, however, evinces anything but respect for either.

The ideal, as Marco would have it, is for Italian Americans "to be

26. Ibid., 89.

Americans in a Southern Italian mode."[27] Toward this end, he seeks the help of fellow Italian laborers to revive a plot of farmland the Gardellas have allowed to fall into disuse. To Marco, the abandoned farm is symbolic of Italian Americans having abandoned their *contadino* (Italian peasant) roots in the New World in favor of a new middle-class, American ethic. To engage in Emilio's style of passing is to make the mistake of "[t]he olive that jumps to the apple tree." "The olive that shouts that it is an apple"—the olive that passes, in other words—has made a profound mistake: and "olive" here carries two connotations, both biologically deterministic. Literally, it refers to a fruit that can never be grafted onto the tree of another fruit. Metaphorically, "olive" refers to Italians and grants them an immutable racial difference through the color of their skin—not white, not black, but unavoidably somewhere in between. According to Marco's logic, one cannot simply declare oneself an American; rather, "[t]he worry is to work, to produce what you can produce and that is what makes you an American" (*OAT* 295). Then, the Italian American is able to forge an identity out of the materials of his or her Italian past and his American present.

Robert Viscusi writes that "[t]he real problem in this novel is how Italians can find a way to be Americans without doing violence to their natures."[28] Viscusi's use of the essentialic word "nature" is apropos for *Olives on the Apple Tree;* while asserting the ability of Italian immigrants to will their own destinies and forge their own identities, d'Agostino cannot help but use the language of biological determinism to describe the "nature" of these very identities. Marco's explanation of eventual Italian American assimilation relies on an essentialistic theory of "blood mixture." Speaking to Giuseppe, a fellow Italian immigrant, Marco sounds a particularly deterministic note:

> People like you and me! We will never become real American. There is too much behind for us to change. But we can be a part of America. We can give to it just as much as the people who call themselves Americans because it is here where they were born and they have the flag waving outside the window. We bring the blood and the life and the energy that from the beginning made this country something. All the rest of the people who come from the other side of the world!

27. Robert Viscusi, "Professions and Faiths: Critical Choices in the Italian American Novel," 47.
28. Ibid., 45.

Italian, Frenchman, Polish, Swede—there is no difference. They all belong to America—and the Italian just like anybody else. We marry and the blood is in our children. Our children marry and there is the mixture of the blood. And the race becomes stronger and better. (*OAT* 141)

Marco counters the hypodescent racism of Madison Grant, but in no less racialist a fashion; his dream vision of melting pot America relies as much on blood as does Madison Grant's nightmare vision of the "passing of the great race." One might dismiss Marco's thoughts as simple *contadino* wisdom, but a character as assimilated and educated as Elena Gardella subscribes to similar notions. When Emilio insists to his sister that his children will "grow up to think their ancestors came over on the Mayflower," Elena jokingly replies, "That'll be funny. Olive-skinned Yankees," as if Italian Americans would be forever racially marked and separated from the American mainstream by the insurmountable barrier of skin color (*OAT* 133). Thus, Marco's story of self-determination is complicated not only by painfully obvious divisions of class and ethnicity, but also by a deterministic racial discourse that early-twentieth-century white ethnic authors seemed unable to escape.

"A Pan-Angle of the Purest Type": Ludwig Lewisohn's Autobiographical Passage from the Melting Pot to Trans-National America

If the "ethnic impersonator autobiography" is an archetypically American form due to its celebration of Emersonian self-reliance and Franklinian self-determination, then for these same reasons, I would argue, it is also easily adaptable to realist epistemology and narrative structure. In *Up Stream: An American Chronicle,* Ludwig Lewisohn (1883–1955) chronicles his ethnic journey from immigrant to passer to ardent anti-assimilationist. In so doing, he transforms his very novelistic autobiography into a culturally pluralistic polemic—a transformation emblematic of immigrant literature's shifting status as literature and vital social rhetoric. Steven J. Rubin explains that "[t]he title suggests the movement of salmon who, having matured, swim upstream—against the current—to find their breeding ground"; in other words, the salmon upstream serves as an apt metaphor for the happy, but arduously attained, end of the narrative.[29] However, Lewisohn can be viewed in such a fashion through-out the entire course of text; for when he opts to pass for white, he swims against the current of German Jewish tradition, and when he opts to iden-tify as Jewish American, he swims against the current of "100% Ameri-canism." Nevertheless, the sense is that, in the end, he has made the right decision: that by sacrificing the potential benefits of a fully assimi-lated American identity, he has retained something of moral and cultural value.

Born in Berlin in 1883, Lewisohn grew up in a culturally astute and relatively well-off family. Most importantly, the Lewisohns were, to a large degree, assimilated into the German mainstream. Lewisohn recalls, "In truth, all the members of my family seemed to feel that they were Germans first and Jews afterwards." Although the Lewisohns did not conceal their Jewish roots, they also "had assimilated, in a deep sense, Aryan ways of thought and feeling. Their books, their music, their political interests were all German." In 1890 the Lewisohns emigrated to the United States—to St. Matthews, South Carolina, disguised as "St. Mark's" in the narrative (US 37).[30] Once there, Lewisohn begins to sense the assimilative pattern of the community; indeed, it seems a microcosm of melting-pot America. He reminisces that "[t]he people of the village . . . came of various stocks—English, Scotch-Irish, German, even French and Dutch. But they were all descended from early nineteenth century set-tlers and had become thorough Americans" (US 42). Lewisohn and his family hope to follow suit: they make close Gentile friends, preferring the "better sort of Americans in the community"—an elitism that would produce for Lewisohn a sad and profound "alienation from [his] own race" (US 44). Lewisohn recounts his struggle to learn English and his subsequent initiation into the experience of English-language literature.

His cultural assimilation becomes advanced at an early age when both he and his family stop observing Jewish religious customs and begin observing Protestant ones. The effects of the conversion are, for Lewisohn, profound; he confesses that, almost without thought, he begins breaking once dear familial and social bonds (US 51). In 1892 the Lewisohns move to Charleston, South Carolina—"Queenshaven" in the autobiography

29. Laura Browder, *Slippery Characters: Ethnic Impersonators and American Identities*, 2–3; Steven J. Rubin, "American-Jewish Autobiography," 291.

30. Ludwig Lewisohn, *Up Stream: An American Chronicle*, 17. Hereafter cited in the text as *US*. Ralph Melnick, *The Life and Work of Ludwig Lewisohn: "A Touch of Wild-ness,"* 37.

(*US* 56).[31] The family continues its assimilatory practices, refusing to join German American or Jewish social groups. Lewisohn admits that while his first-generation parents could not assimilate fully, he, the second-generation "rebel" (to use Irvin Child's terminology), was able to make considerable headway in this regard.

The abuse he suffers at "Queenshaven High School" for "being a foreigner and a Jew" only strengthens his resolve to fit in (*US* 65). He makes American friends and completely stops speaking German. By his final year of high school, he could proclaim, "my Americanization was complete": he was like his Southern classmates in every regard except his indifference toward sports (*US* 73). A committed Methodist, Lewisohn comes to fancy himself a Southern gentleman and adopts all the obligatory beliefs that come with this new identity: "a gentleman believed that the South was right in the War between the States, that Christianity was the true religion[,] that the Democratic party was the only means, under Providence, of saving the White Race from obliteration by the Nigger, that good women are sexless—'sweet and pure' was the formula—and that in a harlot's house you must keep on your hat. And we were trained to be 'young gentlemen.' ... I was a young gentleman" (*US* 74). Indeed, "at the age of fifteen, I was an American, a Southerner and a Christian" (*US* 77). Lewisohn relates that as he became "hostil[e] to everything either Jewish or German," he experienced a continual desire "to live in harmony with the society of which, by virtue of its English speech and ideals, [he] felt [him]self so integral a part"; Lewisohn, like Emilio Gardella, becomes the consummate Anglo conformist—a fact aptly symbolized by his desire one day to become a professor of English literature (*US* 78–79).[32]

At Queenshaven College (College of Charleston), Lewisohn comes under the tutelage of a Professor Ferris (Lancelot Minor Harris), a scholar of English literature whose Southern background and cosmopolitan tastes would provide an apt model for the young undergraduate to follow.[33] The epitome of what Lewisohn wished to be, Ferris teaches the young man a great deal, but likely "never ... quite forgave [him] for being what [he was]" (*US* 83). Nevertheless, in his elite American posturing, Lewisohn comes to consider himself "a Pan-Angle of the purest type" (*US* 87). The language of racial purity is indeed strange; after

31. Ibid., 39.
32. The degree to which Lewisohn actually assimilated is well documented in Stanley F. Chyet, "Ludwig Lewisohn in Charleston (1892–1903)."
33. Melnick, *The Life and Work of Ludwig Lewisohn*, 53, 55.

all, Lewisohn had just told the reader—four pages previously—that an impassable divide separated Ferris from himself because of "what he was." Apparently Lewisohn's ethnic background is not wholly secret to everyone: he tells of being excluded from a Greek fraternity for being Jewish, an indignity that wounds him but does not deter his drive. He graduates with simultaneous bachelor's and master's degrees in English literature and applies successfully for further graduate studies in literature at Columbia University. Before his departure for New York, he describes his sense of alienation from Anglo American culture in tellingly racial terms: "I was passionately Anglo-American in all my sympathies, I wanted above all things to be a poet in the English tongue, and my name and physiognomy were characteristically Jewish. I had ill-cut, provincial clothes and just money enough to get through one semester. Such was my inner and outer equipment for pursuing in a metropolitan graduate school the course which was to lead to a college appointment to teach English. No one warned me, no one discouraged me" (*US* 103). In this plaintive catalogue of characteristics—his "inner and outer equipment"—which, despite Lewisohn's pretensions, still separates him from the Anglo American mainstream—his Jewish "physiognomy" is held to be as important as the items he could hope to change: his name, wealth, and clothing. After one year of study at Columbia, he receives a second master's degree. Despite his excellent performance, however, Lewisohn is not allowed a fellowship, scholarship, or teaching appointment—all because, as his friend Professor Brewer tells him in a letter, he is Jewish (*US* 122). After reading the letter, Lewisohn numbly walks the streets of New York, only to enter a bakery and see himself in a mirror, whereupon he projects Jewish racial difference onto the image he sees and finally views himself as undeniably—and immutably—a Jew. As if awoken from a dream, "I . . . noted with dull objectivity my dark hair, my melancholy eyes, my unmistakably Semitic nose. . . . An outcast" (*US* 122–23). With the narrator's "dull," "objective," and scientifically positivist gaze directed toward himself, many familiar signs of racial in-betweenness begin to assert themselves: his "dark hair," his "melancholy eyes" that recall David Levinsky's sense of his own racially derived temperament, and his "unmistakably Semitic nose"—all of which conspire to render him necessarily "an outcast." The narrator's retroactive projection of Jewish racial difference onto the image he confronts in the window nicely accords with Matthew Frye Jacobson's concept of white ethnic racial perception, in which "visible Jewishness"—and all the physical and mental traits that come with it—only become essentialistically apparent after it is known that the observed is Jewish.[34]

With the narrator's realization, the grip of Anglo American culture begins to loosen within him, and he begins to understand his alienation from it in both racial and cultural terms. After being fired from an unfulfilling job on the editorial staff of Singleton, Leaf and Company, Lewisohn works as a freelance writer, determined to earn a living writing fiction. His Jewish background, however, is still viewed as a significant problem, and one of his friends suggests, "Maybe you could get stuff into the magazines more easily if you used a pseudonym. Your name's very Jewish." Lewisohn "ponder[s] the matter" in a passage reminiscent of classic realist scenes of agency: "I did not know how absurd his notion was. Should I use a pseudonym? Should I—it was possible—make my name less foreign by a change in spelling?" (*US* 133). For someone once so committed to passing thoroughly into Southern Anglo American culture, a name change would seem among the first orders of business. He determines not to, and despite his current refusal to pass, Lewisohn is able to secure employment as a literature professor at "Central City University" (Ohio State University).[35] Now having left the realm of the passing narrative, much of the autobiography's remainder consists of a polemical attack on the banality and jingoistic bigotry of American culture as he witnesses it in post–World War I events, American popular media, and his midwestern students. Lewisohn is particularly stung by the anti-German hatred and "one hundred percent Americanism" fostered by the events of World War I (*US* 199, 231). He is a passer no more, and the end of *Up Stream* issues a call for cultural pluralism. Americanization movements and intellectuals' calls for Anglo conformity are pointless to Lewisohn because:

> [t]hat a nation possessing a compact and autonomous culture should desire recent additions to its population to merge into its cultural life and enrich that life is natural. But the process must come from within. So soon as outer urgency is applied the inner necessity and, therefore, the spiritual justification of the process itself stands in grave doubt. . . . The very existence of an Americanization movement shows—when every allowance for our peculiar conditions has been made—a discord, a prematureness; it shows a crudeness in the fruits

34. Jacobson, *Whiteness of a Different Color*, 174.
35. Seymour Lainoff, *Ludwig Lewisohn*, 11.

of our civilization which not force and clamor but only time and the sun can ripen. Americanization means, of course, assimilation. But that is an empty concept, a mere cry of rage or tyranny, until the question is answered which would never be asked were the answer ripe: Assimilation to what? To what homogenous culture, to what folkways of festival and song, to what common instincts concerning love and beauty, to what imaginative passions, to what roads of thought? We have none such that can unite us. (*US* 235)

Lewisohn's was not the only contemporary voice calling for such a vision of multicultural America. Horace A. Kallen, in his *Nation* article "Democracy versus the Melting-Pot: A Study in American Nationality" (1915), and Randolph S. Bourne, in his *Atlantic Monthly* article "Trans-National America" (1916), are two of the earliest theoretical proponents of a culturally pluralistic understanding of American culture and citizenship. Like Lewisohn, both were writing in response to the nativism, racism, and respectable anti-immigrant sentiment of their day. Kallen regards Americanization as it was then understood to be fundamentally misguided; he explains, quite essentialistically, but no less democratically, that "[m]en may change their clothes, their politics, their wives, their religions, their philosophies, to a greater or lesser extent: they cannot change their grandfathers. Jews or Poles or Anglo-Saxons, in order to cease being Jews or Poles or Anglo-Saxons, would have to cease to be. The selfhood which is inalienable in them ... is ancestrally determined, and the happiness which they pursue has its form implied in ancestral endowment."[36] Indeed, Ludwig Lewisohn adjusted his clothes, politics, religion, and philosophy to suit his image of the ideal Southern Anglo American. According to Kallen's logic, however, Lewisohn would never be able to change the reality of his *ancestry*—from which his sense of selfhood is essentialistically derived. Kallen imagines a future America in which the languages and cultures of all the European nations exist in productive, democratic dialogue. His vision is highly Eurocentric, but at least stands as a limited improvement upon the intellectual status quo that advanced theories of intra-European racial difference and that worked toward the exclusion of European groups that Kallen at least sees as valuable. His ideal America is:

a democracy of nationalities, cooperating voluntarily and autonomously in the enterprise of self-realization through the perfection of

36. Horace M. Kallen, "Democracy versus the Melting Pot: A Study of American Nationality," 91.

men according to their kind. The common language of the common-
wealth, the language of its great political tradition, is English, but
each nationality expresses its emotional and voluntary life in its own
language, in its own inevitable aesthetic and intellectual forms....
Thus "American civilization," may come to mean the perfection of
the cooperative harmonies of "European civilization," the waste, the
squalor, and the distress of Europe being eliminated—a multiplicity
in a unity, an orchestration of mankind. (*US* 92)

The language of "inevitability" smacks of essentialism, even racialism,
while the exclusion of non-European melodies in the "harmonies of
'European civilization'"—reminiscent of Josiah Royce's reluctance regarding the racial aptitude and cultural potential of African Americans—
suggests full-blown racism.[37] However, Kallen's vision is decidedly friend-
lier to a Ludwig Lewisohn than that of the American intellectual
mainstream, and it is this very vision that helped clear the space for the
cultural pluralism of ethnic literature.

Randolph Bourne, a contemporary of Kallen's, sees evidence of "the
failure of the melting pot" in the general xenophobia of World War I.
Among other injustices, Bourne indicts the same anti-German sentiment
Lewisohn would come to criticize in *Up Stream*. Like Kallen, Bourne finds
forced Americanization to be both unhealthy and unrealistic, remarking
that "[w]e act as if we wanted Americanization to take place only on our
terms."[38] Bourne speaks specifically to Lewisohn's plight when he asserts,
"It is not the Jew who sticks proudly to the faith of his fathers and boasts
of that venerable culture who is dangerous to America, but the Jew who
has lost the Jewish fire and become a mere elementary, grasping animal."
Bourne's ideal is "transnational America." No less Eurocentric than
Kallen, Bourne nevertheless argues that "the attempt to weave a wholly
novel international union out of our chaotic America will liberate and
harmonize the creative power of all these peoples and give them the
new spiritual citizenship, as so many individuals have already been
given, of a world."[39] Lewisohn's autobiography certainly can be viewed
as an example of such ethnically specific "creative power" forged through
a deliberate participation in such a "new spiritual citizenship."

Abandoning the belief in the melting-pot model of assimilation he

37. Royce, *Race Questions*, 15. On the racism of Horace Kallen, see Michaels, *Our America*, 64.
38. Randolph Bourne, "Trans-National America," 94.
39. Ibid., 99, 107.

once thought he saw in St. Mark's and, by extension, America, Lewisohn adopts a culturally pluralist sensibility he believes will allow people to develop best according to their ethnic individuality. Lewisohn gains a new awareness of his German-Jewish American identity, and his former assimilationism seems a folly to him. His opinion of the near impossibility of the endeavor strikes this reader as particularly deterministic: "What Anglo-American has lived with the poets who are the sources of his great tradition more closely than I? What Anglo-American has a deeper sense for the order and eloquence and beauty of his own tongue than I? What Anglo-American has a deeper sense for the order and eloquence and beauty of his own tongue than I? But when, in old days, I desired to translate my Americanism in that high and fine sense into action, I was told that I was not wanted" (US 237). Better to maintain a sense of one's ethnic heritage than to pass, and Lewisohn woefully relates the stories of two passers of whom he is familiar. One is a second-generation Jewish American who "knows neither Hebrew nor Yiddish. His English is less foreign than his father's was, but far more vulgar and corrupt. On his clean-shaven face there is an indescribable blending of impudence and cunning, servility and sweetness. He is manager of the Lake City Emporium, makes big money... [and] says, having just made another particularly unscrupulous five-thousand: 'Yes sir, I'm an American all right'" (US 238). Lewisohn also tells of a second-generation German-Jewish American who "has become Americanized. He reads the colored Sunday supplements of the yellow press. He is a baseball 'fan'; his favorite songwriter is Irving Berlin; he drinks whiskey—on the sly.... He has Anglicized his name" (US 238–39). Lewisohn is saddened by such assimilative fervor, and reports that "[t]hese are unhappily not extreme cases." Better to allow the ethnic American "spiritual and intellectual" fulfillment through "cultural continuity" with the Old World; force assimilation upon the ethnic, and "[t]he slow gains of the ages are obliterated in him" (US 239). This closing commentary is strikingly similar to Marco's in *Olives on the Apple Tree*, and with it Lewisohn has demonstrated that after his personal experiment with melting-pot ideology, he has arrived in transnational America. And the net result of his careful negotiation of Old and New World influences is one that is familiar to us by now: as Werner Sollors writes, it is a restatement of "the ethics of wholesome provincialism."[40]

Thus, Lewisohn narratologically weaves together the threads of German Jewishness and "Americanness" into a structurally realist tale of

40. Sollors, *Beyond Ethnicity*, 202.

moral reformation. Lewisohn has written his autobiographical tale with a self-conscious attention to its realism; in the epilogue he proclaims, "All I have written is true. It is true of America. It is true, in other degrees, of mankind.... The facts stand as I have recorded them." However, in 1920s America, "[l]ife among us is ugly and mean and, above all things, false in its assumptions and measures"—a decidedly deterministic assessment. The solution is nothing less than an earnest exercise of moral agency, to "break these shackles and flee and emerge into some beyond of sanity, of a closer contact with reality, of nature and of truth." The message, though, is to some degree mixed; Lewisohn advises against "optimism," for "[t]he hour is dark" (*US* 247). However, he ends the narrative on a positive note: "But that shall not prevent us from working and striving for a better one that may come hereafter" (*US* 248). But this ending, in which the conflict between determinism and moral agency is brought into high relief, mirrors the generic tensions inherent in Lewisohn's seemingly facile story of American self-fashioning and moral refashioning. In the autobiography, Lewisohn grants himself the power to make the moral decision he makes: to assume the identity of a Jewish American critic of American culture. He proclaims, "I am an American and I have spoken strongly for the equally simple reason that the measure of one's love and need is also the measure of one's disappointment and indignation" (*US* 247). Thus, he declares himself not only an American but also an authority who can *speak for* America and even declare his memoirs "An American Chronicle." Yet by his own admission, he has not and in many ways *cannot* assimilate due to a Jewish ethnic difference that he often depicts in racial terms. Barriers of discrimination and anti-Semitic sentiment force him early in life to privatize his ethnic identity, so he freely wills a transformation from second-generation Jewish American to faux Southern Anglo American; he swims "upstream," against the current of Jewish tradition. However, he cannot overcome the barriers his Jewish ethnicity places in his path, so he rejects the rhetoric of "100 percent Americanism" and adopts a Jewish American identity; he now swims against the current of contemporary American intellectual and popular wisdom. But though the decision is figured as a freely willed moral victory, it is won during what Lewisohn perceives to be among the darkest hours of American history.

Lewisohn's tale is told in such an elegant and straightforward manner that such contradictions might at first go unnoticed. However, this seems to be common to the white ethnic male narrative, in which the exigencies of ethnicity and Americanness are cleverly grafted onto a

Howellsian or Franklinian tale of moral growth. But the more strictly policed the boundaries encountered by the ethnic subject, the more complicated and conflicted the story becomes. Consequently, a more *ironic* approach might be necessary to allow the many conflicting narratological cal threads to cohere—or at least *seem* to cohere.

Enter Irony: Samuel Ornitz's *Haunch, Paunch and Jowl*

Among white ethnic male writers, we see the beginnings of this constructive irony in Samuel Ornitz's *Haunch, Paunch and Jowl: An Anonymous Autobiography* (1923), which, according to Laura Browder, "signaled the...death...of the nonironic Jewish immigrant autobiography."[41] Indeed, in *Haunch, Paunch and Jowl*, there is a level of dramatic and structural irony never before seen in European American ethnic literature, and so, for the purposes of this study, it is aesthetically—if not chronologically—a transitional text. (James Weldon Johnson's *The Autobiography of an Ex-Coloured Man*, a heavily ironic faux autobiography, had preceded Ornitz's faux autobiography by eleven years). Realist in subject matter and aesthetics, the ironic distance between the author (and, by extension, the reader) and the protagonist, Meyer Hirsch, works to subvert many of the meanings realism would purportedly seek to reveal.

Haunch, Paunch and Jowl tells the story of Meyer Hirsch, an avaricious petty thug of New York's Ludlow Street gang who, as an adult, rides the corrupt tide of urban ethnic politics to prominent positions as a lawyer, machine politician, and finally, judge of the Superior Criminal Court. The manner in which Hirsch accomplishes this is so disingenuous, so cynical, and so corrupt that the reader cannot but declare him fundamentally irredeemable—even more so than Abraham Cahan's David Levinsky, who at least contemplates with sadness his life of greed and ethnic erasure. Meyer Hirsch is no passer, but undoubtedly finds much of Orthodox Jewish culture to be useless. For example, he recalls of his childhood that "Yiddish, the lingo of greenhorns, was held in contempt by the Ludlow Streeters who felt mightily their Americanism." Hirsch recollects that public school taught him and other second-generation Jewish Americans to devalue their ancestral heritage as pedestrian and foreign (*HPJ* 30). Sufficiently alienated from his ancestral culture, Hirsch is thus able to exploit it cynically for professional and material gain. He

41. Browder, *Slippery Characters*, 156.

performs Jewish ethnicity, donates to Jewish charities, and becomes a "Professional Jew"—all the while deploying the worst techniques of American capitalism. In the "Fifth Period" of the autobiography, Hirsch boasts that he and his colleagues "have come up in the world. I am a lawyer, politician, champion of Jewry and member of a dozen Jewish lodges, societies and charity organizations. I became a Professional Jew in emulation of the successful Irish politician whose principal capital is being a Professional Irishman" (*HPJ* 183). Hirsch's tough talk of success by hook and crook smacks of a "sinister masculinism" that calls into question the wholesomeness of the American success story. However, the seething irony with which Ornitz writes the text disrupts a number of other conventions. Laura Browder argues that the novel "takes for granted the notion that ethnicity is a mask that can be put on and taken off at will. In a country where ethnic performances compete for attention, the winners are those who are best able to consciously manipulate the symbols of ethnic caricature."[42] Thus, the authenticity of wholesome provincialism is called into question by the ironic notion that ethnicity is ultimately a performance—and often a dishonest one at that.

There is one incidental passing character in the text, Dr. Lionel Crane, whose masterful performance of Anglo American whiteness unwittingly shocks Meyer into a consideration of his own ethnic performance. Upon meeting Dr. Lionel Crane, whose given name is Lazarus Cohen, Meyer Hirsch immediately begins to size up the extent of Crane's acculturation, always paying attention to the disjuncture between his performance and his purportedly essential Jewish self:

> Where did he get the bang-up snobbish name—doesn't go with his face. I mulled with distemper the cognomen—too smart-sounding this Lionel Crane to be anything else but a cognomen—that ill-fitted his handsome but pronouncedly Jewish physiognomy.... There actually wasn't anything outstandingly Jewish about him except his nose, and that feature, the after-truth to tell, was a fine example of a Roman proboscis.... On the spot I disliked him.... Like velvet rubbed the wrong way, sickeningly soft, creepily irritating, was his meticulous, modulated speech with its heavy Harvard accent. It cloyed. Inconsonant in *him*, not by his right, therefore an affectation, I felt, as were his distinguished manners—a nicety of deportment shaming mine and calling attention to my *gaucherie*. (*HPJ* 191)

42. Samuel Ornitz, *Haunch, Paunch and Jowl: An Anonymous Autobiography*, 14. Hereafter cited in the text as *HPJ*. Rachel Rubin, *Jewish Gangsters of Modern Literature*, 65; Browder, *Slippery Characters*, 158.

Martin Japtok argues that Meyer does not like Crane because of his New England refinement.[43] There are other things about Crane, however, that disturb Meyer. Meyer is first upset by the inability of Crane's new name to match up to his "pronouncedly Jewish" face. However, unlike the texts previously considered, Ornitz immediately undercuts the certainty of his racialist assessment by having Meyer admit that Crane really is not "outstandingly Jewish" looking. His nose, after all, is viewed as Roman; perhaps Crane, then, could be seen as *Italian.* Meyer is also upset by Crane's bourgeois posturing, his "affectation"—not simply because it is supposedly unbecoming of a Jewish man, but also because his manners exceed those of Meyer. Crane is, in effect, a better performer—a *passer.*

Dr. Crane identifies himself as a "race psychopathologist" who studies "the Jewish Question" (*HPJ* 192). Crane's opinions on this subject allow Ornitz the opportunity to lampoon popular anti-Semitic notions of his day—notions Crane has assimilated as part of his passing performance. He says,

> The Jews will create a Jewish Question in America as long as they cling to their bizarre Jewishness.... What calls immediate, curious attention to the Jews...his outlandish ways and attire—his beards and ear-locks.... He is always the repellent foreigner awakening unpleasant associations of the historically misrepresented Jew...his slovenly, baggy clothes, or his overdressed, bejeweled, flashy appearance; his blatancy and vulgarity...antipathetic assertiveness...his maddening infallible belief in himself as being better, wiser, cleaner, more moral, shrewder, greater; the chosen of the One and Only God, worshiped in the One and Only true way—his way...his contempt of all others, their ways, living, believing, stupidity...and he becomes hateful, unbearable, undesirable. (*HPJ* 198)

Here Dr. Crane provides a veritable catalogue of items representing real and imagined Jewish difference, the entirety of which he believes Jews should rid themselves. According to Dr. Crane, America presents Jews the opportunity to do just this—refashion themselves in the image of America, as Dr. Crane believes he has done. Consequently, Crane indicts "Professional Jews" for promoting Jewish "racial vanity" and perpetuating Jewish difference in the United States (*HPJ* 199).

43. Martin Japtok, "Socialism and Ethnic Solidarity: Samuel Ornitz's *Haunch, Paunch and Jowl,*" 25.

Dr. Crane allows that Jews may "[w]orship as [they] please," but also advises them to "get rid of the foul fungus of the Ghetto. If you do not become an integral, euphonious part of the American nation you will again isolate yourself and stand out yellow-badged among the people of the New World.... The Jew must take himself in hand, see himself as the world sees him. Face historical facts. Face scientific truths. Face medical and pathological findings. Treat himself" (*HPJ* 201). This passage underscores two other circumstances that separate Jews from the American mainstream: geography and biology. However, despite the deterministic cast of Crane's racial rhetoric, he still believes that "we can make it different... Tear down the walls, let out the pent-up people to mingle and mix. Let intermarriage bring in the saving tonic of new blood" (*HPJ* 202). Intermarriage, then—the last stage of structural assimilation, as Milton Gordon would have it—is the means by which Jews could racially work themselves into the melting pot. Dr. Crane's proposal, of course, absurdly suggests that the Jews' only chance of survival in the New World is culturally and racially to cease being Jews. Meyer Hirsch is clearly rankled by Dr. Crane's words and performance, for through them he is reminded not only of his assimilative shortcomings but also perhaps that his own "Professional Jew" posturing is no less artificial than Dr. Crane's aping of bourgeois, Anglo American mannerisms.

Typically in the white ethnic male narrative there is a redemptive voice to counter one such as Dr. Crane's: a Marco or a Ludwig Lewisohn who is capable of demonstrating that there is a possible answer in a wholesome provincialism of Old and New World influences. However, in *Haunch, Paunch and Jowl* there is none. Meyer Hirsch is, to some degree, punished for his life of disingenuousness and avarice. Roundly mocked by New York leftists as "Haunch, Paunch and Jowl," the prominent judge is forced into a marriage with his overtly "ethnic" servant girl Gretel. Rachel Rubin argues that the ending of the novel suggests "a spiritual death by mediocrity": "Gretel offers Meyer 'potted breast' that 'smells good.'"[44] But with this ending, Meyer Hirsch has failed to do what so many misguided ethnic protagonists are *forced* to do in ethnic literature: reconsider their status as ethnics and as "self-made" Americans. Even characters so self-serving as Yekl Podvonik and David Levinsky at least *rethink* the course their lives have taken, even if there is no evidence they change their practices accordingly. With Meyer Hirsch, there is no such

44. Rubin, *Jewish Gangsters*, 68.

self-reflexiveness. The character in the novel who most vocally stands for Jewish cultural preservation—Rov Zucker—is not only seen to be somewhat crazy in his never-ending diatribes but also is violently attacked and henceforth silenced (*HPJ* 57–58). Thus, while the novel takes an ironic stance toward its venal protagonist, this irony doubles back on itself by the manner in which no suitable ethnic alternative is offered. Rachel Rubin argues that Ornitz's radical reworking of the immigrant autobiography "deconstruct[s] the piety of what in 1923 was already a venerable tradition of Jewish American naturalization tales."[45] This decidedly ironic treatment of ethnicity subverts both the earnest ethnic heroism of earlier immigrant texts and the facile, objective veneer of realist literary discourse.

Unlike the previous ethnic texts discussed in this study, the "thesis" of *Haunch, Paunch and Jowl* is more difficult to ascertain. If ethnicity is nothing but a performance, a sham, then what is the function of the ethnic text? But this, perhaps, misses the point. For while *Haunch, Paunch and Jowl* may appear to be taking a step backward with its apparently relativistic double-edged irony, from another perspective this irony marks a step *forward* in literary history. After *Haunch, Paunch and Jowl*, the European American ethnic narrative would no longer be obligated to speak of ethnicity in the essentialistic, racialistic manner favored by not only the intellectual elite but also other ethnic writers. No longer content simply to speak of ethnicity, the irony of *Haunch, Paunch and Jowl* attacks the very assumptions upon which ethnic discourse was constructed and modifies realist notions of a facile, objective reality. Ornitz's innovation vis-à-vis ethnic identity is also directly related to innovations in prose style and genre. Note how, in the extended quotes I have cited, characters uncertainly and inconclusively mull the complexities of ethnic identity in a clumsy, stilted, ellipsis-laden, and often free direct discourse that underscores an awareness of the inability to *describe* ethnic identity according to the fixed aesthetic and epistemological rules of realism.

Given that Jewish American literature is basically a full generation older than the Italian American literary tradition, it is not surprising that the former canon first fell upon these ironic and modernistic innovations. The African American tradition, however, far older and far more mature than its Jewish American and Italian American counterparts, had already broken this barrier by 1912. This becomes even more understandable when one considers that the racial barriers of which the African Amer-

---

45. Ibid., 66.

ican author spoke were far more stark, far more strictly policed, and far more heavily laden with dire consequences than those depicted by his white ethnic counterparts. Therefore, the deconstructive power of the ironic mode is in many ways exactly what was needed to make sense of African American subjectivity—particularly when the African American subject wished to be African American no more.

4

"To Rise Above This Absurd Drama That Others Have Staged"

Race Critique and Genre in Chesnutt, Johnson, and Schuyler

American Negroes have been a race more in name than in fact, or to be exact, more in sentiment than in experience.
—Alain Locke, "The New Negro"

The generic evolution of the African American male-centered passing narrative in the early twentieth century is linked closely with an increased urgency to critique the idea of race, which affected early-twentieth-century African Americans more greatly than any other ethnic group in the United States. This discussion traces racial critique in African American male passing narratives, from the melodramatically tinged work of Charles Chesnutt to the more overtly modernistic work of James Weldon Johnson to the modern satire of George S. Schuyler. In each of the narratives considered, however, an archetypically realist dilemma recurs, in which a light-skinned black character is required to make a choice between openly identifying with an African American ancestral background (which is frequently figured in terms of folk tradition, music, and essentialistic references to "temperament") or else identifying with whiteness and the success it brings in the American mainstream (in turn, "whiteness" comes to be associated stereotypically with greed and moneymaking). On the one hand, the dilemma presented in these narratives is not unlike that of the white ethnic male works examined in chapter 3. On the other hand, the agency exercised by characters who do pass is all the more conflicted by the coercive context in which these characters act, a reality foregrounded by literary representations of racist ideology and law, as well as racially motivated violence—all of which occur to a considerably more severe degree than in Italian American or Jewish American literature. Furthermore, while passing characters of the white ethnic tradition are usually condemned for their acts of cultural betrayal, African American characters must confront not only intraethnic but also interethnic reprisal in the form of antimiscegenation laws and a general hysteria that surrounds black/white racial trespassing. It helps to remember that even though the lynching of African Americans tapered off somewhat as the early 1900s progressed, it still posed a significant threat: 791 blacks were lynched in the first decade of the century, followed by 563 in the 1910s and 281 in the 1920s. Therefore, the author who makes such a set of conflicted racial options cohere into a rational narrative is performing a more unlikely rhetorical feat than the author of the white ethnic male passing narrative. In a sense, the author of the African American passing narrative comes to realize that he or she must, to a considerable extent, refocus attention from a mimetic representation of black social realities—which runs the risk of replicating and reinforcing the race ideologies that plagued African Americans—toward an all-out assault on the idea of race itself.[1]

It is perhaps a truism, though by no means an insignificant one, to suggest that "race" is foregrounded as a problem in African American literature to a far greater degree than it is in the literature of white ethnics. To be sure, white ethnics were branded by racial difference at the time in which these narratives take place, and their literature provides ample and vivid documentation of this. However, the unspoken reality in much of this literature is that race would eventually work in favor of the ethnic groups represented therein. I would argue that the greater tendency of white ethnic authors than African American authors to identify with American success mythology (if also to critique and even to reject it on occasion) is a byproduct of this unspoken reality, as is the greater

1. Gates, Introduction, xx; James Weldon Johnson, *The Autobiography of an Ex-Coloured Man*, 193. Hereafter cited in the text as *AEM*. Davis, *Who Is Black?* 53. As Cathy Boeckmann argues, "attempts to represent race, especially in written language, will reproduce racist assumptions by necessity" (211).

preponderance of a casual racial romanticism to describe what we now take to be ethnic and cultural differences. Of course, African American literature also would continue to be troubled by racial romanticism, but it would not go as unchallenged because an increasingly militant racial critique would figure as a central preoccupation of this tradition in the early twentieth century. The manner in which a critique is issued underscores two realist devices featured in much of this literature: mimesis and the problematizing of received ideologies. To be sure, a more strictly mimetic and, by extension, realistic approach would engender a more cutting examination of race, free of the racial hysteria that clouds earlier African American literary engagements with the subject. However, at least one African American writer, George Schuyler, would conclude that only by a complete abandonment of realistic mimesis and a deployment of a fantastical, though still cutting, satire would he be able to deliver the most devastating blow to race ideologies.

I begin with readings of "The Wife of His Youth" (1899) and *The House behind the Cedars* (1900), by Charles Chesnutt, both of which offer arguably realist treatments of passing with strong melodramatic and romantic tendencies. In Chesnutt, we find the beginnings of an antiracialist irony that questions racist ideology and intraracial snobbery. However, we also discover evidence of a romantic racialism that undercuts the racial critique of the narratives, particularly in the novel. Of all the works considered in this chapter, James Weldon Johnson's *The Autobiography of an Ex-Coloured Man* (1912) is in many ways the pivotal text. While it dramatizes the typical moral passing dilemma and does so in a far less romantic manner than Chesnutt, in both its sharper irony and its entrée into modernist territory, it also demonstrates the limits of realist literary production to effectively critique race ideologies. In *Autobiography*, Johnson creates a character whose classically modernistic alienation from both the "black" and "white" identities he attempts to embody more effectively demonstrates the constructedness of both terms. With *Black No More: Being an Account of the Strange and Wonderful Workings of Science in the Land of the Free, A. D. 1933–1940* (1931), George S. Schuyler entirely abandons realist mimesis in the interest of a futuristic, sci-fi modern satire of the social and financial capital generated by the preservation of the color line in the United States. With this farcical passing novel, Schuyler stages his own "absurd drama" whose incredibility draws the reader's attention away from any anticipated representation of true sociohistorical referents toward the central idea conveyed in the narrative: that race itself is a socially constructed idea rife with cultural pathologies and wholly without merit.[2]

Charles Chesnutt's Realist Romances of Race: "The Wife of His Youth" and *The House behind the Cedars* (John's story)

With "The Wife of His Youth," Charles Chesnutt (1858–1932) seems overtly to have realist aspirations in that the entire story revolves around a central dilemma that reminds the reader of the other classic dilemmas of mainstream American realism. The story begins with a description of the "Blue Vein Society," an organization of elite, light-skinned African Americans in the city of Groveland, which is generally taken to be Chesnutt's native Cleveland, Ohio. The "purpose" of the organization is "to establish and maintain correct social standards among a people whose social condition presented almost unlimited room for improvement."[3] The "social condition" referred to is, of course, caused by the members' black ancestry, which, appearance notwithstanding, places a racial barrier between mainstream America and the "Blue Veins" (so nicknamed because of an unofficial rule deeming "no one...eligible for membership who was not white enough to show blue veins") ("WHY" 1). This barrier can only be overcome by the "maintain[ance]" of "correct social standards"—in other words, the cultural assimilation necessary in order to pass eventually as white. Immediately, then, any racial agency exercised by the Blue Veins must be considered against a backdrop of racism that necessitates this exercise of agency in the first place.

The reader is also quickly introduced to Mr. Ryder, a vigorous aspirant to whiteness, who though "not as white as some of the Blue Veins," still cuts a distinguished figure: "His features were of a refined type, his hair was almost straight; he was always neatly dressed; his manners were irreproachable, and his morals above suspicion" ("WHY" 3, 4). This brief description features both stereotypically "black" (his "almost straight" hair) and "white" (his manners, dress, and morals) signs that underscore

---

2. Gates, Introduction, xviii, xx-xxi. In *Black Skin, White Masks*, Frantz Fanon expresses a desire "to rise above this absurd drama [of race] others have staged round me, to reject the two terms [of biracialism] that are equally unacceptable." Fanon, *Black Skin, White Masks*, 197.

3. Charles W. Chesnutt, "The Wife of His Youth," 1. Hereafter cited in the text as "WHY."

Ryder's need to maintain a level of cultural assimilation that will allow him more convincingly to perform whiteness, which he does with notable success. In accordance with white Victorian/American morality and taste, "[h]e was economical, and had saved money; he owned and occupied a very comfortable house on a respectable street. His residence was handsomely furnished, containing among other things a good library, especially rich in poetry, a piano, and some choice engravings" ("WHY" 4–5). Furthermore, "[h]e could repeat whole pages of the great English poets," particularly Alfred Tennyson, whose poem "A Dream of Fair Women" describes perfectly his love interest, Mrs. Dixon. A widow recently moved to Groveland, Mrs. Dixon is described as an African American gentlewoman who is even "whiter than" Ryder, "better educated," and welcome "in the best colored society of the country" ("WHY" 5). Ryder decides to hold a Blue Vein Society ball in her honor in order to provide the appropriate occasion to propose marriage, the culmination of his "racial fantasy."[4] Mrs. Dixon is not only the symbol of Ryder's assimilative desire but also, more practically, part of the means by which his assimilation is to be effected, as their marriage "would help to further the upward process of absorption he had been wishing and waiting for" ("WHY" 8). To cap off his racial transformation, Ryder has even changed his name. However, Ryder explains his act of transformative will in socially Darwinistic and starkly deterministic terms: " 'I have no race prejudice,' he would say, 'but we people of mixed blood are ground between the upper and the nether millstone. Our fate lies between absorption by the white race and extinction in the black. The one doesn't want us yet, but may take us in time. The other would welcome us, but it would be for us a backward step. "With malice towards none, with charity for all," we must do the best we can for ourselves and those who are to follow us. Self-preservation is the first law of nature'" ("WHY" 7).[5] Standing between opposite poles of whiteness and blackness, and possessing strong, typically male professional aspirations, Mr. Ryder would seem to have much in common with the white ethnic race impostors discussed in the previous chapter; however, given the one-drop racial context in which Ryder acts and Chesnutt writes, in-betweenness is as invalid a social goal for the former as it is a literary goal for the latter. So rather than have Ryder follow the path of the acculturation narrative protagonist,

4. Wonham, *Charles W. Chesnutt: A Study of the Short Fiction*, 58.
5. William L. Andrews, *The Literary Career of Charles W. Chesnutt*, 114.

Chesnutt has him make an all-or-nothing decision, and thus far in the story Ryder has opted for "self-preservation" as a hopefully, soon-to-be-white, middle-class American.

Ryder's conscience is clear until he is confronted, at the door of his ornate home, with a representative of his African American, or as Werner Sollors poignantly phrases it, "pre-American," past: the "wife of his youth," 'Liza Jane. Indeed "everything the Blue Veins have tried to repress about their past," 'Liza Jane is "very black,—so black that her toothless gums, revealed when she opened her mouth to speak, were not red, but blue" ("WHY" 10).[6] Seeming "like a bit of the old plantation life," her "face was crossed and recrossed with a hundred wrinkles," she wears humble traditional clothing, and she speaks a conspicuous Southern/black dialect—signified by apostrophes and contorted phonetic spellings—that Ryder has learned to suppress ("WHY" 10). Significantly, it is in this very dialect that 'Liza Jane reveals the more racially incriminating miscellany of Ryder's past through the story of her twenty-five-year search for her lost husband. The reader learns that though "free-bawn" as "Sam Taylor," Ryder was orphaned at a young age, "'prenticed" by "de w'ite folks" to Liza's master, and made to labor as a slave "in de fiel'" while his wife Liza cooked in the house ("WHY" 12). After being sold down the river, Ryder is able to escape in the chaos created by the Civil War, leaving his wife to search endlessly for him. Unaware that she has found her husband, 'Liza asks Ryder for any assistance he can provide in her quest; predictably, Ryder pretends not to recognize her, but still promises to help. After she leaves, Ryder goes to his room and stands "for a long time before the mirror of his dressing-case, gazing thoughtfully at the reflection of his own face" ("WHY" 17). Ryder's "thoughtfulness" could suggest a certain degree of cognitive dissonance produced by the attempt to reconcile his "white" aspirations—here represented by one of his conspicuously consumed prizes, the dressing-case mirror—with that which he sees in the mirror: namely, his "face" and all the unmentioned signs of racial difference he could either read in, or project onto, it. Ryder would like to see his "racial fantasy" reflected back at him: an unimpeachably white "face" and, by extension, identity. Arguably, though, Ryder sees something quite different.

However one reads this scene, one cannot deny that Ryder is now confronted with a classically realist dilemma, or what Judith Berzon would

6. Sollors, *Beyond Ethnicity*, 163; Sollors, *Neither Black nor White*, 11.

describe as an example of "the crisis experience" of passing fiction: the choice between rejecting 'Liza and continuing to attempt passing, or accepting 'Liza and, by extension, identifying himself as an African American.[7] In other words, with the moral clarity of a realist, Ryder could be self-serving, or he could make the presumably moral, though more difficult, choice. Ryder chooses the latter, but in order to dramatize this choice, Chesnutt guides the narrative into melodramatic territory. At the ball he has planned, Ryder rises to respond to an after-dinner toast and uses the opportunity to tell of his dilemma in a speech generously supplied with the rhetorical appeal of a sentimental novel. Ryder attempts to win his audience's sympathy by speaking generally "of woman as the gift of Heaven to man" and catering to Victorian expectations of female "fidelity and devotion to those she loves" ("WHY" 19). According to one critic, the effect is "of a Sunday school instructional tract."[8] His discourse moves to his afternoon visitor and the story she had told, which Ryder renders "in the same soft dialect," an act significant not only because it demonstrates the ease with which Ryder trades performances of whiteness and blackness, but also simply due to its obvious appeal to the feelings of the audience, who listen "attentively and sympathetically" ("WHY" 20). Ryder relates the dilemma in stark terms, describing 'Liza Jane and her husband as contrastingly as possible and reminding his listeners that their marriage would have to be made official after the war's close (21). The choice becomes all the more heartrending for the audience when Ryder reveals that the husband, "by industry, by thrift, and by study"—in other words, by all the ingredients of Victorian/American social climbing—had "qualified himself . . . to win the friendship and be considered worthy" of those as illustrious as the Blue Veins ("WHY" 21). The sentimental appeal of Ryder's speech, described in terms that remind the reader of Reverend Arthur Dimmesdale's election sermon in Hawthorne's *The Scarlet Letter,* is overwhelming: "There was something in Mr. Ryder's voice that stirred the hearts of those who sat around him. It suggested more than mere sympathy with an imaginary situation; it seemed rather in the nature of a personal appeal." So effective is Ryder's speech that when he asks what the husband should have done, his wife-to-be Mrs. Dixon, "with parted lips and streaming eyes," answers, "He should have acknowledged her" ("WHY" 23). Ryder then voices his agreement and introduces the Blue Veins to "the wife of [his]

7. Berzon, *Neither White nor Black,* 141.
8. Wonham, *Charles W. Chesnutt,* 58.

youth," literally making what the reader is supposed to take to be the correct moral choice, and figuratively reaccepting his culture of "descent" and reclaiming an identity as an African American man ("WHY" 24).[9]

Regarding the ending of "The Wife of His Youth," William L. Andrews makes the obvious comparison to *The Rise of Silas Lapham*: "In taking the 'backward step' toward the uncouth black woman of his past, [Ryder] actually takes a step forward morally, proving his worthiness by his honorable behavior, not by the lightness of his color. Like Silas Lapham, Ryder 'rises' when he sacrifices a narrow notion of public success for a more private moral responsibility."[10] However, the final analysis lies not in the "correctness" of his decision, but in the deterministic social circumstances that narrowed Ryder's options to a troubling dilemma of passing for white on the one hand and living as an African American on the other. A similar claim could be made for Silas Lapham's decision not to defraud English investors interested in relieving him of worthless mill property: a consideration of the morality of Silas's decision is arguably not so significant as a consideration of the Gilded Age market forces and the rapidly evolving American business ethic that established the parameters of the decision. However, once racism becomes a factor, we are confronted with quite a different dilemma indeed, for the decision made bears directly upon a character's very notion of identity, as well as the interplay of both society and the individual in the construction of it. The result is that any facile notions of identity and agency are rendered more complicated, and the reader's focus has shifted from the comparatively frivolous exercise of pondering the morality of the character's decision to examining, perhaps even critiquing, the social forces that compelled the decision.

The House behind the Cedars is similar in its stark rendering of racial decisions based upon social exigencies beyond the characters' control. Chesnutt's only full-length passing narrative, *The House behind the Cedars* is a schizophrenic text that, if one traces the development of John Walden, has the makings of a realist narrative with the requisite plot of social adaptation and ascent. If one focuses upon his sister Rena Walden, then the details of her failed struggle with passing suggest a melodramatic, even naturalistic, plot of decline—a distinction typical of mulatto characters in nineteenth-century fiction.[11] In order to remain within the parameters

9. Sollors, *Beyond Ethnicity*, 160–61.

10. Andrews, *Literary Career of Charles W. Chesnutt*, 115.

11. Siobhan B. Somerville, *Queering the Color Line: Race and the Invention of Homosexuality in American Culture*, 113.

of this chapter, I will leave Rena's story for chapter 6 and focus upon John's, arguing that his successful decision to pass, a reversal of Mr. Ryder's decision *not* to pass in the short story of the previous year, demonstrates that Chesnutt is not so interested in examining the propriety of passing as he is in critiquing the racial logic that makes passing necessary.

The House behind the Cedars begins "a few years after the Civil War" and centers around siblings John and Rena Walden—both part black and both light enough to pass for white. Widower and successful attorney John Walden returns to his hometown of Patesville, North Carolina, in order to attempt to convince sister Rena to return with him to South Carolina to pass and seek her fortune as a white gentlewoman. At first, she agrees, only later to reconsider when she is harshly rebuffed by a prospective Anglo American lover who accidentally learns the secret of her ancestry. John's story begins chronologically in the middle of the novel, and what the reader learns of him is an apt lesson in how "Chesnutt's mixed-race characters . . . manipulate the social fictions of race to become white."[12] John's story begins in 1855 when John Walden, the son of a light-skinned African American Mis' Molly and a white, "rich and liberal" "protector," is fifteen (*HC* 157, 160). Like Mr. Ryder of "The Wife of His Youth," the physical description of John that Chesnutt provides barely hints at the boy's racial "otherness"; for despite his father's patrician features and his mother's *"Indian hair,"* John had "no external sign to mark him off from the white boys on the street" (*HC* 160; italics mine). However, he becomes aware of this "difference" when he is told by a peer that he is "black" (*HC* 160). John vigorously denies the accusation and beats the child, only to be "thrashed" himself the next day when a larger boy makes the same claim about John's ancestry. Indeed, the violence John suffers dramatically foregrounds the racial determinism of his plight.

Convinced that "God, the father of all, had made him white" and "made no mistakes," John concludes that God "must have meant him to be white," so he devotes much of his childhood to immersing himself in the cultural output of European civilization, reading from the immense library left to him by his anonymous benefactor (*HC* 160–61). Intelligent and ambitious, John one day visits Judge Archibald Straight, a friend of the boy's father thought to be a just and benevolent lawman, and

---

12. Charles W. Chesnutt, *The House behind the Cedars*, 1. Hereafter cited in the text as *HC*. Boeckmann, *A Question of Character*, 156.

expresses his desire to become a lawyer. Having just read a pro-slavery pamphlet defending slavery on the grounds of the "hopeless intellectual inferiority of the negro... and the physical and moral degeneration of mulattoes," Straight examines John only to conclude that clearly he is "a lad of good blood" (HC 164, 165). However, the judge's opinion changes when John reveals that Molly Walden is his mother. After expressing incredulity, Judge Straight looks through his door and sees "the son of a leading merchant of the town... whose blood was presumably of the purest strain." Contrary to his racist expectations, Judge Straight finds that "the boy was sallow, with amorphous features, thin shanks, and stooping shoulders"—hardly the epitome of Anglo Saxon masculine poise and physiognomy. Meanwhile, John "was straight, shapely, and well-grown. His eye was clear, and he kept it fixed on the old gentleman with a look in which there was nothing of cringing. He was no darker than many a white boy bronzed by the Southern sun; his hair and eyes were black, and his features of the high-bred, clean-cut order that marks the patrician type the world over" (HC 167). With this description, Chesnutt calls into question the boy's racial purity and, more generally, the entire notion of Anglo Saxon racial superiority (if we can correctly assume that his blood is indeed "of the purest strain"). In either case, Chesnutt attacks a mighty shibboleth of nineteenth-century racialist thought. Judge Straight is not unaware of the cruel determinism of John's plight; in a passage that the reader takes to be the omniscient narrator's rendering of the judge's thoughts, Straight ponders the ethics of depriving African Americans of equal opportunity. He thinks, "Even the law, the instrument by which tyranny riveted the chains upon its victims, had revolted now and then against the senseless and unnatural prejudice by which a race ascribing its superiority to right of blood permitted a mere suspicion of servile blood to outweigh a vast preponderance of its own." The judge here examines the legal constructedness of race, but his analysis is hampered by his assumption that white "blood" would need to "outweigh" any amount of "servile blood" (HC 168). Straight reminds John, "You are aware, of course, that you are a negro?" John wishes to defend himself, but does so according to the very racial logic that oppresses him. Rather than discredit the notion of racial superiority, he insists he is "white" and "free." The judge, however, is unmoved and presents the legal case against John: "You are black, my lad, and you are not free. Did you ever hear of the Dred Scott decision, delivered by the great, wise, and learned Judge Taney?" Judge Straight then proceeds to the *biological* case against John Walden: "that negroes are beings 'of an inferior order'"

(*HC* 169). When John Walden continues to insist that he is white, Straight replies that John is, in fact, "Black as ink. . . . One drop of black blood makes the whole man black"—in accordance with the logic of hypo-descent. Straight completes his argument with an appeal to popular opinion, asserting that "[t]he laws do not permit men of color to practice law, and public sentiment would not allow one of them to study it."

Unwilling to accept this final verdict, John argues that he "might pass for white" (*HC* 170). Straight believes this to be quite "another matter," but having used the law to figure John as racially and legally unfit to become an attorney, he attempts to find legal justification for passing (*HC* 171). He discovers that racial law in South Carolina is different, and that a person—like John—of one-eighth African ancestry is taken to be white (*HC* 172). And although he is hardly free of racism, Judge Straight is still able to realize "that law and custom operate substantially in the establishment of race."[13] Thus vindicated by the law, Judge Straight agrees to allow John to be his servant and thus raise no public suspicions while the young man secretly studies the judge's law books. After two years' service to Judge Straight, John leaves his family for success as a white man in South Carolina. He encounters the "crisis experience" of the passing dilemma, but for John it is hardly a crisis at all. He unwaveringly elects to pass, leaving his mother to tell curious acquaintances simply that "[h]e's gone over on the other side" (*HC* 174). Indeed, for John, no amount of cultural training is so significant as the geographical crossing of borders from North to South Carolina that becomes for him a passage from black to white identities.

John's story chronologically resumes at the beginning of the novel, when he is introduced to the reader by a chapter title as "A Stranger from South Carolina" (*HC* 1). No doubt a stranger to the reader, John "Warwick" (like Mr. Ryder, John changes his name to complete the picture of his reformed identity) is also a stranger to his mother and sister. John's accomplishments bespeak a lifelong exercise of profound moral will, for "with a stout heart and an abounding hope he had gone out into the seemingly hostile world, and made fortune stand and deliver" (*HC* 21). A vivid literary embodiment of the parvenu, John, by leaving home, "had shaken the dust of the town from his feet, and with it, he fondly thought, the blight of his inheritance, and had achieved elsewhere a worthy career" (*HC* 29). However, while the narrator's descriptions of John employ language suggesting possibility, success, and freedom, the

13. Boeckmann, *A Question of Character*, 159.

deterministic descriptions of John's family foreshadow Rena's eventual failure as a passer. To his family, John "was a man come into a household of women,—a man of whom they were proud, and to whom they looked up with fond reverence. For he was not only a son,—a brother— but he represented to them the world from which *circumstances had shut them out*" (*HC* 19–20; italics mine). Furthermore, when John tells of his fortunes, Molly can only see them as the fruits of an "ideal but unattainable life. Circumstances, some beyond her control, and others for which she was herself in a measure responsible, had put it forever and inconceivably beyond her reach" (*HC* 27). The barrier of race and social status that separates him from his family is obviated in their contrasting furnishings: John sees that "[t]he kitchen was different from the stately diningroom of the old colonial mansion where he now lived." Nevertheless, it is still "homelike" and "familiar," though "[o]ne who had gained so much ought not to complain if he must give up a little" (*HC* 30). Thus, what becomes a heartbreaking sacrifice for some passing characters is but a trifle to John—all part of the nobler ideal of Victorian work and sacrifice to which he assimilates.

Chesnutt's examination of racial logic, coupled with a strong narrative desire to replace romantic racial hysteria with rational inquiry, bespeaks at least a partial commitment to the aesthetic and rhetorical program of American literary realism. To be sure, critics have generally treated Chesnutt's works as ur-texts in African American social realism—even when they have done so at the expense of considering contemporaries such as Frances E. W. Harper and Pauline Hopkins. A sampling of criticism on the author reveals this long-enduring tendency to view him as a realist. William Dean Howells, for example, in a 1900 *Atlantic Monthly* review of *The Wife of His Youth and Other Stories of the Color Line*, praises Chesnutt for his "unerring knowledge of the life he had chosen in its peculiar racial characteristics." Howells admires Chesnutt's realist "self-restraint" and the manner in which "[h]e sees his people very clearly, very justly, . . . show[ing] them as he sees them." To Howells, Chesnutt composes "realistic fiction" of the "highest order." Fifty-three years later, in an article aptly entitled "Social Realism in Charles W. Chesnutt," Russell Ames claims that "Chesnutt's portrayal of Southern life is far more inclusive, truthful, complex, interesting, and artistic than Faulkner's." Ames goes on to declare Chesnutt a direct predecessor to black social realists of the twentieth century. In 1974, J. Noel Heermance described Chesnutt's literary aesthetics and politics as products of "the literary milieu of" the late nineteenth century, which "was governed largely by the moral-oriented precepts of William Dean Howells." "Coming under Howells's influence," Heermance argues, Chesnutt "saw the subtle, positive changes which literature could effect in a society." Like Heermance, Sylvia Lyons Render views Chesnutt as a product of the realist zeitgeist of the late nineteenth century and considers him "among the best of the local-color writers."[14]

Recently, however, Joseph R. McElrath has begun to consider Chesnutt's occasional ventures into the melodramatic, coupled with his occasional lapses into second-person polemicism, as evidence that realism may *not* have been the generic motivation for Chesnutt's work. In his interesting article "Why Charles W. Chesnutt Is Not a Realist," McElrath argues that Chesnutt was not "at all interested in, much less committed to, the Realist agenda. His typical subject matter choices, didactic intentions, and considerable imaginative powers were better suited to the medium of romance, and he wrote accordingly."[15] The argument is oddly compelling, but one could easily make a similar case for Mark Twain, whose realist aspirations would continually be rendered problematic by a wild romantic imagination (*Adventures of Huckleberry Finn*), an eventual naturalistic pessimism (*A Connecticut Yankee in King Arthur's Court*), and a proto-modernist sense of alienation (*No. 44, The Mysterious Stranger*). McElrath argues that Chesnutt's characterization was largely romantic, often employing stereotypical characters for purely polemical purposes, but one could make a similar claim of William Dean Howells, whose Reverend Sewell of *The Rise of Silas Lapham* serves as a veritable mouthpiece for the author's views on moral and aesthetic realism.

Nevertheless, there undoubtedly is much romance in Chesnutt's work, enough for Eric J. Sundquist to suggest that "Chesnutt's color line stories . . . are dominated by melodrama." This would certainly describe Mr. Ryder's speech to the Blue Veins in "The Wife of His Youth," as well as Rena's "maudlin" tale of racial fate, emotional turmoil, and death in *The House behind the Cedars* (something I will consider in more detail in chapter 6), in which McElrath finds "little of the Realistic." However, such generic indeterminacy should not be so much a call for Chesnutt's "eviction" from the "House of Howells" as a willingness to see Chesnutt as capable of performing a multiplicity of authorial roles and an awareness of what the implications of these roles are. Sylvia Lyons Render has argued correctly, "Chesnutt cannot be neatly labeled as a Classicist,

14. Howells, "Chesnutt's Stories," 699, 700; Russell Ames, "Social Realism in Charles W. Chesnutt," 152, 153; J. Noel Heermance, *Charles W. Chesnutt: America's First Great Black Novelist*, 139; Sylvia Lyons Render, *Charles W. Chesnutt*, 47.

15. Joseph R. McElrath, Jr., "Why Charles W. Chesnutt Is Not a Realist," 92.

Romanticist, Realist, or Naturalist."[16] When he fictionalizes the social constructedness of race in the United States, Chesnutt is clearly playing the role of the realist, and an often ironic one at that (witness, for example, the racialism of Judge Straight.) However, there are moments when Chesnutt lapses into an unironic racial romanticism that undercuts both the aesthetic and political project of his work. For example, the narrator's explanation for John Walden's middle-class aspirations is that "[t]he blood of his white fathers, the heirs of the ages, cried out for its own, and after the manner of that blood set about getting the object of its desire" (*HC* 163).

Nevertheless, it is in the result of the decidedly realist "crisis experience" that Chesnutt levels his most damning attack on race ideologies. The agency exercised in the "crisis experience" is certainly significant, and Chesnutt arguably "present[s] passing and intermarriage . . . as deliberate acts, chosen by mature and respectable Afro-Americans for justifiable social, economic, and political reasons." But the reader comes to discover that it is not a character's resolution of this "crisis experience" that matters. Mr. Ryder of "The Wife of His Youth" elects not to pass and is thus the hero of the story. John Walden of *The House behind the Cedars*, however, elects to pass and is rewarded not only with the fruits of hard work but the clear conscience of moral rectitude. This marks a fundamental difference between white ethnic passing fiction and African American passing fiction. While white ethnic authors issue fictional critiques of passing characters, occasionally employing racially romantic rhetoric to advocate an abiding sense of ethnic allegiance, African American authors are less likely to offer so facile a view of the passing act. Thus, "The purpose of [Chesnutt's] mulatto-oriented fiction . . . would be neither the explicit advocacy nor condemnation of passing or miscegenation. Rather, it would be to create an awareness of and public responsiveness to the social, economic, and psychological causes for such acts, thereby enlisting sympathy toward those who, because of a 'social fiction,' must suffer tragedy in many cases in their pursuit of the American Dream." The moral focus is not so much upon "right" and "wrong" choices—between the "white race" and social mobility on the one hand and the "black race" with its rich cultural offerings on the other—rather, the focus is upon race itself. William L. Andrews aptly summarizes Chesnutt's racial and generic program: "To Chesnutt, the realists' pragmatic attitude toward

16. Sundquist, *To Wake the Nations*, 397; McElrath, "Why Charles W. Chesnutt Is Not a Realist," 91, 98; Render, *Charles W. Chesnutt*, 123.

social morality, along with their sympathetic view of the individual inevitably implicated in a social context not of his or her making, made possible the portrayal of the mixed blood's situation in new and liberating ways."[17]

Chesnutt's essays are frequently examined as examples of the author's genuine commitment to dismantling the intellectual legacy of soft racial thinking. In "What Is a White Man?" (1889), Chesnutt establishes that it is by "fiat" of "the wise men of the South"—and not by any corresponding biological fact—"that the 'all-pervading, all-conquering Anglo-Saxon race' must continue forever to exercise exclusive control and direction of the government of this so-called Republic." Having handily dispatched the notion of Anglo Saxon superiority, Chesnutt turns to another romantic Southern shibboleth, Anglo-Saxon purity, arguing that "it is evident that where the intermingling of the races has made such progress as it has in this country, the line which separates the races must in many instances have been practically obliterated." In this essay, Chesnutt also elegantly establishes the legal construction of race, providing specific examples to demonstrate that "[t]he states vary slightly in regard to what constitutes a mulatto or person of color, and as to what proportion of white blood should be sufficient to remove the disability of color"; this, of course, anticipates a central theme of *The House behind the Cedars*. In "The Future American: What the Race Is Likely to Become in the Process of Time" (1900), Chesnutt not only reiterates his rejection of the idea "of a pure Aryan, Indo-European race" but also offers views on topics that in the twentieth century would come to be known as "cultural pluralism" and "race formation." In this often-cited essay, Chesnutt critiques a "popular theory" in which "the future American race will consist of a harmonious fusion of the various European elements which now make up our heterogeneous population"; this would become the exclusionary and not-so-antiracist "cultural pluralism" of Horace M. Kallen and Randolph S. Bourne in the 1910s. In this theory's stead, Chesnutt proposes a more fully pluralistic, yet also assimilatory "future American ethnic type… formed of a mingling, in a yet to be ascertained proportion, of the various racial varieties which make up the present population of the United States." Not simply a melting pot of European strains, this "future American race" will be made up of "white, black and Indian" "broad types." These two essays demonstrate that Chesnutt is not so interested in criti-

17. Andrews, *The Literary Career of Charles W. Chesnutt*, 143, 144; Andrews, Foreword, xv.

cizing passing—especially given the inevitability of racial coabsorption; rather, Chesnutt is interested in critiquing nearly every received notion of race.[18]

Put simply, late-nineteenth and early-twentieth-century African American literature exhibits a greater urgency to critique the premises of racialism than white ethnic American literature of the same time period. One could only speculate as to the reasons why. Perhaps it is because African Americans were victimized by racialism to a greater degree, and certainly for a longer time, than their white ethnic counterparts. Perhaps it is because first- and second-generation European ethnic writers were too busy experiencing and understanding the jarring clash of Old and New World cultures to devote sufficient intellectual and literary attention to the ideological bases of the racialism that would hinder, and eventually enhance, their social status. Maybe it is because the idea of race did not carry the same danger for white ethnics that it did for African Americans: for while European immigrants and their progeny often viewed their discriminatory treatment as "race prejudice," they also drew on problematic notions of race to explain cultural difference. Finally, perhaps it is because African American literature was simply an older tradition than Jewish American or Italian American literature and therefore was more likely to be more ideologically and epistemologically progressive.

What is certain is that Charles Chesnutt and other African American writers devoted much literary energy to destabilizing the ideological structures of race, even if this meant turning a critical eye to the racial misunderstandings of African Americans themselves. Witness, for example, Chesnutt's ironic treatment of intraracial snobbery on the part of the Blue Veins and their "dean," Mr. Ryder ("I have no race prejudice"), in "The Wife of His Youth" and of Miss Molly of *The House behind the Cedars*, who views darker-skinned African Americans with the same air of superiority "her poor white neighbors" exhibit toward her (*HC* 175). Chesnutt's racial critique, however, is far from consistent, and I would submit that this is, at least in part, a matter of generic significance. As sharply critical of race as *The House behind the Cedars* is, Chesnutt cannot avoid making problematic references to black racial difference. For example, when describing the love of the unschooled and undeniably black Frank Fowler for Rena Walden, the narrator opines, "There are depths of fidelity and devotion in the negro heart that have never been fathomed

18. Chesnutt, "What Is a White Man?" 837, 839; Chesnutt, "The Future American: What the Race Is Likely to Become in the Process of Time," 846, 845, 846–47.

or fully appreciated" (*HC* 176–77). This statement is clearly in the tradition of racial romanticism and is used, very suggestively, to preface a sentimental, didactic passage on the "common race,—the human race, which is bigger and broader than Celt or Saxon, barbarian or Greek, Jew or Gentile. Black or white" (*HC* 177). Furthermore, as antiracialist as an essay such as "The Future American" may be, it cannot but explain the future social landscape of the United States in terms of race, even if this future race is of a richer, more inclusive variety. One could make the case that an even more realistic treatment of race is necessary to surpass the nagging romanticisms of Chesnutt. However, this would oversimplify, because realism itself in some ways could be held accountable for preserving problematic racial ideologies through authors, such as William Dean Howells and Charles Chesnutt, who "believed in innate, inherited differences between white and black." Even if we take as a given the superiority of realism over romanticism in combating raced ideologies, there still remains the fact that realist mimesis runs the risk of replicating and thereby reinforcing the very racialist thinking it attempts to dismantle.[19] Therefore, while still more realistic treatments of "the color line" would be attempted in African American literary history, it would eventually take an abandonment of realist mimesis in order to fashion a pure, unmitigated assault on racism.

James Weldon Johnson's *The Autobiography of an Ex-Coloured Man:* Modern "Fiction Founded on Hard Fact"

In a 1912 review, Jessie Fauset enthusiastically praised James Weldon Johnson's (1871–1938) first novel, writing that "[t]he varied incidents, the numerous localities brought in, the setting forth in all its ramifications of our great and perplexing race problem, suggests a work of fiction founded on hard fact."[20] Although this "hard fact" does not suggest a one-to-one correspondence between the narrative and the author's life (as its anonymous 1912 publication might have suggested to the uninitiated reader), it does indicate at least some strategic connection between the "fiction" and the African American sociohistorical realities it purports fictionally to represent. For this chapter, *The Autobiography of an Ex-Coloured Man* is

---

19. Boeckmann, *A Question of Character,* 139, 211.
20. Jessie Redmon Fauset, review of *Autobiography of an Ex-Coloured Man,* by James Weldon Johnson, 38.

both a central and pivotal text in that it marks a clearer step in the direction of realism for three basic reasons: its sustained commitment to verisimilitude (if from the perspective of a narrator and an author with strong bourgeois sympathies), its reduced reliance upon the aesthetic and racial romanticisms of Chesnutt, and its expansion of Chesnutt's project of racial critique.

Johnson could scarcely have avoided the influence of realism, as in the early 1900s he had attended for three years the lectures of Columbia professor Brander Matthews, whose "literary concepts . . . work[ed] a subtle change on Johnson's thinking." According to Eugene Levy, "[L]ike William Dean Howells," Matthews "advocated a realistic portrayal of American life"; Matthews would later compare *Autobiography* favorably to Howells's work in a review. However, Johnson also could not avoid being influenced by the increasingly modernist zeitgeist of the 1910s, and this manifests itself in the "characteristic . . . alienation" of *Autobiography*'s protagonist—alienation, ultimately, from both the black *and* white identities he attempts, though is never convincingly able, to embody.[21] Yet another ingredient to the aesthetic stew is a well-documented, heightened sense of irony in *Autobiography* that not only chafes at the veneer of realistic forthrightness, but also suggests the need for the African American writer to explore new literary modus operandi to carry out an effective critique of race.

In *Autobiography*, the nameless protagonist struggles to understand and culturally assimilate both the black and white potential identities he is ultimately alienated from, given his status as a light-skinned African American in a postbellum United States where racial theories of hypodescent held sway. The protagonist is born illegitimately in Georgia after the end of the Civil War to a light-skinned African American mother and an estranged, though financially supportive, white Southern gentleman who could not marry the protagonist's mother for reasons of social propriety. The ex-coloured man's earliest memories are of his mother and his father, "a tall man with a small, dark moustache," whose bourgeois attire would provide a fashion ideal the protagonist would later learn to

21. Eugene Levy, *James Weldon Johnson: Black Leader, Black Voice*, 125, 127; Gates, Introduction, xviii. On *The Autobiography of an Ex-Coloured Man* as a narrative of passing for both black and white identities, see Samira Kawash, "*The Autobiography of an Ex-Coloured Man*: (Passing for) Black Passing for White"; Neil Brooks, "On Becoming an Ex-Man: Postmodern Irony and the Extinguishing of Certainties in the Autobiography of an Ex-Colored Man"; and Martin Japtok's "Between 'Race' as Construct and 'Race' as Essence: *The Autobiography of an Ex-Coloured Man*."

emulate as a successful, middle-class professional. The protagonist recalls that "his shoes or boots were always shiny, and that he wore a gold chain and a great gold watch with which he was always willing to let me play. My admiration was almost equally divided between the watch and chain and the shoes"; significantly, the young protagonist is more interested in the artifacts of his father's conspicuous consumption than his father himself (*AEM* 5). The father's estrangement from his African American lover and son foreshadows the ex-coloured man's later alienation from "African Americanness" once he achieves the bourgeois ideal embodied by his father.

In order to successfully negotiate the rules of middle-class American masculinity, the protagonist would have to undergo the requisite training, and this begins when he moves with his mother to Connecticut and lives "almost luxuriously" in a "little cottage" with lush furnishings, a piano, and a well-stocked library (*AEM* 6). Indeed, the protagonist explains that he is moved North not only because of his father's impending marriage to a Southern gentlewoman but also because his father "intended to give [him] an education and make a man of [him]" (*AEM* 43). Hitherto unaware of his African American ancestry, the ex-coloured man encounters a black student named Shiny whom he describes stereotypically: "His face was as black as night, but shone as though it were polished; he had sparkling eyes, and when he opened his mouth, he displayed glistening white teeth" (14). However, this stereotype is deployed for rhetorical purposes, for it is quickly met by its antithesis: Shiny, it turns out, is the best-performing student in the class (*AEM* 14). Nevertheless, Shiny, like the other African American students, is still treated rudely by his white classmates. When the protagonist inevitably learns the word "nigger" from the students' racist banter, the protagonist is harshly rebuked by his mother for using it; still, the ex-coloured man's mother does not reveal her son's ancestry to him. He only learns when he is told by the schoolteacher, after which some white schoolchildren "jeer" him for being "a nigger too" (*AEM* 16). After this "cruel...sword-thrust," the protagonist hurries home to hold the verity of the accusation to the standard of his senses:

> I rushed up into my own little room, shut the door, and went quickly to where my looking-glass hung on the wall. For an instant I was afraid to look, but when I did, I looked long and earnestly. I had often heard people say to my mother: "What a pretty boy you have!" I was accustomed to hear remarks about my beauty; but now, for the first time, I became conscious of it and recognized it. I noticed the

ivory whiteness of my skin, the beauty of my mouth, the size and liquid darkness of my eyes, and how the long, black lashes that fringed and shaded them produced an effect that was strangely fascinating even to me. I noticed the softness and glossiness of my dark hair that fell in waves over my temples, making my forehead appear whiter than it really was. (*AEM* 19, 17)

This passage recalls Mr. Ryder's self-examination in "The Wife of His Youth," only here the protagonist has yet to learn with certainty the truth of his ancestry, and so the act of self-examination is embellished with descriptive detail that underscores the fascination of a new discovery. Very typically, the description is supplied with signs of both whiteness ("ivory whiteness of my skin") and racial "otherness" ("liquid darkness of my eyes"; "long, black lashes"; "dark hair"; and "forehead appear[ing] whiter than it really was") (*AEM* 17). Indeed, the ex-coloured man's physiognomy is not unlike that of a racially in-between white ethnic; later in the narrative, the protagonist would speak of his "Italian-like complexion" (*AEM* 199). However, the idea of passing for a racially in-between *Italian* never occurs to the protagonist, who spends his life bound by his allegedly authentic black identity and the lure of whiteness. Two determinisms begin to suggest themselves in this scene: first, a social determinism in the form of a "racist environment" that "mandates his creation of an identity which is *either* white *or* black" and, secondly, the psychological impact the "empty signifier of race" has on the narrator, despite the fact that his appearance could lend itself to the performance of more than one racial or ethnic identity.[22]

Immediately after the self-examination, the protagonist sees his mother and retroactively detects evidence of racial difference in her appearance: "And then it was that I looked at her critically for the first time. I had thought of her in a childish way only as the most beautiful woman in the world; now I looked at her searching for defects. I could see that her skin was almost brown, that her hair was not so soft as mine, and that she did differ in some way from the other ladies who came to the house; yet, even so, I could see that she was very beautiful, more beautiful than any of them." Very tellingly, the protagonist here catalogues only signs of racial "otherness": her skin color, her hair texture, and her "difference" from the "ladies." Yet, he cannot view these differences as "defects"; his

22. John Sheehy, "The Mirror and the Veil: The Passing Novel and the Quest for American Racial Identity," 404; Kawash, *"The Autobiography of an Ex-Coloured Man,"* 71.

mother is still beautiful to him, much as he is beautiful to himself. Here Johnson debunks the verity of self-evident, racially determined beauty standards: for the protagonist, any notion that black is *not* "beautiful" would have to be learned. When the protagonist asks his mother if he is a "nigger," she replies, "no" and goes on to defend his ancestry on racialist grounds, admitting that while she herself is "not white," the protagonist's "father is one of the greatest men in the country"; as she insists, "the best blood of the South is in" the young ex-coloured man (*AEM* 18).

From this day forward, the protagonist becomes acutely aware of the psychological determinism of race: "for I did indeed pass into another world. From that time I looked out through other eyes, my thoughts were coloured, my words dictated, my actions limited by one dominating, all-pervading idea which constantly increased in force and weight until I finally realized in it a great, tangible fact" (*AEM* 20–21). In this passing from the white "world" to the black, the protagonist attains a DuBoisian double-consciousness that allows him not only to reflect on his image from the perspective of both whites and blacks but also eventually to understand the constructedness of the "one dominating, all-pervading idea" of race, which "increase[s] in force and weight" and becomes "a great, tangible fact" only through its continual recurrence in the mind of the protagonist (and, by extension, society in general).[23]

Throughout the remainder of the novel, the protagonist alternates between attraction and repulsion to both black and white identities, never feeling fully at home with either. At school, the protagonist recalls an initial "strong aversion to being classed with" fellow African Americans (*AEM* 23). Not fully accepted by the white students and not comfortable with the company of the black students, the protagonist's classically modernist alienation drives him toward more introverted endeavors, literature, which he reads voraciously, and music, which he masters at a young age. Hearing Shiny's graduation speech, however, causes the protagonist to rethink his Negrophobia: "I felt leap within me pride that I was coloured; and I began to form wild dreams of bringing glory and honour to the Negro race. For days I could talk of nothing else with my mother except my ambitions to be a great man, a great coloured man, to reflect credit on the race and gain fame for myself" (*AEM* 46). The pro-

23. On DuBoisian double-consciousness and *Autobiography,* see Sheehy, "The Mirror and the Veil," 406–8, and Warren, "Troubled Black Humanity in *The Souls of Black Folk* and *The Autobiography of an Ex-Colored Man*."

tagonist immerses himself in African American history, but his newfound attraction returns somewhat to revulsion when he encounters poor, rural African Americans for the first time as an Atlanta University student. An ardent classist, the ex-coloured man recalls that "[t]he unkempt appearance, the shambling, slouching gait and loud talk and laughter of these people aroused in me a feeling of almost repulsion. Only one thing about them awoke a feeling of interest; that was their dialect. I had read some negro dialect and had heard snatches of it on my journey down from Washington; but here I heard it in all of its fullness and freedom" (*AEM* 55–56). This is not the only time the protagonist speaks of fellow African Americans with the cool, objective gaze of a sociologist. In a detailed passage, he describes what he considers to be the "three classes" of African Americans: the desperate class, domestic servants, and the black middle class—an important factor in the book's irony in that this "detachment" reveals the ex-coloured man's reluctance to believe he is truly black (*AEM* 76, 78).[24]

Still, much of the novel describes the protagonist's somewhat pathetic attempts to be black. After his money is stolen and he is unable to attend classes in Atlanta, the protagonist travels to Jacksonville to look for work, and though he is told he could pass for white, the protagonist still elects to stay at a "respectable boarding-house for coloured people" (*AEM* 66). In true Algerian style, the protagonist supports himself through work at a cigar factory, and then as a private music teacher. Through his occasional church visit, the ex-coloured man is "acquainted with the best class of coloured people in Jacksonville." Not having been comfortable among poor African Americans, the protagonist's association with the black middle class marks his true "entrance into the race." In surprisingly constructionist terms, he explains that this "was my initiation into what I have termed the freemasonry of the race. I had formulated a theory of what it was to be coloured; now I was getting the practice" (*AEM* 74). This parallels an actual occurrence in James Weldon Johnson's life, as revealed in his autobiography *Along This Way* (1933), in which he writes of learning to become an African American while living among them as a new student at Atlanta University preparatory school: "Indeed, it was in this early period that I received my initiation into the arcana of 'race.' I perceived that education for me meant, fundamentally: preparation to meet the tasks and exigencies of life as a Negro, a realization of the

24. Robert E. Fleming, *James Weldon Johnson*, 36.

peculiar responsibilities due to my own racial group, and a comprehension of the application of American democracy to Negro citizens."[25] Johnson's use of scare quotes around the word "race" is telling, for it is indicative of his literary attempt, in both *Autobiography* and *Along This Way*, to complicate, even destabilize, racial thought.

In *Autobiography*, Johnson, in part, substitutes essentialistic notions of black *racial* difference for African American *cultural*, perhaps *ethnic*, difference. For example, while the protagonist is somewhat discomfited by association with ordinary African American folk, he exhibits a great deal of pride in African American "originality and artistic conception" as evidenced in Uncle Remus stories, Jubilee songs, ragtime, and the cakewalk. Significantly, the protagonist uses this figuration of *ethnic* distinctiveness to "refute the oft-advanced theory that [African Americans] are an absolutely inferior *race*" (*AEM* 87; italics mine). The ex-coloured man interprets the international popularity of ragtime as evidence of the applicability of "lower forms of art . . . to the higher forms" (*AEM* 87). As patently condescending as this notion of fusing "lower art" and "higher art" might seem, it can also be taken as representative of the ex-coloured man's assimilative drive.[26] However difficult to accept as it may have been for him, the protagonist knows himself to be ancestrally black and, at this point in the narrative, had just begun to learn the meaning of being *culturally* or *ethnically* black. However, his bourgeois taste—even outright snobbery—reveals a strong impulse on his part to adapt to the cultural mores of the American mainstream. To achieve some kind of equilibrium of ethnic identity vis-à-vis his national identity, the protagonist believes he can apply an African American cultural awareness to his European American sensibility. His approach to music reflects this understanding: he learns to play ragtime by applying African American musical stylings to the forms of Western art music. He becomes so famous as a composer and performer that a wealthy white man hires him to be a private pianist for parties. While in the employ of the wealthy patron, the ex-coloured man does not mind identifying as black, though he never sheds his elitism (at his favorite jazz club, he dismisses an uncouth African American rival for the attentions of a beautiful widow as a "surly, black despot" who clearly did not possess the protagonist's "native gallantry,"

25. James Weldon Johnson, *Along This Way: the Autobiography of James Weldon Johnson*, 66.

26. On the ex-coloured man's culturally synthetic musical project and its sociohistorical context, see Cristina L. Ruotolo, "James Weldon Johnson and the Autobiography of an Ex-Colored Musician."

"delicacy," "artistic temperament," and "skill") (*AEM* 123, 122). When the wealthy patron tours Europe, the ex-coloured man accompanies him and continues to identify himself as an African American, astonishing socialites with his classically tinged ragtime. It is at this point in the narrative that the ex-coloured man comes closest to achieving ethnic equilibrium, a wholesome provincialism of learned African American and American cultural influences—something Johnson himself valued in his promotion of a "positive racial identity among blacks," coupled with "an implicit belief in the American 'success ethic'" that never really "reject[ed] the desirability of ultimate assimilation."[27] The novel, then, comes close to realizing the discursive equilibrium of the acculturation narrative.

While in Germany, the protagonist begins to feel as though he is "wasting [his] time and abusing [his] talent." A German man had played one of the protagonist's ragtime pieces in all the varieties of Western art music; the result, for the ex-coloured man, is nothing short of an epiphany. Rather than play "classic music" embellished with African American folk influences, the protagonist decides to do the opposite—to use African American musical forms as his starting point, and invent a new kind of "classic music" out of them. Thus, the protagonist comes to identify with his black ancestral past more than ever before in the narrative. In order to gather the musical raw materials for his project, the ex-coloured man decides to leave Europe "to go back into the very heart of the South, . . . live among the people, and drink in my inspiration firsthand" (*AEM* 142).

The wealthy patron, upon hearing of the protagonist's desire, is dismissive of it on the grounds that the ex-coloured man is, for all intents and purposes, white and will jeopardize his future as a musician as an openly black man; this quite unintentionally provides the ex-coloured man with a rationalization for passing as white in the United States, even if he only intended to convince the ex-coloured man to stay in Europe as an African American (*AEM* 144). The ex-coloured man will not be dissuaded and returns to the United States, passing only occasionally for convenience or unintentionally. While passing for convenience on a train from Nashville to Atlanta, the protagonist is sickened by a racist conversation he overhears in which a Texan's social Darwinist, Anglo supremacist argument ("If he's inferior and weaker, and is shoved to the wall, that's his own look out . . . That's the law of nature") is reduced to absurdity by a former Union soldier who argues that "racial supremacy

27. Levy, *James Weldon Johnson*, 137, 142.

is merely a matter of dates in history" (but still "wouldn't consent to [his] daughter's marrying a nigger") (*AEM* 161, 163). Still, the protagonist generally identifies himself as an African American and is often bemused when in some unfamiliar town he is "taken for and treated as a white man" only to be treated differently "when it was learned that [he] was stopping at the house of the coloured preacher or school-teacher" (*AEM* 172). He immerses himself in many aspects of Southern black culture in Georgia, including African American sermons and gospel music.

The protagonist's ethnic idyll is shattered when he witnesses a lynching one night, which he describes in all its grisly detail. His light skin and unknown identity allow him to satisfy his voyeuristic curiosity with impunity. Ironically, it is not "discouragement or fear," but "humiliation and shame" that occur to the protagonist after the horrific spectacle: "Shame that I belonged to a race that could be so dealt with; and shame for my country, that it, the great example of democracy to the world, should be the only civilized, if not the only state on earth, where a human being would be burned alive" (*AEM* 190, 187–88). Significantly, the "shame" extends to both the ethnic and civic components of his once balanced identity; thus, he is confronted with "the crisis experience," the decision whether to remake himself anew. Furthermore, with this jarring plot twist, Johnson signposts his inability to sustain the tension of the acculturation narrative—a tension that, in an African American context, leads almost necessarily to violence and a reversion to the trope of passing.

In a scene reminiscent of the classic realist scene of agency, the ex-coloured man sits and ponders his course of action for "perhaps an hour or more." Soon, the protagonist rides a train to Macon, buys a ticket for New York, and ponders the morality of "the step which [he] had decided to take." He explains his reasoning: "I argued that to forsake one's race to better one's condition was no less worthy an action than to forsake one's country for the same purpose. I finally made up my mind that I would neither disclaim the black race nor claim the white race; but that I would change my name, raise a moustache, and let the world take me for what it would; that it was not necessary for me to go about with a label of inferiority pasted across my forehead" (*AEM* 190). Having identified himself as an African American, and continually pressured by the psychological determinism of race, the protagonist views his choice as tantamount to "forsak[ing] one's race." Although in theory he does not *actively* "disclaim" either of his racial inheritances, in practice this will mean he could be taken as white. Significantly, he decides to "raise a

moustache" so as better to emulate his father, who is now the embodiment of the ex-coloured man's ideal. Kathleen Pfeiffer argues that the
ex-coloured man's passing "claims a full of measure of individualism"
and "evokes the Emersonian self-reliance found in such [realist] fictional
contemporaries as Isabel Archer and Lily Bart." According to this view,
"passing offers the Ex-Colored Man access to a particularly American
form of success: financial security, social prominence, personal independence." However, the protagonist's exercise of agency is not so simple,
as the explanation of his own rationale indicates: he would culturally
assimilate ("raise a moustache," "neither disclaim the black race nor
claim the white race"), but only society can allow his eventual structural
assimilation ("let the world take me for what it would"). Indeed, he can
only be viewed as "a free man aggressively asserting his individuality,
yet trapped within a social system that denies him the rights of an individual."[28] And this passage is further literary evidence that the act of
passing is firmly rooted within contradiction, vis-à-vis not only race but
also the agency we expect to find exhibited by characters attempting to
live by the rules of the American success myth.

Although the protagonist claims not to have passed for the "search
for a larger field of action and opportunity," he rationalizes, "since I was
not going to be a Negro, I would avail myself of every possible opportunity to make a white man's success," which he stereotypically conceives
as "money" (*AEM* 193). In order to do so, he returns to New York City,
the place where the ex-coloured man had previously immersed himself
in African American cultural ferment, in order to begin life anew as a
successful white man. Earlier in the narrative, the protagonist describes
New York in conflicting terms of both opportunity and coercion:

> New York City is the most fatally fascinating thing in America. She
> sits like a great witch at the gate of the country, showing her alluring
> white face and hiding her crooked hands and feet under the folds of
> her wide garments—constantly enticing thousands from far within,
> and tempting those who come from across the seas to go no farther.
> And all these become the victims of her caprice. Some she at once
> crushes beneath her cruel feet; others she condemns to a fate like that
> of galley-slaves; others she favours and fondles, riding them high on
> the bubbles of fortune; then with a sudden breath she blows the bub-
> bles out and laughs mockingly as she watches them fall. (*AEM* 89)

28. Kathleen Pfeiffer, "Individualism, Success and American Identity in *The Autobiography of an Ex-Colored Man*," 405, 417; Brooks, "On Becoming an Ex-Man," 25.

Of course, race has much to do with whether one becomes a "victim"; as David C. Geollnicht writes, "the fact that the narrator and thousands like him feel the necessity to pass for white stands as testament to the fact that the North is not an ideal space where bondage has been exchanged for freedom, where African Americans have changed their status from property to personhood."[29] So as not to become one of the "galley-slaves," the ex-coloured man goes to business school, becomes a clerk, saves his money, and enters into real estate, in which he holds a high-paying position (*AEM* 196). The protagonist's structural assimilation is advanced: he enters into New York high society and marries a woman "as white as a lily," who overcomes her initial hysteria and racial squeamishness when she discovers the truth of the ex-coloured man's ancestry (*AEM* 198). The novel ends with the ex-coloured man expressing regret for having passed. Comparing himself to race leaders such as Booker T. Washington, the ex-coloured man "feel[s] small and selfish": "I am an ordinarily successful white man who has made a little money. They are men who are making history and a race. I, too, might have taken part in a work so glorious." The protagonist recalls the aging manuscripts of his abandoned musical project and considers them "the only tangible remnants of a vanished dream, a dead ambition, a sacrificed talent." Ultimately, he believes he has "sold [his] birthright for a mess of pottage" (*AEM* 211).

This conclusion has been typically viewed as an authorial condemnation of passing not unlike that found in the Italian American and Jewish American texts discussed earlier. Recently, some critics have suggested that the authorial point of view is not so uncomplicated; for example, John Sheehy has argued that the novel both condemns and "celebrates the ex-colored man's transgress[ions]." However, it is difficult to imagine Johnson advocating passing, for although he was a firm believer in the twin American myths of success and "individualism," Johnson also believed that success should never come at the cost of one's African American identity. He never could renounce his anticipation of a "future 'glorious and grand' Negro race in America"; his commitment to ragtime composition and dialect poetry are but two examples of his belief in the "higher cultural ideals" evinced by African American creative potential. In his autobiography, Johnson's condemnation of passing is unequivocal. Recalling having been asked by a white man what he would give to be white himself, Johnson writes, "That same remark, implied if

29. Donald C. Geollnicht, "Passing as Autobiography: James Weldon Johnson's *The Autobiography of an Ex-Coloured Man*," 25.

not expressed, has many times since been thrown at me. I judge that every intelligent Negro in the United States has met it in one form or another. And it is most likely that all of us have at some time toyed with the Arabian Nights–like thought of the magical change of race. As for myself, I find that I do not wish to be anyone but myself. To conceive of myself as someone else is impossible, and the effort repugnant."[30]

Rather than simply suggesting that Johnson "celebrates" or "condemns" passing, it might be more accurate to postulate that Johnson, no doubt, uses the trope of passing as a means to critique racial disloyalty, but more importantly, also the idea of race itself—something Johnson spends far more literary energy examining in the text, anyway. For while explicit regret for passing is expressed only once—at the end—the protagonist, throughout the narrative, issues a number of critiques of the idea of race in America. For example, the protagonist addresses the absurdity of skin color as a determiner of personal worth: "So far as racial differences go, the United States puts a greater premium on colour, or, better, lack of colour, than upon anything else in the world" (*AEM* 154–55). Toward the end of the narrative, the ex-coloured man exhibits an awareness that his ability to succeed at passing directly contradicts racist theories of hypodescent: "The anomaly of my social position often appealed strongly to my sense of humour. I frequently smiled inwardly at some remark not altogether complimentary to people of colour; and more than once I felt like declaiming: 'I am a coloured man. Do I not prove the theory that one drop of Negro blood renders a man unfit?'" (*AEM* 197). Furthermore, the protagonist's "constant fear that [his wife] would discover in [him] some shortcoming which she would unconsciously attribute to [his] blood" underscores the fact any racial difference perceived could be done so only retroactively, once the ex-coloured man's ancestry was already known. Indeed, only when he reveals his ancestry and his lover reacts hysterically does the protagonist feel "that [he] was growing black and thick-featured and crimp-haired" (*AEM* 204).

Johnson's autobiography features intelligent commentary that reveals his understanding of the constructedness of race. With a revealing use of quotes around the word "race," Johnson explains the significance of his first encounter with poor, rural African Americans as a teacher in rural Georgia:

30. Berzon, *Neither White nor Black*, 159; Sollors, *Neither Black nor White*, 269; Warren, "Troubled Black Humanity," 273; Sheehy, "The Mirror and the Veil," 408; Levy, *James Weldon Johnson*, 19, 70–71; James Weldon Johnson, *Along This Way*, 136.

It was this period which marked ... the beginning of my knowledge of my own people as a "race." That statement may not be entirely clear; I mean: I had in the main known my own people as individuals or as groups; and now I began to perceive them clearly as a classified division, a defined section of American society. I had learned something about the Negro as a problem, but now I was where I could touch the crude bulk of the problem itself with my own hands, where the relations between Black and White in the gross were pressed in upon me. Here there were no gradations, no nuances, no tentative approaches; what Black and White meant stood out starkly.

Having established race as a social construct, Johnson theorizes that racial superiority is also a figment of society's imagination: "the 'race problem' is paradoxical; and, with all my inexperience, I could not fail to see that this superior status was not always real, but often imaginary and artificial, bolstered by bigotry and buttressed by the forces of injustice." Given Johnson's outspoken antiracialism, critics have often suggested that his use of passing "challenges the received notions of race" and "establish[es] the fact that [racial] identities are entirely socially constructed."[31] This is certainly true, but it is important not to overstate Johnson's antiracialism and racial constructionism because evidence from both the *Autobiography* and *Along This Way* demonstrates that Johnson never completely renounced racialist theories of cultural difference. The novel is somewhat conflicted in this regard, as indicated by an early passage that scoffs at the "basic, though often dormant, principle of the Anglo-Saxon heart, love of fair play" and then immediately refers to "Shiny" as a "natural orator ... so common in his race" (*AEM* 45). Similarly, near the close of the narrative, the protagonist admits, "Sometimes it seems to me that I have never been a Negro, that I have been only a privileged spectator of their inner life; at other times I feel that I have been a coward, a deserter, and I am possessed by strange longing for my mother's people" (*AEM* 210). Contradictorily, the idea that he has "never been a Negro" calls into question any notion of absolute racial identities, while his occasional sense that he is a "deserter" relies upon a reification of a racial identity he has evaded by the "cowardly" act of passing. One is tempted to attribute this oversight to the fictional narrator, whose elitist snobbery already renders him somewhat ridiculous and unreliable to the contemporary reader.

31. Johnson, *Along This Way*, 119; Kawash, "*The Autobiography of an Ex-Coloured Man*," 62; Gates, Introduction, xvi.

However, Johnson's own autobiography reveals traces of self-contradictory racialism within an otherwise constructionist framework. Johnson's description of Southern blacks' laughter mirrors a passage in *The Autobiography of an Ex-Coloured Man*, in which the protagonist admits being astounded by "this ability to laugh heartily": "Why *did* they laugh so? How *could* they laugh so? Was this rolling, pealing laughter merely echoes from a mental vacuity or did it spring from an innate power to rise above the ironies of life? . . . I found no complete answer to these questions. Probably, some of all the elements suggested entered in" (*AEM* 56). Conversely, the novel also posits materialism and selfishness as being "'essentially' connected to whiteness." Thus, Johnson's work is "double-pronged" in that it "shows racial identity as socially constructed" but "also insists that certain traits are inherent to 'whiteness' or 'blackness.'"[32] According to Martin Japtok, this dualistic approach allows for Johnson simultaneously to critique racialism and celebrate African American cultural difference. However, contemporary readers realize this is generally an imperfect approach because it relies upon a problematic understanding of race that is in no way corrected by a focus upon positive racial difference as opposed to racially derived inferiority or depravity.

Part of the problem lies in the deployment of generic conventions. To be sure, *The Autobiography of an Ex-Coloured Man* marks a decisive step away from the racial romanticism, even melodrama, of Chesnutt. Stylistically, the novel's deadpan rendering of events references realism, while thematically, the novel "runs [a] gamut of color-line experiences." Indeed, the narrator's four excursions back and forth across the color line engender a more rational and probing examination of that very color line. Also, as Robert E. Fleming argues, "[t]he low-keyed ending of the novel is much more effective and realistic than the melodramatic conclusions so typical of earlier black novels on the 'tragic mulatto' theme." Finally, the novel's well-documented use of sustained irony—directed at racist ideology and arguably the narrator himself in his racial snobbery and self-congratulatory elitism—allows for an honest examination of the idea of race, but inadvertently suggests that only through a *more* ironic, if less realistic, approach would the African American author be able to level a more devastating attack on the very idea of race. Indeed, Johnson was ultimately unable to shed the racial romanticisms found in Chesnutt. However, despite the fact that Johnson's novel "leaves behind some

32. Johnson, *Along This Way*, 120; Japtok, "Between 'Race' as Construct and 'Race' as Essence," 39, 46, 33.

sentimental features of nineteenth-century versions of [passing] literature," it is insofar that Johnson is *realistic* that he seems unable, through
mere mimesis, to avoid replicating the raced ideologies he is attempting
to critique.[33] Thus, with regards to the African American male passing
narrative, *The Autobiography of an Ex-Coloured Man* arguably still reveals
the limitations of realism to issue such a critique. It would only be
through the abandonment of mimesis, coupled with the initiation of a
full-fledged ideological assault on racialism and racism, that George
Schuyler would be able to pick up where Chesnutt and Johnson left off.

"Hold That Race Stuff":
George Schuyler's *Black No More* and the Limits of Realism

With *Black No More* (1931), George Schuyler (1895–1977) stages his
own "absurd drama" in order to counteract the prevailing contemporary myths of race—a central function of the twentieth-century satirical
African American novel. "[A]n ambitious attempt to rhetorically dismantle any and all claims to permanent and essential racial differences,"
Black No More contains all the requisite "crisis experiences" and dramatizes the deterministic context in which characters resolve them, but the
plot is so patently absurd as to place the text well outside the pale of
realism. This was, of course, Schuyler's intent, for while the novel may
not have been, as its author believed, the first work "to treat the subject
[of race] with levity," it was "simultaneously the first completely satirical novel written by and about African Americans and the first extended
work of science fiction by a black author." Schuyler's use of a sustained
reductio ad absurdum of race defies realist notions of verisimilitude and
propriety, and throughout the narrative, allegorical characters with ridiculous Dickensian names are placed in improbable situations to demonstrate the absurdity of racialist thought and the racist social order. The
result is akin to M. M. Bakhtin's notion of "Rabelaisian laughter," which
rhetorically "destroys traditional connections and abolishes idealized
strata," or in this case, idealized *racial* strata.[34]

33. Fauset, review, 38; Fleming, *James Weldon Johnson,* 40. For a discussion of the
novel's irony, see Roxanna Pisiak, "Irony and Subversion in James Weldon Johnson's *The Autobiography of an Ex-Coloured Man.*" Sollors, *Neither Black nor White,* 266.
34. Darryl Dickson-Carr, *African-American Satire: The Sacredly Profane Novel,* 16,
57; Stacy Morgan, "'The Strange and Wonderful Workings of Science': Race Science
and Essentialism in George Schuyler's *Black No More,*" 331; George Schuyler, *Black*

Schuyler underscores the novel's satire in his brief preface for the original printing. He opens by relating the story of a man in Asbury Park, New Jersey, who produced and sold "Kink-No-More," a "preparation for the immediate and unfailing straightening of the most stubborn Negro hair." Schuyler does not explicitly condemn the substance, but rather writes that "[w]ith America's constant reiteration of the superiority of whiteness, the avid search on the part of the black masses for some key to chromatic perfection is easily understood. Now it would seem that science is on the verge of satisfying them."[35] Thus, with this brief but thoroughly ironic passage, Schuyler signals the central concern of the novel—the notion of racial superiority—and the means by which he will address it—satire.

The novel proper begins with a "damnably blue" Max Disher standing outside the Honky Tonk Club in Harlem on New Year's Eve, 1933. Schuyler describes Disher as both unmistakably and stereotypically black. "Dapper" and with "smooth coffee-brown" skin, Max possesses "Negroid features" of "a slightly satanic cast" that meet stereotypical expectations of African American innate depravity while his "insolent nonchalance" meets expectations of African American laziness (*BNM* 17). Max's companion Bunny Brown is described equally stereotypically, if more grotesquely, as "[a] short, plump, cherubic black fellow" (*BNM* 18). Dressed flamboyantly, the two are easily identifiable as "gay blades in black Harlem"—and this quickly becomes a problem (*BNM* 19). Presumably too dark for his "[s]tuck on... color," "high 'yallah'" girlfriend Minnie who has left him, Max is harshly rejected inside the club by a "strawberry blonde" white woman from Atlanta of whom he requests a dance (*BNM* 17, 22). That night, Max recalls her "icy" rebuff—"I never dance with niggers"—before drifting off into a dream in which he wins the woman's attention only to be pursued by a "screeching, fanatical mob" with the obvious intent to lynch him for his racial indiscretion (*BNM* 24).

and Conservative: The Autobiography of George S. Schuyler, 170; Michael W. Peplow, *George S. Schuyler,* 72. See James A. Miller, Foreword to *Black No More,* 8–9, in which the author lists a number of allegorical characters and their real-life counterparts; among the most immediately recognizable are Dr. Shakespeare Agamemnon Beard/ W. E. B. DuBois, Dr. Jackson/James Weldon Johnson, Mr. Walter Williams/Walter White, and Santop Licorice/Marcus Garvey. M. M. Bakhtin, *The Dialogic Imagination,* 170.

35. George Schuyler, *Black No More: Being an Account of the Strange and Wonderful Workings of Science in the Land of the Free, A. D. 1933–1940,* 13. Hereafter cited in the text as *BNM.*

The next day, Bunny tells Max of a *New York Times* article about Junius Crookman, an African American physician who has developed a medical procedure named Black-No-More to make blacks appear white. For Max, this seems almost too good to be true as he catalogues all the advantages of passing: "No more jim crow. No more insults. As a white man he could go anywhere, be anything he wanted to be, do most anything he wanted to do, be a free man at last . . . and probably be able to meet the girl from Atlanta. What a vision!" (*BNM* 26). With interest fully piqued, Max visits Junius Crookman at a hotel ironically named after Phyllis Wheatley—that first exemplar of literary African American racial pride. There Dr. Crookman tells Max that a former sociology teacher had once given African Americans three options: "To either get out, get white or get along." Crookman believes that the only solution to "the American race problem" would be for blacks to "get white," hence his procedure (*BNM* 27). No believer in absolute racial differences, Crookman actually becomes a mouthpiece for Schuyler's ardent racial constructionism. The doctor explains to Max, "there are plenty of Caucasians who have lips quite as thick and noses quite as broad as any of us. As a matter of fact there has been considerable exaggeration about the contrast between Caucasian and Negro features. *The cartoonists and minstrel men have been responsible for it very largely*" (*BNM* 31; italics mine).

Thus given both the rationalization and means for passing, Max agrees to undergo the procedure. Just before it is about to begin, Max comes to his "crisis experience" and sentimentally ponders the permanence of his decision: "He thought of the Elks' excursion every summer to Bear Mountain, the high yellow Minnie and her colorful apartment, the pleasant evenings at the Dahomey Casino doing the latest dances with the brown belles of Harlem, the prancing choruses at the Lafayette Theater, the hours he had whiled away at Boogie's and the Honky Tonk Club, and he hesitated" (*BNM* 33–34). Here Max runs through a list of primary group relationships he would be obligated to renounce once he becomes white. However, the thought of "his future as a white man, probably as the husband of the tall blonde from Atlanta" gives him the "firm resolve" needed to continue (*BNM* 34). Once the procedure is completed, the change is miraculous—not only in Max's appearance, but also in the new social status Black-No-More has conferred upon him: "White at last! Gone was the smooth brown complexion. Gone were the slightly full lips and Ethiopian nose. Gone was the nappy hair that he had straightened so meticulously ever since the kink-no-more lotions first wrenched

Aframericans from the tyranny and torture of the comb. There would be no more expenditures for skin whiteners; no more discrimination; no more obstacles in his path. He was free! The world was his oyster and he had the open sesame of a pork-colored skin!" (*BNM* 35). However, this very status is described in more conventionally realist passing narratives as the result of an arduous process of cultural, and then structural, assimilation; in Schuyler's satire, however, the color line is crossed easily (and is thereby more easily discredited) through a fifty-dollar medical procedure. A mere six hours after undergoing Black-No-More, Max is "through with coons" and already feels decidedly "superior" to the long line of African Americans waiting to undergo Black-No-More (*BNM* 35–36). Max's venture into the "great world of whiteness" immediately pays off—quite literally—when he is given one thousand dollars by a reporter for *The Scimitar* to tell his story. Indeed, the ability "to mingle with white people in places where as a youth he had never dared to enter" makes him feel "[a]t last" "like an American citizen" (*BNM* 48).

As Black-No-More becomes widespread, it proves to have devastating effects for those on either side of the "color line." As blacks become white, interest wanes in African American civil rights groups and businesses; Madame Sisseretta Blandish's "hairstraightening shop" loses business while the National Social Equality League (a thinly disguised NAACP led by Dr. Shakespeare Agamemnon Beard, an equally thinly disguised W. E. B. DuBois) loses contributions (*BNM* 59). Eventually, African American society is reduced to "turmoil and chaos": "The colored folk, in straining every nerve to get the Black-No-More treatment, had forgotten all loyalties, affiliations and responsibilities. No longer did they flock to the churches on Sundays or pay dues in their numerous fraternal organizations. They had stopped giving anything to the Anti-Lynching campaign. Santop Licorice [Marcus Garvey], head of the once-flourishing Back-To-Africa Society, was daily raising his stentorian voice in denunciation of the race for deserting his organization" (*BNM* 85–86). Meanwhile, white supremacists are also aghast; a Tallahassee *Announcer* editorial complains that "[d]ay by day we see the color line which we have so laboriously established being rapidly destroyed," as if to draw attention to the fact that the color line is more important than that which it separates. This, in fact, becomes a central thesis of the narrative: that the color line is a completely arbitrary social construct used to justify social dominance. When the ability either to police or to profit from this artificial color line is disrupted, trouble ensues. The same *Announcer* editorial informs readers that the whiteness produced by Black-No-More is not hereditary, and thus, "your daughter, having married a supposed white man, may find herself with a black baby!" (*BNM* 50).

In the meantime, Max Disher moves to Atlanta to find the strawberry blonde who had rebuffed him. By the time of his obligatory name change, Max Disher, reborn as Matthew Fisher, has structurally assimilated enough to be able to associate freely "in almost every stratum of Atlanta society" (*BNM* 62). The experience disillusions him greatly, and the narrator's expression of this disillusionment provides Schuyler an opportunity to deconstruct directly the idea of immutable racial differences and the logic of racism: "As a boy [Max] had been taught to look up to white folks as just a little less than gods; now he found them little different from the Negroes, except that they were uniformly less courteous and less interesting." As a white Atlantan socialite, Max is "infuriated" by "[t]he *unreasoning* and *illogical* color prejudice of most of the people with whom he [is] forced to associate" (*BNM* 63; italics mine).

Nevertheless, Max decides to profit from Southern racism, so he introduces himself as an "anthropologist" to the Reverend Henry Givens, Imperial Grand Wizard, in order to "get in" with The Knights of Nordica, Schuyler's satirical stand-in for the Ku Klux Klan (*BNM* 66–67). Once a speaker of hip Harlem slang, Max proves adept at adopting the discourse of polite, early-twentieth-century academic racism. Max, "in his best salesman's croon," tells Givens, "As an anthropologist, I have, of course, been long interested in the work with which you have been identified. It has always seemed to me that there was no question in American life more important than that of preserving the integrity of the white race. We all know what has been the fate of those nations that have permitted their blood to be polluted with that of inferior breeds" (*BNM* 68–69). Of course, Max "ha[s] no belief in the racial integrity nonsense" and simply wishes to use poor whites for profit (*BNM* 70–71). Meanwhile, the reader discovers that, in private company with his wife, Reverend Givens is notably crude in his manners and speaks a Southern dialect that Schuyler intentionally renders as indistinguishable from the speech of poor Southern African Americans (*BNM* 71). Dr. Junius Crookman anticipates this earlier in the novel when he argues that "[t]here is no such thing as a Negro dialect, except in literature and drama. . . . There are no racial or color dialects; only sectional dialects" (*BNM* 31). Max's speech to the Knights of Nordica, in which he carefully employs the necessary white supremacist rhetoric, solidifies his reputation as a learned white supremacist. He eventually becomes the "Grand Exalted Giraw of the Knights of Nordica" and reaches the final stage of structural assimilation—intermarriage—when he marries Helen Givens, who, as luck would have it, is the very woman who had refused him a dance at the Honky Tonk Club in Harlem (*BNM* 105).

Max is able to use his influence in the Knights of Nordica to secure a job in the organization for his friend Bunny, who has recently undergone Black-No-More. Max sends Bunny to New York to check up on Santop Licorice; it is revealed that Licorice has been on the Knights of Nordica's payroll so as to fight less radical African American leaders such as Dr. Shakespeare Agamemnon Beard and thereby fragment black civil rights leadership. With this ridiculous plot twist, Schuyler seems to be suggesting that African American leaders, with their appeals to racial rhetoric, participate willy-nilly in the perpetuation of racism. When Bunny is "amazed" that "the old crook sold out the race," Max replies, "Hold that race stuff, you're not a shine anymore"; Max later explains to Bunny that while the two must outwardly support the white supremacist agenda, they must covertly not allow either "side"—white or black—to "put the other side out of business" (*BNM* 114–15, 116). Rather, Max wants a racial status quo that will continue to provide a raison d'etre for the Knights of Nordica and maximize the profit potential of the race industry. Thus, Schuyler again underscores a central thesis of the narrative: the idea that the color line is far more significant than the "races" it purportedly separates. Having demonstrated that African Americans can readily "become" white by virtue of a medical procedure and imitation, and that Southern Anglo Americans, if not explicitly identified as white, "sound" just like Southern blacks, Schuyler seems to be suggesting that the racial hierarchy does not correspond to any demonstrable cultural difference between whites and blacks but, rather, is preserved only by the strict maintenance of a socially constructed color line. Thus, with *Black No More*, Schuyler moves into more radically antiracialist territory than Chesnutt and Johnson—whose literature and beliefs retained vestiges of racialism—and, further, anticipates a theory of ethnicity Fredrik Barth would articulate in his 1969 introduction to *Ethnic Groups and Boundaries: The Social Organization of Culture Difference*. Barth argues that it is "the ethnic *boundary* that defines the group, not the cultural stuff that it encloses," which is mutable, arbitrary, and can disintegrate over time anyway. Samira Kawash originally applied Barth's model of ethnicity to African American literature—more specifically Johnson's *The*

Autobiography of an Ex-Coloured Man and especially Nella Larsen's *Passing*, in which "Barth's idea is taken to its limit."[36] I would submit, however, that Schuyler is the most explicit in terms of demonstrably voiding either side of the color line and thereby drawing attention to the almost magical powers of the line itself. Schuyler suggests that the maintenance of this boundary is more than socially pathological; further, it can be exploited for profit, as Max learns from his repeated success in labor racketeering. He collects fifteen thousand dollars from German industrialists to break a strike by publicly questioning the racial purity of the strikers; when Swanson, a white labor leader, is told of the rumors, he protests, in stereotypically black dialect, "Ah haint no damn nigger a-tall . . . Ah'm a white man an' kin prove hit" (*BNM* 125, 126).

This is one of many reversals Schuyler enacts throughout the latter portion of the novel in order to turn soft racial thinking on its head. Temporarily, organized white supremacy rides a wave of public support culminated by the merger of Arthur Snobbcraft's Anglo-Saxon Association with the Knights of Nordica and the 1936 Democratic presidential nomination of Henry Givens with Snobbcraft as the vice-presidential nominee. However, New York insurance company statistician and white supremacist Dr. Samuel Buggerie, with the financial backing of the Anglo-Saxon Association, completes a "nationwide investigation" to "disclose the various non-Nordic strains in the population": contrary to expectations, he discovers that most presumably Anglo "social leaders" have slaves in their family tree (*BNM* 156, 178). When news breaks that Givens and Snobbcraft themselves have black ancestry, there is such a public outcry that the two are compelled to flee the country by airplane. When they run out of fuel and crash-land in rural Mississippi, they blacken up with shoe polish, believing blacks to be so few and far between as to go unnoticed; however, they meet an ironic and gruesome end when they find themselves in the middle of a religious revival whose attendants regret the disappearance of African Americans and are anxious for a lynching (*BNM* 201, 216–18).

Meanwhile, Max Disher's ancestry is revealed when Helen gives birth to a visibly black child. She worries that she has "disgraced" Max, but Max assures her that he is, in fact, "the guilty one." Helen's response to the news is surely an intentionally ironic reversal of convention; rather than experience the usual fit of a hysteria, "Helen felt a wave of relief go

36. Fredrik Barth, "Ethnic Groups and Boundaries," 300; Kawash, *Dislocating the Color Line*, 155.

over her. There was no feeling of revulsion at the thought that her husband was a Negro. There once would have been but that was seemingly
centuries ago when she had been unaware of her remoter Negro ancestry. She felt proud of her Matthew. She loved him more than ever. They
had money and a beautiful brown baby. What more did they need?"
(*BNM* 192). The three move to Mexico and live happily, but this national
recognition of shared ancestry generally does not relieve racial tension.
Rather, it reappears, albeit in a new form, when Dr. Junius Crookman
makes public his discovery that Black-No-More whites are actually *lighter*
than "real" whites. Thus, too-pale whites become the new social pariahs,
and although this reversal of color *hierarchy* seems "staggering" "[t]o a
society that had been taught to venerate whiteness for over three hundred years," it is endurable so long as the color *line* is preserved (*BNM*
219). Predictably, lighter-skinned whites are discriminated against while
those with too-light skin scramble for ways to appear darker so as not to
draw suspicion. A return to racial equilibrium, though heavily ironic, is
suggested by Sisseretta Blandish's return to the beauty industry, this time
as Mrs. Sari Blandine, who begins selling skin stain to "enthusiastically
mulatto-minded" customers (*BNM* 221–22).

Schuyler's racial critique is about as thorough and cutting as it could
have been, and his treatment of race provides one means by which to
understand his generic evolution beyond the conflicted literary antiracialism of Chesnutt and Johnson. According to Stacy Morgan, "Schuyler
approached issues of racial essentialism not with . . . forthrightness . . . ,
but rather through the indirection of an outrageously comic prognosti-
cation of an America quite literally bereft of blacks." Thus, *Black No More*
eschews a realist approach with its emphasis on "the specific and the
detailed in favor of [a] general critique" of race in the United States.
As has been established, any representation of "the specific and the
detailed" from the early twentieth century runs the risk of articulating
racialist thought—something Schuyler generally avoided.[37] At the very
least, Charles Chesnutt could not completely avoid it, and Johnson's
decidedly more ironic, even modernistic, faux *Autobiography* reinforces
racialist ideas the author reiterates in his *real* autobiography. Schuyler's

37. Indeed, much criticism on Schuyler's *Black No More* has focused upon the
novel's satirical war against racial pseudo-science. See Jane Kuenz, "American
Racial Discourse, 1900–1930: Schuyler's *Black No More*" and Morgan, "'The Strange
and Wonderful Workings of Science.'" Morgan, "'The Strange and Wonderful Workings of Science,'" 348; Dickson-Carr, *African-American Satire*, 27; Kuenz, "American
Racial Discourse, 1900–1930," 186.

ideological and aesthetic departure from Johnson is perhaps best under-scored by the former's satirical representation of the latter in *Black No More,* in which Johnson, renamed Dr. Jackson, "wrote long and learned articles, bristling with references, for the more intellectual magazines, in which he sought to prove conclusively that the plantation shouts of Southern Negro peons were superior to any of Beethoven's symphonies and that the city of Benin was the original site of the Garden of Eden" (*BNM* 93). Mocking Johnson's accent, Schuyler has Dr. Jackson give a speech to the National Social Equality League that accuses Crookman and Black-No-More of doing irreparable damage to "the integrity of Negro society" (*BNM* 93–94).

James Weldon Johnson, of course, promoted the appreciation of African American cultural output: the ex-coloured man's failure to do this becomes a grievous shortcoming. But Schuyler, in his drive for com-plete antiracialism, "vehemently rejected the notion that there were major cultural or racial differences between so-called white and black Americans."[38] He had little use for culturally specific approaches to art as championed by writers such as Langston Hughes, who, in "The Negro Artist and the Racial Mountain" (1926), calls for a "true Negro art in America" accomplished by the "truly great Negro artist ... who is not afraid to be himself." In this essay, Hughes praises jazz as "one of the inherent expressions of Negro life in America," coming dangerously close to racial essentialism when he tells of "the eternal tom-tom beating in the Negro soul." This essay was originally published in the *Nation* as a response to Schuyler's infamous critical manifesto, "The Negro-Art Hokum" (1926), in which the author argues that "Negro art 'made in America' is ... non-existent" and that "the Aframerican is merely lamp-blacked Anglo-Saxon" not unlike the culturally assimilated, latter-generation, European American immigrant. According to Schuyler, it is "sheer nonsense to talk about 'racial differences'" between blacks and whites, and by extension, between black art and European American art. Slave songs, spirituals, blues, ragtime, jazz, and the Charleston are more properly known as the "contributions of a caste in a certain section of the country." To argue for the existence of a distinct African American art is to commit a softer version of the same racist sin as white suprema-cist "'scientists' like Madison Grant and Lothrop Stoddard." Jane Kuenz summarizes Schuyler's position well: "Schuyler knows that though ... declarations of difference were the dogma of a good portion of Harlem

38. Hutchinson, *The Harlem Renaissance,* 294.

Renaissance aesthetics, they were also frequently forthcoming from white speakers where they were often prefaced by concerns for preserving the racial integrity of white America, by which is meant its economic and social privilege."[39] Thus, claims to artistic cultural specificity merely give credence to the more virulent forms of racialism.

Occasionally *Black No More* gives voice to a troubled sense of "a rapidly disappearing way of life": namely, the depletion of African American culture due to Crookman's medical procedure.[40] For example, when Max Disher first experiences white New York night life after Black-No-More, he finds "something lacking in these ofay places of amusement or else there was something present that one didn't find in the black-and-tan resorts in Harlem. The joy and abandon here was obviously forced" (*BNM* 40). Max also experiences an occasional "slight feeling of regret that he had left his people forever"—a feeling usually interrupted by bitter memories of his experiences in New York (*BNM* 63). However, these sentiments could easily be dismissed as the interpretations of a fundamentally flawed character. The narrative comes closest to sentimentality during the initial spread of Black-No-More when the narrator relates that "Negro society was in turmoil and chaos. The colored folk, in straining every nerve to get the Black-No-More treatment, had forgotten all loyalties, affiliations and responsibilities," including fraternal organizations, political organizations, and businesses (*BNM* 85–86). The narrator laments, "Gone was the almost European atmosphere of every Negro ghetto: the music, laughter, gaiety, jesting and abandon. Instead, one noted the same excited bustle, wild looks and strained faces to be seen in a war time soldier camp, around a new oil district or before a gold rush. The happy-go-lucky Negro of song and story was gone forever and in his stead was a nervous, money-grubbing black, stuffing away coin in socks, impatiently awaiting a sufficient sum to pay Dr. Crookman's fee" (*BNM* 87). Stacy Morgan points out that the "almost European atmosphere" resists ascription to "a single *racial* (black) disposition" and is, therefore, consistent with Schuyler's antiracialism; however, she also argues that "these seeming lapses in Schuyler's anti-essentialist stance suggest that he was hardly blind to the presence of distinctively African-American lifeways, even if he suppressed their importance in essays like 'The Negro-Art Hokum.'" But "The Negro-Art

39. Langston Hughes, "The Negro Artist and the Racial Mountain," 1268, 1270; Schuyler, "The Negro-Art Hokum," 1171, 1172, 1174; Kuenz, "American Racial Discourse," 182.
40. Miller, Foreword, 7.

Hokum" makes clear that what many commentators take to be *ethnically* or *racially* derived expressions of cultural difference, Schuyler took to be the products of *caste* and *region*. Indeed, as Morgan points out, Schuyler "assiduously eschewed any direct or 'natural' correlation between race and culture." Furthermore, these "seeming lapses" may not be lapses at all when the reader factors in irony. I would submit that the above quote is from a scene in which Schuyler has placed a great deal of ironic distance between himself and the narrator. In reality, Schuyler believed that the aforementioned "happy-go-lucky Negro" was really the creation of "a few writers with a paucity of themes [who have] seized upon imbecilities of the Negro rustics and clowns and palmed them off as authentic and characteristic Aframerican behavior." What African Americans become in *Black No More*—money-grubbing blacks, and then money-grubbing whites—is more a commentary on the universal greed of humanity than it is the elegizing of a lost African American culture. Regardless of what Max Disher or even the narrator may say, Schuyler issues no lament here whatsoever, for, as Kuenz points out, any hint of "racial romanticism" in the novel "is qualified . . . by the fact that the entrance of several million African Americans into the daily mainstream of white America fails to produce any kind of transformative or ennobling effects therein."[41]

Thus, while one might not agree with Schuyler's dismissal of ethnically or racially derived art, in his sustained irony throughout *Black No More* he at least remains theoretically consistent in his attack on racial logic. At the end of the novel—after "black" becomes "white" and "white" becomes, to a significant degree, "black"—all claims to absolute racial difference are discredited. "Whiteness" is revealed to be (as it was for Chesnutt and Johnson) "an essentially empty thing," no longer exclusively linked to acquisitiveness and easily achieved by anyone with the ambition to do so; "blackness" is only so much "hokum"—simultaneously a meaningless honorific and a deadly pejorative. The only thing that remains is the ineffable racial boundary. Fredrik Barth may as well have been addressing *Black No More* when he stated, "boundaries persist despite a flow of personnel across them."[42] However, Schuyler even destabilizes the boundary itself by introducing elements into the text that render the racial binary problematic: for example, the presumably Italian American electrical engineer named Bela Cati, who, in a letter to the

41. Morgan, "'The Strange and Wonderful Workings of Science,'" 341, 342; Schuyler, "The Negro-Art Hokum," 1173; Kuenz, "American Racial Discourse," 186.
42. Kuenz, "American Racial Discourse," 186; Barth, "Ethnic Groups and Boundaries," 294.

NAACP, admits that "[o]nce I myself was very strongly tanned by the sun and a European rural population thought that I was a Negro, too." Although he "did not suffer much," "the situation was disagreeable," and he believes that any "surplus of . . . pigment" could in fact "be removed" (*BNM* 14). Also, when Black-No-More deprives Madame Blandish of nearly all her business, the only remaining customers are "two or three Jewish girls from downtown who came up regularly to have their hair straightened because it wouldn't stand inspection in the Nordic world" (*BNM* 60). Thus, Schuyler not only critiques "whiteness" and "black-ness" in and of themselves, but he also problematizes the location of the boundary that purportedly separates the two. Where *do* those Jews and Italians belong?

While Schuyler's critique of race is undoubtedly thorough, it may be equally troubling to the contemporary reader, influenced as he or she may be by multiculturalism, models of ethnicity, and theories of literary cultural specificity. Schuyler may have been ahead of his time in his progression beyond the nagging essentialisms of Chesnutt and Johnson, but his figuring of African Americans as "lampblacked Anglo-Saxons" and his reduction of a black aesthetic to "hokum" certainly may "appear scandalously heretical," as Werner Sollors would later describe the reception of Fredrik Barth's idea of the ethnic boundary. However, Schuyler's radical deconstruction of race is valuable to the contemporary reader in that it encourages him or her to remain cognizant of the often invisible, or at least seemingly benign, essentialisms that may lie at the heart of every ethnic/racial identity. Walter Benn Michaels has thoroughly addressed this problem in *Our America: Nativism, Modernism, and Pluralism* (1995), in which the author argues that contemporary notions of culturally constructed ethnic identities—as opposed to the now thoroughly discredited notions of biologically constructed racial identities—still rely upon essentialistic appeals to national origin for their very existence. He writes, "The modern concept of culture is not, in other words, a critique of racism; it is a form a racism. And, in fact, as skepticism about the biology of race has increased, it has become—at least among intellectuals—the dominant form of racism." But, as has been amply documented, radical antiracism is easily adaptable, via the phenomenon of neoconservatism, to the wholesale rejection of certain forms of group based activism and policy. At the very least, it can engender an unproductive wishful thinking whereby "racial distinctions . . . might otherwise disappear were we to summon the collective will to renounce race as a philosophical basis of identity." Clearly Schuyler, who later became a McCarthy apologist and regularly attacked Martin Luther King, Jr., in his editorials, reinserted his previously militant antiracialism into a lately adopted paradigm of ultraconservatism. To wit, Schuyler writes in his autobiography, "Relegating spurious racism to limbo, in our future America we need to stress the importance of the individual of whatever color. At best, race is a superstition. There will be no color war here if we will work not to have one, although some kind of color line there may always be, as there is elsewhere in the world."[43]

Thus, a choice presents itself to the student of racial theory: do we engage in antiracialist "wishful thinking" that at best is impractical and at worst denies the "social weight" of race in America; or, do we acknowledge the impact of race, even if this means unavoidably making reference to the theoretically shoddy foundation upon which race's structure is built? By Schuyler's own admission, he lived in a United States in which the "color line" he had theoretically discredited "may always be"; as much as he would have liked to will away the "superstition" of "race," in his life's work, from "The Negro-Art Hokum" to *Black No More* to *Black and Conservative,* he was ultimately unable to avoid the *idea* of race. And the same could certainly be said of Michaels. Ultimately, the work of Schuyler and Michaels is useful not only as an unwitting reminder of the continuing significance of race but also as inspiration to further reworkings of the idea of ethnicity. Like it or not, ethnicity is not going to "go away" any time soon, and those who choose (or are made) to identify as "Italian American," "African American," or "Jewish American" generally do so on the grounds of some collective social narrative that, more or less, corresponds with palpable lived experience.[44] Insofar

43. Sollors, "Foreword: Theories of Ethnicity," xxii; Michaels, *Our America,* 129. For brief statements of Michaels's views on race, both as a "reality" and as a "social construction," see also Michaels, "Response" and "Autobiography of an Ex-White Man: Why Race Is Not a Social Construction." Michael Omi and Howard Winant, *Racial Formation in the United States: From the 1960s to the 1990s,* 128–32; Wald, *Crossing the Line,* 10; Schuyler, *Black and Conservative,* 330, 350, 352.

44. Dickson-Carr, *African-American Satire,* 26; Hutchinson, *The Harlem Renaissance,* 61, 299. Of course, Michaels is not unaware of the everyday import of popular notions of ethnic/racial difference. But his response to critiques of his views that come from social constructionist or multiculturalist perspectives is to sidestep the pragmatics of "ethnicity," "culture," and "race" and to continue to reassert his *theoretical* opposition to them. In a recent interview, he says, "Ever since I started doing *Our America,* people have come along and said, maybe on some level your argument against identity is right, but practically speaking, shouldn't we recognize our identities are in fact important; even though they're in some deep sense wrong, they're socially-constructed; we have them with us, we just can't wish our way out of them?

as these ethnic categories—by choice, or particularly in the case of African Americans, by a combination of choice and external factors—persist, we must attempt to understand them through methodologies that are attentive to the cultural dialectics (indeed, the "cultural stuff" Fredrik Barth summarily dismisses) and the biological essentialisms that produce ethnic identities in the first place. Put simply, future reworkings of ethnicity must acknowledge both the experientially real and the theoretically problematic.

But it's not as if accepting these identities is making things better. I mean, I'm interested in the political consequences of these ideas, but I have no idea of how you go about making the world more consonant with my ideas. Michaels, "Against Identity: An Interview with Walter Benn Michaels."

5

"As If I Were Dead"

Passing into Subjectivity in the Writings of
Ets, Antin, Yezierska, and Barolini

But to marry myself to a man that's a person, I must first make myself
for a person.
— Sara Smolinsky of *Bread Givers*, by Anzia Yezierska

I will make a real human being out of you.
— Alberto Morosini to Marguerite of *Umbertina*, by Helen Barolini

The trope of passing, given the kinds of authorial decisions it requires, reveals larger trends in white ethnic women's realist literary production that are traceable over time. Taken collectively, Marie Hall Ets's *Rosa: The Life of an Immigrant* (1970), Mary Antin's *The Promised Land* (1912), Anzia Yezierska's *Bread Givers* (1925), and Helen Barolini's *Umbertina* (1979) mark a distinct progression in white ethnic female subjective options in American literature. Each of these representative texts reveals varying degrees of engagement with realism and its commitment to detail and the creation of a free-willing subject. However, on their journeys toward self-defined subjectivity, the protagonists encounter not only the nativism described in chapter 3 but also gender subordination derived from both Old World traditions and the New World social order. Each of the four texts exhibits an aesthetic conflict between the protagonist's agency and

her "two-fold . . . struggle . . . against the ethnic barriers set up by the predominant culture in America" and the "double-layered" problem of ethnic and American patriarchy.[1] These texts also demonstrate that as ethnic
American women attain a better sense of self-reflexive awareness—which
can be attributable individually to a better exposure to the liberalizing
influences of education and collectively to a more heightened sense of
place within an ethnic literary tradition—they come to view passing (at
least in the literature they produce) as a possible means to relieve the
tensions of the classic Old World/New World conflict and escape the
patriarchal boundaries both worlds impose. However, ethnic women's
writings in the realist mode ultimately feature characters who come to
reject passing: Italian American and Jewish American women find, for
psychological and sometimes biological reasons, that to shed Old World
attributes is to undergo a kind of cultural "death" that is either undesirable or impossible.

Rosa: The Life of an Immigrant features a woman at the earliest stage of
Italian American—and arguably ethnic—female subjectivity. Generally
uneducated, battered by contentious circumstances, and desperately
struggling to survive in America, Rosa is not allowed the self-reflexive
space to consider passing an option. An apt representative of a white
ethnic women's narrative of acculturation, *Rosa* features a woman who
adapts to American ways by using the freedom she discovers in the United
States along with some retained Old World folkways to fight patriarchy
and to empower herself in the New World. As a literary representation
of early immigrant experience, *Rosa* is distinct from important Jewish
American women's texts such as Antin's *The Promised Land* and Yezierska's *Bread Givers* in that the latter two depict women with greater access
to education and therefore the ability to imagine worlds apart from the
ethnic enclave. The option of passing makes its first appearance in the
Jewish American women's literary tradition with these texts, but it is
deployed unsuccessfully in both cases—in spite of what the author says
in *The Promised Land* and by the author's clear admission in *Bread Givers*.
In both narratives, Old World traditions—to a far greater degree than in
white ethnic male texts—form a deterministic influence the protagonist
is unable to overcome, and this failure is especially bitter in the *Bread
Givers*. Passing does not make its entrée into the Italian American
women's tradition until 1979 with Helen Barolini's *Umbertina*, which features a second-generation woman who attempts to pass as a mainstream

1. Tamburri, *A Semiotic of Ethnicity*, 54.

American. Like *The Promised Land* and especially *Bread Givers*, this text reveals a heightened feminist consciousness in its realistic portrayal of issues of pertinence to ethnic women over four generations. To be sure, *Umbertina* is evidence that "[f]or Italian American women who write, the category of gender functions as an equally necessary lens through which to interpret their negotiation between the Italian familial culture and the American milieu."[2] However, unlike *The Promised Land* and *Bread Givers*, *Umbertina* exhibits a latter-generation tendency to view ethnic heritage not so much as a patriarchal burden—although this possibility is certainly there—but as a generative tool that, when strategically employed, can prove ultimately liberating and empowering.

Rosa and the Uses of *La Via Vecchia*

Rosa: The Life of an Immigrant is in no way a passing narrative, but is rather an acculturation narrative of early immigrant life that is significant in the manner by which it depicts a woman negotiating *la via vecchia* (literally, "the old way," rooted in Italian peasant traditions) and *la via nuova* ("the new way," or the myths and traditions encountered in the United States) in order to adapt to new surroundings in America. However, while traditional accounts of immigration figure the attainment of the latter as coming at the expense of the former, *Rosa* tells the story of a first-generation immigrant Italian woman actively employing the folkways of *la via vecchia* in order better to situate herself as a free agent in the New World. The story was narrated by Rosa Cassettari (1866?-1943) to Marie Hall Ets between 1918 and 1931 when both lived at the Chicago Commons, the former as an elderly tenant, part-time cook, and cleaner, the latter as a graduate student and social worker.[3] As Ets grew acquainted with the friendly Cassettari and her evocative storytelling, she began transcribing the aging immigrant's personal narratives. The result is *Rosa*, an autobiography of Rosa Cassettari's (renamed Cavalleri) girlhood in Bugiarno, Italy; her abusive forced marriage; her emigration to Missouri; and her eventual remarriage and settlement in Chicago, where she endured the burdens of both motherhood and hard wage labor in her fight for survival.

2. Bona, *Claiming a Tradition*, 6.
3. On the reassertion of Old World influences as a means to adjust to life in the New World, see Ferraro, *Ethnic Passages*, chapters 1 and 2. Vaneeta-Marie d'Andrea, "The Life of Rosa Cavalleri: An Application of Abramson's Model of Rootedness/Rootlessness," 116.

Although this text might seem chronologically out of place, its inclusion is defensible on two grounds. First, any discussion of Italian American women's literature that deals with first- and second-generation ethnic women will seem historically anachronistic simply due to the fact that Italian American women did not begin publishing literature on the Italian American experience until 1949 with Mari Tomasi's *Like Lesser Gods*, an account of assimilative problems encountered by immigrant men and women in a Vermont laboring community of stonecutters. Following Tomasi's deft lead in depicting literary characters struggling to make sense of a New World existence despite Old World influences, other Italian American women have committed themselves to ethnic subject matter and the literary possibilities it provides. Scholars such as Helen Barolini, Mary Jo Bona, Edvige Giunta, Mary Ann Vigilante Mannino, and Mary Frances Pipino have uncovered and described a tradition of Italian American women's literature—including works such as Octavia Waldo's *A Cup of the Sun* (1961), Diana Cavallo's *A Bridge of Leaves* (1961), Marion Benasutti's *No Steadyjob for Papa* (1966), Dorothy Bryant's *Miss Giardino* (1978), Helen Barolini's *Umbertina* (1979), and Tina De Rosa's *Paper Fish* (1980)—which, as time progresses, reveals a willingness to explore a variety of aesthetic and political strategies, most notably modernism and feminism. Despite its historical lateness, *Rosa* uncannily serves as a kind of after-the-fact ur-text for an Italian American women's literary tradition composed of authors considered to be "literary descendants of Rosa and her experiences." Aesthetically, like much immigrant literature, *Rosa* is equal parts fictive realism and historical autobiography in its depiction of the immigrant's immediate experience of migration and adaptation. In keeping with the text's realistic thrust, Ets is carefully attuned to speech patterns and attempts, as closely as possible in English, to convey a sense of Rosa's dialectic flair. There is also a keen sense, as one finds in much realism, of the author's necessary mediation in the depiction of "reality." Ets's introduction readily confesses this, for though the author wished directly to convey Rosa's "heavy dialect," "this proved too difficult for the reader." Therefore, Ets "corrected and simplified the text, trying at the same time not to lose the character and style of [Rosa's] spoken words."[4]

---

4. An earlier American woman writer of Italian descent, Frances Winwar (Vinciguerra), generally avoided Italian American subject matter in novels such as *The Ardent Flame* (1927), *The Golden Round* (1928), and *Pagan Interval* (1929). Mary Frances Pipino, "I Have Found My Voice": The Italian-American Woman Writer, 34. Rudolph J. Vecoli, Introduction, vi; Marie Hall Ets, *Rosa: The Life of an Italian Immigrant*, 7. Hereafter cited in the text as *R*.

The story that follows is clearly the stuff of immigrant realism. Through Ets, Rosa tells of having been left for adoption in a Milan hospital, only to be adopted by Papa Giulur and Maddalena Cortesi of Bugiarno, Italy. Her girlhood is characterized by fond memories of village existence— the vivid storytelling of the men, Beppo playing on his concertina, the unconditional love of her adopted parents—scattered against a back-drop of poverty and hardship. Rosa is put to work early in order to as-sist in the upkeep of the family. As a young girl, she is sent to a convent where she becomes skilled as a silkmaker.

Early in life, Rosa is schooled in the determinisms of racism and gen-der oppression. She is claimed by her real mother, a well-to-do Milanese actress named Diodata. At first sight, Diodata cannot believe that Rosa is her child, for she has "the brown skin of a peasant"—a physiognomic sign of Rosa's class status (R 53). Diodata takes Rosa anyway, but Rosa bravely manages to escape back to Bugiarno. Rosa is taught at an early age that women are providentially subservient to men. She asks her Zia Teresa, "Why are the men always so mean?" Her aunt replies, "The woman is made to be the servant of man. . . . The man is the man and the woman must obey him, that's all" (R 80). Don Dominic explains to Rosa that wives should not "talk back" to their husbands because "God gave the man the right to control the woman. . . . It's a sin for the wife not to obey" (R 82). Even as children the Italian peasants must behave accord-ing to prescribed gender roles. Rosa explains, "Girls were not allowed to speak to boys. The boy and the girl, they were like the rich and the poor together, like the man and the woman, like the North Italian and the South Italian—the boy was so much higher than the girl. You didn't dare do anything to a boy" (R 86). Thus, the divide between males and females is as gaping as that between the rich and poor of late-nineteenth-century Italy and as fixed as the racial difference suggested by the referencing of northern Italians and their presumably inferior southern counterparts. Indeed, "Rosa's narrative is filled with fear of men and of the Italian authorities who imposed their will upon her. This power of men to con-trol women comes from God." It is partially through his providential determinism that *Rosa*, like Giuseppe Cautela's *Moon Harvest*, starts to take on romantic overtones. Mary Frances Pipino attributes this mix of romance and realism in Italian American literature to power brokers of American literary culture who have traditionally favored the romantic mode and have required that authors do the same, even as they pay "loving attention to the detail of Italian immigrant life." I would add that part of this very "detail" involves the description of Italian folk beliefs, in which God, the Virgin Mary, and the saints are viewed as active agents in everyday life; *mal occhio* ("evil eye") is an invisible but nonetheless legitimate threat to one's well-being; and a fatalistic sense of *destino* ("destiny") pervades individual and collective consciousness. Furthermore, insofar as the Italian American narrative is rooted in the oral traditions of southern Italian villages, with their "vivid tales of saints and miracles, of ogres and witches, of wars between Christians and Saracens," a palpably romantic hue is unavoidably added to otherwise realistic texts.[5]

In *Rosa*, Italy is depicted as a place of impossibility, in which God-given barriers of race, gender, and class restrict the freedom of the lowly. As a silkmaker, Rosa feels unable to talk to her boss and is surprised when he initiates conversation with her: "a high man like that talking to a poor girl like me!" (*R* 141). Likewise, Rosa is unable to resist an arranged marriage with the abusive and grotesque Santino. He leaves the village to work in Missouri iron mines while Rosa stays behind, giving birth to a son, Francesco. When Santino sends for her, her mother insists she go, lest she sin against God's will (*R* 160). Once in America, Rosa takes on one of the lowliest of immigrant subject positions as a woman, an Italian, and an uneducated peasant.[6] However, the New World also represented for many European immigrants freedom from Old World restrictions. As an American, Rosa uses the libratory tendencies of America along with strategically deployed aspects of Old World folkways to survive in the New World.

Rosa had taken note when a "poor man" who had been to America not only "talk[ed] back" to an unjust landlord but also won a court case against him. The women of Bugiarno had explained to Rosa, "That's what America does for the poor!" (*R* 120). Rosa believes that America granted her the power to speak through hitherto impermeable barriers. For example, she says that "[a]fter living in America I was not afraid to talk to the rich" as she had been in Italy (*R* 118). In *Rosa*, America is figured traditionally as a land of opportunity for the oppressed, "where everyone could find work! Where wages were so high no one had to go

---

5. Gardaphè, *Italian Signs*, 35; Pipino, *"I Have Found My Voice,"* 34. On southern Italian folk religion, see Gambino, *Blood of My Blood*, chapter 6; Lawrence Di Stasi, *Mal Occhio: The Underside of Vision*; and Lucia Chiavola Birnbaum, *Black Madonnas: Feminism, Religion and Politics in Italy*. On Rosa's religiosity, see Gardaphè, *Italian Signs*, 33. Vecoli, "The Italian-American Literary Subculture: An Historical and Sociological Analysis," 7.

6. Mary Ann Mannino, *Revisionary Identities: Strategies of Empowerment in the Writing of Italian/American Women*, 20.

hungry! Where all men were free and equal and where even the poor could own land!" (*R* 164). Furthermore, to Rosa, America is a place where, unlike Italy, "the people are not afraid" and where "the high people teach the poor people and tell them not to be so scared" (*R* 189).

Rosa's narrative suggests that she uses this newfound freedom as a means to create agency for herself, despite her lowly status. However, she also retains her Italian folk religious beliefs—arguably her most enduring link to her ethnic past—and uses them to fight patriarchal oppression in the New World. In other words, Rosa's "social and self-reconstruction emerge through both the American emphasis on individualism and the Italian religious humanism she has been taught but never received." Ironically, it was Don Dominic, practically a personification of traditional Italian patriarchy, who provided Rosa with the very means by which she would fight gender oppression. He had taught her that "[o]nly God and the Madonna come first. Only when the husband wants his wife to sin against God and the Madonna she must not obey him" (*R* 82). Thus, when the foulmouthed, blasphemous Santino crudely asks his wife to remove the crucifix from the couple's bedroom because he wishes to "sleep with his own wife without God watching him from the wall," she refuses (*R* 174). Likewise, when Santino buys a brothel and wants Rosa to manage it, she again refuses, exclaiming: "Never! Never! I belong to God and the Madonna! You can't give me to the Devil!" (*R* 198–99). Soon, Santino becomes so insufferably violent toward Rosa and their children that she leaves for Chicago with a man named Gionin, who eventually marries her after she divorces Santino. Thus, "Rosa leaves her husband and overcomes oppressions of class and dogma. For her, that [involves] an ongoing reintegration of humanistic folk and religious values with democratic ideals."[7]

Loathe to accept charity, Rosa relies upon her resourcefulness and her Catholic "good faith"—along with the occasional strike of good fortune—to give her strength in an America where she fears the people have lost their "faith" and "strong religion" (*R* 213, 44). Her religious faith even allows her to face death stoically: "When it's my time I will die willing, without fighting God," she insists (*R* 253). The narrative concludes with Rosa's reaffirmation of the Madonna's role in "tak[ing] care of us poor women," followed by an apt summary, in Rosa's distinct Italian Ameri-

---

7. D'Andrea, "The Life of Rosa Cavalleri," 119–20; Josephine Gattuso Hendin, "Social Constructions and Aesthetic Achievements: Italian American Writing as Ethnic Art," 15.

can dialect, of her acculturation. In her view, the New World has not only granted her the agency to take control of her own life but also allowed her to see anew her Old World experience, which can never be fully forgotten: "Only one wish more I have: I'd love to go in *Italia* again before I die. Now I speak English good like an American I could go anywhere— where millionaires go and high people. I would look the high people in the face and ask them what questions I'd like to know. I wouldn't be afraid now—not of anybody.... They wouldn't dare hurt me now I come from America. Me, that's why I love America. That's what I learned in America: not to be afraid" (*R* 254). If *Rosa* functions partially as a reclamation of *italianità*, it can also be viewed more generally as a narrative of the "emergent self." But Rosa's limited education, coupled with the sheer hardship of much of her life, did not fully allow her the space—perhaps even the desire—to understand herself self-reflexively as an Italian American. However, second-generation Italian American women writers— such as Mari Tomasi and Marion Benasutti—"enjoyed greater control of the language of the new country" and were thus "better able to forge an identity that essentially was a synthesis of [Italian and American] worldviews." With this greater access to the fruits of the social and educational mainstream comes the recognition of passing as a potential lifestyle option and literary trope. The Italian American women's immigrant tale, with its firm rooting in Old World oral culture, does not allow for this. In fact, passing does not emerge as a viable literary device in Italian American women's literature until Helen Barolini's *Umbertina*. The Jewish American women's literary tradition, however, is notably different in this regard, as Jewish American women writers "tend to stress the possibilities for change and positive self-creation"—even more so than "their male counterparts," who "are often more ambivalent about the relocation."[8] Indeed, "change and positive self-creation" are central thematic features of the next two texts considered.

"When I Passed as an American Among Americans": Mary Antin in the Promised Land

Mary Antin (1881–1949) was born in Polotzk, Russia, and immigrated as a girl to Boston, only later to live in New York. She is known for her advocacy of immigrant interests, her progressivism, and also her strict

8. Pipino, *"I Have Found My Voice,"* 8; Gardaphè, *Italian Signs,* 36; Priscilla Wald, "Of Crucibles and Grandfathers: The Eastern European Immigrants," 60.

assimilationism, expressed most famously in her autobiographical *The Promised Land* (1912). Unlike *Rosa, The Promised Land* is a full-fledged passing narrative since the will to fully de-ethnicize exists in a manner it could not possibly for Rosa Cassettari. Still, the two texts, though published some fifty-eight years apart, are comparable. Both are autobiographies, and both involve emigration, at roughly the same time period, to urban America—Rosa to the Midwest, Mary Antin to the Northeast. Much of the difference between the two texts derives from the differing life circumstances of Antin and Cassettari. Compared to Rosa, Antin was younger, more literate, and better educated; therefore, she had a better sense of the cultural options available to her in the New World.

Cultural histories of Jewish American women share a consensus on the value of public education in the assimilation of the immigrant, which generally encouraged a removal of all indications of ethnic difference. Part of this involved learning a new language, and Jewish children proved especially adept at this. Young Jewish women were no less enthusiastic than men about American education, as they were very likely to have acquired some literacy in Eastern Europe. The same could not be said of Italian American young women, who, for both cultural and economic reasons, were far less likely to have received the amount of education enjoyed by their Russian Jewish counterparts. First, while Jewish American women were conditioned in a shtetl culture that valued literacy, intellectualism, and learning for its own sake, southern Italian women came from a mostly oral, and generally illiterate, background. Thus, "Jewish culture . . . , because of its appreciation of education, enabled . . . immigrants to benefit from American schools" in ways southern Italian culture could not. Second, unlike southern Italian *contadini,* Jewish immigrants, though poor, were far more likely to have professional experience as craftsmen or business owners—experience that required literacy. This business experience made Jews better equipped financially to send their children to schools in America. Furthermore, Jewish American women benefited more educationally from co-ethnic organizations—often established by better-assimilated German Jewish predecessors—than did Italian American women. Some scholars have even suggested that, overall, Jewish American women were products of a "centripetal" family culture that encouraged "involvement in American society," as opposed to the "centrifugal," "insular" family dynamics of Italian Americans.[9]

9. Sydney Stahl Weinberg, *The World of Our Mothers: The Lives of Jewish Immigrant Women,* 113, 169; Rose Laub Coser, Laura S. Anker, and Andrew J. Perrin, *Women of*

These findings are certainly consistent with the immigrant narratives of this chapter, for while Rosa Cassettari empowers herself through an active retention of Old World folkways, Mary Antin of *The Promised Land* and Sara Smolinsky of *Bread Givers* attempt to overcome the adversity of the New World by carrying the centripetal orientation toward its logical extreme—by passing. Sydney Stahl Weinberg cites case studies reporting that young Italian women tended to view themselves as "passive" and family-oriented while Jewish women "described themselves as active agents with control over their own lives."[10] This is witnessed not only in the ability of Antin and Yezierska to tell their own stories (as opposed to Rosa Cassettari, whose story is told through Marie Hall Ets), but also in the unabashed manner by which they attempt to transcend their Old World origins.

Antin's often-cited opening paragraph starkly dramatizes the doubly significant act of will signaled by rendering one's own story of self-fashioning into narrative: "I was born, I have lived, and I have been made over. Is it not time to write my life's story? I am just as much out of the way as if I were dead, for I am absolutely other than the person whose story I have to tell. Physical continuity with my earlier self is no disadvantage. I could speak in the third person and not feel that I was masquerading. I can analyze my subject, I can reveal everything; for *she*, and not *I*, is my real heroine. My life I have still to live; her life ended when mine began." Indeed, Antin believes that she has been "made over"—that is, she has passed—so successfully as to be "absolutely other" than her former immigrant self, who can now be subjected to an icy sociological gaze not unlike that of Dr. Olney or the ex-coloured man. Because of declarations such as this, a number of scholars have located Antin within a general tendency of immigrant writers to absorb unquestioningly American mythology. However, Kirsten Wasson has noted that "there are cracks in [Antin's] 'conversion,'" most notably expressed in her descriptive nostalgia for her native Russia.[11] Indeed, Antin's own assertions in

---

Courage: Jewish and Italian Immigrant Women in New York, 4, 36, 44–45, 48; Miriam Cohen, *Workshop to Office: Two Generations of Italian Women in New York City, 1900–1950*, 139, 142; Kathie Friedman-Kasaba, *Memories of Migration: Gender, Ethnicity, and Work in the Lives of Jewish and Italian Women in New York, 1870–1924*, 134, 187.

10. Weinberg, *The World of Our Mothers*, 190.

11. Mary Antin, *The Promised Land*, xix. Hereafter cited in the text as *PL*. Dearborn, *Pocahontas's Daughters*, 71–72; Janet Handler Burstein, *Writing Mothers, Writing Daughters: Tracing the Maternal in Stories by American Jewish Women*, 28; Browder, *Slippery Characters*, 151–52; Kirsten Wasson, "Mary Antin (1881–1949)," 17.

The Promised Land contradict the notion that she has fully converted. For all of her insistence that she has passed into the mainstream and become "absolutely other," Antin views herself as the "spiritual offspring of the marriage within [her] conscious experience of the Past and the Present" (*PL* xix). At the very least, then, her sense of self is still informed by a "Past" she had supposedly jettisoned. As an immigrant, she believes she is one of the "strands of the cable that binds the Old World to the New" (*PL* xxi). But the Old World is not only unforgotten but also still influential; by her own admission, she wishes to "be of to-day," for "[i]t is painful to be consciously of two worlds." Even her impulse to assimilate is expressed as a product of her essentialistically conceived ethnic difference: "The Wandering Jew in me seeks forgetfulness" (*PL* xxii).

But "forgetfulness" is not to be had, for the memories of the Old Country are too strong. And these memories create a general sense of the Russian Pale of Settlement as a place of confinement, oppression, and impossibility—much like Rosa's peasant Italy. In addition to poverty, hardship, and ignorance, however, Antin and family had to contend with the anti-Jewish violence that plagued late-nineteenth-century Russia. Antin's recollections of the Russia she both dwelled within and was alienated from are often blunt and direct: "in Russia lived the Czar, and a great many cruel people; and in Russia were the dreadful prisons from which people never came back" (*PL* 3). When she first learns of the term "Pale of Settlement," she learns to understand it in terms of confinement: "within this area the Czar commanded me to stay, with my father and mother and friends, and all other people like us. We must not be found outside the Pale, because we were Jews" (*PL* 5).

However, in the Pale of Settlement, Mary is given the cultural tools that will eventually aid her assimilation in the New World. Beyond "physical comfort and social standing," Mary's parents sought to give their daughters a liberal education that would allow them to imagine cultural alternatives beyond the ones in which they currently lived. Antin attributes her parents' motivation to the liberalizing influence of the intellectual urban centers her father had visited in Russia (*PL* 75–76). In this regard, then, Antin holds a distinct advantage over Rosa Cassettari, whose one earlier exposure to secular urban modernity in the Milan apartment of her biological mother produces a sensation akin to horror that leaves her praying to the Madonna for deliverance (*R* 63–64). Antin, on the other hand, revels in the educational opportunities made available to her. In a chapter entitled "The Boundaries Stretch," Antin lives with relatives in Vitebsk for an extended period of time, during which she comes into contact with secular books and learns to love literature. This has a profoundly liberalizing effect on her outlook that helps prepare her for her eventual journey to America. Her father had gone alone to the United States, hoping to earn enough to send for his whole family. When he manages to scrape together enough money for the passage, Antin's expectations of America are typical of immigrant literature: "So at last I was going to America! Really, really going at last! The boundaries burst. The arch of heaven soared. A million suns shone out for every star. The winds rushed in from outer space, roaring in my ears, 'America! America!'" (*PL* 162). In Antin's imagination, America will break the confinement that has defined her life.

At first the tenements of Boston—with their "unkempt, half-washed, toiling, unaspiring foreigners"—seem to replicate the confinement and subservience Antin knew in the Russian Pale of Settlement. But Antin assures the reader that this spiritual residence within the urban American Pale is only temporary: "The well-versed metropolitan knows the slums as a sort of house of detention for poor aliens, where they live on probation till they can show a certificate of good citizenship" (*PL* 183). While on "probation," Antin engages in the requisite cultural assimilation that will allow her to enter the American mainstream. In fact, a significant portion of the plot is propelled by Antin's many acts of cultural assimilation. The children begin to learn English in public schools (*PL* 186). Then, in a "dazzlingly beautiful palace" of a department store— that quintessential locale of American capitalism and democratic self-fashioning—Mary and her siblings "exchanged our hateful homemade European costumes, which pointed us out as 'greenhorns' to the children on the street, for real American machine-made garments." Antin associates the changing of clothing with the changing of names: "With our despised immigrant clothing we shed also our impossible Hebrew names" (*PL* 187). With this curt statement, Antin suggests that both acts are two equally important parts of the assimilation of the immigrant, and that both acts must be conducted as passionlessly as possible. By and large, second-generation Jewish American children gladly took Anglicized versions of Jewish names in order to better fit in.[12] Accordingly, after consulting with a "committee of our friends," "Maryashe" becomes "Mary," and her "impossible" surname becomes the shortened, Anglicized, and "dignified" "Antin" (*PL* 187–88). As if to demonstrate further her growing Anglophilia, Antin devotes a chapter aptly entitled "Initiation" to her

12. Weinberg, *The World of Our Mothers*, 114.

budding love affair with the English language and the literature written in it (*PL* 207–8). Significantly, Antin becomes fascinated with American literature: the stories of Louisa Alcott and the verses of Longfellow are mentioned specifically (*PL* 257, 215).

Unlike Rosa Cassettari, Antin secularizes herself to the point that religion no longer holds any significance for her (*PL* 241, 331–32). Instead, Antin learns to find answers in modes of secular inquiry she associates with America, as opposed to the religious orthodoxy of the Russian Pale. Unworried by the secularism she encounters in America, she praises the constitutional separation of church and state (*PL* 244). This is one of many instances in which Antin demonstrates the extent of her assimilation by declaring unequivocal love for American traditions and institutions. In a chapter called "My Country," Antin talks of voraciously reading patriotic literature: George Washington, the consummate American in her eyes, becomes a role model for her (*PL* 224–25). Later in the narrative, Antin praises the fairness of the American justice system: "'Liberty and justice for all.' Three cheers for the Red, White, and Blue!" (*PL* 260). Antin also celebrates the myth of American social mobility, which she sees as an effective means to counter the restriction and immobility of the Russian Pale. To Antin, "[p]overty was a superficial, temporary matter; it vanished at the touch of money. Money in America was plentiful; it was only a matter of getting some of it, and I was on my way to the mint" (*PL* 297). Antin unequivocally accepts the American myth of success, proclaiming, "That is what America was for. The land of opportunity it was, but opportunities must be used, must be grasped, held, squeezed dry" (*PL* 353). Antin's journey into the world of success American-style goes by way of Barnard College in New York City, where the narrative concludes. In a concluding chapter filled with patriotic declarations entitled "The Heritage," Antin describes entering college—the narrative's final act of cultural assimilation—as the means by which she emerges from the "endless ages" of the Old World and enters the New World. Not merely Antin's ticket into the white middle class, college will allow her full participation in an American democratic heritage she has grown to cherish (*PL* 364).

However, the limits to her assimilation are evidenced in her inability to understand her American experience except through comparison to the Old World. It may be that her "spirit is not tied to the monumental past," but that does not stop her from continuing to lay claim to it even in the narrative's final sentence (*PL* 364). She is continually troubled by memories of Russia. Earlier in the narrative, she confesses, "In after years, when I passed as an American among Americans, if I was suddenly made aware of the past that lay forgotten,—if a letter from Russia, or a paragraph in the newspaper, or a conversation overhead in the street-car, suddenly reminded me of what I might have been,—I thought it miracle enough that I, Mashke, the granddaughter of Raphael the Russian, born to a humble destiny, should be at home in an American metropolis, be free to fashion my own life, and should dream my dreams in English phrases" (*PL* 197). Antin claims to "pass as an American"—even going so far as to use the very terminology of passing—but cannot understand her ostensibly new identity except through reference to the old. As the "granddaughter of Raphael the Russian," Antin holds to an essentialistic notion of Jewish identity, in which the "wandering Jew" of the first chapter later admits to entertaining the possibility that "the faith of Israel is a heritage that no heir in the direct line has the power to alienate from his successors. Even I, with my limited perspective, think it doubtful if the conversion of the Jew to any alien belief or disbelief is ever thoroughly accomplished" (*PL* 249). So there are, by Antin's own admission, limits to the ability of Jews to pass in America. In fact, the whole of Antin's often contradictory assertions about identity seems to suggest that Jewish Americans occupy a racial middle ground between the white mainstream and other more visually marked ethnicities. In the chapter titled "A Child's Paradise," Antin casually assumes that if she were a Jewish boy, she would probably be in a street gang that occasionally harassed "Chinky Chinaman" at the local laundry (*PL* 261).

In the narrative, Antin expresses the will to pass, and even suggests that she has succeeded at doing so. After all, the mere publication of her memoirs indicates she indeed can "dream [her] dreams in English phrases." However, as I have tried to show, her other statements about the nature of Jewish identity and about her native Russia evince a continual need to view the New World through her experience of the Old; the very title's referencing of Exodus is further evidence of this. According to Priscilla Wald, this coexistence of oaths to the completeness of assimilation and evidence to the contrary is not only unsurprising, but typical of immigrant narratives, which "manifest in varying degrees both the effort to suppress it and the impossibility of doing so."[13] This very impossibility greatly mitigates Antin's would-be narrative of American success and self-fashioning. Of course, considerations of gender would further complicate the picture, but this is conspicuously understated in

13. Wald, *Constituting Americans*, 249.

the autobiography. In Anzia Yezierska's *Bread Givers*, however, the story is considerably different; in fact, female gender not only contributes to a strong deterministic undercurrent in the narrative but also hampers the full assimilation the narrator desires.

The Weight of Generations:
Anzia Yezierska and the Ineludible Jewish Essence

The history of ethnic American women's literature reveals a history of women attempting to write themselves into subjectivity, or as Mary Dearborn would have it, a history of the mute Pocahontas's literary descendants giving voice to the exigencies of ethnic female selfhood. For early Jewish American women writers, any such narrative that purports to invest the protagonist with any degree of agency necessarily involves resisting the oppressive patriarchy of Orthodox Judaism, which is often personified in a father figure whose characterization skirts the boundary between realist description and romantic biblical typology. *Bread Givers* is perhaps the best fictionalization of the many struggles undergone by the Jewish American female protagonist who seeks to fight the double-marginalization of ethnic womanhood, and many scholars have examined Anzia Yezierska's writing from this very perspective. I would argue that the struggles associated with ethnic difference and gender are more clearly and dramatically delineated in *Bread Givers* than in *The Promised Land*. First, protagonist Sara Smolinsky confronts an unsympathetic American society that looked upon the immigrant with suspicion. Second, Sara must resist the "pious tyranny" of her father, Reb Smolinsky, and by extension all of Orthodox Jewish patriarchy. Third, in order for Sara to achieve her career goals, she must resist becoming like her mother, who is, if not thoroughly, at least generally submissive to her role as a Jewish American woman. This struggle was by no means simple, for "women who wanted to break out of these old patterns violated not only the expectations of their own immigrant community, but also American social prescription that confirmed dependent roles for women at the turn of the century."[14]

14. Dearborn, *Pocahontas's Daughters*, Introduction and chapter 1; Gay Wilentz, "Cultural Mediation and the Immigrant's Daughter: Anzia Yezierska's *Bread Givers*," 33–34; Carol B. Schoen, *Anzia Yezierska*, 7–8; Louise Levitas Henriksen, *Anzia Yezierska: A Writer's Life*, 216; Burstein, *Writing Mothers*, 7; Sylvia Barack Fishman, "The Faces of Women: An Introductory Essay," 27; Alice Kessler-Harris, Introduction, xix.

The novel begins in an immigrant household in a Jewish ghetto of Lower East Side New York. In *Bread Givers*, Reb Smolinsky expects his daughters to work—in effect, to be the "bread givers" of the household—while he stays home to study the Talmud, the holiest and most noble of occupations according to Orthodox Jewish standards. The sheer fury of Reb Smolinsky's commands and the utter disdain he shows for his wife and daughters present Sara with nothing short of a "development dilemma of a woman whose studious rabbinical father never affirmed, or encouraged, or supported her desire to study: never recognized her as a subject like himself."[15]

More basic than the struggle for subjectivity, however, is the struggle for survival: the Smolinsky family lives in desperate poverty. When the novel begins, they are anxiously expecting Bessie, the hardest-working daughter, to find a new job in order to make rent.[16] Meanwhile, sister Mashah returns home with a new hat—a gross extravagance for the Smolinskys—and stories of the middle-class life the family desires. It is here that the realist convention of cataloguing middle-class consumption comes not in the form of objects already owned, but in the desire for them: "Mashah came home with stories that in rich people's homes they had silver knives and forks, separate, for each person. And new-ironed tablecloths and napkins every time they ate on them. And rich people had marble bathtubs in their own houses, with running hot and cold water all day and night long so they could take a bath any time they felt like it, instead of having to stand on a line before the public bath-house, as we had to do when we wanted a bath for the holidays. But these millionaire things were so far over our heads that they were like fairy tales" (*BG* 5–6). Mashah may seem somewhat ridiculous in her desire for extravagance when basic need is the more pressing concern; however, her material desire is nonetheless consistent with the family's drive toward the middle class, which as Thomas J. Ferraro has convincingly argued, is the determining factor in the novel's status as immigrant social realism.[17]

The daughters and mother, however, already beleaguered by inferior class and ethnic status, are further oppressed by the strict patriarchal order of their household, which is continually expressed in Reb Smolinsky's angry oaths and orders. Thus, an aspect of Jewish American womanhood that is barely implied in *The Promised Land* is made explicit in

15. Burstein, *Writing Mothers*, 30.
16. Anzia Yezierska, *Bread Givers*, 1. Hereafter cited in the text as *BG*.
17. See Ferraro, *Ethnic Passages*, chapter 2.

Bread Givers. Narrator Sara explains, "The prayers of his daughters didn't count because God didn't listen to women. Heaven and the next world were only for men. Women could get into Heaven because they were wives and daughters of men. Women had no brains for the study of God's Torah, but they could be the servants of men who studied the Torah. Only if they cooked for the men, and washed for the men, and didn't nag or curse the men out of their homes; only if they let the men study the Torah in peace, then, maybe they could push themselves into Heaven with the men, to wait on them there" (*BG* 9–10). Any woman struggling for self-definition and success independent of the family necessarily confronted the father's tyranny. Ferraro has argued that Reb Smolinsky's strictly enforced patriarchy stems not only from his attempt to transplant Old World traditions into a New World context but also from his attempt to use these very traditions for capitalistic gain.[18] He becomes first a traditional matchmaker for daughters Bessie, Fania, and Mashah, then a matchmaker for profit. Reb Smolinsky is not unlike Rosa Cassettari, who uses Old World religious faith in order to survive in the New World. However, while Rosa uses these traditions to resist patriarchy, Reb uses them to replicate it in his new surroundings. And his ambitions are clearly greater than Rosa's. When he buys a grocery store (that the reader later learns is empty of goods—one of many mistakes Reb makes as business owner and matchmaker), he fancies himself in the tradition of Gilded Age magnates like "Rockefeller, or Morgan, or any of those millionaires [who] made their start in America . . . with empty hands" (*BG* 133).

Confronted with their father's tyranny, the Smolinsky daughters are presented with a choice as applicable to the logic of social realism as to their family's economic motivations: to obey or to resist their father's demands. After selecting lovers on their own, each of whom Reb Smolinsky cruelly rejects, Bessie, Fania, and Mashah consent to arranged marriages with a grotesque fish peddler, a free-spending gambler, and a fake-diamond salesman, respectively—each of which proves disastrous. Sara, however, had long since believed herself to be "different from [her] sisters": while they obediently endure his abuse, Sara discovers she is increasingly unable to (*BG* 65). In a brazenly rebellious passage, Sara lashes out at her father and God—the ultimate symbol of the Orthodox Jewish patriarchy she has come to loathe. If she takes a lover, it will be "an American-born man who was his own boss. And would let me be my own boss"—a feminist riff on the assimilative/sexual desire of the

18. Ibid., 60.

male characters of chapter 3, who wish to claim ownership of American-ized women as part of their project of social mobility (*BG* 66).

Sara appeals to the libratory power of the New World in order to resist the patriarchy of the Old. When she considers leaving the household, she recalls all that she and her sisters had endured for seventeen years: "Should I let him crush me as he crushed them? No. This is America, where children are people," Sara concludes (*BG* 135). Unlike Rosa Cassettari, Sara has no use for Old World traditions, for they have not abated but have only contributed to gender oppression in her life. Thus, she attempts to will not only her own success but also her very subjectivity by utterly rejecting all Old World influences. According to Sara, only in America can she and others like her be "people." Reb Smolinsky—who dubs his prodigal daughter "*Blut-und-Eisen*," or "blood and iron," for her stubborn resistance—attempts to reassert his patriarchal authority. When Sara tells him of her desire to leave home, he says, "No girl can live without a father or a husband to look out for her. It says in the Torah, only through a man has a woman an existence. Only through a man can a woman enter Heaven" (136–37). Sara responds with a powerful statement of realist free will from a decidedly feminist perspective: "I'm smart enough to look out for myself. It's a new life now. In America, women don't need men to boss them" (*BG* 137). And later, "Thank God, I'm not living in olden times. Thank God, I'm living in America! You made the lives of the other children! I'm going to make my own life! . . . My will is as strong as yours. I'm going to live my own life. Nobody can stop me. I'm not from the old country. I'm American!" (*BG* 137–38).

Sara's rebellious choice reaps hard-earned rewards her sisters would never know. In a classic example of the generic conflictedness one finds in immigrant realism, Sara's sisters enter plots of naturalistic decline precipitated by their unhappy marriages to unworthy husbands their father chose for them. Bessie is miserable and overburdened with childbearing and housework, Fania is a trophy wife for Morris Lipkin, and Mashah's experience with "the grind of poverty harden[s] her face" (*BG* 149). Toward the end of the narrative, the once-beautiful Mashah is described as a "ragged *yenteh*" while the plain Bessie looks "grayer and drabber than ever before" (*BG* 247).

The first part of *Bread Givers* is entitled "Hester Street," to signify the geographical and ethnic rooting of Sara and her family. The second part, "Between Two Worlds," depicts Sara's hard-fought struggle to resist the fate of her sisters and make a new life for herself in the New World. She takes work as an ironer and attends night school, dreaming of one day going to college—"her own ticket into the middle classes"—to become a schoolteacher.[19] Unlike her sisters, Sara views professional success—which she views as part of her struggle for subjectivity—as a prerequisite for even considering marriage. As she tells her mother, "Don't worry. I'll even get married some day. But to marry myself to a man that's a person, I must first make myself for a person" (*BG* 172). Unlike her sisters, she is able to reject a potential suitor, Max Goldstein. Sara discovers that Goldstein knows only "the boom, boom, boom, of his real-estate schemes" and cares little for her interests (*BG* 195). A somewhat more sympathetic reworking of David Levinsky, Lipkin "could buy anything," and Sara worries she would "only be another piece of property" to him (*BG* 199). In this way, she resists falling into the naturalistic plots of decline followed by her sisters.

Part of her personal transformation involves creating the visual effect of having entered the New World. Like Mary Antin, Sara goes to an American department store to buy the necessary clothing and accoutrements, and in yet another scene of self-evaluation before the mirror, Sara tells us:

> I took my little penny savings, and during lunch hour I went to the nearest department store. I bought lipstick, rouge, powder. A lace collar for my waist. Even red roses for my hat. Late into the night I spent fixing myself up, pinning the roses on my hat, trying on my lace collar this way and that, to show off the whiteness of my throat. A wildness possessed me to make up for the pale, colourless years. I saw myself in bright red and dazzling green and gold.... My fingers trembled, and my eyes burned through the mirror as I began daubing on lipstick and rouge. I looked in the glass at the new self I had made. Now I was exactly like the others! Red lips, red cheeks, even red roses under the brim of my hat. Blackened lashes, darkened eyebrows. Soft, white lace at my neck. Ah! What a different picture! No old maid here! A young girl in the height of her bloom![20] (*BG* 182)

The very next day at the laundry, Sara is mocked by fellow workers and she, at least temporarily, rejects the idea of being a "dolled-up dummy" for "the shame that [she] had tried to be like the rest and couldn't" (*BG*

19. Ibid., 72.
20. For a discussion of the importance of fashion in the literary construction of American identity and its implications for Jewish American women, see Meredith Goldsmith, "'The Democracy of Beauty': Fashioning Ethnicity and Gender in the Fiction of Anzia Yezierska."

183). The obviously gaudy description above does more than establish Sara's failure to mimic American taste standards; the notion that she "couldn't . . . be like the rest" foreshadows her later conclusion that she possesses a Jewish essence that she somehow violated by attempting to acculturate.

Sara discovers that shedding Jewish tradition and cultural influence is not easy. Like Antin, she continues to read her experience in the New World through the lens of the Old. After she rejects Max Goldstein, she concludes that her father would approve of her decision on the grounds that she had refused the proverbial "mess of pottage" of the story of Jacob and Esau. Sara even believes that her refusal was caused by an "ingrained something" she had inherited from her father, whom she feels a "sudden longing" to see. At least momentarily, Sara is akin to Rosa Cassettari in her use of Old World religion to resist patriarchal influence. At the very moment when Sara makes this appeal to Jewish religion, she feels a nostalgic longing for her father's "words of wisdom" (*BG* 202). Predictably, though, Reb Smolinsky does not view Sara's action the same way. Furious that his "lawless daughter" has ruined "the one chance of [her] life," Reb Smolinsky declares, "Woe to America where women are let free like men. All that's false in politics, prohibition, and the evils of the world come from them" (*BG* 204, 205). According to Sara, "I no longer saw my father before me, but a tyrant from the Old World where only men were people. To him I was nothing but his last unmarried daughter to be bought and sold" (*BG* 205). Indeed, Reb Smolinsky continues to resist his daughter's appeals to independence on the grounds of Orthodox Judaism. He tells her: "It says in the Torah, Breed and multiply. A woman's highest happiness is to be a man's wife, the mother of a man's children. You're not a person at all" (*BG* 206). So, only shortly after Sara feels her appeal to Jewish religious tradition might bridge the gap between herself and her father, his continual scorn renders the differences between the two as starkly as ever. Sara explains: "I saw there was no use talking. He could never understand. He was the Old World. I was the New" (*BG* 207).

At college, Sara's urge to pass returns with a vengeance. As she gazes at the well-dressed students, Sara thinks, "So these are the real Americans": "They had none of that terrible fight for bread and rent that I always saw in New York people's eyes. Their faces were not worn out with the hunger for things they could never have in their lives. There was in them that sure, settled look of those who belong to the world in which they were born" (*BG* 210–11). With this observation, Laura Wexler argues, Sara Smolinsky "comes to embody a version of Americanization as a self-transformation that requires the obliteration of historical memory." Indeed, Sara's intent to pass is expressed shortly afterward. She desires not only full cultural assimilation but also the structural assimilation she hopes will follow: "How could I most quickly become friends with [the students]? How could I come into their homes, exchange with them my thoughts, break with them bread at their tables? If I could only lose myself body and soul in the serenity of this new world, the hunger and the turmoil of my ghetto years would drop away from me, and I, too, would know the beauty of stillness and peace" (*BG* 211). Sara, then, expresses a desire to rid herself of every internal and external marker of ethnic difference, which in early-twentieth-century America would have been perceived as *racial* difference. At college, she observes and absorbs the mannerisms of her fellow students. Fully aware that "character or brains" were not all that mattered, Sara again returns to collecting the consumer items, especially clothes and accessories, that will allow her to effect passage into the American mainstream and serve "as testimony of an immigrant's new American status, the external proof of economic and cultural viability"[21] (*BG* 220, 221).

Significantly, Sara's arrival in the "New World" (the third and final part of *Bread Givers*)—after which she has graduated, won an essay contest, and secured a job as a schoolteacher—is punctuated by another visit to a department store for a new, American suit of clothes. After selecting a plain serge suit and matching hat, Sara feels that "[f]or the first time in [her] life [she] was perfect from head to foot" (*BG* 240). This chapter, entitled "My Honeymoon with Myself," brings together a number of themes central to the novel's progression. First, it begins with the declaration that she has "changed into a person"; that is, she has finally achieved the self-defined subjectivity she had always wanted (*BG* 237). Second, she declares herself visually "perfect"; in her eyes, she has passed successfully. Third, by becoming a teacher, Sara celebrates a "honeymoon" more significant than that with any man: "the honeymoon of [her] career" (*BG* 241). Thus, in one celebratory chapter, feminist sensibility, passing, professional success, and subjectivity converge to create the "stillness and peace" Sara had always craved: it is not long lasting.

When her mother dies, Sara visits her father's household more fre-

---

21. Laura Wexler, "Looking at Yezierska," 159, 167; Katherine Stubbs, "Reading Material: Contextualizing Clothing in the Work of Anzia Yezierska," 157.

quently to attend to the aging and now somewhat pathetic patriarch—
this marks the beginning of Sara's seemingly inevitable return to the
Old World. Sara's reconciliation with her Jewish ancestral heritage continues with her courtship of second-generation Jewish American Hugo
Seelig, the principal of the school at which she teaches. The two discover
that they enjoy conversing about their families and their Russian Jewish
backgrounds (*BG* 277). When Sara discovers her father pitifully selling
wares on the street, she helps him back home, weeps for having "hated
him and tr[ying] to blot him out of [her] life," and decides to live with
him to care for him in his old age; in an added gesture of reconciliation,
Hugo asks Reb Smolinsky to teach him Hebrew. And although Sara pities
her immovably Old World father for "his fanatical adherence to his traditions," she finds she must return to them, if only in part (*BG* 296). The
narrative concludes with the ominous observation that "[i]t wasn't just
my father, but the generations who made my father whose weight was
still upon me"—a decidedly deterministic statement in a work that otherwise celebrates the strength of individual will (*BG* 297). Some critics
have even suggested that this ending leaves Sara on more or less equal
footing with her Old World mother. Sara, however, is clearly different
from her mother; after all, she is an educated, professional, self-supporting
woman who has selected a lover independently of her father's influence.
However, female gender is clearly a mitigating factor in her quest for
self-definition. Even if one makes the case that Sara's return to the Old
World folkways is voluntary, it is hardly insignificant that while Hugo is
allowed access to the fruits of Jewish tradition (when he learns Hebrew
from Reb Smolinsky), Sara is required to bear its burdens (caring for her
ailing and still tyrannical father).[22]

Much of the determinism in this return to ethnic tradition is figured
biologically, which is not inconsistent with Yezierska's understanding of
Jewish difference. Carol Schoen cites an unpublished manuscript called
"We Can Change Our Moses But Not Our Noses," in which a young
Jewish woman attempts to pass to secure a job. The narrator concludes,
"I couldn't get away with it. . . . the day I gave up my Jewish name, I
ceased to be myself. I ceased to exist. A person who cuts himself off from
his people cuts himself off at the roots of his being, he becomes a shell, a

22. Melanie Levinson, "'To Make Myself for a Person': 'Passing' Narratives and
the Divided Self in the Work of Anzia Yezierska," 7; Tobe Levin, "Anzia Yezierska
(1880–1970)," 486; Wexler, "Looking at Yezierska," 177.

cipher, a spiritual suicide."[23] The title suggests, of course, that while the Jewish American may culturally assimilate by changing religions, there are *biological* limitations to his or her ability to blend into American society—here stereotypically expressed in the telltale Jewish nose. In addition to gender, then, racial determinism becomes another mitigating factor in the fictionalization of free will in *Bread Givers*. This is expressed not only in Sara's offhand comment on Hugo Seelig's "Jewish face," but more significantly in the biological attachment she senses between her father and her personality. She openly wonders, "Can I hate my arm, my hand that is part of me? Can a tree hate the roots from which it sprang? Deeper than love, deeper than pity, is that oneness of the flesh that's in him and in me. Who gave me the fire, the passion, to push myself up from the dirt? If I grow, if I rise, if I ever amount to something, is it not his spirit burning in me?" (*BG* 286). In a strange ironic twist, Sara wonders if even her own accomplishments are attributable to her father's influence. At the very least, the "weight" of her "father" and "the generations who made [her] father" exercise more influence over her than she had ever imagined.

In the final analysis, *Bread Givers* reveals limitations in the ability of Jewish American women to free themselves from the demands of ancestral heritage and succeed on their own terms. As in *The Promised Land*, there is a sense in *Bread Givers* that a biologically conceived Jewish essence may permanently render full assimilation impossible. Unlike *The Promised Land*, however, the workings of gender are stated far more explicitly, and this undoubtedly contributes to the greater sense of determinism one gets from the later work. Mary Dearborn has lumped the two authors together as examples of ethnic women who "struggle to cast off their own literal fathers to become children of America." While this is true, it should also be noted that Yezierska's novel, the obviously more deterministic text, marks an explicit step back toward Old World influence—to a fictionalization of what we would now consider a "Jewish American" identity (as opposed to Antin's ostensible new "American" self). Yezierska is hardly a naturalist; generally speaking, there is too great a sense of moral and material accomplishment among her protagonists to warrant the "naturalist" label. Therefore, I tend to agree with Carol Schoen when she argues that Yezierska, though employing some of the logic of natu-

23. Schoen, *Anzia Yezierska*, 7. For an interpretation of this passage as a rejection of passing, see Martin Japtok, "Justifying Individualism: Anzia Yezierska's *Bread Givers*," 23.

ralism in her novels, ultimately "pulled away from the logical conclusions of the tradition," which suggested a kind of nihilistic fatalism to which she could never subscribe.[24] What the progression from *The Promised Land* to *Bread Givers* does suggest, though, is that realist depictions of ethnicity, particularly when female gender becomes a factor, live within contradiction. Sara's Jewish American identity is actively claimed, but in a sense, it is also forced upon her. Hence, as early as the 1920s, there is a nascent sense that a new generic approach is needed to handle the contradictory threads of ethnic female experience.

Helen Barolini's *Umbertina* and the Ends of *La Bella Figura*

Helen Barolini's *Umbertina*, originally published in 1979, marks the first instance of a passing character in Italian American women's literature. By no means a total passing narrative, the novel traces four generations of Italian American women, from Umbertina, the poor *contadina* from Castagna, Calabria, to second-generation Carla Longobardi, to third-generation Marguerite, and, finally, to fourth-generation Tina. The novel is divided into three parts. The first covers the life of Umbertina (1860–1940), a hard-working goat girl who, after marrying Serafino Longobardi, emigrates to upstate New York where she builds a successful grocery business from the ground up. Part 2 describes the life of Marguerite, an ethnically confused Italian American living in Italy who cannot come to terms with her feminist sensibility as a woman always living for the emotional and professional needs of men—as husband to Alberto Morosini, lover to Massimo Bontelli, and literary translator for both. Part 3 of the novel develops the life of Tina Morosini (1950–), a fourth-generation Italian American who, in becoming a scholar of Italian literature, establishes herself as a professionally independent Italian American woman; that is, she is depicted as a successful negotiator of the exigencies of ethnicity and gender in the United States.

Understandably, second-generation Carla Scalzo has garnered little critical attention. After all, in the classic conflict between traditional first-generation mothers and individualist second-generation daughters, Carla responds by passing: to the very best of her ability, she rids herself of all emotional and intellectual ties to *italianità* and the unwanted differences they tend to confer upon the Italian American. In an interview, Helen

24. Dearborn, *Pocahontas's Daughters*, 96; Schoen, *Anzia Yezierska*, 48.

Barolini has herself said that the "second generation . . . is not as interesting to me as the old generation because they were so into Americanizing. And they have a *less* interesting life because they have no struggle. They simply are materially well off." Furthermore, Carla is an antifeminist character in a work Barolini considers as primarily "a feminist statement."[25]

However, Carla is indeed "interesting" in the context of this study, not simply because she is a passing character, but also because she is a useful commentary on the performative nature of ethnicity for Italian American women specifically. Richard Gambino, in *Blood of My Blood,* devotes an entire chapter to "La Serietà—The Ideal of Womanliness" as understood by Italian Americans. According to Gambino, *serietà* (literally, "seriousness") involves proper public conduct, devotion to family, and an abiding sexual morality that would prevent *la buona femmina* (the good woman) from being viewed as *una disgraziata* (a "disgrace"). The means by which *serietà* is effected is, in part, through a close, continual maintenance of appearances, commonly known as *la bella figura,* a complex of behaviors through which one puts on—literally and metaphorically—a "good face" in order to mask immorality, incompetence, ulterior motives, ill will, discontent, or literally anything that could mar one's public image. The opposite of *la bella figura, la brutta figura* ("ugly face"), is to be avoided at all cost—even at the risk of dishonesty. Although *la bella figura* applies to both Italian American men and women, it carries different meanings and requirements for both: for while *la bella figura* allows Italian American men to effect strength and honor, it instills in Italian American women the burden of effecting chastity. Traditionally conceived, this appeal to proper appearances assumes a continual rooting within Italian folkways. According to Gambino, the Italian American "female learned and taught serietà, which included not only the crucial economic and social roles of womanhood, but also the manner and style of the fine woman *as interpreted in her culture.* From the age of seven a female cultivated precise ways of behavior until they formed the true and visible exterior of her personality. She developed a manner of dressing, grooming, posture, walking, and talking—in short all of the obvious elements of social behavior." However, recent scholarship has examined the ways *la bella figura* can modify, revise, and even subvert tradition. Given that *la bella figura* is wholly performative—that is, it is a "social construction of identity that depends upon public performance for its reification"—its limits are quite endless, and it can become a powerful means by which Italian American

25. Dorothée von Huene Greenberg, "A *MELUS* Interview: Helen Barolini," 95, 93.

women linguistically and performatively "construct roles of power for themselves."[26]

It is my contention that Carla Scalzo can be understood according to the logic of *la bella figura*. Nearly every reference to Carla in the novel reveals her to be continually concerned about proper appearances. However, perennially embarrassed by her immigrant parents, she comes to understand such appearances ideally as being devoid of *italianità*. Carla's thorough assimilation can therefore be viewed as *la bella figura* gone awry—at least in the traditional sense of it.[27] Not wishing to be viewed as Italian American, Carla manipulates her appearance, beliefs, and mannerisms so as to appear properly "American."

Umbertina's realist credentials are many, and critics have made note of them, especially regarding the "traditional" nature of the novel's storytelling and its deeply historical subject matter. Barolini's professed commitment to mimetic accuracy is also notable: in a 1983 essay, she takes Mari Tomasi to task for her lack of realism, particularly regarding the Italian American woman's experience, in *Like Lesser Gods*. I would add that *Umbertina* is further akin to realism in that the plot is motivated entirely by the ongoing struggle of Italian American women to exercise free will in often hostile surroundings. Like Rosa, Umbertina, with her Old World understanding of things, lives in a reality where free will is practically nonexistent. Don Antonio explains—as the broker of both knowledge and power in Umbertina's native village of Castagna—that "God's will" makes the contadini poor subjects of the northern Italian empire.[28] The tumultuous nature of peasant life seems to confirm this lack of free will. According to Umbertina, class and gender oppression are part of unmovable reality: "everything was as ordained and set as the square kerchief she folded over her head and the black felt caps her father and brothers wore—these were their badges, as the hats of the

26. Gambino, *Blood of My Blood*, 162–63, 170 (italics mine); Gloria Nardini, *Che Bella Figura!: The Power of Performance in an Italian Ladies' Club in Chicago*, 16, 20, 127.

27. I am indebted to Josephine Gattuso Hendin for this postmodern interpretation of literary *bella figura*. See Hendin, "Festas and Foodfights: Italian-American Postmodernism as a Feast of Words," 110: "In recent fiction, narrative closure is subverted into the gray area of postmodern speculation and suggests how the entire issue of proper public presence and behavior is exploded into paradoxes. The *bella figura* sign, which reflects cultural agreement about just what proper public presence is, meets its match in the American notion of self-fashioning, self-justifying and individualized behavior."

28. Bona, *Claiming a Tradition*, 128; Edvige Giunta, *Writing with an Accent: Contemporary Italian American Women Authors*, 40; Helen Barolini, "The Case of Mari Tomasi," 183–84; Barolini, *Umbertina*, 27. Hereafter cited in the text as *U*.

gentry were theirs. Men were over women in her world, and the rich over the poor. Over everyone was God, and His minister was Don Antonio. It was God's will that girls should marry and work for their husbands and bear children, so that life could be endlessly repeated" (*U* 33). This reminds the reader of Don Dominic's understanding of things in *Rosa*. Also like *Rosa* is *Umbertina*'s figuring of the as-yet-unseen New World as a place where the downtrodden peasant could claim free will for him or herself. Evoking the language of Antin, Serafino tells Umbertina that "for some people it will be a promised land.... It is a place where, if you speak the language, you call everyone 'you'; there is no special way of addressing the priest or the boss" (*U* 42–43).[29] The very trip across the Atlantic is viewed "as a great defiance of Providence" (*U* 56). Not long in the United States, Umbertina realizes that "[i]f there was one thing she was learning about American life, it was the need to be her own boss" (*U* 65). Her success is contingent upon becoming—literally and figuratively—her own boss.

Second-generation Carla Scalzo seems to carry this advice to an extreme. In order to underscore her modernity, Barolini gives Carla's birth date as 1900: "She is truly a child of fortune to be born not only in the year of the new century but in the new era of progress" (*U* 108). Carla grows up during the peak of the Longobardi family's wealth and well-being in fictional Cato, New York. Fully exposed to the American popular culture she loves to consume and given educational opportunities unheard of for Rosa or Umbertina, Carla is allowed far more latitude in imagining cultural alternatives to *la via vecchia*. According to the narrator, as a girl Carla takes a trip to Oriskany Falls where she eats a molasses cookie. Having "eaten Italian food all her life," eating the cookie becomes "her Americanization" (*U* 114). This understated rendering is undoubtedly comical, but it also underscores the importance of consumption—indeed, the *ability* to consume—in becoming part and parcel of the consumed culture. As Carla grows up, her tastes fall into accordance with bourgeois, WASP standards. She is given charge accounts for shopping sprees unimaginable to most Italian American women of the early twentieth century. Unwilling to work at the wholesale store, she wishes to finish high school and attend college (*U* 135). When her family moves into a less impressive house, she views it as "a ruinous and improper idea" (*U* 118). In fact, Carla is embarrassed by the perceived pedestrian

29. Rosa here speaks of the informal, second-person "*tu*," as opposed to the formal "*Lui*" or "*Lei*."

nature of her parents. A local newspaper reporter asks Umbertina what the Italian Americans "have given their new country in return," and Umbertina replies, "Hard work . . . and good bread." The answer embarrasses Carla, who wonders, with a hint of northern Italian elitism, "Wasn't there something else? Could they mention Marconi or the poet Carducci who had won a Nobel Prize? But no, the famous Italians were in Italy and they certainly weren't Calabrians, anyhow; for the first time Carla wondered what they, the Italians of America, could point to beside their cars and furs and big houses" (*U* 136). The irony here is threefold. First, Carla seems oblivious to the fact that most Italian Americans of the early twentieth century did not enjoy an overabundance of "cars and furs and big houses." Second, she also proves incapable of interpreting her mother's expression of Old World pragmatism and pride in work. Third, her thoughts reflect a kind of cultural idealism that she will later disdain when she encounters it in the words of her third- and fourth-generation progeny.

Whatever feminist sensibility is arguably extant in Carla's careerist desire to attend college is squelched by her marriage to Sam Scalzo, a similarly assimilationist businessman. During one reflection on adulthood, Carla finds she has begun to redefine her sense of her own possibilities: "The splendid old days of getting on and up in the world had stopped with marriage, and real life had begun; there was housework and child-rearing in a new place and in a new era called the Depression. . . . Now, as a woman, Carla learned that there was an end to expectations, to going forward, to always succeeding and wrestling destiny to the ground. And it didn't depend on one's character, . . . it depended also on outside forces before which they were powerless" (*U* 140). With this deterministic assessment, Carla learns the limitations to her self-definition. "As a woman," the obligation to marry, which Umbertina considers a duty, proves too great to resist (*U* 135). And, as a second-generation Italian American, she can only carry her assimilation so far, regardless of how enthusiastically she pursues it. She marries a fellow Italian American, teaches some Italian to her children so they can speak to their grandmother, and even feels a longing for the Longobardis when she moves fifty miles away (*U* 144, 141).

As she grows older, however, her hostility to all things Italian seems to intensify. Carla and Sam teach daughter Marguerite to be an Italophobe: "Marguerite learned that it was not nice to look too Italian and to speak bad English the way Uncle Nunzio did. Italians were not a serious people, her father would say—look at Jimmy Durante and Al Capone;

Sacco and Vanzetti. Italians were buffoons, anarchists, and gangsters, womanizers. 'What are we, Dad, aren't we Italian?' she would ask. 'We're Americans,' he'd say firmly, making her wonder about all the people in the shadows who came before him. Grandma Umbertina was exempt, even though she didn't speak English, because she had made good" (*U* 150). Although Marguerite would later come to reject this message, it would have a long-lasting influence upon her in her continued confusion about her ethnic identity.[30] As Marguerite grows into young adulthood, her parents develop stereotypically "WASP-ish" views, interests, and tastes. When Marguerite complains, "I'm not some damn Homecoming Queen. All you want me to do is smile, play golf, and have dates as if that's what life is all about," Carla answers, "What is life about?" (*U* 152). The Scalzos' house—"Carla's idea of Home"—is part of their performance of middle-class American whiteness: "There was a sweeping staircase down to the hall, a paneled study where the Harvard Classics were displayed, a glassed-in flagstone sunporch, a breakfast room, a fireplace downstairs and another in the master bedroom, a rock garden, a goldfish pond, and a two-car garage" (*U* 153).

Marguerite begins to feel thoroughly alienated from her parents with their total subscription to "the American way of progress: college fraternities, Rotary Club, country clubs, *Ladies' Home Journal*" (*U* 153). Even something as basic to Italian American existence as familial cohesiveness is, from Sam and Carla Scalzo's perspective, rendered in stereotypically "WASP-ish" terms of "commercial transaction": "Children *owed* parents respect; children *paid back* what was done for them by studying hard and leading good lives; children had to *capitalize* on their talents; doing so bore *dividends* in life; you didn't go around with certain people because there was no *profit* in it. The family motto could have been 'Money Talks'" (*U* 154). Carla even avoids the Scalzo family for years because of "their Italianness" (*U* 155). In fact, it seems that nearly every appearance of Sam or Carla—two obviously marginalized characters in the text—is to express some anti-Italian sentiment. When Tina tells her grandfather that she is pursuing a Ph.D. in Italian, he asks "in bewilderment," "What will that fit you for?" Unable to fathom "this infatuation with Italy," Sam asks Tina, "What has Italy ever done for the world?" (*U* 397). Thus, Tina comes to understand her grandparents with a kind of sociological detachment; this fear of "*italianità*" "was ... the burden of the second generation, who had been forced too swiftly to tear the Old World from them-

30. Giunta, *Writing with an Accent*, 45; Mannino, *Revisionary Identities*, 134.

selves and put on the New. They were the sons and daughters ashamed of their illiterate, dialect-speaking forebears—the goatherds and peasants and fishermen who had come over to work and survive and give these very children, the estranged ones, America. Tina was torn between compassion and indignation: She understood [her grandfather], why couldn't he understand her?" (*U* 397, 398).

What Tina perhaps does not understand is that Carla might simply be using the lessons of her mother for quite unexpected ends. As a first-generation Italian mother, Umbertina has schooled Carla in the importance of *bella figura*, of keeping the appearance of Italian American female propriety. For example, when Carla, as a young woman, entertains the notion of going to college, Umbertina says, "No daughter of mine is going off to sleep out of town under strange roofs. Girls should be married"—an assertion that reinforces the need to preserve chastity (*U* 135). However, as Carla's tastes and desires become more mainstream and less recognizably Italian, she learns to apply the logic of *bella figura* to the performance of this new "American" self she has claimed. Thus, in a bizarre reversal of *bella figura*'s traditional intent, to seem too Italian is to *fa una brutta figura*. However, to imitate middle-class WASP mannerisms is the new motive of *bella figura* carried to a logical extreme in which the artifice it encourages works to the very detriment of the cultural tradition it is supposed to serve. It is a most confusing legacy for the third and fourth generations, Marguerite and Tina, who seek self-definition partially out of an adamant unwillingness to detach themselves from Italian culture.

Numerous critics have closely examined Umbertina, Marguerite, and Tina, discussing in considerable detail these characters' rhetorical functions as differing but still related fictionalizations of Italian American female experience.[31] Critics have typically viewed Tina as a character who fulfills the feminist potential of Marguerite. And while I shall not go into great detail about Marguerite and Tina here (which, at this point in Italian American critical history, runs the risk of becoming redundant), I believe that a brief mention of these characters' subjective journeys as Italian American women can help us better understand generic shifts in white ethnic American literary production.

Undeniably, Sam and Carla provide Marguerite with little help in what would later become a crisis of ethnic identity. Having grown up

31. See, for example, Gardaphè, *Italian Signs*, 123–31; Tamburri, *A Semiotic of Ethnicity*, 47–64; Giunta, *Writing with an Accent*, 39–51; Bona, *Claiming a Tradition*, 126–45; Pipino, "*I Have Found My Voice*," 97–114; and Mannino, *Revisionary Identities*, 129–54.

with the Italophobic passing of her parents, and then having reacted against it by embracing Italian culture, Marguerite learns to view ethnicity as an all-or-nothing affair. She feels she is "a failure both as an American woman and as an Italian" (*U* 196). Indeed, this is symptomatic of her tendency "to fit [her]self into abstractions," as she complains to her therapist (*U* 19). The synthetic, potentially evolutionary logic of "Italian American" does not hold as much influence over her. Of course, as Anthony Julian Tamburri has convincingly argued, Marguerite's ethnic confusion is only part of the problem. Gender also problematizes things, particularly when one recalls that the gender biases stem from both her ethnic group and, generally speaking, from the Italian and American societies in which she alternately lives. Marguerite, perennially attached to the emotional and professional needs of other men (first, husband Alberto Morosini, and then lover Massimo Bontelli), never emerges victorious from this struggle. Husband Alberto Morosini had arrogantly promised Marguerite, "I will make a real human being out of you," echoing Reb Smolinsky's insistence to Sara that, without a man, a woman cannot come into her own as a person (*U* 177).[32] Her ultimate failure is rendered final in her death at the end of part 2—from either an accidental, or suicidal, car wreck. Thus, like Bessie, Fania, and Mashah of *Bread Givers*, Marguerite is a naturalist character within an otherwise realist text.

La bella figura has significant implications for Marguerite. At the beginning of her separation from Alberto Morosini, Marguerite angrily rejects a friend's suggestion to return to him by saying she does not "care about making a *brutta figura*" (*U* 222). In fact, her commitment to "authentic" Italianness and "authentic" Americanness will not allow for the performative possibility of *la bella figura*. "Italian" and "American," in effect, become two more "abstractions" she attempts to force herself into, never successfully negotiating the two. Significantly, just before Marguerite dies, she comes to an existential conclusion that, if properly put into use, could have helped her break free of both the internally and externally imposed "abstractions" that have impeded her:

> You have to pretend the truth to children and keep your word to them because they don't know yet that life is flux; that nothing can be promised; that Absolutes are a mirage for desperate beings; that truth cannot be caught and redelivered, still living, at a future date. For each moment is a different truth, sliding into the next as in a kaleidoscope. Children can't understand that circumstances change ...

32. Tamburri, *A Semiotic of Ethnicity*, 54, 56.

that different external factors act on decisions, relationships, ideas, like the natural forces on the earth...that persons act upon persons in a perpetual chain of being. Not because, no longer childlike, we want to be inconstant, changing, mobile; but because we are.

So we must be nimble to bend with the swirl or else we break. Maturity—what else is it but this flexing? We learn not to depend on anything, and with this nondependence comes the final freedom: the sense that all we see cannot be counted on to last. (*U* 277)

The passage holds significance for Marguerite's sense of self, because in its emphasis on constant change it encourages a dialectics of subjectivity—of acting and being acted upon, of "Italian" and "American," etc.—that her absolutism will ultimately not allow. At one point in the narrative, Marguerite had even thought of herself as "[a]n ex-American, a non-Italian, a crossbreed...unfixed and directionless"—as if her only options were to be non-American, non-Italian, or some genetically certain mixture of American and Italian, here pejoratively described as a "crossbreed" (*U* 184). Sadly, she could never apply her discovery to the circumstances of her own life.

Fred L. Gardaphè has argued that while "Marguerite dies, pregnant with the possibilities of finding her own place," "Tina is the self finally realized."[33] Unlike her mother, she achieves an integrated sense of herself as an Italian American woman—an identity resilient enough to endure the hardships of everyday life. And in the novel there is a palpable progression toward this identity. Early in part 3, Tina's section of the narrative, Tina confesses to a friend, "I've never understood where I belong. It tears my whole life apart each time—I mean I go through this absolute trauma of trying to decide here or there: Italian like my father or American like my poor mom" (*U* 298). The "absolute trauma" of this either-or decision reveals that, at least temporarily, she is trapped within the absolutism of her mother. Later in part 3, Tina responds to embarrassing Italian American tourists she encounters in Rome by imagining explaining to others that "she was not Italian-American. My father is Italian and my mother is a third-generation American who never heard Italian until she got to Italy to study; I am part Italian and part American, *not* Italian-American"—as if the conceptual coexistence of the two irreparably diminished both (*U* 315). Here, Tina's idea of her ethnic identity is not unlike her mother's pejorative notion of the "crossbreed." However, her notion of ethnic subjectivity develops to the point that she is able to

33. Gardaphè, *Italian Signs*, 129.

tell her lover Jason that "I have these two things in me that are beginning to be worked out, my work and my Italian-American identity" (*U* 359). And, thus, Barolini cleverly creates a sense of urgency in ethnic identity by inextricably relating it to Tina's lifework as an Italianist scholar. Toward the end of the novel, as she eats with her upstate New York family, Tina compares her sense of ethnic identity with that of her relatives: "Tina saw the faces of her relatives: relaxed, comfortable, unperplexed by existential problems, and for a few moments she envied their condition of security and well-being. They had never wrestled with an Italian identity—if you asked who they were, why, they were just American.... They had friends, continuity, and a sense of their living space. They were good people. Almost imperceptibly Tina shook her head as if consulting with herself: It was not enough. One had to get more out of life than the slot where one was born. Positioning meant moving" (*U* 398–99). And this idea of "positioning" through "moving" applies not only to place, but also to the very meanings of "Italian" and "American." In order for them to continue to make sense in changing contexts and times, they must be more resilient than any absolutist notion of them will allow.

Tina is depicted as successful not only in achieving this resilient sense of Italian American identity but also as a professional woman. Unlike her mother, she insists she is "not going to be just dragged along as baggage on my husband's career" (*U* 360). And, toward the end of the novel, in a letter to her sister Weezy, Tina writes the novel's feminist manifesto: "I think it is important for us as women to cultivate our strengths, to grow, and to move on with purpose whatever our goals" (*U* 419). Here, the novel is most forcefully given universal significance, for this advice can be applied not only to one's ethnic identity but also quite literally to anything one does.[34] This advice is the means by which Tina puts the too-late existential discovery of her mother to practical use. Like her mother, she may be "unfixed," but she is certainly no longer "directionless, even in her aspirations" (*U* 184).

As with the other narratives discussed in this chapter, there is a sense that the influence of the Old World is long lasting, even irresistible. Carla and Sam Scalzo—though not thoroughly unsympathetic characters—are

34. Helen Barolini has written that *Umbertina* was intended "as an American novel about what it is to become an uneasy American"; the Italian American subject matter was added to give interest to this otherwise universal framework. She believes that critics' overenthusiasm to read it—or ignore it—solely on its "ethnic" grounds has led to its marginalization. See Barolini, "*Umbertina* and the Universe," 129.

depicted as living somewhat empty lives in their "right and proper, . . . well-to-do American" homes (*U* 396). Ultimately, they even seem somewhat dishonest: for all their attempts at passing, they retain the telltale vowel at the end of their surname and can never quite break the requisite ties with their Italian American families. Of course, according to the logic of *Umbertina*, this is not even desirable, and here is where this novel distinguishes itself from *Bread Givers*, in which the return to the Old World is viewed somewhat bitterly. By the 1970s, Italian Americans had reached a level of social and material success that allowed them to look toward their ethnic pasts comfortably, and even to view them as a source of strength. As Marcus Hansen observes, what was a bitter pill for the second generation to swallow becomes a source of pride for the third (and fourth) generation. Even further, ethnic identity lately has become a generative source of a number of useful literary and political discourses. Gardaphè has argued that the contemporary autobiographical, or by extension semi-autobiographical, Italian American women's literature exhibits "an intense politicization of the self, rare even among men in the old world. Frequently this politicized expression emerges in combative voices, representative of the intense struggle Italian American women have waged in forging free selves within the constraints of a patriarchal system." Furthermore, as Edvige Giunta has argued, even if "Italian American," contemporarily speaking, becomes an "empty" concept, "up for grabs for anyone interested in ascribing certain political beliefs and agendas" to it, it is still useful as such. In fact, it is certainly possible for Italian American women to "reclaim [the] signs" of an imagined ethnic past and give new and personally significant life to them. Thus, far from accepting Old World patriarchy, laying claim to "Italian American" becomes part of constructing a viable feminist present out of a usable past, something Micaela di Leonarda has termed "fighting with symbols of *italianità*"—but not necessarily in a completely adversarial sense. Rather than figuring their identities as involving a choice between absolute "immanence," or following "commitments to family and kin networks," and "transcendence," or a complete liberation from ethnic sensibility, Italian American women who wish to consider themselves as such "choose a combination of both perspectives. They take advantage of the malleability of symbols to construct sets of meanings—symbolic idiolects— to interpret their lives."[35] Tina's reclamation of "Italian American"—

35. Gardaphè, "Autobiography as Piecework: The Writings of Helen Barolini," 20–21; Giunta, *Writing with an Accent*, 1, 91; Micaela di Leonardo, *The Varieties of Ethnic*

even as she is fully aware of the many differences between herself and the Italian Americans who precede her—is a vivid literary enactment of this very project.

Coming to Tina's realization, however, involves attaining the cultural and financial capital necessary to consider passing an option—an option that is ultimately rejected for its ostensible falsehood. What becomes clear is that for ethnic American subjectivity to make any contemporary sense, it must be prepared to deal with the fluid realities of the postmodern world, in which the Rosas and Umbertinas have long since died, and ethnic discourse can only be constructed from the textuality of an imagined ethnic past. Clearly, a purely realist aesthetic is no longer useful in such a historical context, and *Umbertina* is an excellent example of an ethnic text stretching the boundaries of realist discourse in order to account for the realities of ethnic experience. It is not insignificant that Marguerite's existential discovery is conveyed in an aesthetically modernist and dream-like manner that anticipates Tina de Rosa's *Paper Fish* and shows how the literary "struggle against the fixed identities [of] both old world families and new world exploitation" engenders "innovative forms" to dramatize this struggle. Marguerite is, after all, engaging in the typically modernist exercise of attempting to make contemporary sense out of the disordered fragments of the past. Now that Umbertina is dead, Tina's malleable sense of Italian Americanness, the textuality of which is expressed through her study of Italian *literature,* suggests a postmodern Italian American future in which "Italian American," if not ultimately "empty," may at least be one of many options contemporary American writers of Italian descent exercise. Generically speaking, as the fiction of Josephine Gattuso Hendin, Dorothy Bryant, Tina De Rosa, Carole Maso, and Rita Ciresi has shown us, social realism is only one of many options available to fictionalize Italian American women's experience. And, as I have argued, new understandings of ethnic subjectivity—which come in part from the material luxury to consider them—have led to new aesthetic means of conveying this very subjectivity. It remains to be seen whether the signs of white ethnicity will continually retain literary pertinence in years to come. After all, Italian American women have them-

---

Experience: Kinship, Class, and Gender among California Italian-Americans, 170, 208, 228. On the use and reworking of southern Italian tradition as a means to self-empowerment in a North American context, see Nardini, *Che Bella Figura!* and Giovanna Del Negro, *Looking through My Mother's Eyes: Life Stories of Nine Italian Immigrant Women in Canada.*

selves arguably "'passed' into mainstream America," a fact that has proven materially fruitful, but that also has deprived them of coethnic authorial communities and "generate[d] a perception of cultural invisibility." Still, this reality coexists with a contemporary drive, spawned by academic multiculturalism, to reclaim and utilize the inheritances of an ethnic past. Contemporary Italian American critical discourse must be ever mindful of this contradiction, which is no more apparent than in the trope of passing, in which the enthusiastic and generally successful desire to replace white ethnic "presence" with ethnic "absence" has now resulted in its literary opposite.[36]

36. Boelhower, *Through a Glass Darkly*, chapter 4; Hendin, "Social Constructions and Aesthetic Achievements," 18. On this "postmodern prerogative" of contemporary Italian American writers, see Gardaphè, *Italian Signs*, 153. Pipino, "*I Have Found My Voice*," 167; Giunta, *Writing with an Accent*, 73. On the subject of contemporary literary ethnic recovery, see Gardaphè, "Italian American Fiction: A Third Generation Renaissance." For an excellent discussion of assimilation and contemporary Italian American women's literary discourse—which references the trope of passing in the work of Rose Romano, Kym Ragusa, and Maria Laurino, among others—see Giunta, *Writing with an Accent*, chapter 4.

6

Women "Caught between Two Allegiances"

The Drive toward Modernism in Chesnutt, White, Fauset, and Larsen

> Many of the key works of the past century are hybrid texts of indeterminate genre; the female writer has often worked as an amalgamator of disparate registers and forms.
>
> — Guy Reynolds

Historical consensus holds that urban-dwelling African American women of the late nineteenth and early twentieth centuries had a far more difficult time sustaining themselves than did their white counterparts. In the premigration urban South, black women were generally restricted to low-wage domestic labor. Then, in the early-twentieth-century North, African American women, though desirous of steady factory jobs, routinely encountered last-hired, first-fired discriminatory practices. Sadly, black women who wished to take the path to success that clerical work had cleared for their white female contemporaries met not simply with discrimination, but "complete exclusion." As a result, middle-class status in the early African American women's literary tradition is not imagined to be so likely in the free market—as we find in men's realism and even in women's ethnic realism—as it is in the marriage market. This social reality is well represented in the realistic fiction of African Americans from 1899 to 1929, in which "the constrictions and limitations of the world a middle-class black woman inherited" provides a stark contrast to the

"relative ease" of movement experienced by "the characters in the literature of white women." Unsurprisingly, marriage becomes "a form of
social empowerment" that brings with it a degree of "respectability,"
material comfort, and freedom.[1] As members of an intellectual elite themselves clinging tenuously to middle-class status, New Negro Renaissance fiction writers were sensitive to the strategies employed by men
and women alike to survive in their new urban settings. These very strategies propel the plots of the realistic fiction of Walter White, Jessie Fauset,
and Nella Larsen.

George Hutchinson has made perhaps the most compelling case for
the predominant realism of New Negro Renaissance fiction, the verisimilitude of which was thought to be capable of promoting "interracial
understanding" and countering the predominant racism with a culturally pluralistic Bournean transnationalism. Hutchinson argues that
Harlem Renaissance authors' avoidance of overtly modernistic technique—even to the point of being "'realistic' in an almost old-fashioned
sense"—is largely due to "their objective social position vis-à-vis the
dominant language differ[ing] from the modernists." African American
realities (and to a considerable degree, Jewish American and Italian
American realities) simply demanded realistic treatment, "[t]he very
voicing" of which is plausibly viewed as "an intervention in the settled
language of literature no less 'new' and disruptive than the experiments
of the avant-garde."[2]

This chapter makes an argument similar to that of chapter 4: that early
1900s African American fiction moves steadily from a melodramatic
realism suitable for a turn-of-the-century context to a more unabated
social realism appropriate for the 1920s. As in the previous chapters, the
authors considered here generally are motivated to create characters
who emerge victoriously from their travails and claim a certain degree

1. Jacqueline Jones, *Labor of Love, Labor of Sorrow: Black Women, Work, and the Family, from Slavery to the Present,* 111, 154, 160–61, 178; Mary Helen Washington, "The
Mulatta Trap: Nella Larsen's Women of the 1920s," 163, 165. On the "marriage market" and the marriage plot in Jessie Fauset, see Wald, *Crossing the Line,* 41–46. Thadious
M. Davis, *Nella Larsen, Novelist of the Harlem Renaissance: A Woman's Life Unveiled,* 128.
2. Hutchinson, *The Harlem Renaissance,* 42, 105, 118, 119. On African American
writers' tendency toward "social realism" in the 1920s, see also Edward E. Waldron,
Walter White and the Harlem Renaissance, 32. I would, however, differ with his assertion that this "trend . . . did not involve black writers fully until the twenties." While
I agree that African American fiction writers did become more realistic throughout
the 1920s, I am hesitant to disregard the earlier realistic efforts of, for example,
Charles Chesnutt and James Weldon Johnson.

of agency for themselves. Passing, then, is part and parcel of "a seizing of those rights to which all American women...are entitled."[3] And, as in chapter 4, race is figured not only as a deterministic element in the text but also as a subject for explicit critique—something I find to be generally absent from the texts examined in chapters 3 and 5. However, the complicating factor of female gender—most certainly central to the texts in chapter 5—when coupled with perceived and/or psychologically experienced "blackness," creates a unique set of deterministic circumstances that the logic of social realism seems no longer adequate to encompass. Therefore, while social realism is undoubtedly and understandably an attractive literary mode for writers of black woman–centered texts, it eventually gives way to a more modernist approach capable of understanding and appropriately representing the multifaceted and contradictory aspects of African American female subjectivity. In turn, we find that African American authors understandably wish to free black womanhood from the melodramatic, tragic, even naturalistic plot of Rena Walden in Chesnutt's *The House behind the Cedars.* Walter White's *Flight* (1926) could certainly be read this way: more conventionally realistic than Chesnutt's novel, though certainly not uninfluenced by the modernist mainstream, its ending is perhaps dishonest in its singular insistence that protagonist Mimi Daquin is "Free! Free! Free!" Like *Flight*, Jessie Redmon Fauset's *Plum Bun* (1928) pays acute attention to the motives, means, and ethical dilemmas of passing, but in the perhaps more objective hands of a female author, the ending is not allowed to be quite so uncomplicated for passer Angela Murray, who in the end is not "Free! Free! Free!" from male influence.

Ultimately, with Nella Larsen's *Passing* (1929), the reader encounters the most decisive step toward existential and aesthetic modernism. Since the story begins *after* protagonist Clare Kendry has elected to pass, attention is focused not so much upon the *means* of passing as the irresolvable ethical dilemmas it creates. Like Angela Murray of *Plum Bun,* Clare Kendry's story seems to follow the standard path of social ascent we often find in social realism, but her death from indeterminate circumstances at the end of the novel represents the inability of not only her foil Irene Redfield, but of realism itself, to make sense of the oppressively deterministic and contradictory circumstances of her life. Much has been made recently of Clare Kendry's destabilizing influence upon the text—

3. Mary Condé, "Passing in the Fiction of Jessie Redmon Fauset and Nella Larsen," 104.

how she opens it up and renders it more "writerly"—and I do not intend to be redundant. Rather, I would like to suggest that *Passing*'s treatment of agency and subjectivity directly relates to the generic options available to African American writers. Given that writers of female-centered African American texts find it difficult to lend agency to characters according to the conventional logic of social realism, they discover they must seek such freedom in more modern, perhaps even postmodern, understandings of subjectivity. Thus Clare Kendry's enigmatic nature succeeds not only in opening up the text but also in opening the representational possibilities of African American literature itself.

"A Pretty Woman along the Border-line":
 The House behind the Cedars (Rena's Story)

As we have seen, Rena Walden, the daughter of a deceased "liberal protector" and a free woman of mixed blood named Molly, is encouraged by brother John Walden to do just as he has: move from North Carolina to South Carolina (where blood laws deem her "white"), pass, and hopefully prosper in an otherwise hostile, postbellum Southern context. Rena's description is of the sort we have come to expect; that is, she is young, beautiful, and seemingly "white" with some potentially, but not self-evidently, "black" characteristics: "The girl's figure . . . was admirably proportioned; she was evidently at the period when angles of childhood were rounding in to the promising curves of adolescence. Her abundant hair, of a dark and glossy brown, was neatly plaited and coiled above an ivory column that rose straight from a pair of gently sloping shoulders" (*HC* 7). Complementing this image of feminine perfection is Rena's voice—"soft," "sweet," "clear," and "quite in harmony with her appearance"—and her "singularly pretty face" (*HC* 9).

Upon his return to Patesville, North Carolina, John Walden (now "John Warwick") recommends that Rena change her "old name with the old life" and pass as white in South Carolina. Upon changing her name to Rowena Warwick, Rena undergoes one year of boarding school to acquire the necessary cultural knowledge and attempts to integrate herself into the South Carolina social elite. Happily, Rena's "year of instruction . . . distinctly improv[es] her mind and manners" (*HC* 56). However, this does not help her nearly as much as her attendance of a medieval style tournament held by the Clarence Social Club. In an obvious lampoon of both Southern chivalry and romantic literary conventions, a Sir George

Tyron wins the tournament and selects Rena as his "Queen of Love and Beauty," an epithet that cannot but be intended ironically (*HC* 55).[4] Although the women of Clarence are envious of "Rowena," the "queen-ship...gain[s] for her a temporary social prominence" that had been helped by—quite significantly—her brother's respected status in the community (*HC* 67). In other words, unlike John, Rena's journey to middle-class success comes not so much from her own efforts as through her attachment to other men—a reality that is nearly predetermined since her mother's "highest ambition" is simply "to see her married and comfortably settled in life" (*HC* 197). Indeed, from George Tyron's perspective, "this tall girl, with the ivory complexion, the rippling brown hair, and the inscrutable eyes" —likely described by the narrator as "inscrutable" because they effect one racial status while "hiding" another—is best suited as the "queen of his home and mistress of his life" (*HC* 69–70).

Predictably, for Rena the courtship is somewhat hampered by her racial "secret," and, according to the narrator, she can never culturally assimilate completely due to the psychological burden of her racial self-knowledge: "It had not been difficult for Rena to conform her speech, her manners, and in a measure her modes of thought; but when this readjustment went beyond mere externals and concerned the vital issues of life, the secret that oppressed her took on a more serious aspect, with tragic possibilities" (*HC* 74). Of course, this "secret" is hardly a burden to John Walden, as he is not socially and materially dependent upon the adulation and support of a potentially racist suitor. Nevertheless, the courtship proceeds without incident until Rena returns to Patesville to visit her mother and Tyron unexpectedly follows after her. While John Warwick had "test[ed] the liberality" of Rena's lover—who encouragingly had opined that "there is a great deal of nonsense about families" —Tyron finds he agrees with a racist medical report he reads in a Patesville market (*HC* 83, 105–6). Then, when Tyron visits his relative Dr. Green, he is lectured on Anglo superiority (*HC* 136). "All negroes are alike," says Dr. Green, who allows ironically that "now and then there's a pretty woman along the border-line" (*HC* 112). Tyron, who believes he is "engaged to be married to the most beautiful white woman on earth," feels "[h]e could not possibly

4. The narrator adds, "The influence of Walter Scott was strong upon the old South. The South before the war was essentially feudal, and Scott's novels of chivalry appealed forcefully to the feudal heart" (*HC* 45). The commentary here reveals a motive similar to Mark Twain's when he named a wrecked ship the *Sir Walter Scott* in *Adventures of Huckleberry Finn*.

have been interested in a colored girl, under any circumstances"—
"border-line" or otherwise (*HC* 113).

Tyron, however, is unexpectedly disillusioned when he finds, quite by
accident, that a "colored woman" who visits Dr. Green turns out to be
Rena (*HC* 139). The hysterical reaction is typical of turn-of-the-century
passing narratives: Tyron's face, not insignificantly, turns "pale as death"
and his eyes express sheer "astonishment and horror" (*HC* 140). Even
upon reflection, Tyron's thoughts on the significance of the discovery
begin with the personal—the hurt of being the "victim" of social "fraud"
("A negro girl had been foisted upon him for a white woman")—and
magnify hysterically to the universal: "no Southerner who loved his poor,
downtrodden country, or his race, the proud Anglo-Saxon race which
traced the clear stream of its blood to the cavaliers of England, could tolerate the idea that even in distant generations that unsullied current could
be polluted by the blood of slaves. The very thought was an insult to the
white people of the South" (*HC* 143–44). Miraculously, Tyron retains
some feelings for Rena but ultimately decides he cannot marry her.

Unlike John, Rena is punished for her racial transgression: she is
heartbroken, falls ill from the trauma of discovery, and must remain in
Patesville. Her experience, however, gives her compassion for her fellow
African Americans, whom she had once hated for their darker skin and
former slave status (*HC* 193). Like Iola Leroy, Rena feels obligated to help
less fortunate blacks, so she becomes a schoolteacher, a profession significant not only because it was one of the only white-collar options
for black women in the postbellum South but also because it "implicitly
involved a commitment to social and political activism."[5] While a schoolteacher, Rena meets and becomes interested in a well-to-do mulatto
named Jeff Wain. When George Tyron, after reconsideration, visits Patesville, he sees Rena dancing with Wain; in one final, angry judgment,
Tyron's thoughts underscore and conjoin the racism and sexism Rena is
utterly unable to escape:

> To-night his eyes had been opened—he had seen her with the mask
> thrown off, a true daughter of a race in which the sensuous enjoy-
> ment of the moment took precedence of taste or sentiment or any of
> the higher emotions. Her few months of boarding-school, her brief
> association with white people, had evidently been a mere veneer
> over the underlying negro, and their effects had slipped away as soon

5. Jones, *Labor of Love*, 143.

as the intercourse had ceased. With the monkey-like imitativeness of the negro she had copied the manners of white people while she lived among them, and had dropped them with equal facility when they ceased to serve a purpose. (*HC* 223)

Ironically, while Rena had experienced difficulty finding common emotional ground with poor blacks—especially after her experience as an elite white woman—Tyron, with "eyes" fully "opened," sees her as the living embodiment of white Southerners' stereotype of the unlearned, lower-class "negro" (*HC* 213). To Tyron, Rena had been wearing a "mask," passing not only as a white, but also as a respectable woman when her "black blood" makes the two mutually exclusive. When Wain turns out to be a scoundrel, the heartbroken Rena is left alone and later dies just before Tyron—*again* having reconsidered and now fully aware of the "tyranny" of "custom"—arrives at her home to visit her (*HC* 292, 294).

One would be hard-pressed to find a more self-consciously melodramatic ending, and later passing narratives focusing upon African American female selfhood would necessarily have to address this literary precedent in the tradition. It seems that writers of black woman–centered novels would continue to place a high priority on detailing the double burden of race and gender at the same time as they attempted to invest protagonists with the agency necessary to conquer adversity. In order to do so, they would seek to avoid Chesnutt's tragic and somewhat melodramatic plot of decline while at the same time revising Frances E. W. Harper's comparatively optimistic plot of unfettered success. *Flight* can be read as Walter White's attempt to do just this through protagonist Mimi Daquin, who tries to succeed professionally in a strange Northern urban environment that often restricted access to employment for African American women.

Is Mimi Really "Free! Free! Free!"?: Walter White's *Flight*

The Harlem Renaissance ushered in "the creation of *real* black characters," and Mimi Daquin is the direct result of Walter White's attempt to "treat his characters more realistically." Although written by a man—of nearly full white ancestry, at that—*Flight* is undeniably a black woman–centered text that marks an attempt to move past the melodramatic realisms of the 1890s—optimistic in Harper's case and pessimistic in Chesnutt's—toward a more "lusty vigorous realism" as Alain Locke described it in 1925. According to Locke, with the novels of Jessie Fauset,

Walter White, and others, "reason and realism have cured us of sentimentality."[6] The character Mimi Daquin could certainly be viewed in
this 1920s literary context: neither a passive, naturalistic victim like Rena
Walden nor a perfectly righteous Iola Leroy, Mimi's story involves a deft
negotiation of her self-proclaimed agency and the deterministic forces
that both restrict her movement and compel her to act.

The novel begins in 1906 with the light-skinned black teenager Mimi
Daquin, her fun-loving Creole father, Jean Daquin, and her no-nonsense
Chicagoan stepmother, Mary, in transit from New Orleans to Atlanta.
Mary's father, a well-to-do African American physician and real-estate
speculator, had secured Jean a job at a black insurance company, thus
necessitating the move from the ostensibly lazy, premodern environment
of New Orleans to the ostensibly professional, modern environment of
Atlanta. Jean had been reluctant to leave the familiarity and warmth of
his Creole surroundings, but Mary had insisted upon the move to a
more "progressive" city where Jean could succeed and she would no
longer be subjected to the prejudice of light-skinned Creoles who had
treated her as a dark "outsider."[7]

The house Mr. Robertson provides for the Daquins in Atlanta is closely
described; spacious, with parlors, extra bedrooms, and exquisitely crafted
furnishings, it is the very epitome of bourgeois domestic existence (F
14–16). Mr. and Mrs. Daquin will not be equally happy living in it, though,
for the two are described as ethical opposites from the very beginning.
While Mary shares her father's bottom-line approach to professional
and social life—in which "the wisdom or folly of associating with this
man or that one, of joining one fraternal order or the other one, of doing
this thing or the other... revolv[es] around the one desideratum—will it
pay?"—Jean is suspicious of accumulating capital for its own sake (F 26).
"Money—money—money—how much is it worth?" Jean thinks, imi-
tating Mr. Robertson. "[H]ow much can I make out of it?—these were
the first, last and intermediate stages of Mr. Robertson's every thought,
every statement, every action." "I'll go through with [the job]," thinks
Jean, "but I'll never let my soul be turned into a moneygrubber's" (F 11).
While Jean prefers his former "easy-going" Creole life, Mary feels an
obligation to detach herself from any imagined ethnic past and claim a
place in the American mainstream (F 31). Likewise, while Mary hates
the thought of the old Creole neighborhoods, even suggesting that Jean

6. Waldron, *Walter White*, 32, 83; Alain Locke, "Negro Youth Speaks," 50, 52.
7. Walter White, *Flight*, 22, 29. Hereafter cited in the text as *F*.

renounce his Catholicism so as to better assimilate, Jean continually uses his Creole past as a reference point by which to understand his present (*F* 46, 35). An apt raconteur of African American and French history and culture in Louisiana, Jean reminds Mimi that "when you run up against hard situations later on in life—and we all do—the knowledge of what's back of you will give you strength and courage" (*F* 38). In order to explain Creole cultural distinctiveness, Jean makes use of a romantic racialism White was unlikely to have shared: "You have warm blood in your veins," he tells Mimi (*F* 41). However, Jean's racialism does counter contemporary theories of hypodescent and white supremacy: "The white Louisianian will tell you the Creole is white with ancestry of French or Spanish or West Indian extraction. There may be some of that kind—but I'm not sure—but most Creoles are a little bit of everything and from that very mixture comes the delightful colourfulness which is their greatest charm" (*F* 40).

It is through Jean Daquin that White is able to establish the reductive, but popular, literary dichotomy between "whiteness," modernity, and moneygrubbing on the one hand and "blackness," premodernity, and cultural richness on the other. Jean lashes out against upwardly mobile blacks in Atlanta: "Here are these coloured people with the gifts from God of laughter and song and of creative instincts . . . [A]nd what are they doing with it? They are aping the white man—becoming a race of money-grubbers with ledgers and money tills for brains and Shylock hearts" (*F* 53–54). Jean's indictment extends to the entire modern condition and the social Darwinism it has engendered: "The whole world's gone mad over power and wealth. The strongest man wins, not the most decent or the most intelligent or the best. All the old virtues of comradeship and art and literature and philosophy, in short, all the refinements of life, are being swallowed up in this monster, the Machine, we are creating which is slowly but surely making us mere automatons, dancing like marionettes when the machine pulls the strings and bids us prance" (*F* 54). This passage is central to the text's significance not simply because it reveals an increasing influence of modernism on African American literature in its use of machine imagery but also because it establishes a deterministic undercurrent that runs throughout the entire text and complicates any notion of free will Mimi later adopts.

Indeed, Mimi quickly learns about racism in Atlanta, but the narrator extends the standard lament about racism to the pathologies and contradictions of race itself: "In New Orleans she had thought all people were hers—that only individuals mattered. But here there were sharp, unchanging lines which seemed to matter with extraordinary power. This one was white—that one black. Even though the 'white' one was swarthy while the 'black' one might be as fair as the whitest of the white" (F 54). The narrator relates, "All this perplexed Mimi. She was too young and inexperienced to know that [blacks] were in large part the victims of a system which made colour and hair texture and race a fetish. Nor did she know how all too frequently opportunity came in a direct ratio to the absence of pigmentation" (F 55). White would later use his auto-biography as a means to continue his critique of race ideologies. Near the end of *A Man Called White* (1948), White confesses, "at the root of my anger and my frequent deep discouragement, is the knowledge that all race prejudice... is founded on one of the most absurd fallacies in all thought—the belief that there is a basic difference between a Negro and a white man. There is no such basic difference" (F 363–64). *Flight* can be read in part as Mimi's intellectual journey toward this realization.

Mimi and her family grow "accustomed" to the "slights" they experience in Atlanta, though Mimi does not fully identify with African Americans until she witnesses a man die gruesomely in a race riot (F 64, 73). Walter White himself came to identify as an African American as a result of the 1906 Atlanta Riot, despite his knowledge that he was one sixty-fourth black and therefore legally white nearly everywhere in the United States. Set off by newspaper accounts of "alleged rapes and other crimes committed by Negroes," the riot, White claims, "opened up within me a great awareness; I knew then who I was. I was a Negro, a human being with an invisible pigmentation which marked me as a person to be hunted, hanged, abused, discriminated against, kept in poverty and ignorance, in order that those whose skin was white would have readily at hand a proof of their superiority."[8] Strangely, while Mimi had formerly viewed race as "a relative matter, something that did exist but of which one was not conscious except when it was impressed upon one," the incident further essentializes race for her; "I too am a Negro!" she thinks (F 74). From that moment forward, "the old order had passed" and "she was now definitely of a race set apart" (F 77).

This race consciousness lapses into a "blind race obsession" that disturbs her father; however, it also develops, with the help of her culturally astute acquaintance Carl, an interest in African American culture (F 78).

8. Waldron, *Walter White*, 3; White, *A Man Called White: The Autobiography of Walter White*, 5, 11. On this biographical connection to *Flight*, see Neil Brooks, "We Are Not Free! Free! Free!: *Flight* and the Unmapping of American Literary Studies," 376.

Increasingly fascinated by "the song, the laughter, the deep religious faith and the spontaneous humanity" of African Americans, Mimi comes to adopt an essentialistic, racially romantic view of black culture as an antidote for the mechanization of modernity (F 91). When Mimi hears a chain gang singing one day, she "marvel[s] at their toughness of fibre which seemed to be a racial characteristic, which made them able to live in the midst of a highly mechanized civilization . . . and yet keep free that individual and racial distinctiveness which did not permit the surrender of individuality to the machine" (F 94).

Carl and Mimi take an excursion through African American culture, attending church services and listening to black spirituals. As a result of these experiences, Mimi becomes more of a realist vis-à-vis race, which is directly linked to White's rhetorical and aesthetic goals in the novel. "Before I came to Atlanta I never thought much about 'white people' or 'coloured people,'" Mimi admits to Carl, tracing her intellectual development. "I just thought of people as people. And then came that terrible night of the riot. After that I hated all white people and began to think every Negro was perfect even though my common sense told me I was foolish. Now I begin to see the good and the bad, in white people and coloured people—and that's something" (F 109). The relationship between the two develops into love, but Mimi decides to leave Carl when she discovers that her friend Hilda also loves him. Thinking she has done something "noble" and "sacrificial," Mimi is made miserable by the break-up, and Carl loses himself in drink and dereliction (F 105).

Now alone, Mimi contemplates her situation as a young adult, and her thoughts state explicitly the double marginalization of race and gender: "Here I am, she mused, a woman, a Negro. Life for me if I were white would be hard enough, but it's going to be doubly so when I have race problems added to my own difficulties as a woman" (F 125–26).[9] She briefly contemplates passing but decides against it (F 126). However, Mimi's dilemma intensifies when she discovers she is pregnant. Becoming angry when Carl suggests she abort, Mimi decides the baby will be hers only. Rejecting the marriage plot Rena Walden had taken for granted in The House behind the Cedars, Mimi leaves for Philadelphia to seek her fortune pregnant with the son she later names Petit Jean. Mimi works for a while as a domestic servant and rears the newly born Petit Jean herself, but leaves her job when she is approached sexually by her coarse, racist employer. Mimi rejects him decisively, telling him she has

9. Brooks, "We Are Not Free! Free! Free!" 376–77.

no intention of "falling back on the sentimental melodramatics of the 'poor working girl'": the narrator's language here is significant, for Mimi's avoidance of "sentimental melodramatics" is also White's (*F* 167).

Upon her Aunt Sophie's glowing recommendation, Mimi moves to New York City, but first places Jean in a Baltimore orphanage, vowing to reclaim him when she raises enough to support them both. A fair-skinned child, Petit Jean becomes the first passing character of the novel when Mimi elects to keep secret his ancestry, fully expecting his French surname to be not only a protection but also a benefit (*F* 182). Soon after her move to the "idyllic...Negro city" unto itself that Harlem appears, Mimi takes a job sewing (*F* 192). Initially Mimi thinks she will "work as hard as a mortal could toil, save her money," and eventually succeed according to the dictates of the American myth of success (*F* 182). An acquaintance, Mrs. Rogers, tells Mimi about occupational racism and the many inducements for light-skinned African Americans to pass, concluding cynically, "'honesty, hard work, sticking to the job.' That's bunk!"; Mrs. Rogers scoffs at the Algerian notion of "self-made" men succeeding by "pluck! pluck! pluck!" (*F* 206). When gossip regarding Mimi's out-of-wedlock child follows her from Atlanta to Harlem, Mimi decides to pass as white, a painful and difficult decision for her that involves using her light skin, her French name, and her middle-class upbringing to her advantage (*F* 207–8). For Mimi, passing also involves a geographical move from Harlem, in effect "leaving coloured people for good." Explicitly aware of her doubly marginalized status and somewhat disabused of simplistic Algerian notions, Mimi's changed plans reveal the conflicted sense of agency that now informs her thinking: "I'll live my own life, make more money than I can here, I'll be able sooner to have Jean with me, and— *well, there's no other way out*" (*F* 208; italics mine). Similarly, Mimi later reflects that passing is "a mean and dishonourable thing. She would do so, *she determined, for there was no other course open to her*" (*F* 212; italics mine).

Passing comes at a cultural price, though, for as a white woman Mimi "miss[es] the spontaneity, the ready laughter, the naturalness of her own...Here there was an obsession with material things that crowded out the naturalness that made life for her tolerable" (*F* 212). Once again the text draws a distinction between "the lively, graceful spirit of the black community" and the perceived "somber, mechanical life of the white world."[10] Thus, passing does not allow Mimi to escape the psychological

10. Waldron, *Walter White*, 89.

burden of racial discourse. Moreover, the reader comes to realize that Mimi has herself internalized racial prejudice. When she takes a job as a finisher at Francine's, an upscale women's clothier, she meets an outgoing and self-supporting Jewish American worker named Sylvia Bernstein, who passes for white as "Sylvia Smith." "Ambitious, too. Just like a Jew," Mimi thinks of the woman with the "mark of Israel" on her face, only to feel shame for having thought so of "Sylvia's *race*" (F 220, 219; italics mine).

Mimi's newly adopted "whiteness" allows her to save much-needed money, and her success is given an extra boost when Madame Francine decides to turn over the shop to Mimi upon retirement. Mimi insistently defends her hard-earned freedom. When she is pursued by Jimmie Forrester, a man she meets on a business trip to Paris with Madame Francine, Mimi initially rejects him. Upon receiving an earnest love letter from Jimmie some time afterward, Mimi contemplates the deterministic circumstances of her life from which she had emerged successfully: "She had been flung this way and that, buffeted by winds that often threatened to capsize the tiny boat which was her life. But with it all her lot had not been as hard as it might have been. There had been compensation— Jean and *Petit* Jean, her work, the love of people . . . But all the things hitherto now seemed easy, for through them all she had kept her soul free. Now she was threatened with inundation, the great rising of a wave that rose up—up—up and, bursting into a million silver bubbles, took shape again and formed the face of Jimmie Forrester" (F 255–56). The obvious allusion to the naturalistic imagery of Stephen Crane's "The Open Boat" (1897) underscores the importance to Mimi of maintaining some semblance of free will and foreshadows the threat Jimmie Forrester will pose to it as the two begin a relationship. Unable to tell Jimmie Forrester her "secret," the two marry and live a bourgeois existence with Mimi abandoning her work and having no responsibilities beyond supervising the couple's maids—a situation that reminds the reader of tragic heroine Edna Pontellier in Kate Chopin's *The Awakening*. Mimi soon discovers that Jimmie is a virulent racist, heaping scorn upon "kikes and Catholics and niggers" and reading "Stoddard" (likely *The Rising Tide of Color against White World-Supremacy* from 1920) (F 265, 272).

Unsurprisingly, Mimi quickly becomes discontent with the "[b]athtubs," "radio," and "big business" that now define her life and social surroundings, and her unhappiness is expressed through a number of typically modernist laments common to 1920s writing: "Again she came back to the figure of countless millions of worried and insignificant little people obeying blindly the implacable bidding of a huge, insatiable machine" (F 265, 286).[11] She is saddened by the idea of "[r]estless crowds plying themselves with sex or drink or drugs or silly diversions to forget the implacable demands of the forces that drove them on," concluding that modern people "have thrown overboard . . . all the spiritual anchorages which gave them security in the past and made them strong" (F 287). Given that the novel has already established a dichotomy between "whiteness" and modernity on the one hand and "blackness" and premodernity on the other, Mimi's reclaiming of agency would seem to lie in some sort of return to African American culture. Her future certainly does not lie with Jimmie Forrester with his empty moneymaking and his dislike of "Jews or Japanese or Italians or any other group that wasn't his own" (F 289). At a social function, a Chinese man tells Mimi that "only your Negroes have successfully resisted mechanization" (F 282). This later inspires her to visit a black cabaret in Harlem for the first time since her initial departure; on her way to the cabaret she wonders why she had sacrificed experiencing the multicultural beauty of New York ("where French and Italian and Gipsy and Jewish people lived") in order to adapt herself to Jimmie Forrester's comparatively drab existence (F 294).

At the end, Mimi and Jimmie go to Carnegie Hall to watch a pianist and vocalist performing classics from both the Western art music and African American folk music traditions—exactly the fusion celebrated in *The Autobiography of an Ex-Coloured Man*. The music is spiritually moving to Mimi, and in the most aesthetically modernist sequence of the novel, the music causes her practically to hallucinate a series of images that enact the "absurd drama" of race the novel has hitherto attempted to deconstruct. Mimi has a vision of black trees whitening to the point of invisibility, which is obviously representative of the notion that passing has the capability of erasing not only one's identity but also one's entire lineage, as symbolized by the tree imagery (F 297). Next, Mimi sees exotic black and white dancers, the latter's faces "covered with some white substance to make them more terrible"—another obvious symbolic commentary on passing. A fight ensues between the two groups of dancers with the "white" dancers, not insignificantly, overcoming the black. Her hallucination concludes with a horrific vision of steerage and slavery that—as an "overtone of hope" begins to dominate the music—gives way to feelings of "faith, a faith strong and immovable, a faith unshakable,

---

11. Ironically, Jimmie Forrester blames Mimi's unhappiness on the novels of Theodore Dreiser and Sinclair Lewis (265).

a faith which made a people great" (*F* 299). Mimi decides to leave Jimmie, and as she exits the performance, she says to herself "Free! Free! Free! . . . *Petit* Jean—my own people—and happiness!" (*F* 300). Unwilling to deny herself "the familiar warmth of black life" any longer, Mimi decides to stop passing, to reclaim her son, and to raise him as the son of a single black mother.[12]

Despite the arguably pat ending, White accomplishes a number of things in *Flight*. By giving due description to (and even explicitly stating) the double marginalization of black female subjectivity and dramatizing Mimi Daquin's efforts to assert her agency—to declare herself "Free! Free! Free!"—White steers a middle course between the diametrically opposed melodramas of Chesnutt and Harper. Along with Fauset's *There Is Confusion* (1924), *Flight* marks a bringing up to date of black female literary subjectivity. If representations of the "New Woman" constitute one of many hallmarks of modernism, then Mimi—a woman who could certainly be described as "independent, educated, (relatively) liberated, oriented more toward productive life in the public sphere than toward reproductive life in the home"—can certainly be viewed as emblematic of modernistic influences entering into the African American tradition. Additionally, the extended use of machine imagery "puts [*Flight*] in tune with much of the literature of White's contemporaries."[13] Furthermore, while Mimi's middle-class aspirations place her within the pale of American realism, her intellect is palpably modern. At one point, she wonders "Conscience? Right? Honour? Justice? Truth? What were all these except little shibboleths which man had created in his own mind like little gods and before which he prostrated himself in abject groveling?" (*F* 125). Indeed, "race" could certainly be added to this litany of shibboleths, as the novel is clearly representative of a trend in early-twentieth-century African American literature to critique not only racism as an evil, but, more broadly, race as a coherent idea. The critique is somewhat restricted by the pat essentialisms of Jean Daquin and Mimi's stereotypical notions of "whiteness" and "blackness"; however, it is arguably most damning in the closing scene, when the details of everyday existence recede and the "absurd drama" of race and racial performativity is enacted before Mimi's eyes in a hallucinatory vision. But it is in this aesthetically modernist, even antirealist, sequence that the limits of this critique, and the freedom it potentially provides for Mimi, are discovered.

12. Sollors, *Neither Black nor White*, 274.
13. Marianne Dekoven, "Modernism and Gender," 174; Waldron, *Walter White*, 92.

When Mimi declares herself "Free! Free! Free!" the narrative ends conveniently before the ramifications of this "freedom" are even considered, much less enacted. As Neil Brooks has pointed out, "Mimi can never be completely free because she remains both black and white in a society that insists she must be one or the other." Furthermore, Mimi is a single black mother entering not only a hostile labor market but also a hostile social scene: she had, after all, spent a majority of the narrative after her pregnancy pretending Petit Jean did not exist. Thus, while White steers Mimi away from the melodramatic marriage plot of Chesnutt and grants her a certain amount of freedom and success in the public sphere, he does so without fully explaining how this freedom and success is to be attained. Ultimately, Mimi's spiritual resuscitation through African American art and her personal declaration of independence amount to a "self-fictionalizing" that is significant not so much in the "real world" as "into an aesthetic world . . . where the real-world narratives of race and gender no longer restrict her." As we shall see, other 1920s writers of African American fiction would continue to struggle with the problem of accurately negotiating characters' agency and the multilayered determinisms of race, gender, and class that militate against any coherent notion of agency. While describing American literature of the 1930s, David Minter argues, "The most self-consciously experimental works of the era . . . directly engage poverty, race, gender, sex, caste, and class as critical social problems that are also crucial correlates of selfhood."[14] It seems that the increasingly bewildering and disorderly nature of these correlates would demand a more modernist treatment. However, when the ethical and epistemological problems of passing are added to the mix, it becomes even more inevitable that authors would need new modes of characterization and representation to create a sense of agency—even if that very agency exists more in the world of art than anywhere else.

"Sick of Tragedy": Jessie Redmon Fauset's *Plum Bun*

Jessie Redmon Fauset (1882–1961) first fictionally addressed passing in her debut novel, *There Is Confusion* (1924), which traces the intellectual and professional development of protagonist Joanna Marshall, her siblings Sylvia and Philip, and her future husband, Peter Bye. *There Is Confusion* introduces a number of themes that would remain important throughout

14. Brooks, "We Are Not Free! Free! Free!" 383, 382; David Minter, *A Cultural History of the American Novel: Henry James to William Faulkner*, 159.

her oeuvre, including assimilation, passing, African American female double marginalization, the marriage market, and the American success myth versus the perceived "futility of labor and ambition." Stylistically the novel set a standard for her later works—*Plum Bun* (1928), *The Chinaberry Tree* (1931), and *Comedy: American Style* (1933)—in its thickly described, novel-of-manners social realism. However, for our purposes *There Is Confusion* is not as useful given its relatively cursory treatment of passing (which Joanna does in order to succeed as a dancer toward the end of the narrative), which is not to mention the critical consensus that labels *Plum Bun* Fauset's most important work. Indeed, *Plum Bun* is Fauset's most detailed treatment of the rationale behind, the decision making for, the experience with, and the consequences of passing vis-à-vis one protagonist.[15] It is also the most explicit about the connections between passing, the marriage market, and the likelihood of independent fulfillment—socially, professionally, and materially—for African American women in the early twentieth century. Structured entirely around a children's rhyme—"To Market, to Market/ To buy a Plum Bun;/ Home again, Home again,/ Market is done"—*Plum Bun* is divided into five sections—"Home," "Market," "Plum Bun," "Home Again," and "Market Is Done"—each of which corresponds with a particular stage in protagonist Angela Murray's ethical, intellectual, and professional journey. Fauset's use of realism stems from her desire to represent clearly and thoroughly the double burden of race and gender endured by early-twentieth-century African American women. It also stems from her noted love of Victorian literature and her continual attempts to adapt its traditional forms to contemporary circumstances—despite a literary context that often demanded a more modernist approach.[16] *Plum Bun* is perhaps the best example of this.

Part 1, "Home," establishes not only a sense of emotional and spiritual centeredness for Angela Murray but also the basis for her intellectual views and social aspirations. The novel begins with a description of Philadelphia's Opal Street, a street with modest houses owned by the "unpretentious little people" who are so typically the subject of social realism.[17] Light-skinned Mattie and dark-skinned Junius Murray, along with their two daughters, Angela and Virginia, are described as comfort-

15. Fauset, *There Is Confusion*, 20, 33; Kathleen Pfeiffer, "The Limits of Identity in Jessie Fauset's *Plum Bun*," 79; Carlyn Wedin Sylvander, *Jessie Redmon Fauset: Black American Writer*, 168–69.

16. Wall, *Women of the Harlem Renaissance*, 66.

17. Fauset, *Plum Bun: A Novel without a Moral*, 11. Hereafter cited in the text as *PB*.

ably middle class, with an Opal Street home that, for the parents, "represented the *ne plus ultra* of ambition" (*PB* 12). Mattie and Junius inculcate their children with a narrative of hard work and fastidious saving, but Angela also learns early in life about the determinisms that plague easy existence: namely, that "the good things of life are unevenly distributed; merit is not always rewarded; hard labour does not necessarily entail adequate recompense. Certain fortuitous endowments, great physical beauty, unusual strength, a certain unswerving singleness of mind—gifts bestowed quite blindly and disproportionately by the forces which control life,—these were the qualities which contributed toward a glowing and pleasant existence" (*PB* 12–13). Nevertheless, she still aspires to more than her parents—who once had known unspeakable hardships surviving—are able to give her.

While Angela wishes to be a painter, she ironically realizes that "[c]olour or rather the lack of it seemed to the child the one absolute prerequisite to the life of which she was always dreaming"; this recalls a very similar line in *The Autobiography of an Ex-Coloured Man*, a novel Fauset had praised in a 1912 *Crisis* review (*PB* 13). Given that Angela, unlike sister Virginia, is very light-skinned, "colorlessness" is a performative ideal to which she could more easily aspire. Of course, any potential aspiration in this regard is immediately established as only partly self-willed, given that "colour" is among the deterministic but no less "fortuitous endowments of the gods." However, Angela, with her "mother's creamy complexion" and "soft cloudy, chestnut hair," inherits not only physiognomic whiteness from Mattie but also ideological whiteness: that is, a sense of "the possibilities for joy and freedom which seemed . . . inherent in mere whiteness" (*PB* 14). Mattie's tastes are stereotypically "white" and decidedly middle-class. She passes, "employ[ing] her colour" and "practi[cing] certain winning usages of smile and voice to obtain indulgences," as well as access to the clothing shops, "tea-room[s]," hotels, and concert halls she frequents (*PB* 15). Given this training, it is unsurprising that Angela absorbs her mother's class and race elitism. She comes to two conclusions: "First, that the great rewards of life—riches, glamour, pleasure,—are for white-skinned people only. Secondly, that Junius and Virginia were denied these privileges because they were dark" (*PB* 17–18). Ultimately, and uncritically, Angela comes to believe "that coloured people were to be considered fortunate only in the proportion in which they measured up to the physical standards of white people" (*PB* 18).

Mattie Murray often passes for both fun and convenience and does not mind if Angela also avails herself of this opportunity, even if at the cost of publicly denying her relation to Junius and Virginia. Although Junius does not mind enduring this occasional insult, he does fall ill and passes away shortly after one such episode, in which Mattie denies knowing her husband. Grief-stricken, Mattie herself dies soon after her husband, and these deaths both symbolize the cultural death passing requires and foreshadow the danger therein for Angela. Racist incidents early in Angela's life cause her to reflect on the "curious business [of] colour"— the beginnings of the novel's explicit critique of not simply passing or racism, but race itself. She learns of both the constructedness and the social value of "whiteness": "it seemed to Angela that all the things which she most wanted were wrapped up with white people. All the good things were theirs. Not, some coldly reasoning instinct within was saying, because they were white. But because for the present they had power and the badge of that power was whiteness, very like the colours on the escutcheon of a powerful house" (PB 44, 73). Repeated experiences with both job and social discrimination—indeed, the "accumulation of the slights, real and fancied, which her colour had engendered throughout her lifetime"—bring Angela to view passing for white as more than a mere "lark," as her mother had, but rather the only key to success, which her parents had achieved without the crutch of feigned "whiteness" (PB 77, 73). Even at the cost of abandoning Virginia, Angela decides to leave Philadelphia and all she had previously known in order to pass as a white woman in New York City. Virginia would hold the memory of Angela's departure "beside that other tragic memory of her mother's deliberate submission to death"; thus, Fauset again links the cultural death effected by Angela's passing with Mattie's physical passing.

Part 2 of *Plum Bun*, "Market," begins with Angela relishing the bustle of Manhattan and the life she hopes to make for herself there as an artist and a "quintessentially American individualist."[18] Her assessment of her situation speaks to both racial and gendered barriers; although she believes she could live "without restrictions or restraint" as a "free, white and twenty-one[-year-old]" adult, she would need to be a man in order to live wholly without limitations. "If I were a man," she thinks jokingly, "I could be president." Her desires are lofty: "If she could afford it she would have a salon, a drawing-room where men and women, not necessarily great, but real, alive, free and untrammeled in manner and thought, should come and pour themselves out to her sympathy and magnetism." However, in order to have the necessary "money and influence,"

18. Pfeiffer, "The Limits of Identity," 81.

Angela believes she must seek her fortune not in the free market, but rather the marriage market: "indeed since she was so young she would need even protection; perhaps it would be better to marry...a white man....If she were to do this, do it suitably, then all that richness, all that fullness of life which she so ardently craved would be doubly hers" (*PB* 88).

Angela signs up for an art class and changes her name to "Angèle Mory" to reflect her ostensible change of identity. If one accepts that a certain amount of creative talent is necessary to succeed at the self-fashioning Angela attempts, then it is unsurprising that she meets another passer in the art class: a man with both Latino and African ancestry who has changed his name from Anthony Cruz to Anthony Cross (*PB* 95). Not wishing to be discovered, Angela avoids a fellow African American female student named Rachel Powell whose "ugly beauty" (in Angela's assessment) is evidence of the protagonist's ability already to view "coloured life...objectively" (*PB* 94, 96, 97).

Angela continues to dream of "position, power, wealth" as an artist and continues to believe that "[m]arriage" to a white man "is the easiest way for a woman to get those things" (*PB* 112). This "white man" arrives in the form of Anglo American multimillionaire Roger Fielding, "a blond, glorious god" to Angela who would certainly expect his future bride to be "blue blood and the Mayflower" (*PB* 129, 128). When Fielding takes an interest in Angela, she romantically views her success as nothing short of "a fairy tale" (*PB* 131). Angela's romantic desire for the "happily-ever-after fantasy marriage of which fairy tales are made" will henceforth become a target for Fauset's realistic, even ironic, deflation.[19]

Predictably, Fielding is an unabashed racist who hates "coons" and "darkies," and Angela briefly leaves Fielding because of it only later to declare herself "sick of tragedy": "she belonged to a tragic race. 'God knows it's time for one member of it to be having a little fun'" (*PB* 133, 143–44). She decides to return to Roger, consoling herself that she is merely "play[ing] a game" women need to play to empower themselves (*PB* 145–46). The irony is, obviously, that her "game against public tradition"—one that ostensibly would allow her to avoid the tragedy plot of Rena Walden—causes her to submit not only to racism but also to traditional gender expectations. Fauset accentuates the irony by couching Angela's situation in the terms of self-willed success common to

19. Ann duCille, "Blues Notes on Black Sexuality: Sex and the Texts of Jessie Fauset and Nella Larsen," 435.

male-centered narratives: "she had conquered, she had been the stronger. She had secured not only him but an assured future, wealth, protection, influence, even power. She herself was power,—like the women one reads about, like Cleopatra" (*PB* 151). Thus Fauset employs a traditional marriage plot, but at the same time, ironically critiques it.

Angela's "game" becomes quite serious for her when she must protect her secret by rebuffing not only Rachel Powell but also her sister Virginia. Having disguised herself in order to meet Virginia in New York, Angela, quite by surprise, sees Roger and must pretend not to know her sister. The incident causes Angela to become guiltily self-reflexive for the first time, and she wonders if her aspirations are worth "the sacrifice of a sister" (*PB* 159). It also provides Fauset with an opportunity to level a blow against race in general when Angela feels "[a] sick distaste" not only "for her action, for her daily deception," and "for Roger and his prejudices" but also for "a country and a society which could create such an issue" (*PB* 162). Virginia is deeply hurt by the rebuff, and her bitter attribution of it to the "extra infusion of white blood in [Angela's] veins" (*PB* 168) can be read as "Fauset's parodic commentary on the stereotype" of the literary mulatto, which would ordinarily hold that white blood brings positive qualities.[20]

However, the moral introspection does not last very long, as part 3, "Plum Bun," finds Angela achieving that for which she had gone to market in the first place—a successful courtship with Roger Fielding, who becomes "more than a means" to social ascension and survival, but, rather, Angela's end: "Before her eyes he was changing to the one individual who was kindest, most thoughtful of her, the one whose presence brought warmth and assurance" (*PB* 199). Angela becomes entirely dependent upon Roger, "[h]er whole being turned toward him as a flower to the sun" (*PB* 203). Most damagingly, "[f]or a while his wishes, his pleasure were the end and aim of her existence; she told herself with a slight tendency toward self-mockery that this was the explanation of being, of her being; that men had other aims, other uses but that the sole excuse for being a woman was to be just that,—a woman. Forgotten were her ideals about her Art" (*PB* 203–4). And while Angela's art only occasionally blossoms during "Roger's frequent absences," Virginia enjoys a career as a successful teacher and socializes with "a happy, intelligent, rather independent group of young colored men and women" (*PB* 208, 209). When Roger loses interest and ends the relationship, Angela is forced into an

20. McLendon, *The Politics of Color*, 29.

honest reassessment of the social "conventions" she had made use of to the detriment of "generosity," "kindness," and "unselfishness" (*PB* 228). Angela becomes aware of "the apparently unbridgeable difference between the sexes" that grants "everything [to] men" and nothing "to a woman unless the man chose to grant it" (*PB* 229). Significantly, Angela secures a job for herself at a fashion journal, and although the work is "a trifle narrow, a bit stultifying," it does earn her a "fair salary" independent of a man (*PB* 235).

Part 4, "Home Again," marks Angela's metaphoric return to both her sister and African Americans in general. She vows to return to "Jinny" and develops a more sophisticated sense of how to negotiate the dialectics of race; Angela decides, à la Jean Toomer, that "when it seemed best to be coloured she would be coloured; when it was best to be white she would be that" (*PB* 253). Angela's thoughts soon turn to her classmate Anthony Cross, with whom she begins a relationship and contemplates marrying, first "as a means of avoiding loneliness" (now that it would no longer be "a source of relief from poverty"), and then, in a notable regression, "as an end in itself": "the only, the most desirable and natural end. From this state a gifted, an ambitious woman might reach forth and acquit herself well in any activity. But marriage must be there first, the foundation, the substratum" (*PB* 262, 274). Race reintroduces itself as a problem when Angela finds that she is unsure not only of Anthony's racial background (black? Spanish? a mixture?) but also of how to broach the topic of her own ancestry, if at all. But no sooner does Angela resolve to reveal her black ancestry than Anthony sends Angela a letter ending the relationship, for "more than race divides them": in fact, Anthony is engaged to be married to Virginia Murray, quite unaware of her relation to "Angèle Mory" (*PB* 295). When Anthony finds out, he consoles Angela through a bitterly deterministic statement: "Poor Angèle. As though you could foresee! It's what life does to us, leads us into pitfalls apparently so shallow, so harmless and when we turn around there we are, caught, fettered" (*PB* 304). As Angela recovers from the initial heartbreak, she comes to view African Americans as a testament to the power of free will over the "odds . . . a cruel, relentless fate had called on them to endure": "And she saw them as a people powerfully, almost overwhelmingly endowed with the essence of life. They had to persist, had to survive because they did not know how to die" (*PB* 309). Angela concludes that passing was not necessarily wrong but rather one possible means of "survival . . . she had been forced to take"; in Angela's view, forsaking her sister was wrong (*PB* 308).

Angela does not immediately cease passing, but she does become notably more suspicious of race as an idea. When Jewish American friend Rachel Salting laments her father's unwillingness to allow her to marry a Catholic, Angela declares "race and creed and colour" to be "tommyrot" (*PB* 312). Thus, in Angela's intellectual development, "racial difference," which was once viewed as an "absolute . . . societal barrier," becomes "a false distinction of value to be overcome, ignored, and re-placed."[21] Rachel agrees when this is applied to notions of intra-European racial difference, but she "wouldn't marry a nigger in any circumstances"; Angela, who had once been puzzled by the "ritual[s] inherent in [Rachel's] racial connections," can only laugh hysterically at the bitter irony (*PB* 213, 313). Even more ironic, however, is an earlier, unchallenged narra-tional description of Rachel's "unquenchable ambition" as "her racial dowry"—perhaps the most glaring inconsistency in the novel's racial critique (*PB* 214).

Unattached to any man, Angela resumes painting with great fervor and resolutely rejects a marriage offer from an apologetic Roger Field-ing. "Market Is Done," declares the title of part 5, in which Angela pur-sues her own interests and "courageous self-definition is made precisely against society's false values of race, sex, and wealth."[22] Angela and Rachel Powell are awarded a substantial prize for urban-themed paintings they had done: art school at an American college in Paris. However, when the college discovers that Rachel Powell is black, it revokes her prize, leav-ing Angela with a difficult moral choice. She elects not to accept the prize and announces to reporters that she too is black; in the ensuing local media scandal, Angela loses her job at the fashion firm. However, the heroic action pleases Rachel Powell, who reminds Angela that while she is only black when she chooses to be, "I'm black and I've had it all my life. You don't know the prizes within my grasp that have been snatched away from me again because of colour" (*PB* 348). Virginia, to whom Angela literally and metaphorically returns, is also pleased with Angela, and in one of their conversations, Angela says that "the matter of blood seems nothing compared with individuality, character, living"—Fauset's parting shot at racial ideology (*PB* 354). Despite losing the funding, Angela plans to travel to Europe using her own savings. Before Angela departs, she returns to her former home in Philadelphia and sees Opal Street African Americans again. Although Angela will occasionally pass for

21. Sylvander, *Jessie Redmon Fauset*, 188.
22. Ibid., 185.

convenience, she fully aligns herself with African Americans when she declares, "I am on the coloured side" (*PB* 373). The novel ends in Paris with Angela meeting and presumably rekindling a relationship with Anthony Cross, who is no longer engaged to Virginia.

There is reason to believe that Fauset's ending is "optimistic" in Angela's victorious assertion of individuality over the deterministic forces of race and gender. I would suggest that the ending, like that of *Flight*, is a bit facile; indeed, "while we have the illusion of clear resolution, too many of the novel's troubling complexities remain unresolved." It is unclear whether Angela's seeming return to the marriage plot offered by Anthony is done from a position of professional or social equality. Currently unemployed, there is no telling of the difficulties Angela will encounter now that she has more firmly rooted herself "on the coloured side" (*PB* 373). Furthermore, although Angela more than once bemoans the baffling ethical and logistical "complications" of passing, these very complications remain unresolved in the novel's happy ending (*PB* 354, 373). What is suggested here is not so much a failure on the part of Fauset as on the part of the mimetically straightforward, socially realistic novel of manners to contain, aesthetically and thematically, the multifaceted "complications" created by literary passing. As in *Flight*, *Plum Bun* occasionally exhibits a modernist manner of thinking, if not representing. Kathleen Pfeiffer, for example, has made the case that Angela's move from Philadelphia to "New York and her simultaneous passing for white . . . reflect a transition from an identifiable community to an undifferentiated mass society."[23] However, the descriptively sparse, psychologically astute realism of Nella Larsen would mark the most decisive step toward modernism in African American women's fiction to date. More free of the realist's burden to create self-consistent, well-made fiction, Larsen leaves African American female identity an open question, making use of both the modernist's sense of subjective fragmentation and, arguably, the postmodernist's sense of the self as forever in process.

Nella Larsen's *Passing* into Modernism

Nella Larsen (1891–1964) revealed some of her aesthetic motivations in an angry letter to the editor of *Opportunity* (the Urban League's periodical) disputing a negative review of *Flight*, a book she had liked. According to

---

23. Pfeiffer, "The Limits of Identity," 87, 92.

"Nella Imes," " 'Flight' is a far better piece of work than [White's bombastically naturalistic debut,] 'The Fire in the Flint.' Less dramatic, it is more fastidious and required more understanding, keener insight. Actions and words count less and the poetic conception of the character, the psychology of the scene more, than in the earlier novel. 'Flight' shows a more mature artistry." Each of the items in Larsen's description of White's work could easily apply to her own long fiction. To be sure, her writing is firmly rooted in a social realism that describes the mores of the urban black middle class, a fact that has encouraged comparisons to the works of Theodore Dreiser and Sinclair Lewis, as well as other American fictional representations of bourgeois consumption. However, Larsen's psychologically rich work—especially *Passing*—is arguably more "modern in tone" than that of Fauset and better equipped to represent the subjective complexities inherent in literary passing. Thadious M. Davis goes so far as to say that Larsen "was without a female peer in the modernity and complexity of her fictional vision."[24]

Larsen's first novel, *Quicksand* (1928), features a light-skinned African American female protagonist named Helga Crane who attempts "to fashion an individual identity" in a number of contexts: as a college instructor at a fictional Southern black school called Naxos College, as a secretary in Chicago and New York, and as a traveler in Denmark. However, Helga is ultimately unsuccessful as she finds herself always to be defined by someone else's standards for her. Deemed as having too flamboyant a personality for the conservative Naxos College, Helga finds herself to be treated as an exotic sex object by suitor Axel Olsen and others in Copenhagen. Helga returns to America, has a "conversion experience" in which she develops a fellow feeling for African Americans, marries a traditional Southern minister named Reverend Pleasant Green, and—when the novella ends—lives unhappily in Alabama raising four children and pregnant with a fifth. Critics have frequently noted the racial and gendered determinisms of the narrative and Helga's inability to exercise agency and forge a viable identity in the face of "the competing ideological and iconographical forces that ultimately render her invisible." Thadious M. Davis notes that Helga's "loss of autonomy and self-determination is

24. Nella Imes, letter to the editor, 295. See Davis, *Nella Larsen*, 201–8, for a close reading of this letter. Davis, *Nella Larsen*, 3, 311; Meredith Goldsmith, "Shopping to Pass, Passing to Shop: Bodily Self-Fashioning in the Fiction of Nella Larsen," 97–99. Goldsmith specifically references Crane's *Maggie*, Dreiser's *Sister Carrie*, Yezierska's *Bread Givers*, and Fauset's *Plum Bun*. David Levering Lewis, *When Harlem Was in Vogue*, 235; Davis, *Nella Larsen*, 3.

signed by her inability to control her own body and by the debilitating efforts of reproduction and motherhood." Thus, it would seem that *Passing*, Larsen's second novel, is a literary attempt to rework black female agency and "the dynamics of racism and sexism."[25]

According to Martha J. Cutter, Helga Crane's problem lies in the fact that as she moves from one occupation to another—from "committed teacher" to "exotic Other" to "dutiful mother," etc.—she always retains a "unitary sense of identity" "structured around . . . one role that somehow corresponds to her 'essential self,'" ultimately defeating the purpose of freeing herself from the proscriptive "enclosures of a racist, classist, and sexist society." This is, in effect, highly reminiscent of the plight of Marguerite in *Umbertina*. Clare Kendry of *Passing*, however, "chooses not to be confined by any one signification, be it of race, class, or sexuality" and replaces any notion of an "essential self" with an infinite array of performances that "destabilizes the narrative as a whole."[26] I would add that this, in effect, marks the most decisive step toward modernism in African American women's literature—a step that was taken necessarily due to the unresolved, uncontainable complexities of race, gender, and passing.

Part 1, "Encounter," begins in New York with Irene Redfield considering a letter from Clare Kendry, a light-skinned African American friend from Chicago she had not seen in years. The letter requests that the two old friends meet, and Irene's hesitance sets off an extended flashback to a similar request and subsequent meeting in the couple's native Chicago two years earlier. The "mysterious and slightly furtive" "illegible scrawl" using "[p]urple ink" on "[f]oreign paper of extraordinary size" foreshadows the exotic otherness that will come to be associated with Clare in the narrative. Irene's memory of Clare as "[s]tepping always on the edge of danger" foreshadows the perceived brashness of Clare's social transgressions.[27] Irene's memories also establish Clare's talent for passing, as evidenced by her "catlike" ability to adopt any required demeanor: "Sometimes she was hard and apparently without feeling at all; sometimes she was affectionate and rashly impulsive" (*P* 144–45).

So talented is Clare, we discover in the lengthy flashback, that Irene had not even recognized the woman she had seen at the fictional Drayton Hotel as her friend. The first description of Clare, through the eyes

25. DuCille, "Blues Notes on Black Sexuality," 432; Davis, *Nella Larsen*, 8, 271.
26. Martha J. Cutter, "Sliding Significations: Passing as a Narrative and Textual Strategy in Nella Larsen's Fiction," 75, 89.
27. Nella Larsen, *Passing*, 143. Hereafter cited in the text as *P*.

of Irene, not only evokes the racial uncertainty typical of African American passing narratives but also establishes a palpable homosexual subtext well documented by critics: "An attractive-looking woman, was Irene's opinion, with those dark, almost black, eyes and that wide mouth like a scarlet flower against the ivory of her skin" (P 148).[28] Irene is herself passing at the whites-only Drayton, confident that her "warm, olive cheeks" will shield her from the suspicion of white patrons, who typically take her for a racially in-between "Italian," "Spaniard," or "gipsy" (P 145, 150). Clare recognizes and approaches Irene, who "studie[s] the lovely creature standing beside her for some clue to her identity," but is unable to decipher the "intangible something" that renders Clare both strange and enticingly "familiar" (P 151).

Clare wishes to reestablish her friendship with Irene, who though initially hesitant, had never stopped being curious about the pragmatics of passing: "There were things that she wanted to ask Clare Kendry. She wished to find out about this hazardous business of 'passing,' this breaking away from all that was familiar and friendly to take one's chances in another environment, not entirely strange, perhaps, but certainly not entirely friendly. What, for example, one did about background, how one accounted for oneself. And how one felt when one came into contact with other Negroes." In their conversations Clare and Irene directly address passing and the physical requirements and cultural investments it involves. While Irene is married to a light-skinned African American man named Brian Redfield and passes only occasionally for convenience, Clare has passed fully into the white middle class and "wonder[s] why more coloured girls . . . never passed over themselves" (P 157). "It's such a frightfully easy thing to do," she says. "If one's the type [phenotype?], all that's needed is a little nerve" (P 157–58).

When the skeptical Irene asks about the matter of "background," Clare speaks with barely concealed irony of her white aunts who inculcated her with the values necessary to effect middle-class whiteness. Their Christian morality, work ethic, racism, and "talks on morals and thrift and industry" had educated Clare in the necessary cultural codes, and though her assertion that her aunts "made me what I am" is undeniably sardonic, it does carry a certain amount of personal truth for Clare, who "was determined to get away, to be a person and not a charity

28. On this homosexual subtext, see McDowell, Introduction and David L. Blackmore, "'That Unreasonable Restless Feeling': The Homosexual Subtexts of Nella Larsen's *Passing*."

or a problem, or even a daughter of the indiscreet Ham," even at the cost of losing African American companionship (*P* 159). Clare also makes clear that passing was a means by which she was able to escape poverty, confessing that she hated the middle-class blacks of South Chicago and was "determined" to be like them (*P* 159). Thus, by "exploiting light-skin privilege," "embrac[ing]" a "willfully inauthentic, performative sel[f]," and marrying a wealthy white man, Clare "enter[s] a fluid, seemingly boundless state" presumably unfettered by racial and class boundaries.[29] Irene agrees to visit Clare for tea in an elegant Chicago hotel room whose description is a partial catalogue of "all the things [she] wanted and never had"—yet another instance of interior description as a metaphor of assimilative desire (*P* 159, 165). Tea begins with Irene, Clare, and Clare's friend Gertrude—each of whom is African American and at least occasionally passes—conversing about the practical and emotional difficulties of passing. Clare's attention to middle-class fashion and ritual is notable: she serves her guests attentively and avoids "thorny subjects" in conversation (*P* 170). Larsen's treatment of the marriage plot takes a heavily ironic turn when Clare's husband, John Bellew, enters the room. Virulently racist, Bellew jokingly calls his wife "Nig" due to her dark skin; boasts of having "No niggers in my family"; and lectures on the innate criminality of "black scrimy devils" (*P* 171, 172). Irene is aghast, but, along with Gertrude and Clare, says nothing. Later, she leaves for her current home in New York City thinking she had forever rid herself of Clare and her "innate lack of consideration for the feeling of others" (*P* 178, 177).

Part 2, "Re-Encounter," takes the reader back to the present in New York City, where Clare is visiting because white husband John Bellew has business there. We learn that Clare misses her "own people" and wishes, with the help of Irene, to socialize with African Americans again, an idea Irene dismisses as both selfishness and dishonesty on the part of Clare. "Clare was acting," Irene thinks. "Not consciously, perhaps—that is, not too consciously—but none the less, acting" (*P* 182). This can be read as Larsen explicitly referencing the performativity of passing. Clare *is* acting, and very successfully; from the moment Irene cautiously agrees to see Clare again until the end of the narrative, Clare "acts black" in the company of African Americans and retains her access

29. On the influence of Clare Kendry's aunts, see Neil Sullivan, "Nella Larsen's *Passing* and the Fading Subject," 375. Goldsmith, "Shopping to Pass," 97; Davis, *Nella Larsen*, 308.

to the "white world" she has presumably entered. What is remarkable and revolutionary about Clare is that, of all the characters discussed in this study (perhaps with the exception of the ex-coloured man), she is easily the most successful in alternating between "black" and "white" personas. Furthermore, compared to Mimi Daquin, Angela Murray, and Irene Redfield—who at first lies about having passed ("No. Why should I?") and then later admits to passing "for the sake of convenience, restaurants, theatre tickets, and things like that"—she is also indisputably the least apologetic (*P* 160, 277).

Thadious M. Davis writes that Larsen "tak[es] a bemused stance toward matters of race" and "reflect[s] an ironic vision of life, a willingness to dissent from acceptable racial discourse, and a complicated understanding of the racial definitions."[30] Like *Flight* and *Plum Bun*, *Passing* issues an explicit critique of both racism and racial ideology in general; it could be read, in part, as a novel of ideas in which notions of race are discussed, their problems becoming increasingly apparent. Larsen allows characters to contradict themselves in their opinions on race, as if to demonstrate the limitations of "race" as an idea and to underscore its simultaneous presence and absence for light-skinned African Americans such as Irene and Clare. For example, within the course of one conversation with Irene, Brian Redfield admits not "know[ing] what race is," but then explains passing as the "[i]nstinct of the race to survive and expand" as if he *did* know (*P* 186). Similarly, Irene, when pondering whether to allow her friend back into her life, thinks, "Clare Kendry cared nothing for the race. She only belonged to it," as if one could biologically *belong* to a "race" and not "care" about it, or, in other words, participate in any notion, albeit socially constructed, of what that "race" is (*P* 182). But then Irene dismisses Brian's "instinct of the race" theory as "[r]ot!" "Everything can't be explained by some general biological phrase," Irene says, directly critiquing the universal applicability of biological determinism. And then, in an amusing reversal, Brian's reply—"Absolutely everything can. Look at the so-called whites, who've left bastards all over the known earth. Same thing in them. Instinct of the race to survive and expand"—both reifies the taxonomic certainty of race and, through the dismissal of racial purity and the use of the adjective "so-called," undermines it (*P* 186). Indeed, Brian's confused uncertainty about race can be attributed to the fact that "race is founded not on being but on the para-

30. Davis, *Nella Larsen*, 12.

noid conflation of being and appearance," with the latter simultaneously giving life to the former and rendering it indeterminate.[31]

Irene's and Brian's relationship to domestic servant Zulena allows
Larsen an opportunity to represent ironically "the triumph of racist
signification in Irene's own thinking."[32] Irene and Brian discuss the
ethics of passing while Zulena, a "mahogany-coloured creature" they
ignore, serves them breakfast; thus, Larsen subtly underscores the sad
irony of intraracial racism and reminds readers that while passing is an
enticing if morally troubling option for some African Americans, it is
not even a consideration for most (P 185). Despite these oversights, Irene
does exhibit an awareness of the contradictions of passing; presumably
speaking for all African Americans, Irene says, "It's funny about 'passing.' We disapprove of it and at the same time condone it. It excites our
contempt and yet we rather admire it. We shy away from it with an odd
kind of revulsion, but we protect it" (P 186). Thus, Irene can never completely renounce Clare, who manipulates the very contradictions of
passing and forges an indeterminate identity that indeed excites Irene's
contempt and admiration. When Irene plans to attend an upscale, socially
significant Negro Welfare League dance, she cannot refuse Clare's company, despite the fact that Clare plans to pass for white and Irene fears
"the unpleasantness and possible danger" that could result (P 199).

Indeed, Clare seemingly has an "ability to secure the thing she wanted
in the face of any opposition, and in utter disregard to the convenience
and desire of others. About her there was some quality, hard and persis-
tent, with the strength and endurance of rock, that would not be beaten
or ignored" (P 201). Clare manages to create an extraordinary amount
of freedom for herself despite the highly deterministic circumstances
explicitly stated in the novel. Irene tries to warn Clare that associating
with African Americans again is plainly "not safe" given "Mr. Bellew's
attitude" and much of the general public's attitude for that matter;
Clare's social transgressions simply carry more "perils" than they do for
the female characters discussed in chapter 5 (P 195, 192). Even as the
novel explicitly critiques race—reducing it almost to an empty signifier—
it affirms and reaffirms the psychological burden it places upon Irene.
Clare's racial escapades threaten Irene's sense of morality and security

31. Brian Carr, "Paranoid Interpretation, Desire's Nonobject, and Nella Larsen's
Passing," 292.
32. Sullivan, "Nella Larsen's *Passing*," 376.

to the point that she considers telling John Bellew of his wife's ancestry "to be free of her" (*P* 224). She is ultimately unable, and the thing that prevents her is "race," a term Irene understands in two ways: as representative of a specific subgroup and as an overarching metanarrative of social control: "She was caught between two allegiances, different, yet the same. Herself. Her race. Race! The thing that bound and suffocated her. Whatever steps she took, or if she took none at all, something would be crushed. A person or the race. Clare, herself, or the race." Irene thinks specifically about "the burden of race," echoing similar laments in *Flight* and *Plum Bun:* "It was . . . enough to suffer as a woman, an individual, on one's own account, without having to suffer for the race as well. It was a brutality, and undeserved" (*P* 225). But while Irene, on one hand, is to a large degree preoccupied with "race"—talking frequently about it and belonging to the Negro Welfare League—Clare, on the other, significantly avoids race as a subject of conversation (*P* 170). According to the narrative's logic, while Irene is stifled by her inability to "separate individuals from the race," Clare transcends the ostensibly "instinctive loyalty to a race" and creates a surprising amount of social freedom for herself (*P* 227).

But Larsen's ending suggests that Clare's approach can only be successful for so long: that "[t]he material realities of the black female body that [Clare] attempts to escape through costume, performance, and self-adornment ultimately prove inexorable." Somehow John Bellew discovers his wife's ancestry and arrives at a Harlem party she is attending. "So you're a nigger, a damned dirty nigger!" John says, causing some of the partygoers to step between Clare and him (*P* 238). In the ensuing chaos, during which Irene runs to Clare and "lay[s] a hand on [her] bare arm," Clare falls through an open window to her death under indeterminate circumstances: it is unclear whether Clare falls—intentionally or accidentally—due to the force of Bellew, Irene, or herself (*P* 239). Some critics argue that Irene, who could never come to terms with the "revolutionary possibilities inherent in Clare's character," is the killer. Irene is, after all, the only person clearly said to have touched Clare before her death. Also suspicious is Irene's initially hysterical, but then simultaneously chilly and guilty, reaction to the death: "Gone! The soft white face, the bright hair, the disturbing scarlet mouth, the dreaming eyes, the caressing smile, the whole torturing loveliness that had been Clare Kendry. That beauty that had torn at Irene's placid life. Gone! The mocking daring, the gallantry of her pose, the ringing bells of her laughter. Irene wasn't sorry. She was amazed, incredulous almost. What would the others think? That Clare had fallen? That she had deliberately leaned backward? Certainly one or the other. Not—" (*P* 239). Whatever the specific circumstances of Clare's death, as the final action in the novel, it allows the racial and gendered determinisms that Clare had been trying to escape to reassert themselves—in John Bellew's racist rage and in the novel's fade to black as Irene faints ("Then everything was dark" is the final line) (*P* 242). Much of the criticism on *Passing* documents, even laments, the ultimate supremacy of these deterministic elements in the novel.[33]

However, as Cheryl Wall points out, though Clare's "death is typical of the tragic mulatto fate"—as witnessed in *The House behind the Cedars*, for example—she "breaks the mold in every other respect." Indeed, Clare's ability to adopt both "white" and "black" public personas depending on her social context, her "floating racial identity" as David Levering Lewis phrases it, is evidence of Clare's avoidance—at least until the moment she dies—of "a unitary sense of identity" that would subsume her under one racial, gender, or, as some critics have pointed out, sexual classification. Critics such as Deborah McDowell and David L. Blackmore have noted a subtextual sexual attraction between Clare and Irene set off by the former's flirtation and documented through the narrative's description of the latter's uneasy thoughts. Larsen's biographer Thadious M. Davis has argued for the historical viability of this reading: "Lesbianism as a theme in a popular work" and as a visible cultural presence was "neither unfamiliar nor shocking in Larsen's [Harlem Renaissance] milieu."[34] Certain oft-cited passages of the text also seem to validate this reading. Clare's initial written plea to Irene contains all the desperate rhetorical flourishes of a love letter: "For I am lonely, so lonely... cannot help longing to be with you again, as I have never longed for anything before; and I have wanted many things in my life... It's like an ache, a pain that never ceases... [A]nd it's your fault, 'Rene dear. At least partly. For I wouldn't now, perhaps, have this terrible, this wild desire if I hadn't seen you that time in Chicago" (*P* 145). Then, one of the earliest descriptions we read of Clare is through Irene's desirous eyes: "She'd always had that pale gold hair, which, unsheared still, was drawn

33. Goldsmith, "Shopping to Pass," 117; Jennifer DeVere Brody, "Clare Kendry's 'True' Colors: Race and Class Conflict in Nella Larsen's *Passing*," 1064; Washington, "The Mulatta Trap," 165; Corrine E. Blackmer, "The Veils of the Law: Race and Sexuality in Nella Larsen's *Passing*," 113; Guy Reynolds, *Twentieth-Century American Women's Fiction: A Critical Introduction*, 103.

34. Wall, *Women of the Harlem Renaissance*, 123–24; Lewis, *When Harlem Was in Vogue*, 235; Cutter, "Sliding Significations," 75; Davis, *Nella Larsen*, 326.

loosely back from a broad brow...Her lips, painted a brilliant geranium-red, were sweet and sensitive and a little obstinate. A tempting mouth...[T]he ivory skin had a peculiar soft luster. And the eyes were magnificent! dark, sometimes absolutely black, always luminous, and set in long, black lashes. Arresting eyes, slow and mesmeric, and with, for all their warmth, something withdrawn and secret about them" (*P* 161). And, then, as their first meeting at the Drayton comes to an end, Irene finds it "a dreadful thing to think of never seeing Clare Kendry again. Standing there under the appeal, the caress, of her eyes, Irene had the desire, the hope, that this parting wouldn't be the last" (*P* 162).

However, like every other aspect of Clare's multifaceted identity, this reading is not wholly conclusive, and the textual result underscores a change in approaches to African American female subjectivity as expressed in literature. Martha J. Cutter writes, "In a world of fixed identities, Clare is such a powerful presence because she denies all the boundaries that the other characters work so hard to establish and maintain; she denies divisions of race, class, and even sexuality. Clare's plural identity destabilizes others' sense of identity, but it also destabilizes the narrative as a whole"—arguably more so than any other protagonist in the passing narratives discussed. Thus through the unprecedented indeterminacy of Clare Kendry—that is, through the fictionalization of the "never...coherent," "never self-identical" subject—Larsen "create[s] a text that remains open and uncontainable"—more "writerly" to use Roland Barthes's terminology—and makes the most decisive step toward modernist representation in African American women's literature in the 1920s.[35]

The killing of Clare, however, arguably reveals an unwillingness to complete the step. I would suggest that the threat Clare poses to Irene—not merely sexually but vis-à-vis her entire public persona—is analogous to the threat posed to the literary realist by the social dislocations of the late nineteenth and early twentieth centuries. Critics have noted that since *Passing* is rendered in a third-person narrative that generally relates Irene's perspective of things, much of the text reveals Irene's inability to comprehend and thereby control Clare and the anxiety this produces—anxiety that has been linked to Clare's "resistance to the concomitant knowledge of her own self-difference." The novel's course of events—from Irene's inability to recognize her friend at the Drayton to her continual unease about Clare's passing to her inability to identify that "quality" driving Clare's actions—brings Irene to the "realiz[ation]

---

35. Cutter, "Sliding Significations," 89, 97; Butler, *Bodies That Matter*, 190.

that she cannot 'master' Clare," who comes to represent not only sexual impropriety, but more generally, "the embodiment of [Irene's] fantasies and of her worst nightmares." Irene with her "world of rising towers, conventional romance, and stable class structure" has no way of accounting for Clare, and I argue that Irene's failure to do so can be read as a failure of literary realism with its complicity in upholding Irene's sense of propriety and stability.[36] Clare ultimately escapes Irene's stable, self-consistent realist narrative of what a middle-class African American woman should be (which should certainly remind us of Marguerite's idea of Italian American womanhood in *Umbertina*) and thereby becomes a vehicle for Larsen's exploration of new generic options for black female literary production.

If we accept that "the destruction of Clare Kendry suggests the intractable artistic limits that confronted" Larsen, then it may be that *Passing* also suggests, if it does not realize, new approaches to black female subjectivity in American literature. In effect, Larsen manufactures a "fantastic realm" and imagines subjective possibilities through art that were unthinkable in the real world. Thus, Larsen can be said to be engaging in a kind of "self-conscious . . . aesthetic[ism]" that has come to be associated with modernism given that genre's general distrust of literature as a means to progressive reform and its valorization of art as an end in and of itself. Clearly, Larsen's representative fragmentation of Clare Kendry into indeterminate components of race, class, and sexuality reveals a modernist notion of subjectivity to be held in contrast with Irene's stable, arguably "realist" view of herself. If Clare is indeed an incorrigibly "problematic signifier" open to new interpretations with every reading, then we might say that Larsen uses her to hint at a kind of postmodern subjectivity: namely, as "something in process, never as fixed and never as autonomous, outside history. It is always a gendered subjectivity, rooted also in class, race, ethnicity, and sexual orientation."[37] Thus, Larsen

36. McDowell, Introduction, xxx; Blackmore, "'That Unreasonable Restless Feeling,'" 475, 483; Caughie, *Passing and Pedagogy*, 129; Sullivan, "Nella Larsen's *Passing*," 378; Brody, "Clare Kendry's 'True' Colors," 1062, 1064.

37. Blackmer, "The Veils of the Law," 112; duCille, "Blues Notes on Black Sexuality," 442; Dekoven, "Modernism and Gender," 175; Frederick J. Hoffman, *The Twenties: American Writing in the Postwar Decade*, 24; Cutter, "Sliding Significations," 96, 98. Many contemporary discussions of *Passing* play upon variations of this theme. See, for example, Kawash, *Dislocating the Color Line*, 155, for a reading of Clare as a "disruption of knowledge" itself and Carr, "Paranoid Interpretation," 290, which argues that the novel, largely through Clare, "insistently foregrounds the impossibility of objects." Linda Hutcheon, *The Politics of Postmodernism*, 39.

can be viewed as taking the most radical step from Pamela L. Caughie's first cultural notion of passing—the substitution of one unitary identity for another—to the latter cultural notion, in which passing encompasses all the performative choices of postmodernity. However, Clare's death, it would seem, defers until the future any self-empowering use of such a notion of subjectivity.

Larsen can be viewed as a transitional figure in the African American literary tradition between the genteel realism of Chesnutt, Johnson, and Fauset and the high modernism of Zora Neale Hurston and Ralph Ellison. Guy Reynolds writes that Larsen's work "seems at first ... an evenly toned social realism" but "mutates generically. As their explorations of identity deepen, [her] novels shift towards a hallucinatory and almost anti-realistic mode; Larsen's fictions about identity crisis prefigured the African-American existentialist novel which is often thought of as coming-into-being with Ralph Ellison's *Invisible Man* (1952)."[38] Indeed, Clare Kendry's awareness of the fragmented self as an unavoidable and even beneficial corollary of modern existence anticipates the proto-postmodern conclusion the Invisible Man reaches vis-à-vis subjectivity. Furthermore, the confident sense of self-empowerment Clare claims for herself antici-pates Janie of Hurston's *Their Eyes Were Watching God* (1937)—a charac-ter who, in a significant development, does *not* meet the same tragic fate as some of her culturally defiant literary predecessors. *Passing* would be Nella Larsen's last novel. Stung by a plagiarism accusation regarding her short story "Sanctuary" (1930) and the infidelity of her husband, Elmer Imes, which led to their 1933 divorce, Larsen returned to nursing, the profession she had originally trained for in the 1910s. Although she died in relative obscurity in 1964, the two major works she contributed to the African American literary tradition are essential to understanding those that preceded them and those that followed.

38. Reynolds, *Twentieth-Century American Women's Fiction*, 90.

Epilogue

Walker, Kessler-Harris, Barolini, and the Literary Politics of Recovery

As civil rights activism of the 1950s and 1960s ushered in an era of vocal African American cultural pride, black passing narratives gave way to antipassing confessionals and essays with titles such as "I Refuse to Pass" (1950), "I'm Through with Passing" (1951), and "Why 'Passing' Is Passing Out" (1952).[1] At the very same time, postwar antiracialism and the upward social mobility of white ethnics as a result of, among other things, college education via the G.I. Bill and the increased availability of white-collar jobs allowed Italian Americans and Jewish Americans to enter the ranks of "white" America. Paradoxically, this "passing" of the white ethnics into the American mainstream provided a measure of social and economic stability that granted them the luxury to explore their cultural inheritances. And while the resultant scholarship of the "ethnic revival"—representatively, Nathan Glazer's and Daniel Patrick Moynihan's *Beyond the Melting Pot* (1963) and Michael Novak's *The Rise of the Unmeltable Ethnics* (1971)—strikes contemporary readers as somewhat less than theoretically elegant, it does highlight a common project of ethnic recovery undertaken by many scholars and creative writers in the second half of the twentieth century. In literary studies, this manifested

---

1. Wald, *Crossing the Line*, 116–51.

itself, in part, through projects of textual recovery that have not only re-
stored the legacies of individual writers but also enriched the ever-
evolving body of works we understand to be "the American Canon."
Influenced by the burgeoning field of African American studies, which
became an established and articulate field in the 1960s, scholars initiated inquiry in what would become Jewish American studies, Italian
American studies, Native American studies, Asian American studies, and
a wide variety of culturally specific fields. I would like to conclude this
study by describing one example of such interethnic influence, in which
textual recovery becomes part of an overall drive to refresh ethnic memory and provoke personal reflection upon the significance of ethnicity.
For some Jewish American and Italian American scholars, this project is
quite urgent, as it helps forestall what they perceive to be the cultural
erasure of passing, which though impossible for the vast majority of
African Americans, is now for white ethnics something that operates
both individually and group-wide. Recovery is also remarkable in that it
relies upon both first cultural and latter cultural notions of passing and
thereby reemphasizes the continual need to understand the simultaneous significance of both in the figuring of identity.

The process of ethnic literary recovery begins with an eerie silence.
For Alice Walker, it began after graduating from Sarah Lawrence College
and realizing that she had encountered no early African American women
writers in her education. Given this silence, Walker set about answering
a burning question: had there been any at all?[2] The question is in some
ways rhetorical: of course, there had been. But the subsequent process
of textual recovery that answers this question does more than simply
replace a literary absence with a presence; it also uncovers the political
and historical reasons that relegated the recovered text to out-of-print
status in the first place. Indeed, Alice Walker's restoration of Zora Neale
Hurston's legacy, in part, has demonstrated the importance of initial
critical reception in determining which texts become fixtures in American literary history and which texts become sociological curiosities, collecting dust and falling into disrepair on library shelves. For example,
Sterling Brown, Alain Locke, and Richard Wright gave generally unfavor-
able assessments of *Their Eyes Were Watching God* after its publication in
1937, preferring hard-hitting black social realism to what they perceived

---

2. Alice Walker, "Saving the Life That Is Your Own: The Importance of Models in
the Artist's Life," 9. Unfortunately, permission was refused for any quotation of
Alice Walker's work.

as Hurston's high-modernist experiment in overtly feminine aestheticism; given this chilly critical reception, the novel soon went out of print.

Walker's experience with Hurston began in 1970 when she was researching Southern black anthropology and folklore in order to write a short story that referenced voodoo practices. The material was written mostly by whites—some of whom were less than covert about their racism—but it was in a footnote in one of these works that Walker first read about Zora Neale Hurston and her work as an anthropologist of Southern black folk culture. Walker then set about learning Hurston's personal history and reading all her published books. She began teaching Hurston's work at Wellesley in 1971 and, two years later, found Hurston's gravestone in Eatonville, Florida. In the celebrated essay "Looking for Zora," Walker tells of giving the stone a new inscription describing Hurston's multifaceted cultural endeavors. Beyond establishing these basic facts, Walker's subsequent work led to her edited Hurston anthology *I Love Myself When I Am Laughing . . . and Then Again When I Am Looking Mean and Impressive,* whose 1979 publication is considered by Mary Helen Washington to be one of the important "literary events [that] made it possible for serious Hurston scholarship to emerge." Rediscovering Hurston and exploring her Southern black cultural and historical context became, for Walker, part of a broader project of being, as both essay and essay collection are titled "In Search of Our Mothers' Gardens"—in other words, seeking out and learning from a historically continuous tradition of black female creativity, which Walker renders through the symbol of her mother's fertile and beautiful garden. Indeed, Zora Neale Hurston was not merely a forgotten writer, but even more significantly someone whose lifework was devoted to preserving African American culture, thereby making recovery of her work all the more essential. This type of project is more than merely personal. To be sure, it certainly provides the individual with a sense of their cultural inheritances and their unique place in history. For example, Walker fondly remembers giving Hurston's work of sociology *Mules and Men* to her relatives only to find that reading it did for them what it had done for her: that is, it vividly re-created folk stories that time, neglect, and assimilation had erased.[3] Recovery, however, also has the ability to transform our collective understanding of American history on the whole—literary or otherwise. The

3. Ibid., 11; Walker, "Looking for Zora," 101; Washington, Foreword to *Their Eyes Were Watching God,* xi; Walker, "In Search of Our Mothers' Gardens," 238–39; Walker, "Zora Neale Hurston: A Cautionary Tale and a Partisan View," 85, 91.

overwhelming amount of scholarship on Hurston since the late 1970s is a testament to this.

At about the same time in the 1970s, there were others doing similar work in their own ethnic subgenres of interest. Two examples would be found in the field of early-twentieth-century immigrant literature, in which scholars directly influenced by the work of African Americanists have engaged in their own projects of literary search and rescue. For instance, in the late 1960s, renowned labor historian Alice Kessler-Harris accidentally discovered Anzia Yezierska's works in a public library while researching her dissertation on the Jews of 1890s New York. Kessler-Harris read all of Yezierska's major works, discovered a collection of personal papers at Boston University, interviewed Yezierska's daughter, and tried repeatedly to get the author's 1925 work *Bread Givers* republished, succeeding finally in 1975 with Persea Books.[4] Since then, the work has stayed in print and Yezierska has been hailed posthumously as one of the most important Jewish American immigrant realists.

That which Alice Kessler-Harris accomplished for Jewish immigrant literature was later repeated by Helen Barolini for Italian immigrant literature, something Thomas J. Ferraro has called one of the "best kept literary secrets of this century." Herself the granddaughter of immigrants, the onetime librarian turned author and scholar wondered why she found so few women of Italian descent in the major literary reference catalogs. Like Alice Walker, Barolini sensed they were there and undertook the task of looking for them herself. In the 1985 introduction of *The Dream Book: An Anthology of Writings by Italian American Women,* Barolini directly references the recovery work of Walker and insists, "There are human documents—oral histories, letters, diaries, memoirs—which, rare as they are among Italian Americans, have to be searched out and preserved more fully than has been done up to now, because therein would be those authentic voices of women so missing as points of contact with our past."[5]

Among these human documents were the works of second-generation Italian American novelist Mari Tomasi, whose best work, *Like Lesser Gods* (1949), a story about Vermont granite workers, is now in print and is recognized as an important representative of labor fiction. In an essay called "Looking for Mari Tomasi," which was named after Walker's essay

4. Alice Kessler-Harris, "Finding *Bread Givers*," v-xi.
5. Thomas J. Ferraro, "Ethnicity in the Marketplace," 398; Helen Barolini, "After-Thoughts on Italian American Women Writers," 37; Barolini, Preface to *The Dream Book: An Anthology of Writings by Italian American Women*, x; Barolini, Introduction to *The Dream Book: An Anthology of Writings by Italian American Women*, 52.

"Looking for Zora," Barolini tells of driving to Vermont in 1973 "to find the flesh and blood memory of . . . Tomasi," who had died eight years earlier.[6] While there, Barolini interviewed Tomasi's surviving sister and examined items the author had left behind, which quite tellingly did not include a personal diary. This silence, coupled with the fact that Tomasi's second and last novel was published in 1949—sixteen years before her death—allowed Barolini to intuit a more general theory of Italian American female literary silence, born of both economic factors and traditional attitudes regarding education and the family in the early twentieth century. This is a theory that Barolini elegantly details in the introduction to her *Dream Book* anthology, which contains fiction, nonfiction, and poetry by fifty-six authors and provides ample evidence that, by the mid-1980s, things had changed considerably since Tomasi's time as an author.

As we have seen, Barolini's own fictional work has been informed by this project of ethnic recovery, most famously in *Umbertina*. As we have also seen, later scholars in the field, such as Edvige Giunta and Mary Jo Bona, have been influenced by Barolini's pioneering work and have noted the connections between Barolini and Walker. But the greatest validation came from Alice Walker herself, who wrote a laudatory endorsement that appeared on the original printing of *The Dream Book*, praising it for its important recovery work.[7]

But beyond recovery, another factor linking Walker, Kessler-Harris, and Barolini is their use of familial metaphors to explain simultaneously the unavoidability and the preciousness of their connection to an ethnic past. For Walker, delving into the African American past involves more than sifting through dusty archives and libraries. Rather, it involves, as she says, being in search of her mothers' gardens: a more "earthy" and, indeed, inviting metaphor for exploring the often stifled creative potential of her black female ancestors who had few legitimate outlets for their intense creativity. Not insignificantly, Walker pretends she is Zora Neale Hurston's niece in order to convince Eatonville locals to help her find the enigmatic author's grave. This is not merely a white lie: rather, it is arguably a powerful expression of affiliation, not only in terms of ethnicity but also of Walker's place in African American literary history. Unsurprisingly, others engaged in the work of recovery have made use of the same familial metaphors. Kessler-Harris, for example, writes of

6. Helen Barolini, "Looking for Mari Tomasi," 73.
7. Giunta, *Writing with an Accent*, 29–30; Bona, *Claiming a Tradition*, 2–3, 201–2n.

Yezierska as "the 'voice of the voiceless' speaking to the generations to come after," figuring the author as a metaphorical grandmother to "the grandchildren of immigrants"—that is, those attempting to make sense of Jewish ethnic difference in the present. Kessler-Harris certainly counts herself among these metaphorical grandchildren, admitting that reading Yezierska caused her to identify with Sara Smolinsky's ethnic cultural dilemma and allowed her to "f[in]d [her] own voice" as a Jewish American woman. Finally, Barolini, though speaking specifically of Italian American women writers, could certainly be speaking for all Italian American women when she, on more than one occasion in *The Dream Book* introduction, views first-generation "grandmothers" as a source of creative power: "We can use the same strength our grandmothers had," she advises. For Barolini, recovery becomes more than a filling-in of literary blanks: rather, it becomes a means by which she and other Italian American women "could recognize the transcultural and transgenerational complexities of who [they] are." Italian American women writers have a unique opportunity in that they

> are in the process of redefining themselves, of redefining family patterns, while all the time they value and hold on to tradition. They are writing to create models that were never there; they are writing to know themselves. They are emerging, not receding, writers. Italian American writers are recombining two cultures into something which is of neither one world nor another, but, belonging to both, forms a third realm of consciousness and expression. These new women identify their Italian background and American foreground, thereby doubling their perceptions. There is an Italian American identity because they have an awareness of it, and this has brought very definite emotional overtones into their work.[8]

Thus, in the work of each of the scholars and writers considered in this epilogue, recovery not only enriches our understanding of American literature—and its respective ethnic subgroupings—but also provides the recovery worker, and presumably others, with the means to better understand and (re)define themselves as ethnic Americans. And

8. Walker, "In Search of Our Mother's Gardens," 233; Walker, "Looking for Zora," 95. Henry Louis Gates, Jr., explores the literary historical connection between Hurston and Walker in *The Signifying Monkey: A Theory of African-American Literary Criticism*, chapter 7. Kessler-Harris, "Finding *Bread Givers*," ix, vi, v; Barolini, Introduction, x, xiii, 34–35, 51.

so recovery would seem to extend beyond the archaeological to the very means by which people live their lives.

Recovery relies upon the coexistence of, and indeed the interaction between, both the first and latter cultural notions of passing, in which the former consists of essentialistic and binaristic formulations of ethnic identity while the latter emphasizes the performativity of ethnic subjectivity. The mere act of recovery is initiated by binaristic, first-cultural logic, according to which ethnic presence over time has been replaced by ethnic absence—a process the recovery worker wishes to reverse lest the ethnic group become something other than what they ostensibly are, or, lest they "pass." Thus, the reclaiming of ethnocultural competencies is governed by the either-or logic of the first cultural notion of passing. But the *performance* of ethnicity that results from recovery work enters the realm of the latter cultural notion of passing. Contemporary notions of subjectivity—and, by extension, passing—focus not so much upon what one *is* as upon what one *does*, and, vis-à-vis ethnicity, one does not possess an essential ethnic core being but, rather, performs ethnicity in accordance with specific cultural norms, many of which are revived through the work of recovery. However, contemporary theory suggests that while this latter cultural notion of subjectivity indicates that passing can be a freely willed "conscious practice," it also acknowledges that much of this very "practice" is extrapolated from social codes beyond the subject's control—something that the tradition of literary passing makes quite clear. If subjectivity is best conceived as the slippage between the voluntary and the reiterative or the "volitional and the performative," and if passing can be come to be seen this way, then we can view recovery as not merely an isolated act, but as part of a process that productively encompasses both components. Recovery itself alternates between the volitional and the performative: that is, it is certainly a freely willed act, but the need to engage in the work in the first place stems from a sense of ethnic affiliation over which, depending upon a number of factors (for example, race, family ties, personal experience, etc.), the recovery worker does not have as much control. (Indeed, the circumstantial differences between the African American and the white ethnic longing for ethnic return would make for an interesting study.) Then, in the recovery of ethnic miscellany—literary texts, primary documents, folk traditions, etc.—the recovery worker makes available a catalogue of ethnic options, which, for the contemporary ethnic subject, may become "a norm or set of norms" to perform (i.e., the performative subject) or to discard or modify (i.e., the volitional subject).[9] Thus, recovery can help the ethnic, who wishes more closely to identify as ethnic, better *perform* as an ethnic. This establishes a beautiful paradox: namely, that in the post-passing era, the consequential projects of recovery have provided the tools with which to better pass as ethnic. But above all, for Walker, Kessler-Harris, Barolini, and all others interested in their work, recovery is as much a serious and ongoing process as it is a labor of love.

9. Caughie, *Passing and Pedagogy*, 31, 33; Butler, *Bodies That Matter*, 12, 15.

Bibliography

Ames, Russell. "Social Realism in Charles W. Chesnutt." In Joseph R. McElrath, ed., *Critical Essays on Charles W. Chesnutt* (New York: G. K. Hall and Company, 1999), 147–54.

Ammons, Elizabeth. "Expanding the Canon of American Realism." In Donald Pizer, ed., *The Cambridge Companion to American Realism and Naturalism* (Cambridge, England: Cambridge University Press, 1995), 95–114.

Andrews, William L. Foreword to *The House behind the Cedars*, by Charles W. Chesnutt, vii–xxii. 1900. Rprt., Athens: University of Georgia Press, 1988.

———. *The Literary Career of Charles W. Chesnutt*. Baton Rouge: Louisiana State University Press, 1980.

Antin, Mary. *The Promised Land*. 1912. Rprt., Princeton, N.J.: Princeton University Press, 1969.

Baker, Houston, Jr. *Workings of the Spirit: The Poetics of Afro-American Women's Writing*. Chicago: University of Chicago Press, 1991.

Bakhtin, M. M. *The Dialogic Imagination*. Translated by Caryl Emerson and Michael Holquist. Edited by Michael Holquist. Austin: University of Texas Press, 1981.

Barolini, Helen. "After-Thoughts on Italian American Women Writers." In Barolini, *Chiaroscuro: Essays of Identity* (West Lafayette, Ind.: Bordighera, 1997), 37–50.

———. "The Case of Mari Tomasi." In Francis X. Femminella, ed., *Italians and Irish in America* (Proceedings of the Sixteenth Annual Conference of the American Italian Historical Association, 1983, Albany, N.Y. Staten Island, N.Y.: AIHA, 1985), 177–86.

———. *Chiaroscuro: Essays of Identity.* West Lafayette, Ind.: Bordighera, 1997.

———, ed. *The Dream Book: An Anthology of Writings by Italian American Women.* New York: Schocken Books, 1985.

———. Introduction to *The Dream Book: An Anthology of Writings by Italian American Women* (New York: Schocken Books, 1985), 3–56.

———. "Looking for Mari Tomasi." In *Chiaroscuro: Essays of Identity* (West Lafayette, Ind.: Bordighera, 1997), 73–82.

———. Preface to *The Dream Book: An Anthology of Writings by Italian American Women* (New York: Schocken Books, 1985), ix–xiv.

———. *Umbertina.* 1979. Rprt., New York: Feminist Press, 1999.

———. "*Umbertina* and the Universe." In *Chiaroscuro: Essays of Identity* (West Lafayette, Ind.: Bordighera, 1997), 129–38.

Barth, Fredrik. "Ethnic Groups and Boundaries." In Werner Sollors, ed., *Theories of Ethnicity: A Classical Reader* (New York: New York University Press, 1996), 294–324.

Barthes, Roland. *Image Music Text.* Translated by Stephen Heath. New York: Hill and Wang, 1977.

———. "Theory of the Text." In Robert Young, ed., *Untying the Text: A Post-Structuralist Reader* (Boston: Routledge and Kegan Paul, 1981), 31–47.

Baskin, Judith R., ed. *Women of the Word: Jewish Women and Jewish Writing.* Detroit: Wayne State University Press, 1994.

Baumgarten, Murray. *City Scriptures: Modern Jewish Writing.* Cambridge, Mass.: Harvard University Press, 1982.

Bell, Michael Davitt. *The Problem of American Realism: Studies in the Cultural History of a Literary Idea.* Chicago: University of Chicago Press, 1993.

Benasutti, Marion. *No Steady Job for Papa.* New York: Vanguard, 1966.

Bennett, Michael, and Vanessa D. Dickerson, eds. *Recovering the Black Female Body: Self-Representations by African-American Women.* New Brunswick, N.J.: Rutgers University Press, 2001.

Berzon, Judith. *Neither White nor Black: The Mulatto Character in American Fiction.* New York: New York University Press, 1978.

Birnbaum, Lucia Chiavola. *Black Madonnas: Feminism, Religion and Politics in Italy.* Boston: Northeastern University Press, 1993.

Birnbaum, Michele. "Racial Hysteria: Female Pathology and Race Politics in Frances Harper's *Iola Leroy* and W. D. Howells's *An Imperative Duty.*" *African American Review* 33 (1999): 7–23.

Blackmer, Corinne E. "The Veils of the Law: Race and Sexuality in Nella Larsen's *Passing*." In Kostas Myrsiades and Linda Myrsiades, eds., *Race-ing Representation: Voice, History, and Sexuality* (Lanham, Md.: Rowman and Littlefield, 1998), 98–116.

Blackmore, David L. "'That Unreasonable Restless Feeling': The Homosexual Subtexts of Nella Larsen's *Passing*." *African American Review* 26 (1992): 475–84.

Bodnar, John, Roger Simon, and Michael P. Weber. *Lives of Their Own: Blacks, Italians, and Poles in Pittsburgh, 1900–1960*. Urbana: University of Illinois Press, 1982.

Boeckmann, Cathy. *A Question of Character: Scientific Racism and the Genres of American Fiction, 1892–1912*. Tuscaloosa: University of Alabama Press, 2000.

Boelhower, William. *Through a Glass Darkly: Ethnic Semiosis in American Literature*. New York: Oxford University Press, 1987.

Bona, Mary Jo. *Claiming a Tradition: Italian American Women Writers*. Carbondale: Southern Illinois University Press, 1999.

———, ed. *The Voices We Carry: Recent Italian-American Fiction*. Toronto: Guernica, 1994.

Bourne, Randolph. "Trans-National America." In Werner Sollors, ed., *Theories of Ethnicity: A Classical Reader* (New York: Oxford University Press, 1996), 93–108.

Boyd, Melba Joyce. *Discarded Legacy: Politics and Poetics in the Life of Frances E. W. Harper, 1825–1911*. Detroit: Wayne State University Press, 1994.

Brodkin, Karen. *How Jews Became White Folks and What That Says about Race in America*. New Brunswick, N.J.: Rutgers University Press, 1998.

Brody, Jennifer DeVere. "Clare Kendry's 'True' Colors: Race and Class Conflict in Nella Larsen's *Passing*." *Callaloo* 15 (1992): 1053–65.

Brooks, Neil. "On Becoming an Ex-Man: Postmodern Irony and the Extinguishing of Certainties in the Autobiography of an Ex-Colored Man." *College Literature* 22, no. 3 (1995): 17–29.

———. "We Are Not Free! Free! Free!: *Flight* and the Unmapping of American Literary Studies." *CLA Journal* 41 (1998): 371–86.

Browder, Laura. *Slippery Characters: Ethnic Impersonators and American Identities*. Chapel Hill: University of North Carolina Press, 2000.

Brown, Julie, ed. *Ethnicity and the American Short Story*. New York: Garland Publishing, 1997.

Brown, William Wells. *Clotel; or, the President's Daughter*. 1853. Rprt. in *Three Classic African-American Novels*, edited by Henry Louis Gates, Jr. (New York: Vintage Books, 1990), 3–223.

Bryant, Dorothy. *Miss Giardino*. 1978. Rprt., New York: Feminist Press, 1997.

Budd, Louis J. "The American Background." In Donald Pizer, ed., *Cambridge Companion to American Realism and Naturalism* (Cambridge, England: Cambridge University Press, 1995), 21–46.

Burstein, Janet Handler. *Writing Mothers, Writing Daughters: Tracing the Maternal in Stories by American Jewish Women*. Urbana: University of Illinois Press, 1996.

Butler, Judith. *Bodies That Matter: On the Discursive Limits of "Sex."* New York: Routledge, 1993.

Cady, Edwin H. *The Light of Common Day: Realism in American Fiction.* Bloomington: Indiana University Press, 1971.

———. *The Realist at War: The Mature Years, 1885–1920.* Syracuse, N.Y.: Syracuse University Press, 1958.

———. *The Road to Realism: The Early Years of William Dean Howells, 1837–1885.* Syracuse, N.Y.: Syracuse University Press, 1956.

Cahan, Abraham. *The Rise of David Levinsky*. 1917. Rprt., New York: Penguin Books, 1993.

———. Yekl *and* The Imported Bridegroom *and Other Stories of Yiddish New York*. 1896, 1898. Rprt., New York: Dover, 1970.

Cammett, John M., ed. *The Italian American Novel*. Proceedings of the Second Annual Conference of the American Italian Historical Association, 1969, New York. Staten Island, N.Y.: AIHA, 1969.

Carby, Hazel. *Reconstructing Womanhood: The Emergence of the Afro-American Woman Novelist*. New York: Oxford University Press, 1987.

Carr, Brian. "Paranoid Interpretation, Desire's Nonobject, and Nella Larsen's *Passing*." *PMLA* 119 (2004): 282–95.

Carter, Everett. *Howells and the Age of Realism*. Philadelphia: J. B. Lippincott Company, 1954.

Caughie, Pamela. *Passing and Pedagogy: The Dynamics of Responsibility.* Urbana: University of Illinois Press, 1999.

Cautela, Giuseppe. *Moon Harvest*. New York: Dial Press, 1925.

Cavallo, Diana. *A Bridge of Leaves*. New York: Atheneum, 1961.

Chametsky, Jules. *From the Ghetto: The Fiction of Abraham Cahan*. Amherst: University of Massachusetts Press, 1977.

Chesnutt, Charles W. "The Future American: What the Race Is Likely to Become in the Process of Time." In *Stories, Novels, and Essays*, edited by Werner Sollors (New York: Library of America, 2002), 845–50.

———. *The House behind the Cedars*. 1900. Rprt., Athens: University of Georgia Press, 1988.

————. *Stories, Novels, and Essays,* edited by Werner Sollors. New York: The Library of America, 2002.

————. "What Is a White Man?" In *Stories, Novels, and Essays,* edited by Werner Sollors (New York: Library of America, 2002), 837–44.

————. "The Wife of His Youth." In *"The Wife of His Youth" and Other Stories* (Ann Arbor: University of Michigan Press, 1968), 1–24.

————. *"The Wife of His Youth" and Other Stories.* 1899. Rprt., Ann Arbor: University of Michigan Press, 1968.

Child, Irvin L. *Italian or American? The Second Generation in Conflict.* New Haven, Conn.: Yale University Press, 1943.

Chopin, Kate. The Awakening *and Other Stories.* 1896, 1892–1898. Rprt., New York: Penguin Books, 1986.

Christmann, James. "Raising Voices, Lifting Shadows: Competing Voice-Paradigms in Frances E. W. Harper's *Iola Leroy.*" *African American Review* 34 (2000): 5–18.

Chyet, Stanley F. "Ludwig Lewisohn in Charleston (1892–1903)." *American Jewish Historical Quarterly* 54 (1965): 296–322.

Clymer, Jeffrey A. "Race and the Protocol of American Citizenship in William Dean Howells' *An Imperative Duty.*" *American Literary Realism* 30, no. 3 (1998): 31–52.

Cohen, Miriam. *Workshop to Office: Two Generations of Italian Women in New York City, 1900–1950.* Ithaca, N.Y.: Cornell University Press, 1992.

Condé, Mary. "Passing in the Fiction of Jessie Redmon Fauset and Nella Larsen." *Yearbook of English Studies* 24 (1994): 94–104.

Conder, John J. *Naturalism in American Fiction: The Classic Phase.* Lexington: University Press of Kentucky, 1984.

Cosco, Joseph P. *Imagining Italians: The Clash of Romance and Race in American Perceptions, 1880–1910.* Albany: State University of New York Press, 2003.

Coser, Rose Laub, Laura S. Anker, and Andrew J. Perrin. *Women of Courage: Jewish And Italian Immigrant Women in New York.* Westport, Conn.: Greenwood Press, 1999.

Crowley, John W. *"The Portrait of a Lady* and *The Rise of Silas Lapham:* The Company They Kept." In Donald Pizer, ed., *The Cambridge Companion to American Realism and Naturalism* (Cambridge, England: Cambridge University Press, 1995), 117–37.

Cutter, Martha J. "Sliding Significations: Passing as a Narrative and Textual Strategy in Nella Larsen's Fiction." In Elaine K. Ginsberg, ed., *Passing and the Fictions of Identity* (Durham, N.C.: Duke University Press, 1996), 75–100.

D'Agostino, Guido. *Olives on the Apple Tree.* 1940. Rprt., New York: Arno Press, 1975.

D'Andrea, Vaneeta-Marie. "The Life of Rosa Cavalleri: An Application of Abramson's Model of Rootedness/Rootlessness." In Rocco Caporale, ed., *The Italian Americans through the Generations* (Proceedings of the Fifteenth Annual Conference of the American Italian Historical Association, 1982, New York. Staten Island, N.Y.: AIHA, 1986), 112–24.

Daugherty, Sarah B. *"An Imperative Duty:* Howells and White Male Anxiety." *American Literary Realism* 30, no. 3 (1998): 53–64.

Davis, F. James. *Who Is Black?: One Nation's Definition.* University Park: Pennsylvania State University Press, 1991.

Davis, Thadious M. *Nella Larsen, Novelist of the Harlem Renaissance: A Woman's Life Unveiled.* Baton Rouge: Louisiana State University Press, 1994.

Dearborn, Mary V. *Pocahontas's Daughters: Gender and Ethnicity in American Culture.* New York: Oxford University Press, 1986.

Dekoven, Marianne. "Modernism and Gender." In Michael Levenson, ed., *The Cambridge Companion to Modernism* (Cambridge, England: Cambridge University Press, 1999), 174–93.

Del Negro, Giovanna. *Looking through My Mother's Eyes: Life Stories of Nine Italian Immigrant Women in Canada.* Toronto: Guernica, 1997.

De Rosa, Tina. *Paper Fish.* 1980. Rprt., New York: Feminist Press, 1996.

Dickson-Carr, Darryl. *African American Satire: The Sacredly Profane Novel.* Columbia: University of Missouri Press, 2001.

Di Donato, Pietro. *Christ in Concrete.* Indianapolis: Bobbs-Merrill Company, 1939.

Di Leonardo, Micaela. *The Varieties of Ethnic Experience: Kinship, Class, and Gender among California Italian-Americans.* Ithaca, N.Y.: Cornell University Press, 1984.

Dimont, Max. *The Jews in America: The Roots and Destiny of American Jews.* New York: Simon and Schuster, 1978.

Di Stasi, Lawrence. *Mal Occhio: The Underside of Vision.* San Francisco: North Point, 1981.

Drake, St. Clair, and Horace R. Cayton. *Black Metropolis: A Study of Negro Life in a Northern City.* Vol. 1. 1945. Rprt., New York: Harper and Row, 1962.

DuCille, Ann. "Blues Notes on Black Sexuality: Sex and the Texts of Jessie Fauset and Nella Larsen." *Journal of the History of Sexuality* 3, no. 3 (1993): 418–44.

Elkins, Marilyn. "Reading beyond the Conventions: A Look at Frances E. W. Harper's *Iola Leroy, or Shadows Uplifted.*" *American Literary Realism, 1870–1910* 22, no. 2 (1990): 44–53.

Elliott, Emory, ed. *Columbia Literary History of the United States.* New York: Columbia University Press, 1988.

Ernest, John. "From Mysteries to Histories: Cultural Pedagogy in Frances E. W. Harper's *Iola Leroy.*" *American Literature* 64 (1992): 497–518.

Ets, Marie Hall. *Rosa: The Life of an Italian Immigrant.* Minneapolis: University of Minnesota Press, 1970.

Fabi, Giulia. "Reconstructing Literary Genealogies: Frances E. W. Harper's and William Dean Howells's Race Novels." In Karen L. Kilcup, ed., *Soft Canons: American Women Writers and Masculine Tradition* (Iowa City: University of Iowa Press, 1999), 48–66.

Fanon, Frantz. *Black Skin, White Masks.* Translated by Charles Lam Markmann. New York: Grove Press, 1967.

Fauset, Jessie Redmon. *Comedy: American Style.* 1933. Rprt., New York: G. K. Hall and Company, 1995.

———. *Plum Bun: A Novel without a Moral.* 1929. Rprt., Boston: Beacon Press, 1990.

———. Review of *Autobiography of an Ex-Coloured Man,* by James Weldon Johnson. *Crisis* 5 (1912): 38.

———. *There Is Confusion.* 1924. Rprt., New York: Boni and Liveright, 1974.

Femminella, Francis X., ed. *Italians and Irish in America.* Proceedings of the Sixteenth Annual Conference of the American Italian Historical Association, 1983, Albany, N.Y. Staten Island, N.Y.: AIHA, 1985.

Ferraro, Thomas J. "Avant-Garde Ethnics." In William Boelhower, ed., *The Future of American Modernism: Ethnic Writing Between the Wars* (Amsterdam: Free University Press, 1990), 1–31.

———. *Ethnic Passages: Literary Immigrants in Twentieth-Century America.* Chicago: University of Chicago Press, 1993.

———. "Ethnicity in the Marketplace." In Emory Elliott, ed., *Columbia Literary History of the United States* (New York: Columbia University Press, 1988), 380–406.

Fishman, Sylvia Barack. "The Faces of Women: An Introductory Essay." In *Follow My Footprints: Changing Images of Women in American Jewish Fiction* (Hanover, N.H.: Brandeis University Press, 1992), 1–60.

Fleming, Robert E. *James Weldon Johnson.* Boston: Twayne Publishers, 1987.

Foreman, P. Gabrielle. "'Reading Aright': White Slavery, Black Referents, and the Strategy of Histotextuality in *Iola Leroy.*" *Yale Journal of Criticism* 10 (1997): 327–54.

Foster, Frances Smith. Introduction to *Iola Leroy, or Shadows Uplifted*, by Frances E. W. Harper, xxvii–xxxix. 1892. Rprt., New York: Oxford University Press, 1988.

———. *Written By Herself: Literary Production by African American Women, 1746–1892*. Bloomington: Indiana University Press, 1993.

Fried, Lewis, ed. *Handbook of American-Jewish Literature: An Analytical Guide to Topics, Themes, and Sources*. Westport, Conn.: Greenwood Press, 1988.

Friedman-Kasaba, Kathie. *Memories of Migration: Gender, Ethnicity, and Work in the Lives of Jewish and Italian Women in New York, 1870–1924*. Albany: State University of New York Press, 1996.

Gaines, Kevin K. *Uplifting the Race: Black Leadership, Politics, and Culture in the Twentieth Century*. Chapel Hill: University of North Carolina Press, 1996.

Gallo, Patrick. *Ethnic Alienation: The Italian-Americans*. Cranbury, N.J.: Fairleigh Dickinson University Press, 1974.

Gambino, Richard. *Blood of My Blood: The Dilemma of the Italian-Americans*. 1974. Rprt., Toronto: Guernica, 1996.

Gans, Herbert J. *The Urban Villagers: Group and Class in the Life of Italian-Americans*. 1962. Rprt., New York: Free Press, 1982.

Gardaphè, Fred L. "Autobiography as Piecework: The Writings of Helen Barolini." In Paola A. Sensi Isolani and Anthony J. Tamburri, eds., *Italian Americans Celebrate Life: The Arts and Popular Culture* (Selected Essays from the Twenty-second Annual Conference of the American Italian Historical Association, 1989, San Francisco. Staten Island, NY: AIHA, 1990), 19–27.

———. "Italian American Fiction: A Third Generation Renaissance." *MELUS* 4, no. 3–4 (1987): 69–85.

———. *Italian Signs, American Streets: The Evolution of Italian American Narrative*. Durham, N.C.: Duke University Press, 1996.

Garland, Hamlin. *Crumbling Idols: Twelve Essays on Art Dealing Chiefly with Literature, Painting and the Drama*. 1894. Rprt., Cambridge, Mass.: Belknap Press of Harvard University Press, 1960.

Gates, Henry Louis, Jr. Introduction to *The Autobiography of an Ex-Coloured Man*, by James Weldon Johnson, v–xxiii. New York: Vintage Books, 1989.

———. *The Signifying Monkey: A Theory of African-American Literary Criticism*. New York: Oxford University Press, 1988.

———, ed. *Three Classic African-American Novels*. New York: Vintage Books, 1990.

————, and Nellie Y. McKay, eds. *The Norton Anthology of African American Literature*. New York: W. W. Norton and Company, 1997.

Geollnicht, Donald C. "Passing as Autobiography: James Weldon Johnson's *The Autobiography of an Ex-Coloured Man*." *African American Review* 30 (1996): 17–33.

Gerstle, Gary. *American Crucible: Race and Nation in the Twentieth Century*. Princeton, N.J.: Princeton University Press, 2001.

Ginsberg, Elaine K. "Introduction: The Politics of Passing." In Ginsberg, ed., *Passing and the Fictions of Identity* (Durham, N.C.: Duke University Press, 1996), 1–18.

————, ed. *Passing and the Fictions of Identity*. Durham, N.C.: Duke University Press, 1996.

Girgus, Sam. *The New Covenant: Jewish Writers and the American Idea*. Chapel Hill: University of North Carolina Press, 1984.

Giunta, Edvige. *Writing with an Accent: Contemporary Italian American Women Authors*. New York: Palgrave, 2002.

Giunta, Edvige, and Samuel J. Patti, eds. *A Tavola: Food Tradition and Community among Italian Americans*. Proceedings of the Twenty-ninth Annual Conference of the American Italian Historical Association, 1996, Pittsburgh. Staten Island, N.Y.: AIHA, 1998.

Glazer, Nathan, and Daniel Patrick Moynihan. *Beyond the Melting Pot: The Negroes, Puerto Ricans, Jews, Italians, and Irish of New York City*. 2d ed. Cambridge, Mass.: Massachusetts Institute of Technology, 1970.

Gold, Michael. *Jews without Money*. 1930. Rprt., New York: Carroll and Graf, 1996.

Goldsmith, Meredith. "'The Democracy of Beauty': Fashioning Ethnicity and Gender in the Fiction of Anzia Yezierska." *Yiddish* 11, no. 3–4 (1999): 166–87.

————. "Shopping to Pass, Passing to Shop: Bodily Self-Fashioning in the Fiction of Nella Larsen." In Michael Bennett and Vanessa D. Dickerson, eds., *Recovering the Black Female Body: Self-Representations by African-American Women* (New Brunswick, N.J.: Rutgers University Press, 2001), 97–120.

Gordon, Milton M. *Assimilation in American Life: The Role of Race, Religion, and National Origins*. New York: Oxford University Press, 1964.

Gould, Stephen Jay. *The Mismeasure of Man*. Rev. ed. New York: W. W. Norton and Company, 1996.

Grant, Madison. *The Passing of the Great Race or the Racial Basis of European History*. Rev. ed. New York: Charles Scribner's Sons, 1919.

Green, Rose Basile. *The Italian-American Novel: A Document of the Interaction of Two Cultures*. Rutherford, N.J.: Fairleigh Dickinson University Press, 1974.

Greenberg, Dorothée von Huene. "A *MELUS* Interview: Helen Barolini." *MELUS* 18, no. 2 (1992): 91–108.

Guglielmo, Jennifer, and Salvatore Salerno, eds. *Are Italians White?: How Race Is Made in America*. New York: Routledge, 2003.

———. "Introduction: White Lies, Dark Truths." In *Are Italians White?: How Race Is Made in America* (New York: Routledge, 2003), 1–16.

Guglielmo, Thomas. "'No Color Barrier': Italians, Race, and Power in the United States." In *Are Italians White?: How Race Is Made in America* (New York: Routledge, 2003), 29–43.

———. *White on Arrival: Italians, Race, Color, and Power in Chicago, 1890–1945*. Oxford, England: Oxford University Press, 2003.

Gurock, Jeffrey. *When Harlem Was Jewish, 1890–1925*. New York: Columbia University Press, 1979.

Harap, Louis. *Creative Awakening: The Jewish Presence in Twentieth-Century American Literature, 1900–1940s*. New York: Greenwood Press, 1987.

Harper, Frances E. W. *Iola Leroy, or Shadows Uplifted*. 1892. Rprt., New York: Oxford University Press, 1988.

Harrison, Alferdteen, ed. *Black Exodus: The Great Migration from the American South*. Jackson: University Press of Mississippi, 1991.

Heermance, J. Noel. *Charles W. Chesnutt: America's First Great Black Novelist*. Hamden, Conn: Archon Books, 1974.

Hendin, Josephine Gattuso. "Festas and Foodfights: Italian-American Postmodernism as a Feast of Words." In Edvige Giunta and Samuel J. Patti, eds., *A Tavola: Food Tradition and Community among Italian Americans* (Proceedings of the Twenty-ninth Annual Conference of the American Italian Historical Association, 1996, Pittsburgh. Staten Island, N.Y.: AIHA, 1998), 107–14.

———. "Social Constructions and Aesthetic Achievements: Italian American Writing as Ethnic Art." *MELUS* 28, no. 3 (2003): 13–39.

Henriksen, Louise Levitas. *Anzia Yezierska: A Writer's Life*. New Brunswick, N.J.: Rutgers University Press, 1988.

Herndl, Diane Price. "Miscegen(r)ation of Mestiza Discourse?: Feminist and Racial Politics in *Ramona* and *Iola Leroy*." In Timothy B. Powell, ed., *Beyond the Binary: Reconstructing Cultural Identity in a Multicultural Context* (New Brunswick, N.J.: Rutgers University Press, 1999), 261–75.

Hoffman, Frederick J. *The Twenties: American Writing in the Postwar Decade*. 1955. Rprt., New York: Free Press, 1965.

Howard, June. *Form and History in American Literary Naturalism.* Chapel Hill: University of North Carolina Press, 1985.

Howe, Irving. *The World of our Fathers: The Journey of the East European Jews to America and the Life They Found and Made.* New York: Harcourt Brace Jovanovich, 1976.

Howells, William Dean. *Criticism and Fiction.* 1892. Rprt. in *Selected Literary Criticism. Volume II: 1887–1897,* edited by Donald Pizer (Bloomington: Indiana University Press, 1993), 293–354.

———. "Mr. Charles W. Chesnutt's Stories." *Atlantic Monthly* 85 (May 1900): 699–701.

———. *The Rise of Silas Lapham.* 1885. Rprt., New York: Penguin Classics, 1986.

———. *Selected Literary Criticism. Volume II: 1886–1897,* edited by Donald Pizer. Bloomington: Indiana University Press, 1993.

———. *The Shadow of a Dream* and *An Imperative Duty.* 1890, 1892. Rprt., New York: Twayne, 1962.

Hughes, Langston. "The Negro Artist and the Racial Mountain." In Henry Louis Gates, Jr., and Nellie Y. McKay, eds., *The Norton Anthology of African American Literature* (New York: W. W. Norton and Company, 1997), 1267–71.

Hurston, Zora Neale. *Their Eyes Were Watching God.* 1937. Rprt., New York: Harper And Row, 1990.

Hutcheon, Linda. *The Politics of Postmodernism.* London: Routledge, 1989.

Hutchinson, George. *The Harlem Renaissance in Black and White.* Cambridge, Mass.: Belknap Press of Harvard University Press, 1995.

Ignatiev, Noel. *How the Irish Became White.* New York: Routledge, 1995.

Imes, Nella, letter, *Opportunity* 4 (September 1926): 295.

Iorizzo, Luciano, and Salvatore Mondello. *The Italian Americans.* New York: Twayne Publishers, 1971.

Jackson, Blyden. "Introduction: A Street of Dreams." In Alferdteen Harrison, ed., *Black Exodus: The Great Migration from the American South* (Jackson: University Press of Mississippi, 1991), xi–xviii.

Jacobson, Matthew Frye. *Whiteness of a Different Color: European Immigrants and the Alchemy of Race.* Cambridge, Mass.: University of Harvard Press, 1998

James, Henry. *Henry James: French Writers, Other European Writers, the Prefaces to the New York Edition.* Edited by Leon Edel. New York: Library of America, 1984.

———. *The Portrait of a Lady.* 1881. Rprt., New York: Signet, 1995.

———. Preface to *The Portrait of a Lady.* 1908. Rprt. in *Henry James: French*

Writers, Other European Writers, the Prefaces to the New York Edition,
edited by Leon Edel. New York: Library of America, 1984, 1070–85.

Japtok, Martin. "Between 'Race' as Construct and 'Race' as Essence: *The Autobiography of an Ex-Coloured Man.*" *Southern Literary Journal* 28, no. 2 (1996): 32–47.

———. "Justifying Individualism: Anzia Yezierska's *Bread Givers.*" In Katherine B. Payant and Toby Rose, eds., *The Immigrant Experience in North American Literature* (Westport, Conn.: Greenwood Press, 1999), 17–30.

———. "Socialism and Ethnic Solidarity: Samuel Ornitz's *Haunch, Paunch and Jowl.*" *MELUS* 24, no. 3 (1999): 21–38.

Johnson, James Weldon. *Along This Way: The Autobiography of James Weldon Johnson.* New York: Viking Press, 1933.

———. *The Autobiography of an Ex-Coloured Man.* 1912. Rprt., New York: Vintage Books, 1989.

Johnson, Jane. Introduction to *Crumbling Idols: Twelve Essays on Art Dealing Chiefly with Literature, Painting and the Drama,* by Hamlin Garland (1894. Rprt., Cambridge, Mass.: Belknap Press of Harvard University Press, 1960), ix–xxviii.

Jones, Jacqueline. *Labor of Love, Labor of Sorrow: Black Women, Work, and the Family, from Slavery to the Present.* New York: Vintage Books, 1985.

Kallen, Horace M. "Democracy versus the Melting-Pot: A Study of American Nationality." In Werner Sollors, ed., *Theories of Ethnicity: A Classical Reader* (New York: New York University Press, 1996), 67–92.

Kaplan, Amy. *The Social Construction of American Realism.* Chicago: University of Chicago Press, 1988.

Kawash, Samira. *"The Autobiography of an Ex-Coloured Man:* (Passing for) Black Passing for White." In Elaine K. Ginsberg, ed., *Passing and the Fictions of Identity* (Durham, N.C.: Duke University Press, 1996), 59–74.

———. *Dislocating the Color Line: Identity, Hybridity, and Singularity in African-American Narrative.* Stanford, Calif.: Stanford University Press, 1997.

Kessler-Harris, Alice. "Finding *Bread Givers.*" Foreword to *Bread Givers,* by Anzia Yezierska (1925. Rprt., New York: Persea Books, 1999), v–xiii.

———. Introduction to *Bread Givers,* by Anzia Yezierska (1925. (Rprt., New York: Persea Books, 1999), xvi–xxix.

Kilcup, Karen L., ed. *Soft Canons: American Women Writers and Masculine Tradition.* Iowa City: University of Iowa Press, 1999.

King, Desmond. *Making Americans: Immigration, Race, and the Origins of the Diverse Democracy.* Cambridge, Mass.: Harvard University Press, 2000.

Konzett, Delia Caparoso. *Ethnic Modernisms: Anzia Yezierska, Zora Neale Hurston, Jean Rhys, and the Aesthetics of Dislocation.* New York: Palgrave MacMillan, 2002.

Koppelman, Susan. "The Naming of Katz: Who Am I? Who Am I Supposed to Be? Who Can I Be? Passing, Assimilation, and Embodiment in Short Fiction by Fannie Hurst and Thyra Samter Winslow with a Few Jokes Thrown in and Various References to Other Others." In Julie Brown, ed., *Ethnicity and the American Short Story* (New York: Garland Publishing, 1997), 229–52.

Kramer, Michael P., and Hana Wirth-Nesher, eds. *The Cambridge Companion to Jewish American Literature.* Cambridge, England: Cambridge University Press, 2003.

Kuenz, Jane. "American Racial Discourse, 1900–1930: Schuyler's *Black No More." Novel* 30 (1997): 170–92.

LaGumina, Salvatore. *Wop!: A Documentary History of Anti-Italian Discrimination in the United States.* 1973. Rprt., Toronto: Guernica, 1999.

Lainoff, Seymour. *Ludwig Lewisohn.* Boston: Twayne Publishers, 1982.

Larsen, Nella. Quicksand *and* Passing. Edited by Deborah E. McDowell. 1928, 1929. Rprt., New Brunswick, N.J.: Rutgers University Press, 1986.

Levin, Tobe. "Anzia Yezierska (1880–1970)." In Ann R. Shapiro, ed., *Jewish American Women Writers: A Bio-Bibliographical and Critical Sourcebook* (Westport, Conn.: Greenwood Press, 1994), 482–93.

Levinson, Melanie. " 'To Make Myself for a Person': 'Passing' Narratives and the Divided Self in the Work of Anzia Yezierska." *Studies in American Jewish Literature* 13 (1994): 2–9.

Levy, Eugene. *James Weldon Johnson: Black Leader, Black Voice.* Chicago: University of Chicago Press, 1973.

Lewis, David Levering. *When Harlem Was in Vogue.* 1979. Rprt., New York: Penguin Books, 1997.

Lewis, Earl. "To Turn as on a Pivot: Writing African Americans into a History of Overlapping Diasporas." *American Historical Review* 100 (1995): 765–87.

Lewisohn, Ludwig. *Up Stream: An American Chronicle.* New York: Boni and Liveright, 1922.

Locke, Alain. "Negro Youth Speaks." In *The New Negro: An Interpretation* (1925. Rprt., New York: Arno Press and the New York Times, 1968), 47–53.

———. "The New Negro." In *The New Negro: An Interpretation*, by Alain Locke (1925. Rprt., New York: Arno Press and the New York Times, 1968), 3–16.

———, ed. *The New Negro: An Interpretation.* 1925. Rprt., New York: Arno Press and the New York Times, 1968.

Lopreato, Joseph. *Italian Americans.* Ethnic Groups in Comparative Perspective. New York: Random House, 1970.

Lott, Eric. *Love and Theft: Blackface Minstrelsy and the American Working Class.* New York: Oxford University Press, 1993.

Lynn, Kenneth S. *William Dean Howells: An American Life.* New York: Harcourt Brace Jovanovich, 1971.

Mangione, Jerre. *Mount Allegro.* 1942. Rprt., New York: Harper and Row, 1989.

———, and Ben Morreale. *La Storia: Five Centuries of the Italian American Experience.* New York: Harper Collins, 1992.

Mannino, Mary Ann. *Revisionary Identities: Strategies of Empowerment in the Writing of Italian/American Women.* New York: Peter Lang, 2000.

Marks, Carole. *Farewell—We're Good and Gone: The Great Black Migration.* Bloomington: Indiana University Press, 1989.

Marovitz, Sanford E. *Abraham Cahan.* New York: Twayne, 1996.

McDowell, Deborah E. "'The Changing Same': Generational Connections and Black Women Novelists." *New Literary History* 18 (1987): 281–302.

———. Introduction to Quicksand *and* Passing, edited by Deborah E. McDowell (1928, 1929. Rprt., New Brunswick, N.J.: Rutgers University Press, 1986), ix–xxv.

McElrath, Joseph R., Jr., ed. *Critical Essays on Charles W. Chesnutt.* New York: G. K. Hall and Company, 1999.

———. "W. D. Howells and Race: Charles W. Chesnutt's Disappointment of the Dean." In *Critical Essays on Charles Chesnutt* (New York: G. K. Hall and Company, 1999), 242–60.

———. "Why Charles W. Chesnutt Is Not a Realist." *American Literary Realism, 1870–1910* 32 (2000): 91–108.

McLendon, Jacquelyn Y. *The Politics of Color in the Fiction of Jessie Fauset and Nella Larsen.* Charlottesville: University Press of Virginia, 1995.

Melnick, Ralph. *The Life and Work of Ludwig Lewisohn: "A Touch of Wildness."* Vol. 1. Detroit: Wayne State University Press, 1998.

Michaels, Walter Benn. "Against Identity: An Interview with Walter Benn Michaels." Interview with Jeffrey J. Williams. *Minnesota Review* 55–57 (2002). January 16, 2002 <http://www.theminnesotareview.org/ns55/michaels.htm>.

————. "Autobiography of an Ex-White Man: Why Race Is Not a Social Construction." *Boundary* 73 (1998): 122–43.

————. *Our America: Nativism, Modernism, and Pluralism.* Durham, N.C.: Duke University Press, 1995.

————. "Response." *Modernism/Modernity* 3, no. 5 (1996): 121–26.

Miller, James A. Foreword to *Black No More: Being an Account of the Strange and Wonderful Workings of Science in the Land of the Free, A. D.,* by George Schuyler (1931. Rprt., Boston: Northeastern University Press, 1989), 1–12.

Minter, David. *A Cultural History of the American Novel: Henry James to William Faulkner.* Cambridge, England: Cambridge University Press, 1994.

Mitchell, Lee Clark. *Determined Fictions: American Literary Naturalism.* New York: Columbia University Press, 1989.

————. "Naturalism and Languages of Determinism." In Emory Elliott, ed., *The Columbia Literary History of the United States* (New York: Columbia University Press, 1988), 525–45.

Moore, Deborah Dash. *At Home in America: Second Generation New York Jews.* New York: Columbia University Press, 1981.

Morgan, Stacy. "'The Strange and Wonderful Workings of Science': Race Science and Essentialism in George Schuyler's *Black No More.*" *CLA Journal* 42 (1999): 331–52.

Myrdal, Gunnar. *An American Dilemma: The Negro Problem and Modern Democracy.* Vol. 1. New York: Harper and Brothers Publishers, 1944.

Nardini, Gloria. *Che Bella Figura!: The Power of Performance in an Italian Ladies' Club in Chicago.* Albany: State University of New York Press, 1999.

Nettels, Elsa. *Language, Race, and Social Class in Howells's America.* Lexington: University Press of Kentucky, 1988.

Novak, Michael. *The Rise of the Unmeltable Ethnics.* New York: Macmillan, 1971.

Olson, Henry Fairfield. "Preface to the New Edition." In Madison Grant, *The Passing of the Great Race or the Racial Basis of European History* (New York: Charles Scribner's Sons, 1919), xi–xii.

Omi, Michael, and Howard Winant. *Racial Formation in the United States: From the 1960s to the 1990s.* 2d ed. New York: Routledge, 1994.

Ornitz, Samuel. *Haunch, Paunch and Jowl: An Anonymous Autobiography.* New York: Boni and Liveright, 1923.

Orvell, Miles. *The Real Thing: Imitation and Authenticity in American Culture, 1880–1940.* Chapel Hill: University of North Carolina Press, 1989.

Pane, Remigio U., ed. *Italian Americans in the Professions*. Proceedings of the Twelfth Annual Conference of the American Italian Historical Association, 1979, New Brunswick, N.J. Staten Island, N.Y.: AIHA, 1983.

Panunzio, Constantine. *The Soul of an Immigrant*. New York: MacMillan Company, 1921.

Payant, Katherine B., and Toby Rose, eds. *The Immigrant Experience in North American Literature*. Westport, Conn.: Greenwood Press, 1999.

Peplow, Michael W. *George S. Schuyler*. Boston: Twayne Publishers, 1980.

Peragallo, Olga. *Italian-American Authors and Their Contribution to American Literature*. Edited by Anita Peragallo. New York: S. F. Vanni, 1949.

Perlmann, Joel. *Ethnic Differences: Schooling and Social Structure among the Irish, Italians, Jews, and Blacks in an American City, 1880–1935*. New York: Cambridge University Press, 1988.

Pfeiffer, Kathleen. "Individualism, Success and American Identity in *The Autobiography of an Ex-Colored Man*." *African American Review* 30 (1996): 403–19.

———. "The Limits of Identity in Jessie Fauset's *Plum Bun*." *Legacy* 18, no. 1 (2001): 79–93.

Pipino, Mary Frances. *"I Have Found My Voice": The Italian-American Woman Writer*. New York: Peter Lang, 2000.

Pisiak, Roxanna. "Irony and Subversion in James Weldon Johnson's *The Autobiography of an Ex-Coloured Man*." *Studies in American Fiction* 21 (1993): 83–96.

Pizer, Donald, ed. *The Cambridge Companion to American Realism and Naturalism*. Cambridge, England: Cambridge University Press, 1995.

———. "Introduction: The Problem of Definition." In *The Cambridge Companion to American Realism and Naturalism* (Cambridge, England: Cambridge University Press, 1995), 1–18.

———, ed. *Selected Literary Criticism. Volume II: 1886–1897*, by William Dean Howells. Bloomington: Indiana University Press, 1993.

———. *Twentieth-Century American Literary Naturalism*. Carbondale: Southern Illinois University Press, 1982.

Powell, Timothy B., ed. *Beyond the Binary: Reconstructing Cultural Identity in a Multicultural Context*. New Brunswick, N.J.: Rutgers University Press, 1999.

———. "Introduction: Re-Thinking Cultural Identity." In Timothy B. Powell, ed., *Beyond the Binary: Reconstructing Cultural Identity in a Multicultural Context* (New Brunswick, N.J.: Rutgers University Press, 1999), 1–13.

Render, Sylvia Lyons. *Charles W. Chesnutt*. Boston: Twayne, 1980.

Reynolds, Guy. *Twentieth-Century American Women's Fiction: A Critical Introduction*. New York: St. Martin's Press, 1999.

Richards, Bernard G. *Introduction to* Yekl *and* The Imported Bridegroom *and Other Stories of Yiddish New York,* by Abraham Cahan (1896, 1898. Rprt., New York: Dover, 1970), iii–viii.

Richards, David A. J. *Italian American: The Racializing of an Ethnic Identity.* New York: New York University Press, 1999.

Roediger, David. *Towards the Abolition of Whiteness: Essays on Race, Politics, and Working Class History.* London: Verso, 1994.

———. *The Wages of Whiteness: Race and the Making of the American Working Class.* London: Verso, 1991.

Rolle, Andrew. *The American Italians: Their History and Culture.* Belmont, Calif.: Wadsworth Publishing Company, 1972.

Royce, Josiah. *Race Questions: Provincialism and Other American Problems.* 1908. Rprt., Freeport, N.Y.: Books for Libraries Press, 1967.

Rubin, Rachel. *Jewish Gangsters of Modern Literature.* Urbana: University of Illinois Press, 2000.

Rubin, Steven J. "American-Jewish Autobiography." In Lewis Fried, ed., *Handbook of American-Jewish Literature: An Analytical Guide to Topics, Themes, and Sources* (Westport, Conn.: Greenwood Press, 1988), 287–313.

Ruotolo, Cristina L. "James Weldon Johnson and the Autobiography of an Ex-Colored Musician." *American Literature* 72 (2000): 249–74.

Russo, John Paul. "From Italophilia to Italophobia: Representations of Italian Americans in the Early Gilded Age." *Differentia* 6–7 (1994): 45–75.

Salerno, Aldo E. "America for Americans Only: Gino C. Speranza and the Immigrant Experience." *Italian Americana* 14 (1996): 133–47.

Sanders, Richard. *The Downtown Jews: Portraits of an Immigrant Generation.* New York: Harper and Row, 1969.

Schoen, Carol B. *Anzia Yezierska.* Boston: Twayne Publishers, 1982.

Schuyler, George. *Black and Conservative: The Autobiography of George S. Schuyler.* New Rochelle, N.Y.: Arlington House Publishers, 1966.

———. *Black No More: Being an Account of the Strange and Wonderful Workings of Science in the Land of the Free, A.D. 1933–1940.* 1931. Rprt., Boston: Northeastern University Press, 1989.

———. "The Negro-Art Hokum." In Henry Louis Gates, Jr., and Nellie Y. McKay, eds., *The Norton Anthology of African American Literature* (New York: W. W. Norton and Company, 1997), 1171–74.

———. Preface to *Black No More: Being an Account of the Strange and Wonderful Workings of Science in the Land of the Free, A. D. 1933–1940,* by George Schuyler (1931. Rprt., Boston: Northeastern University Press, 1989), 13–14.

Sensi Isolani, Paola A., and Anthony Julian Tamburri. *Italian Americans Celebrate Life: The Arts and Popular Culture.* Selected Essays from the Twenty-second Annual Conference of the American Italian Historical Association, 1989, San Francisco. Staten Island, N.Y.: AIHA, 1990.

Shapiro, Ann R., ed. *Jewish American Women Writers: A Bio-Bibliographical and Critical Sourcebook.* Westport, Conn.: Greenwood Press, 1994.

Sheehy, John. "The Mirror and the Veil: The Passing Novel and the Quest for American Racial Identity." *African American Review* 33 (1999): 401–15.

Shi, David E. *Facing Facts: Realism in American Thought and Culture, 1850–1920.* New York: Oxford University Press, 1995.

Sollors, Werner. *Beyond Ethnicity: Consent and Descent in American Culture.* New York: Oxford University Press, 1986.

———. "Foreword: Theories of Ethnicity." In *Theories of Ethnicity: A Classical Reader* (New York: New York University Press, 1996), x–xliv.

———. *Neither Black nor White yet Both: Thematic Explorations of Interracial Literature.* New York: Oxford University Press, 1997.

———, ed. *Stories, Novels, and Essays,* by Charles W. Chesnutt. New York: Library of America, 2002.

———, ed. *Theories of Ethnicity: A Classical Reader.* New York: New York University Press, 1996.

Somerville, Siobhan B. *Queering the Color Line: Race and the Invention of Homosexuality in American Culture.* Durham, N.C.: Duke University Press, 2000.

Speranza, Gino. *Race or Nation: A Conflict of Divided Loyalties.* Indianapolis: Bobbs-Merrill Company, 1925.

Sterba, Christopher M. *Good Americans: Italian and Jewish Immigrants during the First World War.* Cambridge, England: Oxford University Press, 2003.

Stonequist, Everett V. *The Marginal Man: A Study in Personality and Culture Conflict.* New York: Charles Scribner's Sons, 1937.

Stubbs, Katherine. "Reading Material: Contextualizing Clothing in the Work of Anzia Yezierska." *MELUS* 23, no. 3 (1998): 157–72.

Sullivan, Neil. "Nella Larsen's *Passing* and the Fading Subject." *African American Review* 32 (1998): 373–86.

Sundquist, Eric J. "Realism and Regionalism." In Emory Elliott, ed., *The Columbia Literary History of the United States* (New York: Columbia University Press, 1988), 501–24.

———. *To Wake the Nations: Race in the Making of American Literature.* Cambridge, Mass: Belknap Press of Harvard University Press, 1993.

Sylvander, Carlyn Wedin. *Jessie Redmon Fauset: Black American Writer.* Troy, N.Y.: Whitson Publishing Company, 1981.

Tamburri, Anthony Julian. *To Hyphenate or Not to Hyphenate: The Italian/American Writer: An Other Writer.* Montreal: Guernica, 1991.

———. *A Semiotic of Ethnicity: In (Re)cognition of the Italian/American Writer.* Albany: State University of New York Press, 1998.

Tate, Claudia. *Domestic Allegories of Political Desire: The Black Heroine's Text at the Turn of the Century.* New York: Oxford University Press, 1992.

Tomasi, Lydio F. *The Italian American Family.* 1972. Rprt., Staten Island, N.Y.: Center for Migration Studies of New York, Inc., 1991.

Trotter, Joe William, Jr., ed. *The Great Migration in Historical Perspective: New Dimensions of Race, Class, and Gender.* Bloomington: Indiana University Press, 1991.

Twain, Mark. *Adventures of Huckleberry Finn.* 1885. Rprt., Berkeley: University of California Press, 1985.

U.S. Congress. Senate Immigration Commission. *Dictionary of Races or Peoples. Reports of the Immigration Commission.* 61st Cong., 3d sess., S. Doc 662. Washington, D.C.: Government Printing Office, 1911.

———. Senate Immigration Commission. *Emigration Conditions in Europe. Reports of the Immigration Commission.* 61st Cong., 3d sess., S. Doc 748. Washington, D.C.: Government Printing Office, 1910.

Vecoli, Rudolph J. Introduction to *Rosa: The Life of an Italian Immigrant,* by Marie Hall Ets (Minneapolis: University of Minnesota Press, 1970), v–xi.

———. "The Italian-American Literary Subculture: An Historical and Sociological Analysis." In John M. Cammett, ed., *The Italian American Novel* (Proceedings of the Second Annual Conference of the American Italian Historical Association, 1969, New York. Staten Island, N.Y.: AIHA, 1969), 6–10.

Viscusi, Robert. "Professions and Faiths: Critical Choices in the Italian American Novel." In Remigio U. Pane, ed., *Italian Americans in the Professions* (Proceedings of the Twelfth Annual Conference of the American Italian Historical Association, 1979, New Brunswick, N.J. Staten Island, N.Y.: AIHA, 1983), 41–54.

Wald, Gayle. *Crossing the Line: Racial Passing in Twentieth-Century U.S. Literature and Culture.* Durham, N.C.: Duke University Press, 2000.

Wald, Priscilla. *Constituting Americans: Cultural Anxiety and Narrative Form.* 1995. Durham, N.C.: Duke University Press, 1998.

———. "Of Crucibles and Grandfathers: The East European Immigrants." In Michael P. Kramer and Hana Wirth-Nesher, eds., *The Cambridge Companion to Jewish American Literature* (Cambridge, England: Cambridge University Press, 2003), 50–69.

Waldron, Edward E. *Walter White and the Harlem Renaissance.* Port Washington, N.Y.: Kennikat Press, 1978.

Waldo, Octavia. *A Cup of the Sun.* New York: Harcourt, 1961.

Walker, Alice. "In Search of Our Mothers' Gardens." In *In Search Of Our Mothers' Gardens: Womanist Prose* (San Diego: Harcourt Brace Jovanovich, 1983), 231–43.

———. *In Search of Our Mothers' Gardens: Womanist Prose.* San Diego: Harcourt Brace Jovanovich, 1983.

———. "Looking for Zora." In *In Search of Our Mother's Gardens: Womanist Prose* (San Diego: Harcourt Brace Jovanovich, 1983), 93–116.

———. "Saving the Life That Is Your Own: The Importance of Models in the Artist's Life." In *In Search of Our Mothers' Gardens: Womanist Prose* (San Diego: Harcourt Brace Jovanovich, 1983), 3–14.

———. "Zora Neale Hurston: A Cautionary Tale and a Partisan View." In *In Search of Our Mothers' Gardens: Womanist Prose* (San Diego: Harcourt Brace Jovanovich, 1983), 83–92.

Wall, Cheryl A. *Women of the Harlem Renaissance.* Bloomington: Indiana University Press, 1995.

Warren, Kenneth W. *Black and White Strangers: Race and American Literary Realism.* Chicago: University of Chicago Press, 1993.

———. "Troubled Black Humanity in *The Souls of Black Folk* and *The Autobiography of an Ex-Colored Man.*" In Donald Pizer, ed., *The Cambridge Companion to American Realism and Naturalism* (Cambridge, England: Cambridge University Press, 1995), 263–77.

Washington, Mary Helen. Foreword to *Their Eyes Were Watching God*, by Zora Neale Hurston. 1937. Rprt., New York: Harper and Row, 1990.

———, ed. *Invented Lives: Narratives of Black Women, 1860–1960.* New York: Doubleday, 1987.

———. "The Mulatta Trap: Nella Larsen's Women of the 1920s." In *Invented Lives: Narratives of Black Women, 1860–1960* (New York: Doubleday, 1987), 159–67.

———. "Uplifting the Women and the Race: The Forerunners—Harper and Hopkins." In *Invented Lives: Narratives of Black Women, 1860–1960* (New York: Doubleday, 1987), 73–86.

Wasson, Kirsten. "Mary Antin (1881–1949)." In Ann R. Shapiro, ed., *Jewish American Women Writers: A Bio-Bibliographical and Critical Sourcebook* (Westport, Conn.: Greenwood Press, 1994), 15–21.

Weinberg, Sydney Stahl. *The World of Our Mothers: The Lives of Jewish Immigrant Women.* New York: Schocken Books, 1988.

Wexler, Laura. "Looking at Yezierska." In Judith R. Baskin, ed., *Women of the Word: Jewish Women and Jewish Writing* (Detroit: Wayne State University Press, 1994), 153–81.

Wharton, Edith. *The House of Mirth.* 1905. Rprt., New York: Vintage Books, 1990.

White, Walter. *Flight.* New York: Alfred A. Knopf, 1926.

———. *A Man Called White: The Autobiography of Walter White.* New York: Viking Press, 1948.

Wilentz, Gay. "Cultural Mediation and the Immigrant's Daughter: Anzia Yezierska's *Bread Givers.*" *MELUS* 17, no. 3 (1991–1992): 33–41.

Wilson, Kimberly A. C. "The Function of the 'Fair' Mulatto: Complexion, Audience, and Mediation in Frances Harper's *Iola Leroy.*" *Cimarron Review* 106 (1994): 104–14.

Wonham, Henry B. *Charles W. Chesnutt: A Study of the Short Fiction.* New York: Twayne Publishers, 1998.

———. "Writing Realism, Policing Consciousness: Howells and the Black Body." *American Literature* 67 (1995): 701–24.

Wright, Richard. *Native Son.* 1940. Rprt., New York: HarperCollins, 1993.

Yezierska, Anzia. *Bread Givers.* 1925. Rprt., New York: Persea Books, 1999.

Young, Elizabeth. "Warring Fictions: *Iola Leroy* and the Color of Gender." *American Literature* 64 (1992): 273–97.

Young, Robert, ed. *Untying the Text: A Post-Structuralist Reader.* Boston: Routledge and Kegan Paul, 1981.

Index

Acculturation narratives: *Cahan's Rise of David Levinsky* as, 108–12; Cahan's *Yekl* as, 104–7; Cautela's *Moon Harvest* as, 100–103; compared with white ethnic passing narratives, 7, 13, 14, 21, 24, 26, 91; Ets's *Rosa* as, 24, 25, 177, 178–85, 202; Johnson's *Autobiography of an Ex-Coloured Man* as, 155, 156. *See also* Assimilation
Adventures of Huckleberry Finn (Twain), 48, 49–50, 144, 216n4
African American passing narratives: and antipassing confessionals and essays during civil rights era, 247; and assimilation, 13; authors of generally, 2, 3; compared with white ethnic passing narratives, 133–34, 145, 147; and cultural betrayal, 25; irony in, 130–31; and modernism, 26; racial critique in, 7–8, 10, 11, 14, 21–22, 53, 132–35; realism of, 4–8, 45–54; scholarship and literary criticism on, 14–21; by women, 214–15, 227–46. *See also* specific authors and titles
African Americans: alleged inferiority of, 31–32, 42, 42n18; assimilation of, 41–45, 95; deterministic aspects of, in nineteenth century, 75; employ-ment of black women, 83, 212, 223, 246; legal rights for, 41; marriage and middle-class status for black women, 212–13, 231; and one-drop rule, 43, 60, 68, 69, 80, 94, 142; passing by, 1–2, 9–11, 43–45; prejudice against, 42–43; segregation of, 41; urban migration from South by, 41–42; violence against and lynching of, 41, 58, 133, 156

African American studies, 248

Agency: and assimilation, 51–52; in Barolini's *Umbertina*, 176–77; in Cahan's *Rise of David Levinsky*, 109–11; in Cahan's *Yekl*, 106–7, 108; in Ets's *Rosa*, 183; in Harper's *Iola Leroy*, 75, 82–87; in Howells's *Imperative Duty*, 71; in Johnson's *Autobiography of an Ex-Coloured Man*, 58, 157; in Larsen's *Passing*, 237; in Lewisohn's *Up Stream*, 121; and passing narratives, 48–52, 57, 133, 214; and realism, 48–52, 57; in White's *Flight*, 225, 226

Alcott, Louisa, 188

Alexander II, Czar, 38n13

Alexander III, Czar, 38n13

Along This Way (Johnson), 153–54, 158–59, 160, 161, 169